THE ANGLER'S
COMPANION

THE ANGLER'S COMPANION

The Lore of Fishing

compiled by
Brian Murphy

PADDINGTON PRESS LTD

NEW YORK & LONDON

Library of Congress Cataloging in Publication Data
Main entry under title:
The Angler's companion.
   1. Fishing. 2. Fishing stories. 3. Fishing –
Literary collection.   I. Murphy, Brian Michael.
SH439.A42   799.1'08   78–18808
   ISBN 0 7092 0513 9
   ISBN 0 448 22682 0 (U.S. and Canada only)

"Big Two-Hearted River Parts I and II" reprinted from "Big Two-Hearted River" by Ernest Hemingway from *In Our Time* with the permission of Charles Scribners' Sons. Copyright © 1925 Charles Scribners' Sons.

Filmset in England by Tradespools Ltd, Frome, Somerset
Printed and bound in the United States
Designed by Sandra Shafee
IN THE UNITED STATES
PADDINGTON PRESS
Distributed by
GROSSET & DUNLAP

IN THE UNITED KINGDOM
PADDINGTON PRESS

IN CANADA
Distributed by
RANDOM HOUSE OF CANADA LTD

IN SOUTHERN AFRICA
Distributed by
ERNEST STANTON (PUBLISHERS) (PTY) LTD

IN AUSTRALIA AND NEW ZEALAND
Distributed by
A. H. & W. REED

Contents

ACKNOWLEDGMENTS

For permission to reprint the following copyrighted material, Paddington Press are grateful to the authors, their agents, and publishers indicated:

"Early Experiences" by George M. L. La Branche is reprinted with permission of Charles Scribners' Sons from *The Dry Fly and Fast Water*.

"The Early Days" is reprinted with permission of Daniel Farson. © Negley Farson. First published in England in *Going Fishing*. Country Life 1942.

"Sins My Father Taught Me" from *Trout Magic* by Robert Traver. Crown Publishers Inc. ©1974 by John D. Voelker. By permission of the author.

"Aksakov on Fishing" by Arthur Ransome from *Rod and Line* is reprinted with permission of The Arthur Ransome Estate.

"The Fisherman" by W. B. Yeats is reprinted in the UK and Commonwealth with permission of M. B. Yeats, Miss Anne Yeats and the Macmillan Co. of London and Basingstoke, and in the US and Canada with permission of Macmillan Co., Inc. (US). From *Collected Poems by William Butler Yeats*. Copyright 1919 by Macmillan Publishing Co., Inc., renewed 1947 by Bertha Georgie Yeats.

"Big Two-Hearted River Parts I and II" reprinted in the US and Canada from "Big Two-Hearted River" by Ernest Hemingway from *In Our Time* with the permission of Charles Scribners' Sons. Copyright 1925 Charles Scribners' Sons. Reprinted in the UK and Commonwealth from *The First Forty-nine Stories* by Ernest Hemingway, published by Jonathan Cape Ltd., with the permission of the Executors of The Ernest Hemingway Estate.

"The Lure of Opening Day" by Nick Lyons. ©1970 by Nick Lyons. Reprinted by permission of the author, from *The Seasonable Angler*.

"Fly Fishermen: The World's Biggest Snobs" taken from *Trout Magic* by Robert Traver. © 1974 by John D. Voelker. Used by permission of Crown Publishers Inc.

"Two Friends". Copyright 1922 and renewed 1950 by Alfred A. Knopf, Inc. Reprinted in the US and Canada from *The Collected Novels and Stories of Guy de Maupassant* by permission of Alfred A. Knopf Inc and in the UK and Commonwealth by permission of Cassell and Co. Ltd.

Introduction

As a boy I was fat and lazy. Many would say I have not changed all that much. I had little time for sport and was hopeless at making things with my hands. This did not make me very welcome in the company of boys of my own age but this I didn't mind. I was already an addict. The drug that had me in its grip was literature. But that is too grand a name for it – I was devoted to reading. Books of almost any kind had a fascination for me. I read everything I could lay my hands on whether I understood it or not.

My elder brother was disgusted by my lack of interest in all the things he was so good at. He was an excellent sportsman, could built a rabbit hutch, paint a picture and could make a fishing rod – for he was a dedicated angler. Eventually he decided that he had to save me from myself. He tried to make me play football but my fat prevented me running and if the ball happened to come near me, my cowardice ensured that I made no contact with it. He sat over me whilst I made some chicken coops but even the chicken refused to take the resultant lopsided boxes seriously and continued to roost in the apple trees in the orchard. Finally he decided to take me fishing.

Protesting fiercely, I was woken at four in the morning and rudely tipped out of bed. My mood improved somewhat when I saw the large quantity of sandwiches left on the kitchen table by my mother the night before. At least we wouldn't starve. As we cycled through the summer dawn I saw the sun rise for the first time and the early morning mist being drawn from the trees by the growing heat. I knew that we were heading for a series of ponds that lay in some fields a mile or two from an old Roman road, the Fosse Way. In the Middle Ages there had been a monastery nearby and the ponds had been stocked by the monks with carp for their Friday meals.

I protested again when my brother made me leave my bicycle about a mile away from the ponds and loaded me with equipment. He quietened my moans with his usual reasoned approach – a quick clip round the ear. Thus encouraged I crept over the damp stubble and watched as my brother set up his rod and tackle and ground-baited the area which he knew from experience yielded the best fish. I tried to follow his example but found that my line constantly tangled and that I repeatedly hooked either my trousers or the surrounding bushes. Eventually my brother took pity on me, put everything in order and cast for me. We settled down to wait. Apart from the birds all was silent. I felt my first stir of excitement as I saw a fox stealing quietly home along the hedgerow. Then my brother's float rose gently to lie flat on the surface before disappearing under the water in the direction of the reeds. He struck, fought and landed what was to me a magical fish – golden bronze and beautiful. Memory makes it a giant but I do not suppose that it was more than half a pound in weight. I had always known my big brother was a superman; this was certain proof. I couldn't wait for my turn to come. I had to wait. Eventually my float bobbed and moved toward the shore. I struck. Now I would land a fish, finer than my brother's in every way. At last he would have to acknowledge that I was his equal. I reeled in fast but no golden monster broke the surface. Instead something black and orange and shaped like a small dragon appeared. I had caught my first newt. I looked at it in horror. I didn't know what to do with it. I wept with mortification.

After my brother had broken its grasp on my worm, had assured me that it was harmless and had turned it over to show me its beautiful orange belly, I began to feel a strong affection for it. After all it was mine, it might not be a fish but it lived in the water and had chosen my worm. I never did catch a carp that day but I took my newt home and put it in an aquarium which I carefully laid out to create the ideal newt world. Next morning I got out of bed almost willingly, cycled through the countryside greeting the dawn chorus as old friends, crept with exaggerated caution towards the edge of the pond and only caught my trousers twice before I cast my worm close to where my newt had been feeding the day before. I was hoping to catch his mate. To my great surprise I had two carp in the keep net within an hour – stout, golden, beautiful. I was an angler. A new addiction had begun.

I did not desert my first love, however. I soon found that fishing and reading go together. Particularly when I discovered a network of old canals, long bereft of their narrow boats, within cycling distance of my home. Quiet endless days were spent sitting amongst the willow herb on their banks with my rod in its rest and a book in my hand. To the committed reader every fresh book is a possible new world of delights. Within that book each chapter can be savored both in advance and in retrospect. If you are reading a book by a gifted writer, each new page can surprise and delight you – a turn of the plot, a moving phrase, a happy choice of word.

Fishing is surprisingly similar. It gives pleasures of anticipation and memory. The dullest and most uneventful day can suddenly be brought to life by the catching of a fish. No single moment exists that isn't bursting with promise and possible excitement. Nothing may happen for hours, for days even. Commonsense and past experience can prove to you that the time and the hour are totally unlikely to yield a catch but still you hope. What is more, just often enough to keep you a slave to your addiction, something does happen, something quite unlikely, something that starts the blood and heart pounding again.

It may not necessarily be something to do with the fish themselves. My great-uncle Charlie, a farmer of limited imagination, was walking by the river one night to judge the level of the water for the next morning's fishing when he was attacked by a heron for no apparent reason at all. To his great surprise, and pain, it flew at his face and seized his nose in its bill. He had to choke it to death before he could make it release its grip. He always told us boys that it was for this reason that his nose was so red and bulbous at the end. Even in our youth and innocence we didn't accept this as the only reason. My brother said that it was probably the glow from Uncle Charlie's nose in the gathering dusk that had upset the heron in the first place.

It was due to another Uncle that I was first able to bring my two great interests together. Uncle Harry presented me with Izaak Walton's *The Compleat Angler* on my fourteenth birthday. At first I was put off by the fact that it is written in the form of a dialogue between a fisherman, old Izaak himself, a fowler and a hunter. The language was a little too archaic for easy reading but I glanced through it and read first those parts dealing with the catching and the cooking of various fish. Gradually I became at ease with the language and began to appreciate its beauty. Soon I found myself going back to the beginning and reading through it all with the greatest pleasure.

Truth to tell, *The Compleat Angler* is more of a literary treasure than a book of instruction to the angler for Izaak was in no way a sound, all-round fisherman. He had little experience, if any, of fly-fishing and never used a reel. Many of his maxims he had copied from the two great angling writers who preceded him, Dame Juliana Berners (1496) and Thomas Barker (1651). What has ensured that *The Compleat Angler* be printed in more than fifty editions since it was first published in 1653, is the way that

Walton so lovingly details his joy in the river meadows, the country folk, the fishing inns and the effect of the weather upon the angler. The charm of his character and the happiness of his disposition speak out from every page of his book. Never has the sheer pleasure of angling, and all that is attendant upon it, been so well expressed.

My next find amongst fishing books was *Going Fishing* by Negley Farson (1942). This great American foreign correspondent combined good fishing stories with a gift for writing about out of the way places and people. A gift that made you feel he was sitting on the other side of a camp fire and that you were his chosen companion – equally skilled as a fisherman and equally dauntless a traveller. To my great sorrow I lost my copy during the war but was delighted to find the familiar binding quite recently on the shelves of a secondhand book barn in an isolated Cornish village. Somewhere remote and unlikely enough to appeal to Mr Farson.

During my lifetime and up until today I remain a hopeless addict to both books and fishing. Testing the patience and good nature of my family by being totally unable to pass by any bookshop or tackle shop. Such space in my home as is not littered with books is cluttered with rods, fishing bags, keep nets and odd jars or plastic boxes of bait. Fishing and reading both have the great advantage of being year long occupations. You can fish in almost any season and can dress your tackle when fishing is impossible. There is no seasonal bar to reading. The pleasure is equally great whether the book is read before a log fire in Winter or in an apple orchard in the spring. My ideal is to combine my two obsessions and to read books about fishing; I even do it whilst fishing, although this confession will upset purists.

Moving quietly towards my fifteenth year, still stout and not noticeably energetic, I am firmly convinced that the ideal combination leading to a happy life is to have the time to both fish and read. When fishing, it is a pleasure to try out new and untested water, and yet, how often do we return to the waters we have fished a hundred times or more – waters we know and love, whose imperfections we savor as much as their perfections? In making this selection of writing on fishing I have had this in mind. Some of the pieces I have chosen you will know well and greet as welcome old friends. Others come from ancient books on angling and may have been generally unread for a hundred years or more. You will find, I am sure, that there is no generation gap amongst brothers of the angle and that the voice of the enthusiast comes down the years undimmed. Then, as now, the eternal angler will fish whenever he can. When he can not, he will

14

read about fishing. Izaak Walton's great friend and fellow author, Charles Cotton, expressed it perfectly three hundred years ago:

> That man is happy in his share
> Who is warm clad, and cleanly fed,
> Whose necessaries bound his care,
> And honest labour makes his bed;
>
> Who with his angle and his books,
> Can think the longest day well spent,
> And praises God when back he looks
> And finds that all was innocent.

THE
YOUNG ANGLER

CROCKER'S HOLE

R. D. Blackmore

1896

THE CULM, which rises in Somersetshire, and hastening into a fairer land (as the border waters wisely do) falls into the Exe near Killerton, formerly was a lovely trout stream, such as perverts the Devonshire angler from due respect toward Father Thames and the other canals round London. In the Devonshire valleys it is sweet to see how soon a spring becomes a rill, and a rill runs on into a rivulet, and a rivulet swells into a brook; and before one has time to say, "What are you at?" – before the first tree it ever spoke to is a dummy, or the first hill it ever ran down has turned blue, here we have all the airs and graces, demands and assertions of a full-grown river.

But what is the test of a river? Who shall say? "The power to drown a man," replies the river darkly. But rudeness is not argument. Rather shall we say that the power to work a good undershot wheel, without being dammed up all night in a pond, and leaving a tidy backstream to spare at the bottom of the orchard, is a fair certificate of riverhood. If so, many Devonshire streams attain that rank within five miles of their spring; aye, and rapidly add to it. At every turn they gather aid, from ash-clad dingle and aldered meadow, mossy rock and ferny wall, hedge-trough roofed with bramble netting, where the baby water lurks, and lanes that coming down to ford bring suicidal tribute. Arrogant, all-engrossing river, now it has claimed a great valley of its own; and whatever falls within the hill scoop, sooner or later belongs to itself. Even the crystal "shutt" that crosses the farmyard by the wood-rick, and glides down an aqueduct of last year's bark for Mary to fill the kettle from; and even the tricklets that have no organs for telling or knowing their business, but only get into unwary oozings in and among the water-grass, and there make moss and forget themselves among it – one and all, they come to the same thing at last, and that is the river.

The Culm used to be a good river at Culmstock, tormented already by a factory, but not strangled as yet by a railroad. How it is now the present writer does not know, and is afraid to ask, having heard of a vile "Culm Valley Line". But Culmstock bridge was a very pretty place to stand and contemplate the ways of trout; which is easier work than to catch them. When I was just big enough to peep above the rim, or to lie upon it with

18

one leg inside for fear of tumbling over, what a mighty river it used to seem, for it takes a treat there and spreads itself. Above the bridge the factory stream falls in again, having done its business, and washing its hands in the innocent half that has strayed down the meadows. Then under the arches they both rejoice and come to a slide of about two feet, and make a short, wide pool below, and indulge themselves in perhaps two islands, through which a little river always magnifies itself, and maintains a mysterious middle. But after that, all of it used to come together, and make off in one body for the meadows, intent upon nurturing trout with rapid stickles, and buttercuppy corners where fat flies may tumble in. And here you may find in the very first meadow, or at any rate you might have found, forty years ago, the celebrated "Crocker's Hole".

The story of Crocker is unknown to me, and interesting as it doubtless was, I do not deal with him, but with his Hole. Tradition said that he was a baker's boy who, during his basket-rounds, fell in love with a maiden who received the cottage-loaf, or perhaps good "Households", for her master's use. No doubt she was charming as a girl should be, but whether she encouraged the youthful baker and then betrayed him with false *rôle*, or whether she "consisted" throughout – as our cousins across the water express it – is known to their *manes* only. Enough that she would not have the floury lad; and that he, after giving in his books and money, sought an untimely grave among the trout. And this was the first pool below the bread-walk deep enough to drown a five-foot baker boy. Sad it was; but such things must be, and bread must still be delivered daily.

A truce to such reflections – as our foremost writers always say, when they do not see how to go on with them – but it is a serious thing to know what Crocker's Hole was like; because at a time when (if he had only persevered, and married the maid, and succeeded to the oven, and reared a large family of short-weight bakers) he might have been leaning on his crutch beside the pool, and teaching his grandson to swim by precept (that beautiful proxy for practice) – at such a time, I say, there lived a remarkably fine trout in that hole. Anglers are notoriously truthful, especially as to what they catch, or even more frequently have not caught. Though I may have written fiction, among many other sins – as a nice old lady told me once – now I have to deal with facts; and foul scorn would I count it ever to make believe that I caught that fish. My length at that time was not more than the butt of a four-jointed rod, and all I could catch was a minnow with a pin, which our cook Lydia would not cook, but used to say, "Oh, what a shame, Master Richard! they would have been trout in the summer, please God! if you would only a' let 'em grow on". She is living now, and will bear me out in this.

But upon every great occasion there arises a great man; or to put it more accurately, in the present instance, a mighty and distinguished boy. My father, being the parson of the parish, and getting, need it be said, small pay, took sundry pupils, very pleasant fellows, about to adorn the universities. Among them was the original "Bude Light", as he was satirically called at Cambridge, for he came from Bude, and there was no light in him. Among them also was John Pike, a born Zebedee, if ever there was one.

John Pike was a thick-set younker, with a large and bushy head, keen blue eyes that could see through water, and the proper slouch of shoulder into which great anglers ripen; but greater still are born with it; and of these was Master John. It mattered little what the weather was, and scarcely more as to the time of year, John Pike must have his fishing every day, and on Sundays he read about it, and made flies. All the rest of the time he was thinking about it.

My father was coaching him in the fourth book of the *Aeneid* and all those wonderful speeches of Dido, where passion disdains construction; but the only line Pike cared for was of horsehair. "I fear, Mr Pike, that you are not giving me your entire attention", my father used to say in his mild dry way; and once when Pike was more than usually abroad, his tutor begged to share his meditations. "Well, sir", said Pike, who was very truthful, "I can see a green drake by the strawberry tree, the first of the season, and your derivation of 'barbarous' put me in mind of my barberry dye." In those days it was a very nice point to get the right tint for the mallard's feather.

No sooner was lesson done than Pike, whose rod was ready upon the lawn, dashed away always for the river, rushing headlong down the hill, and away to the left through a private yard, where "no thoroughfare" was put up, and a big dog stationed to enforce it. But Cerberus himself could not have stopped John Pike; his conscience backed him up in trespass the most sinful when his heart was inditing of a trout upon the rise.

All this, however, is preliminary, as the boy said when he put his father's coat upon his grandfather's tenterhooks, with felonious intent upon his grandmother's apples; the main point to be understood is this, that nothing – neither brazen tower, hundred-eyed Argus, nor Cretan Minotaur – could stop John Pike from getting at a good stickle. But, even as the world knows nothing of its greatest men, its greatest men know nothing of the world beneath their very nose, till fortune sneezes dexter. For two years John Pike must have been whipping the water as hard as Xerxes, without having ever once dreamed of the glorious trout that lived in Crocker's Hole. But why, when he ought to have been at least on bowing terms with every fish as long as his middle finger, why had he failed to know this champion? The answer is simple – because of his short cuts. Flying as he did like an arrow from a bow, Pike used to hit his beloved river at an elbow, some furlong below Crocker's Hole, where a sweet little stickle sailed away downstream, whereas for the length of a meadow upward the water lay smooth, clear, and shallow; therefore the youth, with so little time to spare, rushed into the downward joy.

And here it may be noted that the leading maxim of the present period, that man can discharge his duty only by going counter to the stream, was scarcely mooted in those days. My grandfather (who was a wonderful man, if he was accustomed to fill a cart in two days of fly-fishing on the Barle) regularly fished downstream; and what more than a cartload need anyone put into his basket?

And surely it is more genial and pleasant to behold our friend the river growing and thriving as we go on, strengthening its voice and enlarging its bosom, and sparkling through each successive meadow with richer plenitude of silver, than to trace it against its own grain and good-will toward weakness, and littleness, and immature conceptions.

However, you will say that if John Pike had fished up stream, he would have found this trout much sooner. And that is true; but still, as it was, the trout had more time to grow into such a prize. And the way in which John found him out was this. For some days he had been tormented with a very painful tooth, which even poisoned all the joys of fishing. Therefore he resolved to have it out, and sturdily entered the shop of John Sweetland, the village blacksmith, and there paid his sixpence. Sweetland extracted the teeth of the village, whenever they required it, in the simplest and most effectual way. A piece of fine wire was fastened round the tooth, and the other end round the anvil's nose, then the sturdy blacksmith shut the lower half of his shop door, which was about breast-high, with the patient outside and the anvil within; a strong push of the foot upset the anvil, and the tooth flew out like a well-thrown fly.

When John Pike had suffered this very bravely, "Ah, Master Pike," said the blacksmith, with a grin, "I reckon you won't pull out thic there big vish" – the smithy commanded a view of the river – "clever as you be, quite so peart as thiccy."

21

"What big fish?" asked the boy, with deepest interest, though his mouth was bleeding fearfully.

"Why that girt mortial of a vish as hath his hover in Crocker's Hole. Zum on 'em saith as a' must be a zammon."

Off went Pike with his handkerchief to his mouth, and after him ran Alec Bolt, one of his fellow-pupils, who had come to the shop to enjoy the extraction.

"Oh, my!" was all that Pike could utter, when by craftily posting himself he had obtained a good view of this grand fish.

"I'll lay you a crown you don't catch him!" cried Bolt, an impatient youth, who scorned angling.

"How long will you give me?" asked the wary Pike, who never made rash wagers.

"Oh! till the holidays if you like; if that won't do, till Michaelmas."

Now the midsummer holidays were six weeks off – boys used not to talk of "vacations" then, still less of "recesses."

"I think I'll bet you," said Pike, in his slow way, bending forward carefully, with his keen eyes on this monster; "but it would not be fair to take till Michaelmas. I'll bet you a crown that I catch him before the holidays – at least, unless some other fellow does."

The day of that most momentous interview must have been the 14th of May. Of the year I will not be so sure; for children take more note of days than of years, for which the latter have their full revenge thereafter. It must have been the 14th, because the morrow was our holiday, given upon the 15th of May, in honour of a birthday.

Now, John Pike was beyond his years wary as well as enterprising, calm as well as ardent, quite as rich in patience as in promptitude and vigour. But Alec Bolt was a headlong youth, volatile, hot, and hasty, fit only to fish the Maëlstrom, or a torrent of new lava. And the moment he had laid that wager he expected his crown piece; though time, as the lawyers phrase it, was "expressly of the essence of the contract". And now he demanded that Pike should spend the holiday in trying to catch that trout.

"I shall not go near him," that lad replied, "until I have got a new collar." No piece of personal adornment was it, without which he would not act, but rather that which now is called the fly-cast, or the gut-cast, or the trace, or what it may be. "And another thing," continued Pike; "the bet is off if you go near him, either now or at any other time, without asking my leave first, and then only going as I tell you."

"What do I want with the great slimy beggar?" the arrogant Bolt made answer. "A good rat is worth fifty of him. No fear of my going near him, Pike. You shan't get out of it that way."

Pike showed his remarkable qualities that day by fishing exactly as he would have fished without having heard of the great Crockerite. He was up and away upon the mill-stream before breakfast; and the forenoon he devoted to his favourite course – first down the Craddock stream, a very pretty confluent of the Culm, and from its junction, down the pleasant hams, where the river winds toward Uffculme. It was my privilege to accompany this hero, as his humble Sancho; while Bolt and the faster race went up the river ratting. We were back in time to have Pike's trout (which ranged between two ounces and one-half pound) fried for the early dinner; and here it may be lawful to remark that the trout of the Culm are of the very purest excellence, by reason of the flinty bottom, at any rate in these the upper regions. For the valley is the western outlet of the Blackdown range, with the Beacon hill upon the North, and Hackpen long ridge to the south; and beyond that again the whetstone hill, upon whose western end dark port-holes scarped with white grit mark the pits. But flint is the staple of the broad Culm Valley, under good, well-pastured loam; and here are chalcedonies and agate stones.

At dinner everybody had a brace of trout – large for the larger folk, little for the little ones, with coughing and some patting on the back for bones. What of equal purport could the fierce rat-hunter show? Pike explained many points in the history of each fish, seeming to know them none the worse, and love them all the better, for being fried. We banqueted, neither a whit did soul get stinted of banquet impartial. Then the wielder of the magic rod very modestly sought leave of absence at the tea time.

"Fishing again, Mr Pike, I suppose," my father answered pleasantly; "I used to be fond of it at your age; but never so entirely wrapped up in it as you are."

"No, sir; I am not going fishing again. I want to walk to Wellington, to get some things at Cherry's."

"Books, Mr Pike? Ah! I am very glad of that. But I fear it can only be fly-books."

"I want a little Horace for eighteen-pence – the Cambridge one just published, to carry in my pocket – and a new hank of gut."

"Which of the two is more important? Put that into Latin, and answer it."

"Utrum pluris facio? Flaccum flocci. Viscera magni." With this vast effort Pike turned as red as any trout spot.

"After that who could refuse you?" said my father. "You always tell the truth, my boy, in Latin or in English."

Although it was a long walk, some fourteen miles to Wellington and back, I got permission to go with Pike; and as we crossed the bridge and saw the tree that overhung Crocker's Hole, I begged him to show me that mighty fish.

"Not a bit of it," he replied. "It would bring the blackguards. If the blackguards once find him out, it is all over with him."

"The blackguards are all in factory now, and I am sure they cannot see us from the windows. They won't be out till five o'clock."

With the true liberality of young England, which abides even now as large and glorious as ever, we always called the free and enlightened operatives of the period by the courteous name above set down, and it must be acknowledged that some of them deserved it, although perhaps they poached with less of science than their sons. But the cowardly murder of fish by liming the water was already prevalent.

Yielding to my request and perhaps his own desire – manfully kept in check that morning – Pike very carefully approached that pool, command- ing me to sit down while he reconnoitred from the meadow upon the right bank of the stream. And the place which had so sadly quenched the fire of the poor baker's love filled my childish heart with dread and deep wonder at the cruelty of women. But as for John Pike, all he thought of was the fish and the best way to get at him.

Very likely that hole is "holed out" now, as the Yankees well express it, or at any rate changed out of knowlege. Even in my time a very heavy flood entirely altered its character; but to the eager eye of Pike it seemed pretty much as follows, and possibly it may have come to such a form again.

The river, after passing through a hurdle fence at the head of the meadow, takes a little turn or two of bright and shallow indifference, then gathers itself into a good strong slide, as if going down a slope instead of steps. The right bank is high and beetles over with yellow loam and grassy fringe; but the other side is of flinty shingle, low and bare and washed by floods. At the end of this rapid the stream turns sharply under an ancient alder tree into a large, deep, calm repose, cool, unruffled, and sheltered from the sun by branch and leaf – and that is the hole of poor Crocker.

At the head of the pool (where the hasty current rushes in so eagerly, with noisy excitement and much ado) the quieter waters from below, having rested and enlarged themselves, come lapping up round either curve, with some recollection of their past career, the hoary experience of foam. And sidling toward the new arrival of the impulsive column, where they meet it, things go on, which no man can describe without his mouth being full of water. A "V" is formed, a fancy letter V, beyond any designer's tracery, and even beyond his imagination, a perpetually fluctuating limpid wedge, perpetually crenelled and rippled into by little ups and downs that try to make an impress, but can only glide away upon either side or sink in dimples under it. And here a grey bough of the ancient alder stretches across, like a thirsty giant's arm, and makes it a very ticklish place to throw a fly, yet this was the very spot our John Pike must put his fly into, or lose his crown.

Because the great tenant of Crocker's Hole, who allowed no other fish to wag a fin there, and from strict monopoly had grown so fat, kept his victualling yard – if so low an expression can be used concerning him – within about a square yard of this spot. He had a sweet hover, both for rest and recreation, under the bank, in a placid antre, where the water made no noise, but tickled his belly in digestive ease. The loftier the character is of any being, the slower and more dignified his movements are. No true psychologist could have believed – as Sweetland the blacksmith did, and Mr Pook the tinman – that this trout could ever be the embodiment of Crocker. For this was the last trout in the universal world to drown himself for love; if truly any trout has done so.

"You may come now, and try to look along my back," John Pike, with a reverential whisper, said to me. "Now don't be in a hurry, young stupid; kneel down. He is not to be disturbed at his dinner, mind. You keep behind me, and look along my back; I never clapped eyes on such a whopper."

I had to kneel down in a tender reminiscence of pasture land, and gaze carefully; and not having eyes like those of our Zebedee (who offered his spine for a camera, as he crawled on all fours in front of me), it took me a long time to descry an object most distinct to all who have that special gift of piercing with their eyes the water. See what is said upon this subject in that delicious book, *The Gamekeeper at Home*.

"You are no better than a muff," said Pike, and it was not in my power to deny it.

"If the sun would only leave off," I said. But the sun, who was having a very pleasant play with the sparkle of the water and the twinkle of the leaves, had no inclination to leave off yet, but kept the rippling crystal in a dance of flashing facets, and the quivering verdure in a steady flush of gold.

But suddenly a May-fly, a luscious grey-drake, richer and more delicate than canvas-back or woodcock, with a dart and a leap and a merry zigzag, began to enjoy a little game above the stream. Rising and falling like a gnat, thrilling her gauzy wings, and arching her elegant pellucid frame, every now and then she almost dipped her three long tapering whisks into the dimples of the water.

"He sees her! He'll have her as sure as a gun!" cried Pike, with a gulp, as if he himself were "rising". "Now, can you see him, stupid?"

"Crikey, crokums!" I exclaimed, with classic elegance; "I have seen that long thing for five minutes; but I took it for a tree."

"You little" – animal quite early in the alphabet – "now don't you stir a peg, or I'll dig my elbow into you."

The great trout was stationary almost as a stone, in the middle of the "V" above described. He was gently fanning with his large clear fins, but holding his own against the current mainly by the wagging of his broad-fluked tail. As soon as my slow eyes had once defined him, he grew upon them mightily, moulding himself in the matrix of the water, as a thing put into jelly does. And I doubt whether even John Pike saw him more accurately than I did. His size was such, or seemed to be such, that I fear to say a word about it; not because language does not contain the word, but from dread of exaggeration. But his shape and colour may be reasonably told without wounding the feeling of an age whose incredulity springs from self-knowledge.

His head was truly small, his shoulders vast; the spring of his back was like a rainbow when the sun is southing; the generous sweep of his deep elastic belly, nobly pulped out with rich nurture, showed what the power of his brain must be, and seemed to undulate, time for time, with the vibrant vigilance of his large wise eyes. His latter end was consistent also. An elegant taper run of counter, coming almost to a cylinder, as a mackerel does, boldly developed with a hugeous spread to a glorious amplitude of swallow-tail. His colour was all that can well be desired, but ill-described by any poor word-palette. Enough that he seemed to tone away from olive and umber, with carmine stars, to glowing gold and soft pure silver, mantled with a subtle flush of rose and fawn and opal.

Swoop came a swallow, as we gazed, and was gone with a flick, having missed the May-fly. But the wind of his passage, or the skir of wing, struck the merry dancer down, so that he fluttered for one instant on the wave, and that instant was enough. Swift as the swallow, and more true of aim, the great trout made one dart, and a sound, deeper than a tinkle, but as silvery as a bell, rang the poor ephemerid's knell. The rapid water scarcely showed a break; but a bubble sailed down the pool, and the dark hollow echoed with the music of a rise.

"He knows how to take a fly," said Pike; "he has had too many to be tricked with mine. Have him I must; but how ever shall I do it?"

All the way to Wellington he uttered not a word, but shambled along with a mind full of care. When I ventured to look up now and then, to surmise what was going on beneath his hat, deeply-set eyes and a wrinkled forehead, relieved at long intervals by a solid shake, proved that there are meditations deeper than those of philosopher or statesman.

Surely no trout could have been misled by the artificial May-fly of that time, unless he were either a very young fish, quite new to entomology, or else one afflicted with a combination of myopy and bulimy. Even now there is room for plenty of improvement in our counterfeit presentment; but in those days the body was made with yellow mohair, ribbed with red silk and gold twist, and as thick as a fertile bumble-bee. John Pike perceived that to offer such a thing to Crocker's trout would probably consign him – even if his great stamina should overget the horror – to an uneatable death, through just and natural indignation. On the other hand, while the May-fly lasted, a trout so cultured, so highly refined, so full of light and sweetness, would never demean himself to low bait, or any coarse son of a maggot.

Meanwhile Alec Bolt allowed poor Pike no peaceful thought, no calm absorption of high mind into the world of flies, no placid period of cobbler's wax, floss-silk, turned hackles, and dubbing. For in making of flies John Pike had his special moments of inspiration, times of clearer insight into the everlasting verities, times of brighter conception and more subtle execution, tails of more elastic grace and heads of a neater and nattier expression. As a poet labours at one immortal line, compressing worlds of wisdom into the music of ten syllables, so toiled the patient Pike about the fabric of a fly comprising all the excellence that ever sprang from maggot. Yet Bolt rejoiced to jerk his elbow at the moment of sublimest art. And a swarm of flies was blighted thus.

Peaceful, therefore, and long-suffering, and full of resignation as he was, John Pike came slowly to the sad perception that arts avail not without arms. The elbow, so often jerked, at last took a voluntary jerk from the shoulder, and Alec Bolt lay prostrate, with his right eye full of cobbler's wax. This put a desirable check upon his energies for a week or more, and by that time Pike had flown his fly.

When the honeymoon of spring and summer (which they are now too fashionable to celebrate in this country), the hey-day of the whole year marked by the budding of the wild rose, the start of the wheatear from its sheath, the feathering of the lesser plantain, and flowering of the meadow-sweet, and, foremost for the angler's joy, the caracole of may-flies – when these things are to be seen and felt (which has not happened at all this year), then rivers should be mild and bright, skies blue and white with fleecy cloud, the west wind blowing softly, and the trout in charming appetite.

On such a day came Pike to the bank of Culm, with a loudly beating heart. A fly there is, not ignominious, or of cowdab origin, neither gross and heavy-bodied, from cradlehood of slimy stones, nor yet of menacing aspect and suggesting deeds of poison, but elegant, bland, and of sunny nature, and obviously good to eat. Him or her – why quest we which? – the shepherd of the dale, contemptuous of gender, except in his own species, has called, and as long as they two co-exist will call, the "Yellow Sally". A fly that does not waste the day in giddy dances and the fervid waltz, but undergoes family incidents with decorum and discretion. He or she, as the case may be for the natural history of the river bank is a book to come hereafter, and of fifty men who make flies not one knows the name of the fly he is making – in the early morning of June, or else in the second quarter of the afternoon, this Yellow Sally fares abroad, with a nice well-ordered flutter.

Despairing of the May-fly, as it still may be despaired of, Pike came down to the river with his masterpiece of portraiture. The artificial Yellow Sally is generally always – as they say in Cheshire – a mile or more too yellow. On the other hand, the "Yellow Dun" conveys no idea of any Sally. But Pike had made a very decent Sally, not perfect (for he was young as well as wise), but far above any counterfeit to be had in fishing-tackle shops. How he made it, he told nobody. But if he lives now, as I hope he does, any of my readers may ask him through the G.P.O., and hope to get an answer.

It fluttered beautifully on the breeze, and in such living form, that a brother or sister Sally came up to see it, and went away sadder and wiser. Then Pike said; "Get away, you young wretch," to your humble servant who tells this tale; yet being better than his words, allowed that pious follower to lie down upon his digestive organs and with deep attention watch. There must have been great things to see, but to see them so was difficult. And if I huddle up what happened, excitement also shares the blame.

Pike had fashioned well the time and manner of this overture. He knew that the giant Crockerite was satiate now with May-flies, or began to find their flavour failing, as happens to us with asparagus, marrow-fat peas, or strawberries, when we have had a month of them. And he thought that the first Yellow Sally of the season, inferior though it were, might have the special charm of novelty. With the skill of a Zulu, he stole up through the branches over the lower pool till he came to a spot where a yard-wide opening gave just space for spring of rod. Then he saw his desirable friend at dinner, wagging his tail, as a hungry gentleman dining with the Lord Mayor agitates his coat. With one dexterous whirl, untaught by any of the many books upon the subject, John Pike laid his Yellow Sally (for he cast with one fly only) as lightly as gossamer upon the rapid, about a yard in front of the big trout's head. A moment's pause, and then, too quick for words, was the thing that happened.

A heavy plunge was followed by a fearful rush. Forgetful of current the river was ridged, as if with a plough driven under it; the strong line, though given out as fast as might be, twanged like a harp-string as it cut the wave, and then Pike stood up, like a ship dismasted, with the butt of his rod snapped below the ferrule. He had one of those foolish things, just invented, a hollow butt of hickory; and the finial ring of his spare top looked out, to ask what had happened to the rest of it. "Bad luck!" cried the fisherman; "but never mind, I shall have him next time, to a certainty."

When this great issue came to be considered, the cause of it was sadly obvious. The fish, being hooked, had made off with the rush of a shark for the bottom of the pool. A thicket of saplings below the alder tree had stopped the judicious hooker from all possibility of following; and when he strove to turn him by elastic pliance, his rod broke at the breach of pliability. "I have learned a sad lesson," said John Pike, looking sadly.

How many fellows would have given up this matter, and glorified themselves for having hooked so grand a fish, while explaining that they must have caught him, if they could have done it! But Pike only told me not to say a word about it, and began to make ready for another tug of war. He made himself a splice-rod, short and handy, of well-seasoned ash, with a stout top of bamboo, tapered so discreetly, and so balanced in its spring, that verily it formed an arc, with any pressure on it, as perfect as a leafy poplar in a stormy summer. "Now break it if you can," he said, "by any amount of rushes; I'll hook you by your jacket collar; you cut away now, and I'll land you."

This was highly skilful, and he did it many times; and whenever I was landed well, I got a lolly-pop, so that I was careful not to break his tackle. Moreover he made him a landing net, with a kidney-bean stick, a ring of wire, and his own best nightcap of strong cotton net. Then he got the farmer's leave, and lopped obnoxious bushes; and now the chiefest question was: what bait, and when to offer it? In spite of his sad rebuff, the spirit of John Pike had been equable. The genuine angling mind is steadfast, large, and self-supported, and to the vapid, ignominious chaff, tossed by swine upon the idle wind, it pays as much heed as a big trout does to a dance of midges. People put their fingers to their noses and said: "Master Pike, have you caught him yet?" and Pike only answered: "Wait a bit." If ever this fortitude and perseverance is to be recovered as the English Brand (the one thing that has made us what we are, and may yet redeem us from niddering shame), a degenerate age should encourage the habit of fishing and never despairing. And the brightest sign yet for our future is the increasing demand for hooks and gut.

Pike fished in a manlier age, when nobody would dream of cowering from a savage because he was clever at skulking; and when, if a big fish broke the rod, a stronger rod was made for him, according to the usage of Great Britain. And though the young angler had been defeated, he did not sit down and have a good cry over it.

About the second week in June, when the May-fly had danced its day, and died – for the season was an early one – and Crocker's trout had recovered from the wound to his feelings and philanthropy, there came a night of gentle rain, of pleasant tinkling upon window ledges, and a soothing patter among young leaves, and the Culm was yellow in the morning. "I mean to do it this afternoon," Pike whispered to me, as he came back panting. "When the water clears there will be a splendid time."

The lover of the rose knows well a gay voluptuous beetle, whose pleasure is to lie embedded in a fount of beauty. Deep among the incurving petals of the blushing fragrance, he loses himself in his joys some times, till a breezy waft reveals him. And when the sunlight breaks upon his luscious dissipation, few would have the heart to oust him, such a gem from such a setting. All his back is emerald sparkles; all his front red Indian gold, and here and there he grows white spots to save the eye from aching. Pike put his finger in and fetched him out, and offered him a little change of joys, by putting a Limerick hook through his thorax, and bringing it out between his elytra. *Cetonia aurata* liked it not, but pawed the air very naturally, and fluttered with his wings attractively.

"I meant to have tried with a fern web," said the angler; "until I saw one of these beggars this morning. If he works like that upon the water, he will do. It was hopeless to try artificials again. What a lovely colour the water is! Only three days now to the holidays. I have run it very close. You be ready, younker."

With these words he stepped upon a branch of the alder, for the tone of the water allowed approach, being soft and sublustrous, without any mud. Also Master Pike's own tone was such as becomes the fisher man, calm, deliberate, free from nerve, but full of eye and muscle. He stepped upon the alder bough to get as near as might be to the fish, for he could not cast this beetle like a fly; it must be dropped gently and allowed to play. "You may come and look," he said to me; "when the water is so, they have no eyes in their tails."

The rose-beetle trod upon the water prettily, under a lively vibration, and he looked quite as happy, and considerably more active, than when he had been cradled in the anthers of the rose. To the eye of a fish he was a strong individual, fighting courageously with the current, but sure to be beaten through lack of fins; and mercy suggested, as well as appetite, that the proper solution was to gulp him.

"Hooked him in the gullet. He can't get off!" cried John Pike, labouring to keep his nerves under; "every inch of tackle is as strong as a bell-pull. Now, if I don't land him, I will never fish again!"

Providence, which had constructed Pike, foremost of all things, for lofty angling – disdainful of worm and even minnow – Providence, I say, at this adjuration, pronounced that Pike must catch that trout. Not many anglers are heaven-born; and for one to drop off the hook halfway through his teens would be infinitely worse than to slay the champion trout. Pike felt the force of this, and rushing through the rushes, shouted: "I am sure to have him, Dick! Be ready with my nightcap."

Rod in a bow, like a springle-riser; line on the hum, like the string of Paganini; winch on the gallop, like a harpoon wheel, Pike, the head-centre of everything, dashing through thick and thin, and once taken overhead – for he jumped into the hole, when he must have lost him else, but the fish too impetuously towed him out, and made off in passion for another pool, when, if he had only retired to his hover, the angler might have shared the baker's fate – all these things (I tell you, for they all come up again, as if the day were yesterday) so scared me of my never very steadfast wits, that I could only holloa! But one thing I did, I kept the nightcap ready.

"He is pretty nearly spent, I do believe," said Pike; and his voice was like balm of Gilead, as we came to Farmer Anning's meadow, a quarter of a mile below Crocker's Hole. "Take it coolly, my dear boy, and we shall be safe to have him."

Never have I felt, through forty years, such tremendous responsibility. I had not the faintest notion how to use a landing net; but a mighty general directed me. "Don't let him see it; don't let him see it! Don't clap it over him; go under him, you stupid! If he makes another rush, he will get off, after all. Bring it up his tail. Well done! You have him!"

The mighty trout lay in the nightcap of Pike, which was half a fathom long, with a tassel at the end, for his mother had made it in the winter evenings. "Come and hold the rod, if you can't lift him," my master shouted, and so I did. Then, with both arms straining, and his mouth wide open, John Pike made a mighty sweep, and we both fell upon the grass and rolled, with the giant of the deep flapping heavily between us, and no power left to us, except to cry, "Hurrah!"

EARLY EXPERIENCES
George M. L. La Branche

1924

FROM MY EARLIEST BOYHOOD I have been devoted to the fly fisher's art, having been inducted into it by my father, who was an ardent angler before me. For more than twenty years I have fished the near-by streams of New York and Pennsylvania; not a season has passed without having brought to me the pleasure of casting a fly over their waters. Each recurring year I find myself, as the season approaches, eagerly looking forward to the bright days when I can again go upon the streams. In the early days of the season, however, I am content to overhaul my gear, to dream alone, or talk with others about the active days to come; for I have never enjoyed going upon the waters so long as the air still holds chill winter's bite.

During the early years of my angling I fished my flies wet or sunk. Such was the manner universally prevailing upon our streams and the manner of my teaching. I had read about the dry fly and knew that its use was general in England, which country may justly be said to be its place of origin. That this is true may not be gainsaid, yet it seems to me remarkable that with all the reputed ingenuity of Americans the present development of dry fly fishing for trout should be almost entirely the work of British sportsmen. That the use of the dry fly on streams in this country has not been more common may be due to a pardonable disinclination upon the part of expert wet fly anglers to admit the weakness of their method under conditions as they now exist. Their method has served them well, as it did their fathers before them, and perhaps they are loath to surrender it for something new. In the earlier days trout were much more abundant in our streams, and the men who fished the streams and wrote upon the subject of fly fishing in this country may have felt that a knowledge of the habits and haunts of the fish was more essential to success in taking them than the employment of any particular method. The merits of up-stream over down-stream fishing caused some discussion among anglers, and some of these discussions found permanent place in angling literature. The discussion, however, seems always to have been confined to the question of position and seems never to have been extended to the manner of fishing the flies. Individual characteristics or experiences led some to advocate a certain manner of manipulating the dropper-fly and others to recommend the sinking of the tail-fly to a greater depth; but the flies seem always to have been manipulated upon the theory that to be effective they must be constantly in motion. It seems to have been conceded by all that the flies should be always under the control and subject to the direction of the rod, thus enabling the angler to simulate living insects by twitching them over or under the surface of the water – a practice that is the exact opposite of the method of the dry fly fisher, who casts a single fly lightly upon the surface of the water and permits it to float with the current over or near the spot where he knows or believes a fish to lie.

Many expert wet fly anglers in this country have been using the floating fly for years, but most of them use it only on water where they consider it may prove more effective than the wet fly – usually upon the quiet surface of a pool or on flat, slow water. Contrary to the prevailing notion, however, the floating fly is not a whit more deadly on water of this character than the wet fly, when the latter is properly fished. The difficulty in taking trout on such water may be ascribed to two causes: (1) When the water is low and clear, or where it has little motion and the surface is unruffled, the fish is likely to perceive the activities of the angler at a greater distance than is possible in rougher water, and is thus sooner warned of his approach. (2) When the angler has been careful to conceal himself from the fish, the fly cast in the usual wet fly manner is likely to be refused because of its unnatural action, the wake made by dragging the flies across the smooth surface being sufficient at times to deter even small fish from becoming interested in it. The floating fly is far more effective than the wet, "jerky" fly, because, as no motion is imparted to it, it is more lifelike in appearance. When such a fly, properly presented, is refused such refusal may be due as much to a disinclination upon the part of the fish to feed as to his suspicion having been aroused. The wet fly fished *sunk*, with no more motion given to it than is given to the floating one (a single fly being used in each case), will prove quite as deadly as the latter on smooth water; and where many casts with the dry fly may be necessary to induce a rise, the sunk fly may appeal upon the first or second attempt, because its taking demands of the fish no particular exertion. The effort of the angler to impart a "lifelike" motion to the wet fly upon the surface will often be quite enough in itself to defeat his purpose. Such effort should never be made on clear, glassy water, for, while it may occasionally be successful, unseen fish are put down.

For many years I was one of those who firmly believed that only the smooth, slow stretches of a stream could be fished successfully with the dry fly. Experience, however, has taught me that the floater, skilfully handled, is applicable to any part of a swift stream short of a perpendicular waterfall. My unorthodox method of using it – which may be described as creating a whole family of flies instead of imitating an individual member thereof – may be characterised by some as "hammering" or "flogging," and condemned as tending to make fish shy because the leader is shown so often. My answer to this is that if the blows struck by the fly are light no harm is done. And, furthermore, if showing gut to the fish really tends to make them more wary, the sport of taking them, in my estimation, is pushed up a peg.

It is not my purpose to contend that the dry fly is more effective than the wet fly, although I do believe that, under certain conditions, the dry fly will take fish that may not be taken in any other manner. I do contend, however, that a greater fascination attends its use. All game birds are pursued with the same weapon, but the more difficult birds to kill have the greater attraction for sportsmen; and my predilection for the dry fly is based on the same principle.

My first dry fly was cast over the Junction Pool – the meeting of the waters of the Willowemoc and the Mongaup – about fifteen years ago, and the fact that I cast it at all was due more to the exigency of the occasion than to any predevised plan for attempting the feat. Every day in the late afternoon or evening I noted four or five fish rising in the pool formed by these two streams, and repeated attempts upon my part to take one of them by the old method absolutely failed me, although I put forth diligent efforts. The desire to take one of these fish became an obsession, and their constant rising to everything but my flies exasperated me to the point of wishing that I might bring myself to the use of dynamite.

One evening in looking through my fly book I found in one of the pockets a clipping from the *Fishing Gazette*, which I had placed there during the preceding winter. If my memory serves me, I think this article was entitled "Casting to Rising Fish". At any rate, the caption was such that it caught my eye, as it seemed to suggest the remedy for which I was searching. The article proved to be an account of the experience of an angler who used the dry fly for trout, and his exposition of the manner of using it seemed so clear that I determined to try it myself upon the pool over the rising fish in the late afternoon. Barring my inability to execute properly the things the author described and that I was called upon to do, the only stumbling-block in my way was the impossibility of my obtaining an artificial fly that resembled the insects upon which the trout were feeding, and the author laid a great deal of stress upon the necessity of using such an imitation. I remember that, in a measure, I was mildly glad of this, because I felt that I would have an excuse for failure if I were unsuccessful. I "doctored" some wet flies into what I thought to be a fair imitation of the dry fly by tying the wings forward so that they stood at right angles to the body, and then sallied forth to the pool. On my way to the stream I went alternately hot and cold betwixt hope and fear. I rehearsed in my mind all the things I had to do, and I think I was coldest when I thought of having to float the fly. The writer had recommended the use of paraffin-oil as an aid to buoyancy, and this commodity was about as easily procurable in Sullivan County at that time as the philosopher's stone; in my then frame of mind the latter would probably have proven quite as good a buoyant. The pool was but a stone's throw from the house, and I arrived there in a few minutes, only to find a boy disturbing the water by dredging it with a worm. Him I lured away with a cake of chocolate, sat down to wait for the rise which came on shortly, and by the time I was ready there were a half dozen good fish feeding on the surface. I observed two or three sorts of flies about and on the water, to none of which my poor, mussed-up Queen-of-the-Waters bore the slightest resemblance. This did not deter me, however, and I waded boldly out to a position some forty feet below and to the right of the pool. My first cast amazed me. The fly alighted as gently as a natural insect upon the surface, and, watching it as it floated down toward the spot where a fish had been rising, I saw it disappear, a little bubble being left in its place. Instinctively I struck, and to my astonishment found that I was fast in a solid fish that leaped clear of the water. The leaping of this fish was a new experience, as I had never seen a trout jump as cleanly from the water. After a few flights and a determined rush or two I netted him – a rainbow trout just over a foot long and the first I had ever taken. This variety of trout had been placed in the stream a few years before as an experiment, and few had been caught. Stowing my prize in my creel, I prepared for another attempt as soon as the excitement in the pool had subsided. The fly I had used was bedraggled and slimy and would not float, so I knotted on another. My second attempt was as successful as the first, and I finally netted, after a tussle, a beautiful native trout that weighed a little over one pound. Four fine fish fell to my rod that evening, all within half an hour, and the fly was taken on the first cast each time. If such had not been the case I doubt very much if I should have succeeded, because I am certain that my confidence in the method would have been much weakened had I failed to take the first fish, and my subsequent attempts might not have been made at all, or, if made, would probably have ended in failure.

For several years after my first experience with the floating fly I used it in conjunction with the wet fly, and until I read Mr Halford's "Dry Fly Fishing," when, recognising his great authority and feeling that the last word had been said upon the subject, I used the dry fly only on such water as I felt he would approve of and fished only rising fish. Some time later on I read George A.B.Dewar's "Book of the Dry Fly". Mr Dewar says: "I shall endeavour to prove in the course of this volume that the dry fly is never an affectation, save when resorted to in the case of brawling, impetuous streams of mountainous districts, where it is practically impossible of application." Here again I felt inclined to listen to the voice of authority and felt that I must abandon the dry fly. I was accustomed to fish such streams as the Beaverkill, Neversink, Willowemoc, and Esopus, in New York; the Brodhead and Shohola, in Pennsylvania; the Saco and its tributaries, in New Hampshire, and others of similar character – all brawling, impetuous, tumbling streams – and it seemed to me that by continuing to use the dry fly on them I was profaning the creed of authority and inviting the wrath of his gods upon my head. Since then, however, I have continued the use of the dry fly on all of these streams, and a number of years ago abandoned the use of the wet fly for all time.

Since I began casting the fly over the streams of the region I have mentioned their character has greatly changed in many particulars, and conditions are not the same as they were twenty years ago. The natural streams themselves have changed; the condition of the water flowing in them has changed; the sorts of fish inhabiting the waters have changed; and the methods of taking the fish have changed, or should change; and it is to show why this last is true that the following pages are written.

The changes that have taken place in the character of our mountain streams may be attributed to many causes, chief of which, however, is the destruction of the timber which at one time covered the hills through which they have their course. During the frequent and long-continued droughts the denuded hills, baked hard as rock, shed the occasional summer showers as readily as the back of the proverbial duck; the streams become turbid torrents for a few hours, after which they run down, seemingly to a lower mark than before. So long as the forests covered the watersheds the rains as they fell were soaked up by the loose and porous earth about the roots of the trees, were cooled in the shade of the leaves and branches, and slowly percolated into the tiny brooklets, through which they were fed to the streams for many days. Under present conditions the temperature of the streams is much higher than formerly, and, while the temperature has seldom risen to a point where it has been fatal to the fish, it has risen in many streams to a point that is distateful to the native brook-trout (*Salvelinus fontinalis*).

It is not unreasonable to assume that the heat of the water has a very deleterious effect upon the vitality of the fish during certain years when the droughts are long sustained and, should the condition have existed for a great length of time prior to the spawning season, that the progeny for the year would probably come into being lacking the vitality necessary to overcome the attacks of natural enemies and disease. A bad spawning season, of course, reduces the hatch for the year, but is ordinarily not noticed by the angler until two or three years later, at which time the unusually small number of immature fish taken becomes a matter of comment among the frequenters of the streams. A native angler who has made it a practice to visit the spawning-grounds of trout for over twenty-five years stated to me that during the season of 1910 the redds were occupied by trout, but that not a fish spawned on any of them in a stretch of nearly a mile of the stream which flows past his home and which was under his constant observation during the entire season. It is difficult for me to believe that such a thing could have been possible, yet I know the man to be a careful and accurate observer, and his statement must be given credence. He seemed frightened at the prospect and alarmed as to the future of the stream, and he besought me for an explanation of the condition – which I was unable to give. My diary for that year had been destroyed, so that I was then, and am now, unable to even theorise as to whether or not the failure to spawn was due to weather conditions prevailing at that time. Let us hope, assuming that my informant was not mistaken, that the curious condition observed by him was confined to the stretch of the stream that he investigated. Let us hope, further, that the fish, even in that stream, will not become addicted to such an ungenerous and unnatural habit.

Great numbers of trout must be destroyed in the periodical freshets that carry masses of ice tearing and grinding over the beds of the mountain streams. When the ice breaks up gradually there is very little danger to the fish; but a sudden and continued thaw, accompanied by a steady fall of warm rain, washes the snow from the hillsides, swells the streams into wild torrents, and rips the very bottom out of them. Any one who has witnessed the forming of an ice-jam and its final breaking must marvel at the possibility of any fish or other living thing in its path escaping destruction, so tremendous is the upheaval. A few years ago a jam and freshet on the Brodhead, besides uprooting great trees along the banks, lifted three iron bridges within as many miles from their stone abutments and carried each of them a hundred yards down-stream, leaving them, finally, mere masses of twisted iron. These bridges were twelve or fifteen feet above the normal flow of the stream, yet, even so, they did not escape destruction. How, then, is it possible for stream life to stand against such catastrophe? Furthermore, this scouring of the beds of the streams by ice and debris carried down during the floods undoubtedly destroys great quantities of the larvæ of the aquatic insects which form an important part of the trout's food, and this, too, indirectly affects the supply of fish available to the angler's rod. After a severe winter and a torrential spring there is a noticeable dearth of fly upon the water – another of the many causes of lament of the fly fisherman of to-day.

Directly or indirectly, all of the conditions above described are the result of the ruthless cutting of the timber from the hills. Happily, there is reason to hope that these conditions are not going to grow worse, because the present movement toward the preservation of the forests seems to be gaining headway; conversation of nature's resources will come to be a fixed policy of our National and State Government, and if the policy is pushed with vigor and persistence our children's children may some day see our old familiar streams again singing gaily through great woods like those our fathers knew.

With the elements, man, beast, and bird all intent upon its destruction, it is a marvel that our native brook-trout survives. But live on he does, though his numbers constantly decrease. The great gaps left in his ranks are being filled by the alien brown trout – his equal in every respect but that of beauty. True, there is a wide difference of opinion in this particular, and there are some who will go so far as to say that the brown trout is, all round, the better fish for the angler. When feeding he takes the fly quite as freely as the native trout, leaps vigorously when hooked, grows rapidly to a large size, and seems better able to withstand abnormal changes in the temperature of the water, which are so often fatal to *fontinalis*. No one deplores the scarcity of our own beautiful fish more than I do; but we must not be blind to the facts that the brown trout is a game-fish, that he is in our streams and there to stay, and that our streams are suited to him. He is a fish of moods and often seems less willing to feed than the native trout; but for that reason alone, if for no other, I would consider him the sportier fish. When both varieties are taking freely and their fighting qualities compared, it is not easy to decide which is the gamer. The leaping of the brown trout is often more impressive than the determined resistance of the native trout, and the taking of a particularly active or particularly sluggish fish of either variety is frequently made the basis for an opinion. It seems to me that, in any event, the taking of even a single fair fish of either variety on the fly is an achievement to be put down as a distinct credit to the angler's skill and something to be proud of and to remember. Our native brook-trout is much loved of man. It has come to be something more than a fish: it is an ideal. It will always hold first place in the hearts of many anglers. I fear, however, that it must yield first place in the streams to its European contemporary, he having been endowed by nature with a constitution fitted to contend against existing conditions and survive.

My many years' experience upon the streams of New York and Pennsylvania have brought me to realise that changed conditions call for an expertness of skill and knowledge that anglers of the past generation did very well without. The streams now are smaller, the fish in them fewer and warier, and the difficulties of the angler who would take them greater. Three flies fished down-stream may still be a permissible method for those who pursue the trout of the wilderness, but the sportsman should now be willing to adopt the use of the single light surface fly when pursuing the trout of our domestic waters; and, if he does adopt it, as he gains in skill he will come at last to realise that it has a virtue not possessed by its wet brother. I can illustrate my point best by quoting an experience of my own that happened several years ago.

One day, while fishing an up-State stream, I met a dear old clergyman, who, after watching me for a long time, came up and said: "Young man, I have fished this stream for nearly forty years, and they will tell you at the house that I have been accounted as good as any man who ever fished here with a fly. I have killed some fine fish, too; but in all that time I have never been able to take trout as regularly as you have taken them in the few days you have been here. I am told that you use the dry fly and have some particular patterns. If it is not asking too much, will you be good enough to give me their names and tell me where they may be obtained?" I gave him the information he asked, and volunteered some instruction by pointing out that his gear was not suitable for the work, convincing him that such was the case by placing my own rod in his hands. We sat in the shade for a couple of hours exchanging ideas, and to prove or explode a theory of mine he agreed to fish a certain pool with me later in the day. He used my rod and rose and killed a brown trout of one pound five ounces, a little later leaving the fly in a heavier fish. He was an expert at placing the fly, but, not being used to the stiffer rod and lighter gut, he struck too hard, with the resultant smash. Being a good angler, he easily overcame this difficulty. He now fishes only with a rod of fine action and power, which enables him to place his fly easily, delicately, and accurately a greater distance than was possible with the "weeping" rod he formerly used. This he abandoned once and for all, and with it the wet fly. He came into the knowledge and enjoyment of the dry fly method, and he has since then frankly admitted to me that he greatly regretted having realised so late in life that the actual taking of trout constitutes but a very small part of the joy of fly fishing.

THE FISHER LAD
John Keats

c. 1820

More did I love to lie in a cavern nude,
Keeping in wait whole days for Neptune's voice,
And if it came at last, hark, and rejoice!
There blush'd no summer eve but I would steer
My skiff along green shelving coasts, to hear
The shepherd's pipe come clear from aery steep,
Mingled with ceaseless bleatings of his sheep:
And never was a day of summer shine,
But I beheld its birth upon the brine:
For I would watch all night to see unfold
Heaven's gates, and Aethon snort his morning gold
Wide o'er the swelling streams: and constantly
At brim of day-tide, on some grassy lea,
My nets would be spread out, and I at rest.
The poor folk of the sea-country I blest
With daily boon of fish most delicate:
They knew not whence this bounty, and elate
Would strew sweet flowers on a sterile beach.

MAY

Sir Herbert Maxwell

1928

I FIND the following in an old note-book: "It was a favourite saying of Dr Alexander Ross that, as sunshine of years long bygone is stored up in coal-measures, so past enjoyment should be garnered in the soul as a source of warmth and light in dark days." Who Dr Ross may have been I cannot now guess; but his metaphor is just, and applies to no reminiscence more aptly than to that of an old angler. Let me jot down in this snug armchair by the fireside a few incidents that rise in retrospect upon days by the waterside.

Of those who were Eton boys in 1860, some survivors may remember the adventure of a small boy named Jodrell with a big trout, resulting in the most singular capture that I have known. A little above the Playing Fields a mill-stream flows into the Thames on the left bank, and just at the junction there was in those days a brick arch through which a large drain discharged sewage from the college. No doubt the Thames Conservancy Board have caused that primitive arrangement to be changed; but so long as it remained, this unsavoury affluent often attracted a large trout to make it his hunting-ground. One day Jodrell, who, although in Remove, was a very small fellow for his years, was fishing for gudgeon, bleak, or other humble quarry, with one of those light lines wound, with a brightly painted float, on a piece of split bamboo that we used to buy from a tackle shop "up town." He had, of course, no reel; the line was tied to the top ring of a cheap rod. His companion, Street, a big hulking fellow "in tails," was not fishing, and at first was only an idle spectator and critic. Just as the two lads arrived opposite the mouth of the sewer, a wave shot across the slack water, scattering the small fry which jumped out of the stream in terror, and splash went a broad tail as a mighty trout turned with a bleak across his jaws.

"I'll try him with another," quoth little Jodrell, and fastening a dead bleak to his perch hook, he flung it across the narrow stream to the deep hole on the far side. Nine hundred and ninety-nine chances against the monster taking any notice of it, and any odds you like against the frail tackle holding him if he did. But there was the thousandth chance, and it came off! the big trout came on and nearly dragged the gimcrack rod out of the fisher's hands. But he held on gamely, and before either fish or fisher had recovered the surprise, lo! the former was wallowing in the shallow on the hither side of the stream. In dashed Street, flung himself flat upon the trout, grasped it in his arms and, struggling up the bank, flung the glittering prize (Thames trout do indeed glitter) high and dry on the grass. The whole affair, from find to finish, lasted less than a minute, and a lusty Thames trout of 9 lb. honest weight had been landed by fair fishing in as short time as would be required to bag a four-ounce roach.

I have never met Jodrell since we left Eton, nor do I know whether his subsequent career as an angler was maintained at the high level of its outset. There was a considerable element of fluke in the exploit; but credit is due to the angler for not having followed Izaak Walton's counsel of despair for dealing with a heavy fish. After "a great old trout," which was "both subtle and fearful," had smashed Venator's line by "running to the rod's end," he addressed his pupil thus:

I would have held him within the bent of my rod, unless he had been fellow to the great trout that is near an ell long, which was of such a length and depth that he had his picture drawn, and now is to be seen at mine host Rickabie's, at the George in Ware; and it may be, by giving that very great trout the rod – that is, by casting it to him in the water – I might have caught him at the long run; for so I always use to do when I meet with an overgrown fish; and you will learn to do so too hereafter, for I tell you, scholar, fishing is an art, or at least it is an art to catch fish.

If Izaak ever saw a reel, it never occurred to him to use one for circumventing an "overgrown fish"; indeed the following passage suggests that he was writing only from hearsay, for he was no salmon-fisher:

Note also that many use to fish for a salmon with a ring of wire on the top of their rod, through which the line may run to as great a length as is needful when he is hooked. And to that end some use a wheel about the middle of their rod or near their hand, which is to be observed better by seeing one of them than by a large demonstration of words.

Jodrell's feat was due to the trout having in its first spasm of terror run aground in the shallow; but there is no doubt that, if an angler has nerve for it, force promptly applied may surprise a fish of considerable weight into capture before it can get fairly under way. One of the best salmon-fishers I ever knew (he is now on the far side of the bourne) used to set me an example which I have never had the nerve to follow. In the river which I often fished in his company there was usually a good run of grilse in July. My friend had little patience with them; so soon as he hooked one, changing his hand, he hauled the fish within reach of a long gaff, carried by his gillie. The mouths of grilse are soft, and no doubt he lost some fish through rough handling that might have been landed if played in the orthodox way; but lightly hooked fish lightly dealt with often break away in the end, and a short shrift with grilse is most likely to contribute weight to the bag.

AN ANGLER IN EMBRYO
Henry Lamond

1911

PERHAPS THERE NEVER WAS a time when we were not interested in things piscatorial. It is not to be wondered at therefore that at the age when most boys begin to draw railway trains and steamboats our favourite composition was a "Portrait of a Gentleman Fishing."

We recall that this angler was attired conspicuously in a top hat, that his rod was in the ratio of about ten to one of his apparent height, and that the line (immeasurably thicker than the rod) was mounted with a cast of three flies of gigantic proportions. We can see even now – for we sometimes come across them unexpectedly in our library – that these works, barring the undue prominence given to the flies and to the tall hat, did some credit to our early powers of observation. Nor did it seem at all to matter to us which book we embellished or whether the picture we amended represented an Italian lake scene or a wreck on the Goodwin Sands. We were convinced that a more vivid interest could be imparted to any subject by the addition of our "Gentleman Fishing." We frankly admit that we knew in our heart of hearts, when our angler with his preposterous outfit was found industriously casting for the "great fish" which occupied the background of the engraving of Jonah in the family Bible, that something more than a mere rebuke might justly on that occasion be administered – as in point of fact it was.

It is certain that our early predilections were fostered by residence at Moffat, where we made our first acquaintance with a "burn." The "Wee Burn" we called it, in contradistinction to the greater volume of the Little Annan, into which it flowed, thence to unite lower down with the Moffat Water and the Evan at "The Meeting of the Waters." But to us, still with others in charge of a somewhat austere nursemaid, these great rivers ran mightily through regions all unknown. The "Wee Burn" gave scope and verge enough.

Between the road bridge – hardly more than a culvert – and the swing fence over the burn at the far end of the field, a fence which could only be negotiated by wading underneath (and that with a sense of adventure), lay many a fair pool and rippling shallow. One "pool" in particular was our favourite. It was vast in extent, perhaps some three yards long from the run above to the shingly tail below. Its translucent waters may have plumbed eighteen inches at the deepest part beneath the overhanging grassy bank. This side was partially muddy where a relatively huge mass of the bank had been so undermined by the current as to topple over, but elsewhere was gravel of jewel-like quality sloping gently up to dry land on the further side.

We never tired of watching the inhabitants of this ideal aquarium. It contained many a curious water insect, from the bustling black beetles which pulled themselves along from weed to weed, like corpulent gymnasts, to mysterious caddises wrapped in their artful gravelly disguises. But the fish which the pool contained interested us more. To begin with, it was the chosen haunt of a great shoal of minnows, which cruised slowly and inquisitively upstream till some sudden alarm would send them sparking and scuttling in all directions back to the broken water lower down, whence, all danger over, they would begin anew their tentative ascent. At other times they would remain in a bunch deep down behind the submerged turf nor would any inducement prevail to move them. Each blunt little nose, with its whitish warty protuberances, would be sullenly held to the mud, and the shoal would sulk as one man, gloomily indifferent to all around.

Then there was a stickleback of brilliant hue but saturnine character, who scorned the shoal of silly minnows or chevied them viciously when they disturbed his meditations. He lay afar off poised in mid-water, with scarce a flicker of his gossamer fins, till abruptly, for no apparent reason, he would disappear suddenly, only to reappear instantaneously a foot or more upstream poised as immovably as before.

A more active and interesting occupant of the pool (to our mind) was a four-inch parr – brilliant with its black and red spots and blue-barred sides. This graceful fish would lie also poised in mid-stream hardly beneath the surface, waving his tail, and no floating object could come within his range but he would rush at a water spider or floating gnat with accumulated energy. Sometimes the visit of a neighbour would be received with pronounced hostility, for the intruder would be harried in a deadly earnest game of "tig" all over the pool, the penalty of the loser apparently being expulsion, for always was the same fish, when we came again (or it may have been the intruder), at the same spot, wagging his tail and throbbing his gills, alert for any edible flotsam.

Until this time, it seems to us, we had discovered no ambition for the slaughter of these innocents, preferring rather to view their proceedings with an inquiring eye. But soon a serpent was to enter into this watery Eden, for one fine day we were horrified to see the morose head of an eel protruding from the muddy bank.

It is difficult to explain why – there must have been something naturally sinister in the eel's appearance – but we clearly felt that Mr Eel must be destroyed. We therefore procured a discarded top joint, tied to its tip some few feet of strong black linen thread, and added a fly hook from which we had carefully clipped the feathers. To this we affixed a worm. Excitement made the rod top quiver as the luscious morsel dangled at the eel's very nose. Nor were we kept long in suspense, for as more eel protruded from the mud the bait suddenly disappeared. A spasmodic jerk caused the evil monster, after describing a quick half-circle in the air, to find itself safely tethered by the thread to a thistle. Physical repulsion (not to say fear of the consequences) forbade the handling of him. To put it briefly, the tackle, minus the hook, was only freed of its capture when the eel had been stamped firmly and finally into the earth. From this incident, we are convinced, dates our fall from the purer atmosphere of Research to the lower level of Sport.

But our present complete moral degradation was not all at once accomplished. Some few days later, on our customary cautious approach to the bank, a sudden little cloud of mud arose in the lower end of the pool and upstream darted and wriggled an active something which disappeared at last under the bank in another little cloud of mud. This was clearly no eel. A sudden stamp of the foot above the spot sent the parr like an arrow into the shelter of the run, caused the stickleback to disappear and reappear with hysterical rapidity, and scattered the astonished minnows as if a mine had exploded in their midst. And then out again darted the wriggling something, to take cover once more in a cloud of mud lower down. But not before we had had time to see the speckled beauty of a trout. Our heart leapt within us. Here indeed was a noble quarry whose very efforts to evade observation challenged the beholder to circumvent him.

Alas! the easy victory over the eel had done its fell work. We decided to capture the trout also. But, though this was our main purpose, we paltered with our conscience. We had heard of trout which, being kept in captivity, were trained to eat from the hand. We would catch, but not kill, this trout, and train him to eat from our hand. The top joint and linen thread were again requisitioned, and (we blame the eel) another fly-hook was surreptitiously abstracted from the parental fly-book.

At first we angled in vain. The trout declined to be lured by any dismembered fly-hook, however craftily garnished it might be, though the minnows voted the worms exciting fare. But we persevered from day to day, while those minnows which were inadvertently captured through choking on the worms were transported in a blue tin pail – inaptly in-scribed "A Present for a Good Boy" – and consigned to a tub which stood in the back premises. But at last perseverance had its reward. A particularly attractive worm had barely lured the silly shoal to the equal feast one fine morning, when out from the bank darted the quarry, right and left fled the minnows and back beneath the bank went the trout, tug, tug, tugging at our top joint. One long stern pull dragged him forth flapping, and in great excitement he was seized and the hook extracted from his lip. The pail was filled amidst general rejoicing, and a proces-sion started for the tub at a steady walk which degenerated into a run, as the trout, having splashed all the water from the pail, began to get exhausted.

Our fell purpose was effected, and to-morrow the trout would be trained to feed from our hand. But it was not to be. On the morrow the captive exhibited a sickly pallor, and on the ensuing day a corpse alone remained, pale in its leprous white. Soap in the tub was blamed for this tragedy, but a summer sun beating remorselessly on the captive's head for two whole days was worse than soap.

Our moral ruin was now assured. That tug, tug, tugging of the trout completed what the eel had begun. The whole shoal of minnows (we bragged), the parr, and at last even the stickleback, fell successive victims to our top joint and disreputable fly. We went further afield for "sport" – even below the culvert – slaying for the very lust of slaughter. All hope of salvation was gone. Before we were seven we had become an Angler.

MY FIRST TROUT
Herbert E. Palmer

1933

MY PARENTS REFUSED to let me go angling or to encourage me with presents of tackle. My mother was convinced that I was not to be trusted, for I was considered to be much too absent-minded, as well as venturesome, foolish, and excitable. My father said I had every sense in the world except common sense, and my mother was convinced that all stretches of water, still or flowing, were the natural gateways into eternity for boys constituted like me. Finally it was agreed that I might go fishing if somebody in the house would consent to accompany me. But my brother had long since lost all interest; and my father, although not particularly hostile, had never had much sympathy with anglers, for he cultivated Samuel Johnson above every other writer, and more than once had been heard to quote his favourite's sarcastic observations about a fish at one end of the rod and a fool at the other. There was nobody willing to watch over me hour after hour while I fumed over tangling tackle or sat still and stared quivering at a float. I had no responsible school companion who ever went fishing, and the angler-miners, who might save me from drowning if I fell in were nearly all guilty of calling a roach a "bloody roach," thereby disqualifying themselves as suitable companions for a growing boy with an impatient temper and a passion for epithets.

This kind of tyranny went on till I was fourteen, when the barriers were removed. About that time we moved into Yorkshire and went to live at Grassington on the River Wharfe; and as I was supposed to have arrived at years of discretion and there was swiftly flowing water everywhere (much of which could not possibly be quite avoided), I was allowed to do rather much as I liked. But we had arrived at Grassington at the end of the trout season, the river season-ticket cost ten shillings, and no cheaper weekly or monthly tickets were issued. Moreover, I had

no gear beyond my brother's old Rudyard Lake rod with its accompanying half-dozen yards of superior string to act as a line, and the attached
little green-and-red wooden float with insufficient gut and hook. There
was nothing for it but to try some simple kind of fishing in one of the little
becks.

I well remember my stroll of inspection along the banks of Linton
Beck, where an amiable farmer had granted me permission to fish for
trout. To me it seemed crowded with really wonderful fishes, and as I
watched them darting along, frequently making that queer corkscrew
motion which a trout terribly frightened generally makes when it is
dashing to cover, I was as thrilled and exalted as a grown man might be
at the beginning of a great love-affair. The trout were nymphs or
exquisite little fairy creatures desiring to get into my school-bag; while
the shallow, sandy beck, strewn with large mosscovered stones, and
babbling delightfully between sharply defined banks, seemed a glassy
gateway into an enthralling fairyland. I would catch one of these
mysterious nymph-like creatures, take it home, and make clear to my
astonished parents the real aim and purpose of my existence. For surely
it was all quite easy. All I had to do was to present a wriggling worm
before a motionless or slowly moving trout, and it would most assuredly
succumb to temptation. If it moved away from me, all I had to do was to
follow it swiftly and slam the worm in front of its retiring nose.

So I bought a shilling trout licence and a big spate hook attached to
two feet of thick and heavily leaded gut. The trout licence I put in the

safest pocket of my old everyday jacket, and the thick gut trace I tied to those half-dozen yards of carefully preserved fishing-line. My brother's old yellow eight-foot ash rod had unfortunately got broken at the top; and, of course, it had no winch fittings by which to attach a reel even if I had possessed one. But I made a small loop of twine where the top ring ought to have been, and carefully tied two and a half yards of the line down the remaining rings. I thought I would fish a short line at first, and afterwards tie the line to the end of the rod if occasion required. Meanwhile a dour Yorkshire "old hand" considerably upset me by telling me that in the low, clear water that had been prevalent since August it was no use fishing anything save "up-stream-worm," and on two small hooks and at least a yard and a half of extremely fine gut. He showed me the extremely fine gut, but did not give me any, feeling, I suppose, that it was a sin and shame to waste so much good material on such an ignorant beginner. But believing in a Power higher than his I added a short, earnest petition to my next day's morning prayers; and then, after I had carefully tested the rod to see how many pounds it would lift without breaking, I set off at seven miles an hour to the beck.

As soon as I passed through the gate (which of course I forgot to close after me) I walked down to the waterside without the slightest attempt at caution, flung the baited line into a most unsuitable place, crouched down, and waited a minute. Nothing happened. Then I stood up and pushed the worm in front of a slowly moving trout. He waved his tail and fled. I tried the same action with another. He fled even faster than the first. The rest of that unhappy morning was spent in chasing the terrified trout up and down the beck.

The next day I tried "up-stream-worm." But my method was a very splashing method, and it consisted of flinging the large worm-covered hook and weighted thick gut-cast into any kind of water four or five feet above me. I was as prominent and aggressive as a gendarme stalking a mad dog with a gun. The trout got more and more panic-stricken, and I more and more despairing. For a solid fortnight I fished that stream in the same way (sometimes with only half a worm on the hook lest the trout should bite off a hanging end without making acquaintance with the hook), though occasionally I did vary my methods by sitting down quietly for ten minutes and waiting for a bite. But the water was gin-clear, and no beneficent spate or freshet ever came to give me a heavenly helping hand. The village boys grinned when I passed them on my way to the beck, and mockingly asked me when I returned home if I had caught anything.

I found that I was subjecting myself to a sort of meaningless daily drill, which my parents soon smilingly recognized, though my eldest sister got scornful and declared aggressively that she was quite sure that I never, never would catch anything, not even if I lived to be a hundred years old. Finally the last day of the season came to put an end to the trouts' terror and my growing discomfiture.

Before the next spring arrived my parents made me a present of a twelve-foot, four-jointed ash rod with a lancewood top, a wooden reel, and twenty yards of cheap line. Their choice was directed by my own wishes and the local tackle-seller, who kept a chemist's shop. The rod was another yellow one, for although all the local anglers fished with brown or dark-green rods I could not quite dissociate angling from the colour yellow. A benevolent aunt even made me a present of some biggish flies on strong gut, which might have caught very hungry trout in a freshet, but which I was quite too unskilled to use, especially on a fishing-rod too stiff to throw a fly properly.

When the new season arrived in March I was granted the privilege of fishing in some preserved water of the Wharfe, and promised instruction. But I was told to wait till the "snow-broth" from the fells had cleared off and the river was running in better flood, when I should be sure to catch something.

The better flood was a long time coming; but a spring rain driving over the fells and moors did one day strongly colour the water, when I was accompanied to the river by an elderly friend and shown how to bait the hook with two worms in the correct local style. Then I was taken to a likely quiet place under some trees, and shown exactly what to do. The bait was thrown out towards the current and allowed to move slowly back to the bank, after which I laid the rod down at my feet and stood still and waited. After a lot of waiting the line slowly moved. Then the rod top waggled. It was an unmistakable bite. "Something has touched it," said my instructor. It waggled again, and yet again. I was beside myself with excitement. "Now," said my instructor, "I think that the trout is on. You must pull him out." I grasped the rod butt with both hands and pulled with all my might. I pulled sideways and so hard that the trout jammed against the overhanging bank and, of course, broke the gut-line. The severed line waved to the wind, and in supreme anguish I saw the trout's disappearing belly gleam golden through the tea-brown flood-water. The worst thing possible had happened; and I made a sudden movement of despair, my whole soul and body gravitating towards the bed of the Wharfe. But it was no use jumping in, no use kneeling down and stretching my hands into the water. Neither the trout nor the foot of line which he had carried off in his mouth was anywhere to be seen. "You shouldn't have done that," said my instructor, dourly and unsympathetically. "That trout must have been quite half a pound, and you have lost him." Yes, I had lost him. After ten years of frustration, burning thirst, and one-sided attempts to preserve my worthless life I had with my own hands flung my hour of triumph madly into the void.

I went home with my heart beating unusually out of tune. I tried to explain to my long-suffering parents and incredulous eldest sister that I had caught a trout after all, but had not been able to bring it home because it had chosen to stay in the river with the hook down its throat. There, of course, I knew it would not swim about long; for it had manifestly swallowed both worm and hook, and in pulling it so wildly against the bank I must have nearly torn out its vitals. I have been haunted all my life by the ghost of that wretched trout, which must have slowly died of agony and starvation.

THE EARLY DAYS
Negley Farson

1942

THE NEW JERSEY COAST lay bleaching under the winter sun. The lighthouse blazed like a white bone. The dune grass stood still. And the green ocean lay like a pond. There were no foot-marks along the sand.

The summer was over, one of those long summers of childhood. I was walking along the tide mark, examining the driftwood and wreckage cast up by a recent pounding storm. There was always mystery in these bits of broken timber and rusted metal, some of which had been lying off the beach for years. The strewn, irregular line of the highest surge of waves was a continuous story after each storm. But I was searching for a specific treasure. It was always the same; a particular type of tackle that we used off that coast – a triangular brass swivel, to one end of which would be left, usually, a broken bit of parted Cuttyhunk line; a three-ply twisted gut cast from another loop; and a four-ounce pyramidal sinker dangling from the other.

This was the rig of the surf-casters, those men who waded far out into the sea, and cast with a stout two-handed greenheart or snakewood, far out, hundreds of feet beyond the on-rushing combers, to where the great striped channel bass lay crunching clams in the dappled lagoons of the sea floor. I found this tackle, entangled around waterlogged planks or twisted in some conglomerate wreckage, chiefly because of the delicacy of this sport. For, making a full-armed cast with the big quadruple reel, this four-ounce sinker was slung like a bullet into the sky. You controlled the spinning reel with your thumb, barely braking; and, if you had a back-lash when the sinker was in full flight – even the Cuttyhunk parted.

You stood there, watching helplessly, as your tackle sailed outwards, having severed all connections with you, to drop into the open sea. Sometimes a channel bass, or a flounder, or a weakfish would take the clam or bit of shedder-crab with which the hook was baited, and ultimately die. These, too, were washed ashore. The storms dug into the sea sands and beat everything up. We once found part of a yard of an old sailing ship. And it was ripping and snarling at one of these bits of decayed fish that I found Joe. The fish was a monstrous thing, with a mouth about a foot wide, ugly teeth, all head, and no tail; we used to call them "all-mouths". Joe was the doughtiest bull terrier I have ever encountered.

As I said, the summer was over. Joe was a castaway himself. I'd like to know what sort of a person his master was, for some people did leave their dogs and cats when they went away. And Joe seemed to have been soured by it. He had, for several days, a grudge against all mankind. But I was out of a dog at that moment, and so flirtation ensued that took me the better part of a dangerous afternoon. The end of it was that Joe followed me home, his hackle rising every time I turned to speak to him, until I got him into the backyard, and shut the gate. Joe was caught.

This was perhaps the finest channel bass season, this tail-end of autumn; and with the setting in of real winter the "frost fish" would come up along the coast, and there would be night after night when, with a bucket of long-necked clams, I would go out and fish for ling. Joe accompanied me, sitting by my side on moonlit nights, pondering in his dog-way, over the mysteries and melancholy of the lonely sea.

It said so many things to me! It was over thirty-five years later, out on

Lake Victoria in Uganda, when I had some natives tell me, wide-eyed, their legends of the Sese Islands (they said to me they had no special name for every kind of fish, they were just "the Things in the Water") that I touched again the fringe of this imagination which used to thrill, depress, and fill me with such breathless meditation on those enchanted nights. I pictured the sea's depths and filled them with every shape, any of which I might hook; these Things in the Water.

That was the right name for them. In the long native canoe on Lake Victoria, I was still wondering what we would catch. The water still held mystery. The anxiety had not diminished. It has not yet.

In those early days fishing was uphill work. There was a certain amount of ignominy attached to it. It was too often associated with failures, with ne'er-do-wells, with not-getting-on; and, in our Calvinistic civilisation, where to be poor was considered almost a crime, such a waste of time as fishing was considered unpardonable. The result was that some of the finest men I have ever known were fanatic fishermen. It took, for some people, great courage.

The female members of my family would rather eat *anything* from the fish-monger than what I caught. For some reason (and they would never reveal it) my fish were suspect. Perhaps they thought them unorthodox.

A true surf-caster is a man who loves the sea. Far beyond the prize of any great fish he might land, is the exhilaration of the waves. In the summer along the New Jersey coast they came in in sets of three, in great, racing combers. You could hear their dull booms far inland. Then there was the smell of the salt marsh. When the wind was off-shore these arching sea-horses raced in with long white manes streaming from their tips. From the marsh at sunset you heard the cry of shore-fowl. The haunting, space-hinting cry of the curlew; is there a more moving call by any sea? There were days of dull mist which blurred the headlands. Then a white fog, with the hot sun behind it, when the hissing surf shone like burnished silver. And then the long hot afternoons when the mirage came and the liners far off the yellow coast came past in streamers, or sailed upside down.

These are the things which fill the eye, and heart, and mind of the veteran surfcaster. These are often all that he brings home after a hard day's work, with the sandpipers dancing along the shore. Surf-casting is not a duffer's sport. And you are sure to catch many more fish from a boat.

For some reason, perhaps experience, we the belief that the striped channel bass always struck best by night. There was a rod-maker along that coast who gave as a prize each year "a handsome snakewood rod", with German silver mounting, and agate guides, to the person who caught the biggest channel bass. One year the man who lived next door to me won it with a 42-pounder. He was very professional, having taken a house where he could command the sea, and having a glass case in that house full of greenheart, snakewood, and split-cane rods. Below the case was a chest of drawers containing Vom Hofe reels, Pfluegers, with ratchet and drag, and cast-off so that the spool could run free without turning the handle. Being an intensely religious man he never fished on Sundays; but that had nothing to do with "practising". So, when other people were at church, he and some of his old cronies would totter stiffly down to the beach and practise casting with just the sinker. For some reason – because of the ecstasy of it, I suppose – he seemed to get his strength back the minute he took his stance to make a cast.

It was a delight to watch the even parabola of his sinker, sailing surely to precisely where he had intended it. A back-lash, from him, would have been sacrilege. But there were other casters, among the summer lot, who were not so skilful. One summer day a novice, making the sweeping sidewise cast among a lot of enthusiasts at the end of our local wooden pier, rotated with all his might to shoot his sinker out to sea, but, unfortunately, caught a Japanese in the ear.

The hook was driven with such force that it pulled the ear forward and entered the Jap's skull. The lead sinker then swiftly spun around his head, and, *clunk!* hit him on the forehead and almost brained him.

But we, we locals, detested pier fishing. It meant a crowd; and that meant you lost the chief thing in surf-casting – the luxury of your own solitude. That, and trying to solve the sea – guessing whether this or that sand-bar had shifted – these things are the very essence of surf fishing. Then, to haul 2- or 3-lb fish up like a bucket is an entirely different thing from beaching a fighting 25-pounder through heavy waves. There, every bit of your skill and intelligence is called upon. And quickly. In these conditions, with a heavy undertow and the last receding wave adding pounds to your line-pull, you can make a mistake only once.

Not able to play Sancho Panza to my revered neighbor, and feeling (quite correctly) that I had little chance of ever winning that fine prize rod myself, I attached myself to the next-best fisherman I knew along that stretch of coast. He was an old ex-German. I did not know what his profession was, or his politics; nor did I care. All I knew was that if I did want to be in at the killing of one of these monster fish, he was the man for me. He felt likewise.

You cannot buy enthusiasm. Nor a small boy who will run a mile to fetch your bait. Or someone who will sit silent, for hours, while you ruminate. Someone who will eagerly hold your rod while you take a snooze. Or, even more wondrous companion, a boy who will collect driftwood for a fire on cold nights, when the driftwood burns green from the copper in it; and you two sit, avidly eating the bait – the fat clams you have roasted in the embers. Clams scorned by the channel bass.

But one moonlit night they did not scorn them. The German had waded far out and made his cast. Now he was drying himself by our fire. He had taken up all slack. With the click on, his rod was leaning over a "Y" that he always brought along to rest it on – for these surf rods are not light things; if you can afford it, you use a heavy belt with a leather cup to hold the butt of your rod against you while you are fighting a fish. *And the reel screamed!*

I did not know a word of German then. But I heard a sputter of them. He was into a big fish. There was no doubt about that, the way the German's rod was bending – *and jerking.* Joe's bark showed that even he had realised this moment's significance. For the German nearly went crazy. What had happened was that he had jammed his reel. If my wealthy neighbor had reels with gadgets that made me envious, this German had tackle which made my heart ache. His reel not only had a drag, but super-super-drags. And one of them had "frozen". The spool was locked solid. The only thing to do now was run back and forth to the surf, or up and down the coast, *as the fish played him!*

In this unforeseen tug-of-war the fat German showed almost an indecent agility. One minute he would be shouting commands to me from atop the sand dunes (though what I could do about it, I could not see!); the next he would be racing past me towards the surf. The bass had made a run out for deep water. The fish had the upper hand for some time. "Big von! Big von!" the German kept shouting at me. But the bend of his rod had already told me that. Finally loud Teuton yelps from the sand dunes announced that the German was beaching him.

And very skilfully he did it! Watching for an incoming wave, he went backwards with it. The fish was tired. The German got him just ahead of the wave and raced shorewards with it, keeping a taut line, bringing the fish with it as the wave surged far up the sands. Then he held it. The wave retreated. And there in the moonlight flapped a huge striped channel bass.

Then I broke the line.

I had tried to pull the fish farther upwards with it. Fatal ignorance! His dead weight snapped the Cuttyhunk forthwith. But I landed it. I ran down and fell upon it, thrusting my hand and arm well up through its gills. A scratchy gesture. But when the next wave came we were holding the prize up in the moonlight – just to look at it.

Every man has a fish in his life that haunts him; that particular big one which got away. Sometimes even I lie awake and groan at nights over an 8 lb. sea trout I had on for 2 hrs and 40 mins on a 3X cast up at Laxo in the Shetlands. It gets a pound bigger every time I tell about it. And how big that German's striped bass would have been, had the next wave carried it back, I cannot say. But when we went down into the town and woke up Mr Seager (the rod maker) in the dead of night, so that he could weigh it while it was still wet, it pulled the spring-scale to only $25\frac{1}{2}$ lb. It did not qualify even among the first three that season. It won no prize. But it won an imperishable place in my memory, for it was the first *big* game fish that I had ever seen killed.

I still see that night, for it was by a flume, with the silent lighthouse on the other side; and in this flume we used to stand on the cross-beams and scoop up the herring, with dip nets, as they tried to rush the fall of peat-coloured water to get into Deal Lake. Our swift, sweeping dips, almost as fast as paddles, ended with a thud when a fish was in our net. We kids sold them around the town for about tuppence each. Then, in the spring, the small fish came out of the lake (probably spawned a couple of years back) about the size of large Marchand sardines. These we caught in masses and sold them for bait, or put some in jam jars and salted them down. (I know that herrings are supposed to spawn in the sea; and that their ova, in jelly-like masses, are alleged to sink to the bottom. Yet these were certainly herring that we caught going up that flume.) Always the same technique: the big hook was inserted through the mouth, out through a gill, then turned round and pulled through the fish again near the tail. On this triangular-swivel tackle the 3-ply cast always had a cork (just an ordinary bottle cork) split and closed over it, so that it could be slid along. By this means we adjusted the ratio of the cast so that the hook could always float several inches clear from the bottom, which kept it away from crabs.

With these we caught weakfish, which, with their hundreds of spots and fine mouths, look like trout, and are actually called Bay Trout as you go southwards along the Atlantic coast, although they do not have the adipose fin. They have a fine, firm white flesh, are magnificent eating, and are one of the gamer sea fish.

We also used crabs for bait. The American crab sheds his shell, I think every year; and he does so in four stages. First he is a hard-shell; then a crack-shell – he is ready to shed; than a "shedder". With this last you may take the two sharp end tips, bend them back, and break him out. There he lies in your hand; the same colouring of dark green, with white and blue claws – but with the essential character that his skin is already so tough – ready to form the hard shell again – that he will stick on your hook; and, unless you are clumsy, stand any amount of casting. He is delicious to eat then; and "Soft-Shell" American crabs, fried in sizzling fat and bread-crumbs, served with Tartar sauce, are a dish to delight any gourmet. These are another of the rewards of a surf-caster's life; for, in the long summer months the shallow salt lagoons are full of these soft-shell crabs, helpless objects, some of which you will see being carried along on the hard-shells' backs.

But to the surf-caster, there is probably nothing that can touch a run of "Bluies". These are a fighting fish of the mackerel family which run in schools. You use a lead "squid". Viewed laterally, it is a sharp-edged, sharp-pointed object, made of lead, very like a double spear point. A cross-section of its centre would be a very sharp-pointed diamond. On one end of this is a heavy black hook. And so fiercely do the "bluies" strike that they will often snap this hook off. You use a wire trace, burnish the lead squid silver-bright with your knife each day before you use it; then you cast this, like a Devon or a Dowegiac, into the tide rip or patch of bay where you think the bluefish are schooling. With your big-spooled, quadruple reel you reel in the instant the squid hits the water. It darts toward you through the green sea like a flashing fish. When a bluie hits that your rod almost leaves your bands. It is always a battle to land him.

Then, on the great sweep of Barnegat Bay, we "chummed" for bluies, sailing a cat-boat with the sheets fairly free, or one of those spoon-bowed sneak-boxes (which we used later duck shooting), towing astern a bag full of crushed-up menhadden – a herring-like fish, which stinks like hell, you think, because about the only other time you see it is when the New Jersey farmers are using it for fertiliser. These oily menhaddens leave a broad streak of oil in the wake of your sailboat. The bluefish love menhaddens. They come racing across the bay towards that tell-tale, promising oil streak – and there, darting through it, is your trolling "squid".

If you are alone in a sneak-box (it is only comfortable for two anyway) you will have your hands full with both sail and fish at the same time.

In the meantime, as the summer days go on, your skin becomes tanned like leather; your eyebrows turn white from salt and sun; and your hair becomes bleached white as a baby Swede's. Drying your line at night, walking along the balcony of the old wooden hotel which used to lie near Barnegat Light, you were so healthy, content, still thrumming with the day's sport, that you felt all this was too good to be true.

Well, it was. Lying there at nights during one of the vacations from my University, watching the beam of the Light, my ears filled with that satisfying sound of the ceaseless surf below me, I knew that my days of long leave would soon be ended. I would have to work pretty soon; the fishing-rods would be put away. Two weeks a year for my own self would be about the most I could hope for. And not these to ooeete s.

But then there is the inland fishing, fresh-water, which brings with it other settings and an entirely different philosophy. I mean, by philosophy, the thoughts and meditations which come to you while you are fishing. For fresh-water thoughts have not the grandeur which comes from viewing the vast Atlantic. You must realise I am not talking now about fishing from piers and jetties, with other people, or even with buildings in sight of you; I speak of what the deep-dyed surf-caster always longs for – just the sea and himself.

And I exempt from this, of course, fishing for sea trout or salmon in the raw sweeps of romantic Scotland, or in the Hebrides, or the Shetlands, when the heather turns wine-red at sunset. No scenes could be grander than those.

But, otherwise, you may become contemplative until you are a very Izaak Walton under your willow tree, or have the grace to meet Nature with an open heart like Lord Grey of Fallodon; but, you must admit, your rewards will be less physically exhilarating. Your philosophical reflections may be – they are almost sure to be – more delicate, perhaps reach a finer perception – the salt sea jars you too much – but they are more on the contemplative than the active side.

In the States we have two fish, the small-mouth and the large-mouth bass, which we Americans feel have never received their proper recognition from fishermen of other countries. We used to think that they were the gamest fish, inch-for-inch and pound-for-pound, that swims. (Except a little fish called the "bonehead" which you find in the shallows of the coral reefs off the Florida Keys.) I used to believe that – until I met the sea trout. Yet even now, inch-for-inch, pound-for-pound, I rather think it is a toss up.

The small-mouth is far and away the gamer of the two bass. To be at his best he ought to be in the cold, clear, spring-fed lakes of upper New York State, or some of the cold northern lakes, such as those in Wisconsin. When he strikes, if he hits a surface, or sub-surface bait, he will leap into the sky like Nijinsky, fighting on the surface all the time until you get him into the boat. And on each of these leaps your heart stops, for you know he is violently flicking his stubborn head, trying to shake out your lure.

For these fine fresh-water game fish you bait-cast. Here again you use the quadruple reel (one turn of the handle means four turns of the spool); and here again your intelligent thumb, ever so delicately braking, must control the spinning reel so that you do not get a back-lash. It is one-handed casting, with a rod seldom over six feet long, with a finely knit un-oiled silk line. This braided, unfinished silk line is the very acme of pliability. And, as I have said, your brains must be in your thumb.

You cast with "plugs". A surface bait like the Wilson Wobbler, a white-painted, cigar-shaped thing, with scarlet fluting; compact, painted Dowegiacs, which look like minnows – and even a white-painted float with a revolving head – which putters along the surface like a tug-boat; and the instant your plug hits the water you must start to reel it towards you. Nobody can prove exactly why the bass do strike at some of these lures – they can't think that white thing zig-zagging through the water is a *fish*. Nor with the Jamison Coaxer, a white, egg-shaped arrangement, with one hook fastened to another, paralleled by a scarlet feather. I myself think they strike from anger. For I have painted a clothes-pin red, cast it over their nests (when the male bass was patrolling them); and had them *wham* at it in perfect fury. Bass are also very fond of small grasshoppers and crickets.

I lived for years on a spring lake in the lower Catskills. I knew bass from the time I was 13 years old. And it was always a struggle, in the more infantile years, not to fish for bass over their nests. This rage of theirs was always their undoing. And here is an interesting thing: the bass (unless there was some freak of Nature that year) never came up to spawn until the temperature of these icy lakes had risen to 52 degrees Fahrenheit. Then, when they had made these round, whitish nests with their tails, the female had laid her eggs and the male had fertilised them with his milt, the female went off. It was always the male bass who was left to patrol the nest. He guarded it against other bass, or alligator-faced pike or pickerel.

These lakes turned blue in certain angles of the sun. They were cloaked in pine or beech or oak or chestnut. Their shores and their islands were grey granite rocks. It was a fine, hard scenery. There was nothing soft about the home of the small-mouth bass. In the autumn, with the turning leaves, these shores were a flame of red and yellow glory. You usually fished from a moving boat. You never anchored – not when you were bait-casting. When you cast your plug skilfully between some granite ledges – and had the fish carry it out of water with his leap – then you had one of the greatest thrills that fishing in the Americas can offer you.

The small-mouth has a hard, fighting mouth. He does not run as big as the large-mouth; a 4-lb. small-mouth, for example, would be considered very fine, almost an exceptional fish, certainly an unusual one, whereas a 4-lb. large-mouth is what we would call "just middling". A good fish, but nothing to brag about.

With the large-mouth, we had a style of fishing which was fascinating. I believe, Leonard in New York now makes a special rod for it. It is split-cane, but short and stiff, like a stumpy trout rod. It is tough, because with this style of fishing, you have to strike with great force to drive the hook in. We used live small frogs.

I know it sounds inhumane. But a "frog-fisher" always looks down on the man who uses the mechanical lures, sneering that he is "fishing with machinery!" And to cast a live frog correctly required a skilled and gentle hand. For many years I fished with one of the finest "frog casters" in the United States. At any rate, he made it almost a matter of course to win every prize given by the big sporting magazines.

But this doctor did not fish for prizes. He was a Southerner, from the Deep South, and a gentleman of the purest heart. He both looked and talked like the old President Theodore Roosevelt, who, he asserted, was what an all-round man should be. And, although he had just enough to keep him comfortable, this fine old doctor didn't care a whoop for either money, fame, even medical distinction; he lived the year round for just one month – July.

Every morning in July, except Sunday, a local man arrived at the doctor's door with 75 small, live frogs in a box. Then the doctor got into his old-fashioned car. Back he would come at sunset, red as a strawberry; and some dozen or so monster bass would be lying under a wet gunnysack. Where he got them from, such a continual supply of big ones, the neighbourhood never could make out. And then, too, the neighbours were not particularly interested; for, as I have said, this was in the money-making age, and most of the wealthy men who had their summer homes around that lake were merely tolerant of the doctor, liking him, but thinking him rather a fool – to go off fishing in the hot sun that way.

But he baited me so often about my "fishing with machinery" that I took to frog-casting in sheer self-defence. I caught his fever.

There was a shallow, sandy-bottomed lake that it took us some hours to get to. A mite too slack, this reedy-marged expanse, for the vigorous small-mouth. There was a sort of back-bone of willows that seemed to grow almost out of the water along the centre of it.

"Negley," the old doctor would say, baiting a fresh frog through its lips, "the big old bass, the wise ones, lie under the shade of those willows in the heat of the day. Now there's one . . . just . . . there . . . that I've stirred once or twice . . ."

As he said "just there" the doctor made his cast – plenty of line already stripped off the reel over the fingers of one hand; the *dressed* silk line, in this case, "shooting" easily through the guides. The art is to cast your frog so that there is no jerk. You mustn't kill him, or take the life out of him, by jerking his head about. You must drop him gently *on the willows*.

"Y-e-e-s . . ." said the doctor, reminiscently; "he must be at least five pounds . . . that fellow under there."

And as he said that he was gently coaxing the frog off the willow branch into the water. The frog dropped. Instantly, it began to swim – with kicks. If the bass didn't take it then, the doctor pulled the line in, strip fashion, so that each pull straightened out the frog's legs, and each pause gave it time to kick again. But usually a big waiting bass was ready for it.

There was a swirl – and the swimming frog was taken under.

"*But you don't strike now, Negley!*"

No, the doctor explained; that would only mean that you pulled the frog out of the bass's mouth. "Because these large-mouth always take a frog, first, sideways. Then they swim off and down a bit, blow it out, then take it in head-on!" So, while he was saying this, I watched with apprehensive stare the line sliding through the big guides of the Leonard rod. The doctor made no attempt to stop it; on the contrary, he was obediently paying it out – so that the bass should feel no pull.

Then there was a pause when the line stopped moving. The doctor's jaw muscles began to set. Then the line started slowly moving out again. Carefully, oh so carefully, the doctor gently took in all the slack; then he leaned back – *struck!*

Well, if you have ever stirred a paddle around in a bath tub, you can imagine the rumpus that was aroused. A huge bass – five, six, possibly eight pounds, had had the hook driven deep into him. He was wild. He came from the surface, the spray flying away from him, arched, turned like a fighting plane in a dog-fight – and crashed back into the water again.

"Away!" shouted the doctor; "get me away from those willows! Work out into the lake! For God's sake – keep your side to him. Wait – don't move – he's making a run! Ah — got you, you beauty!"

The fish had flung out into the sunny air, crashed back again. And, in all these contradictory commands, I had won the valuable space between us and the shore. The art of frog-casting will make you dissatisfied with the artificial lures. Its drama is more visible, because you are watching your frog for most of the time – a thing you seldom get the chance of doing when you are fishing with a live minnow. Always, after the doctor and I had killed a few satisfactory fish, we would deliberately chance losing one merely for the opportunity of watching the bass handle the frog; they always did what the doctor said – took it from the side, then swam off and down to blow it out. You never came closer to watching a fish *thinking* than when you saw one of these deep-shouldered bass eye the frog . . . and bear down on it to swallow it head on. Then, when you struck, at these close distances, you witnessed all the frantic energy you had set in motion.

As to the cruelty of this sport, it cannot be any more unpardonable than baiting a live minnow through the back and letting the doomed thing swim. Sometimes the frogs would come back with their "trousers" ripped off, or long triangular rips in their green and white skin; this meant that a pike or pickerel had taken a snatch at it, with their long rows of slanting teeth. We always killed these frogs immediately and threw them ashore. The doctor, too, had a sense of fair play, even with frogs; he never used one for more than four casts. "Then he's served his time," he would say with a smile, looking at me over the tops of his spectacles; "he's a free frog." So, when we pulled ashore under some shady tree for luncheon, the old man always released a dozen or so lively little ones. *His* gentle casting had not hurt them. A less-skilled man might kill the frog in two casts. And they would grow up, said the doctor, reminding me of Uncle Remus, to sing the booming bull-frog song: "Doncher-believe-'um! Doncher-believe-'um!"

But as one old river character said to me: "Fishing makes you think." There was not a town in the States which did not have its very sect of enthusiasts, with always a "character", very often the town drunk, whose solace was to sit idle days beside some stream, pond, lake, or even marsh, with a rod. The first drink I ever had in my life was from one of these. His name was "Spieler" Welsh. Why the Spieler, I never knew; he neither talked much nor sang. Which last, God forbid! My mind rocks even now when I consider the prospect of that evil old man breaking into song. But Spieler was kind; and, managing to escape from my house, I went with him one misty night to where, perched on a bridge, we sat down to fish for catfish, with raw liver, where an ill-used little stream still went into a swamp. Spieler showed me how to slide my hand up their slippery sides from the tail – so that the back and two side spikes of their fins passed harmlessly up between my fingers – and then grip them, while, with the catfish "gurking", I twisted out the hook. A white-belly catfish can be a very toothsome dish; a bit sweet, like eel; "Catfish & Waffles" were once a celebrated Philadelphia specialty in the inns along the Schuylkill.

Spieler, pleased with our catch, fished a flask of "rot-gut" whisky from his back pocket: "Here, Kid – have some bait." I obediently took a long pull – and nearly blew out a lung: it was, as the Indians correctly called it, firewater!

Beginning with Spieler Welsh, on that misty moonlit night, fish lured me. I was even more drawn to them than they were to my baits. It is a deep pleasure today to walk beside some English stream, without a rod, and watch the trout, and wonder what they are doing, thinking, opening their little mouths as they lie in the food stream. I feel no impatience. I would watch any fish; they fascinate me – even on a fishmonger's plate.

And so, drawn by this lure, I fished in still ponds where the yellow water-lilies never moved in the heat of the day, and miasmic stretches of marshy water where the turtles dropped from the dead branches of fallen trees, *plop-plop-plop*, as your canoe came along; lonely stretches, safe from man, where the red-winged blackbirds sang and built their nests in tufts of reeds and the solitary blue heron stopped his broody fishing to flap away. All these settings said things to me. Then, as I have described, I mastered the art and joined the coterie of fanatic surf-casters; here was a great glory. And then the skill, and the thrills, of bait-casting. I loved them all.

SINS MY FATHER TAUGHT ME
Robert Traver

1974

1

TO PARAPHRASE a deceased patriot, I regret that I have but one life to give to my fly-fishing. I also regret all the years I wasted bait-fishing as well as all the trout I thereby unwittingly maimed or killed by these crude methods. For this is the "sin" my father taught me which I now wish to bewail – the wrong way to fish – though I suppose the way one learns to fish is just as chancy as the color of one's eyes or indeed that one was ever born at all.

In my father's favor I should add that he in turn probably learned his way of fishing from his own father, as I suspect most young fishermen do, and that this tends to happen for a variety of reasons: juvenile hero worship ("My old man's a better fisherman than your old man"); plain simian imitation; a lack of opportunity to learn any other way; and, more practically, the availability of his equipment when the old boy's off at work.

In any case, my youthful corruption began early and soon became total, and by the time I was ten I could wind up and heave a writhing gob of angleworms almost as far as my father could. My first fishing pole was an incredibly long one-piece bamboo number with an askew pigtailed tip, of the kind one used to pick out of bristling stacks that stood in front of hardware stores – your choice, fifteen cents. For I had bait fished many years before I graduated to the decadent luxury of having one of the new steel rods that magically telescoped, the kind my early fly-fishing hero Tommy Cole scornfully called a "collapsible girder."

In a canny effort to make myself indispensable so I'd never be left behind on fishing trips, I also contrived to become something of a neighborhood authority on the collection, preservation, and transportation of all manner of live baits, a dark art in which my father early schooled me. Though I haven't fished any kind of live bait in many years, I still remember most of those I gathered for my father and his fishing pals: chiefly angleworms and night crawlers, of course, and then a more esoteric and sometimes seasonal variety that included bloodsuckers, minnows, snaillike whitish things called grubs, and let's see, oh yes, grasshoppers and helgramites, to name the main ones.

I also learned that each species called for a special stalking and storing technique: night crawlers, as their name suggests, came much faster at night after a shower, especially when stalked like a footpad with a hoodedbeam kerosene lantern with a sliding door (before flash-lights became common) of the kind refined ladies would today doubtless give their eyeteeth to get hold of to plant ivy in. My father also taught me that these crawlers, usually kept in a tub of rich black earth, became so python lively they would even avidly grab a reluctant trout if, the night before your next fishing trip, you cagily transferred the trip's supply into a container of damp caribou moss.

Grasshoppers were best gathered before sunup, I soon learned, when the lively devils were still numb from the chill of night. These were clapped into a wooden bait box with a screen at one end and a sliding door at the other which my father fashioned out of old cigar boxes from his saloon. Then there were homemade minnow traps that one transferred to tricky buckets one was forever changing the water in. And there were the jars within jars for luring bloodsuckers, baited with liver, both a procedure and prey which gave me the creeps.

I pretty well stuck to garden worms and crawlers in my own fishing but my father played the field, using all the baits I've mentioned and others I've doubtless forgotten. He also had a macabre passion for all kinds of "boughten" dead baits, which I also failed to share (probably for economic as well as esthetic reasons), and he was a monthly pushover for the startling variety of pickled and embalmed baits that used to adorn the outdoor magazines, and still may.

A few years ago while I was rummaging through some of my father's old fishing gear I came up with a nostalgic prize: a bottle of what looked like the coveted remains of somebody's operation for tapeworms. Closer inspection of the faded label revealed that I was the proud inheritor of a virginal jar of pickled pork rind peddled by one of the early folk heroes of preserved baits, Al Foss. If any museum of ancient fishing tackle is interested, I'll cheerfully entertain bids ...

My father had one hell of a time trying to switch from bait-fishing to fly-fishing, and he never made it. His youngest son also had one hell of a time making the switch, and he barely made it. My father's first discernible impulse to switch occurred when one of the earliest fly-fishermen I can remember moved to our town from the East. His name was August Ludington and he managed the local Singer Sewing Machine store – that is, when he managed to resist going out fishing with my father. I tagged along on their very first trip to our South Camp and there witnessed another fisherman fishing rings around my father. It was a rare spectacle.

To make it all the more humiliating, this feat took place on Blair Pond, one of my father's and my very favorite brook trout waters (also the setting of one of my earliest fishing stories, "Fishermen at Night," in case anybody gives a damn), though it was Mr Ludington's first visit. I suppose what happened was that an evening fly hatch had come along and the trout were feeding far above my father's inert and ignored gob of worms. It was a lesson I never forgot, and in later years I used to wince when I saw the trout start "jumping" (as we crude bait heavers called it), because this told me they would henceforth pretty much ignore any bottom-fished bait, dead or alive.

Back up at camp I went into my lantern-lit fishcleaning act, and I still recall my father's look of pained incredulity when, after he had dug a few wizened fish out of his giant wicker creel, Mr Ludington calmly poured out an avalanche of glistening trout. My father's eyes bugged and his jaw fell and his lower lip trembled.

"Well I'll be goddamned," he said when he could speak. "You mean you caught all *them* with a measly little fly that ain't even fit to eat?"

"That's right, George," Mr Ludington said. "They were really on the prod tonight."

"My, my. Let's go have a drink – I guess I sorta need one."

When my fish-cleaning chores were done I got back into camp in time to make their third round of whiskey sours. I was also just in time to witness the event I'd all along been waiting for.

"Look, Lud," my father said as they clinked drinks, "where can a fella get hold of one of them there fly outfits?"

"Oh, Chicago or Milwaukee or almost any town back East."

"How much do they run?"

"Oh, twenty or thirty dollars should put you right in business, George."

"You mean the whole works – pole, reel, line – and some of them fake flies?"

"That's right, George, except we fly-fishermen call them *rods*, not poles."

"Hmm . . . Do you think you could get hold of an outfit for me?"

"Sure thing, George," Mr Ludington said, glancing my way. "How about the youngster?"

"Nope, 'way too young for that there fancy new fangled fishing. How long will it take?"

"Should be here in a week, ten days," Mr Ludington said, rising. "Here's bumps to the world's latest convert to fly-fishing."

"Thanks, Lud," my father said, glancing at me. "Step lively and take the man's glass, son – can't you see it's empty? Might so well freshen mine up, too."

But the world's newest fly-fisherman never quite made the grade, as I've said. In fact his grotesque attempts were a disaster from the start, perhaps because his main motivation was wounded pride rather than any genuine feel for fly-fishing. I still have his antique fly outfit: an awesomely long and heavy rod made of ash, I believe; an old level silk line virtually time-glued to the corroded reel; and, the richest prize of the lot, a fat leather wallet full of snelled English flies of unfamiliar patterns, most of them never used, some of them still curled away in their parched soaking pads.

I recently went over these ancient treasures and, as I did, recalled some of the highlights of his gallant efforts to make the switch. Mr Ludington tried valiantly to show him how to cast but my father could not seem to get it through his head that fly-casting was not a matter of brute strength but rather of rhythmic, purposeful timing. And since he was a big powerful man with a magnificently short fuse, sometimes he looked like a man trying to beat up the water into a lathered vat of his brewer father's choicest beer.

When Mr Ludington was with us, out of pride my father pretty well stuck with his flies, but when we two were alone he'd often come sidling over and sheepishly mooch some worms off his youngest son. When the sad day finally came that Mr Ludington had to move away all pretense fled: the fly outfit was reverently laid to rest, without flowers, and the collapsible girder permanently reappeared.

My own conversion to fly-fishing, if not quite so dramatic or traumatic, was in some ways even more prolonged and uncertain. By this I do not imply that all older bait-fishermen are too soaked in sin ever to switch to fly-fishing; in fact, I know two notable proofs that it can be done if one really wants to. One is my old friend, the late L. P. "Busky" Barrett, who was past seventy when we taught him fly-casting; the other, a younger fishing pal, Anthony "Gigs" Gagliardi, was in his mid-forties when he made the switch, last summer further reddening our bourbon-flushed faces by catching the largest brookie of the lot.

Another advantage I had over my father was that by my mid-teens I began to feel a vague but growing disillusion with the *way* I was taking my trout. For one thing, I was getting weary of all the fuss and bother and uncertainty of gathering, preserving, and fishing with live bait. But mostly I felt an increasing distaste for the tied, inert, plunking quality of the way I was fishing compared with the dash and singing grace of men like Mr Ludington.

But still I did not forsake bait-fishing, and after Mr Ludington left town I kept doggedly plunking away, more out of inertia and lack of guidance than anything else, I suspect. By the time I was ready for college my fishing went into sort of an eclipse, my summers being largely devoted to selling everything under the sun – "Good day, Madam, may I please demonstrate the wondrous new housewife-emancipating Mother Goose self-wringing mop?" – and also celebrating my belated discovery that chasing girls was almost as much fun as chasing trout. But one day my schooling was over and I was back home again clutching my diploma and looking around for my old fishing gear.

I found it and shortly after that had the good fortune to meet Tommy Cole on a trout stream. I'd known about little old Tommy for years, of course, as one casually knows just about everyone in a small town. I knew him as one of the town's few dedicated native fly-fishermen as well as a bit of a choosy and aloof loner. Anyway, that day we fell to talking and discovered that both of us fished just about every day, so we made a date to go out together. We did, and hit it off from the start, and soon were fishing together almost daily.

As I look back on it, it seems both fitting and fateful that a chance meeting with a spunky fisherman on a remote trout stream not only changed my mode of fishing but in many ways, I suspect, my whole way of life. I'd now like to try to tell a little about this change and about the remarkable little man who inspired it.

2

Thomas Wellington Cole was a dark, slender little man of Cornish ancestry who had all the natural grace and gentility that as a boy I dreamed only dukes possessed. Though his formal education was both sketchy and brief, when he was not fishing or prowling the woods Tommy was an omnivorous reader and one of the most widely informed people I ever knew. Though I scarcely equate proficiency at word games with the highest cerebral flights, one of Tommy's more baffling feats was his ability regularly to solve the tough *New York Times* Sunday crossword without a dictionary, though I knew a fellow fisherman of his who couldn't even work the northwest corner of same with the help of five feet of encyclopedia.

As a young man Tommy also had a natural aptitude for mechanics and, like many Upper Peninsula of Michigan natives of that First World War era, was lured to the Detroit area to work on Henry Ford's budding assembly lines. Though he liked his job and the high wages, he keenly missed his Lake Superior bush country. When finally we got into the war to make the world safe for democracy (which world, ironically, became more and more totalitarian),·Tommy promptly enlisted and was sent to the front in France where, after much harrowing action, the Germans gassed him and he was ultimately shipped home. Since with his ravaged lungs he could no longer do hard labor, he finally found a job in a nearby town chauffeuring a country doctor.

This chance job opened up whole new fishing horizons for Tommy, for it seemed that when Doctor Moll wasn't delivering babies he was out in the brambles delivering flies over trout. This was a daily ritual, in fact, and since the old doctor took quite a fancy to little Tommy, he soon initiated his new chauffeur into the art of fly-fishing and even taught him to tie his own flies, including the Doctor Trude fly, whose creator Tommy's doctor long knew and had often fished with.

By the time I got to know Tommy the good doctor had transferred his trout fishing to some pastoral celestial realm and Tommy had returned home, resolved never again to bear arms other than a fly rod. This resolve included shunning all steady work and living on his modest disability pension and going trout fishing every day. By then I too was fishing almost daily, so we soon joined forces and started going steady. And from the very first day Tommy began a subtle compaign to wean me away from bait-fishing and win me over to the fly – a rather large, uncertain undertaking as it finally turned out.

Tommy was that rare combination, a gentle man as well as a gentleman, and so he sensibly proceeded not by ridiculing and running down the way I fished, but by trying to make me see that fly-fishing was simply a vastly more exciting, artful, and humane way of wooing a trout. From the outset he conceded that in its way bait-fishing responded as much to patience and skill as did other forms of fishing – something I already ruefully knew from years of fishing with such wily bait foxes as Edward "Bud" Harrington and, later, Bill Gray, a real wizard with bait.

At the same time, Tommy kept pointing out that since the whole strategy of bait-fishing was to let the fish swallow the bait while the fly-fisherman, upon pain of instant rejection, had to strike his fish at once, in practice this meant that the mortality rate of returning bait-caught trout was virtually total, while that of fly-caught trout was virtually nil. The accuracy of Tommy's shrewd observation was borne out later by the field studies of my old fisheries friend, Al Hazzard (with whom I had much exciting fishing while he was still stationed in Michigan), and many others.

Tommy also quietly reminded me – as well as demonstrated almost daily – that the fly-fisherman was rarely plagued by catching such nongame fish as suckers and chubs and the like, though these trash fish were often the annoying bane of the bait-fisherman's existence. One evening after I'd caught such a monotonous procession of stunted perch that I'd run clean out of worms and had to quit, Tommy squinted over my way for a spell, rubbing his chin, and finally spoke. "Look, pal," he said, "if you play your cards right and also promise to clean out my trout I'll be glad to rent you the fly I'm using for only half a buck."

"Go to hell, Cole," I said, folding my girder and sitting there morosely batting mosquitoes while Tommy played and deftly netted still another trout.

During these propaganda sessions, which ran the gamut from the needle to the bludgeon, Tommy also pointed out that though the common angleworm could often be a savage killer when the trout were bottom feeding, there were frequent periods during a fishing day, especially during a good fly hatch, when virtually all the trout were cruising and feeding at or near the top.

"During these periods," he once said, "a plunking bait-fisherman might just as well heave out a stillson wrench."

"Yes, I know," I said, remembering.

He also gently kept harping, and finally made me see, that for a fisherman to restrict himself to fishing the same lure all day – which is essentially what the bait-fisherman does – is as dull and boring and foolishly self-confining as an eccentric fly-fisherman who would regularly go fishing with but a single fly.

"Unless you're a commercial fisherman," he ran on, driving home his point, "the main aim and fun of going fishing at all is the action a guy gets, not the goddam fish – which, like as not, he'll either throw back or give away."

"Yes?" I said, listening closely.

"And as I think I've already shown you, chum, the best way to get action trout fishing is to carry a varied assortment of flies – types, sizes, patterns – so that, if you're lucky, you might finally toss out something they really want." He widened his hands. "It's as simple as that, pard – or do you still fail to see the light?"

"I do *see* it, Tommy," I once all but wailed, probably while threading on still another worm, "but I can't seem to be able to convince myself that a hungry trout will continue to spurn something that's good to eat in preference for grabbing a bare hook adorned with assorted fluff that's fake and no good." I sighed, groping for words. "It seems you're making me a fly-fisherman in my head, Tommy, but not yet in my heart."

"That will come," Tommy solemnly promised

A whole season passed this way, and part of the next with Tommy eloquently preaching the gospel of fly-fishing while I kept doggedly pelting out my "pork chops" – Tommy's scornful generic term for all live bait. Along about mid-season of the second year Tommy seemed to take a new tack: he talked less about the joys and advantages of fly-fishing and instead seemed bent on demonstrating them. Meanwhile, I wondered whether he'd given up on me or was instead trying to shame me into the paths of virtue. Whatever he had in mind, one thing rapidly became clear – almost daily he monotonously beat hell out of me fishing.

It must have been sometime around mid-August (this was before I started keeping daily fishing notes) that Tommy got a tip from a retired fishing pal that there used to be some fabulous late-summer brown fishing on a certain remote stretch of the upper reaches of the Bogdan River, somewhere above the third wooden bridge, and that maybe the place was still worth a shot.

Our own fishing was in a bit of a late-season slump, so the next afternoon we threw my little cedar boat on top of the old Model A (which the tipster had said was needed to reach the place), and headed for the third wooden bridge to have a look. Once there we quickly unloaded the boat and hid the Model A (against the prying eyes of rival fishermen) and were soon pushing our way upstream, using canoe paddles for oars.

We swiftly saw that Tommy's informant was at least partly right: the place was indeed isolated and hard to reach and, after a half-mile or so of maneuvering our way between the lush growth of overhanging tag alders, I was about ready to drown Tommy's tipster, having already accumulated quite enough material to write two books about all the phony fishing tips I'd followed.

Then came a spell of faster and shallower water, during which we several times had to get out and pull the boat, then a long stretch of more depressing tag alders. Then, rounding a slow bend, we came upon a wide, deep, open stretch, really an enormous pool, bounded on both sides by grassy natural meadows – "My friend says the Finnish farm kids used to swim here," Tommy explained – and suddenly we were beholding one of the most spectacular rises of big trout I've seen anywhere, before or since.

"Head her inshore," Tommy tensely whispered, and, once beached, we grabbed our gear and began rigging up with trembling hands. This was back in the gut leader and silk line days so, amidst all the plashing of big rising trout, meticulous Tommy had to go through the daily ritual of dressing out his line and scrubbing his leader and all the rest while all I had to do was uncollapse my girder and impale a crawler on my harpoon and quick plop it in.

At least bait-fishing has one small advantage, I thought as I made my first plop, but this advantage rapidly waned. By the time Tommy was rigged up and ready, I had caught several wriggling chubs and one gasping sucker and was towing in another.

Tommy moved upstream a decent distance and made his first business cast as I was disimpaling my latest sucker. Almost instantly he was on to a tail-thwacking, rod-bending brown, which he quickly creeled. By the time my harpoon was freed and rebaited he had caught and returned two more lovely browns and was fast to another.

Doggedly I arose and flung a writhing new gob of crawlers far out into the steadily dimpling pool. Something grabbed it before my hook had settled and almost wrenched the girder out of my hands as it roared off and away, and I found myself engaged to a threshing tiger.

"It's a real *dandy!*" I hollered, bringing all my bait lore to the playing of my prize, my straining girder almost bent double, while Tommy held his fire and watched me land my epic fish.

"Boy oh boy!" I hollered, deftly thrusting my net under him (my sole concession to Tommy's way of fishing) and straining to hold high, for all the world to see, the slobbiest, yawpiest, most repellent sucker either of us had ever beheld. "Oh," I said in a small voice, abruptly sitting down. "Oh," I repeated, and then I just sat there, dully watching the crazily rising browns.

"If you'd only thought to bring your watercolors," Tommy said after a bit, "you could paint some mighty purty trout spots on it."

"Go to hell, Wellington," I murmured, on the verge of tears, heaving the mammoth sucker far back in the meadow.

Tommy reeled in and moved down my way and thrust out a supple, tanned hand. "Here," he said sharply, motioning with his fingers, "hand over that goddam girder."

"Yessir," I said surrendering my treasure and watching him collapse and toss it clattering into the bottom of the boat.

"Take this," Tommy said, thrusting his precious fly rod out at me, "and go sit your ass in the front of the scow."

"Yessir," I said, automatically obeying.

"Tonight I'm going to make a fly-fisherman out of you," Tommy quietly vowed as he squatted in the stern and grabbed up a paddle, "or you'll never in hell ever make it."

"What d'you mean?" I said, bristling.

"Just what I said. Now shut up and pitch out that fly – without my good eye on it, if you'll please kindly try and manage that."

Before we left the pool I had busted off on two beauties and finally landed a third. Then in the gathering dusk Tommy slowly paddled me down through the narrow lane of tag alders, which by now seemed a boiling cauldron of threshing fish, during which I caught four more browns and lost some more of Tommy's flies, one lost brown seeming almost as large as an overfed water spaniel.

By the time we reached the third wooden bridge my little cedar boat carried a dedicated new convert to fly-fishing. "Tommy," I said, grabbing and pumping his hand when we landed, "thank you for turning your back on one of the most sensational trout rises we've ever seen, just to turn a stubborn bait-fisherman into a fly-fisherman. Tonight, my friend, you really made it and I thank you from the bottom of my heart."

"Cut out the corny sentiment," Tommy said gruffly, "and hold that bloody flashlight steady so a man can see to clean out these trout. Quit shaking, will you?"

"Yessir," I said, watching the kneeling, blurred figure of Tommy through the dancing columns of insects and trying to hold back my convulsive sobs of joy that tonight, thanks to this gallant little man, I was not only a fly-fisherman my head but at last in my heart, the only place I guess it really matters.

THE
ANGLERS OF OLD

J. M. W. TURNER, R.A.

Dr William Russell

c. 1850

THE SOLE RELAXATION which this remarkable man permitted himself, besides certain potations – but it was not till late in life that he at times over-indulged – was fishing. He might be seen wending his way to the river side, dressed in the oddest fashion – a flabby hat, ill-fitting green Monmouth-street coat, nankeen trousers much too short, and highlow boots, with a dilapidated cotton umbrella, and a fishing-rod. From early morning till nightfall would he sit upon the river's bank, under pelting rain, patiently, shielded by his capacious umbrella, even though he did not obtain a single nibble. He was not, however, an unskilful angler, and was very proud of a good day's sport. He often fished in the Thames at Brentford.

JASPER ST. AUBYN

Henry William Herbert

1849

In the mid-1800s, anglers in the USA were advised to follow the style of English fly fishermen in the pursuit of salmon. In illustration, Henry Herbert drew upon his own short story, "Jasper St. Aubyn," then being prepared for *Graham's Magazine.*

IT IS SCARCELY, perhaps, necessary to add that the mode of fishing for the Salmon in England and America are identical, the tackle and implements the same, and the same flies the most killing in all waters, of which singular fact, and other matters connected with which, I shall say more hereafter. Nor, I presume, need I apologise to my reader for the slight anachronism which has attributed to an ideal personage supposed to live in the age of the Second James all the modern improvements and advantages possessed by the anglers of the present day, and all the skill and science which were certainly not to be found at that time in any Salmon-fisher, not excepting even good quaint Father Izaak, whose maxims on Salmon-fishing, and indeed on fly-fishing in general, savour far more of antiquity than of utility.

It was as fair a morning of July as ever dawned in the blue summer sky; the sun as yet had risen but a little way above the waves of fresh green foliage which formed the horizon of the woodland scenery surrounding Widecomb Manor; and his heat, which promised ere mid-day to become excessive, was tempered now by the exhalations of the copious night-dews, and by the cool breath of the western breeze, which came down through the leafy gorges, in long, soft swells from the open moorlands.

All nature was alive and joyous; the air was vocal with the piping melody of the blackbirds and thrushes, carolling in every brake and bosky dingle; the smooth, green lawn before the windows of the old Hall was peopled with whole tribes of fat, lazy hares, limping about the dewy herbage, fearless, as it would seem, of man's aggression; and to complete the picture, above a score of splendid peacocks were strutting to and fro on the paved terraces, or perched upon the carved stone balustrades, displaying their gorgeous plumage to the early sunshine.

The shadowy mists of the first morning twilight had not been dispersed from the lower regions, and were suspended still in the middle air in broad fleecy masses, though melting rapidly away in the increasing warmth and brightness of the day.

And still a faint blue line hovered over the bed of the long rocky gorge, which divided the chase from the open country, floating about it like the steam of a seething cauldron, and rising here and there into tall smoke-like columns, probably where some steeper cataract of the mountain-stream sent its foam skyward.

So early, indeed, was the hour, that had my tale been recited of these degenerate days, there would have been no gentle eyes awake to look upon the loveliness of new-awakened nature.

In the good days of old, however, when daylight was still deemed to be the fitting time for labour and for pastime, and night the appointed time for natural and healthful sleep, the dawn was wont to brighten beheld by other eyes than those of clowns and milkmaids, and the gay songs of the matutinal birds were listened to by ears that could appreciate their untaught melodies.

And now, just as the stable clock was striking four, the great oaken door of the old Hall was thrown open with a vigorous swing that made it rattle on its hinges, and Jasper St. Aubyn came bounding out into the fresh morning air, with a foot as elastic as that of the mountain roe, singing a snatch of some quaint old ballad.

He was dressed simply in a close-fitting jacket and tight hose of dark-green cloth, without any lace or embroidery, light boots of untanned leather, and a broad-leafed hat, with a single eagle's feather thrust carelessly through the band. He wore neither cloak nor sword, though it was a period at which gentlemen rarely went abroad without these, their distinctive attributes; but in the broad black belt which girt his rounded waist he carried a stout wood-knife with a buckhorn hilt; and over his shoulder there swung from a leathern thong a large wicker fishing-basket.

Nothing, indeed, could be simpler or less indicative of any particular rank or station in society than young St. Aubyn's garb, yet it would have been a very dull and unobservant eye which should take him for aught less than a high-born and high-bred gentleman.

His fine intellectual face, his bearing erect before heaven, the graceful ease of his every motion, as he hurried down the flagged steps of the terrace, and planted his light foot on the dewy greensward, all betokened gentle birth and gentle associations.

But he thought nothing of himself, nor cared for his advantages, acquired or natural. The long and heavy salmon-rod which he carried in his right hand, in three pieces as yet unconnected, did not more clearly indicate his purpose than the quick marking glance which he cast towards the half-veiled sun and hazy sky, scanning the signs of the weather.

"It will do, it will do," he said to himself, thinking as it were aloud, "for three or four hours at least; the sun will not shake off those vapours before eight o'clock at the earliest, and if he do come out then hot and strong, I do not know but the water is dark enough after the late rains to serve my turn a while longer. It will blow up, too, I think, from the westward, and there will be a brisk curl on the pools. But come, I must be moving, if I would reach Darringford to breakfast."

And as he spoke he strode out rapidly across the park toward the deep chasm of the stream, crushing a thousand aromatic perfumes from the dewy wild-flowers with his heedless foot, and thinking little of the beauties of nature, as he hastened to the scene of his loved exercise.

It was not long, accordingly, before he reached the brink of the steep rocky bank above the stream, which he proposed to fish that morning, and paused to select the best place for descending to the water's edge.

It was, indeed, a striking and romantic scene as ever met the eye of painter or of poet. On the farther side of the gorge, scarcely a hundred yards distant, the dark limestone rocks rose sheer and precipitous from the very brink of the stream, rifted and broken into angular blocks and tall columnar masses, from the clefts of which, wherever they could find soil enough to support their scanty growth, a few stunted oaks shot out almost horizontally with their gnarled arms and dark-green foliage, and here and there the silvery bark and quivering tresses of the birch relieved the monotony of colour by their gay brightness. Above, the clifts were crowned with the beautiful purple heather, now in its very glow of summer bloom, about which were buzzing myriads of wild bees, sipping their nectar from its cups of amethyst.

The hither side, though rough and steep and broken, was not in the place where Jasper stood precipitous; indeed it seemed as if at some distant period a sort of landslip had occurred, by which the summit of the rocky wall had been broken into massive fragments, and hurled down in an inclined plane into the bed of the stream, on which it had encroached with its shattered blocks and rounded boulders.

Time, however, had covered all this abrupt and broken slope with a beautiful growth of oak and hazel coppice, among which, only at distant intervals, could the dun weather-beaten flanks of the great stones be discovered.

At the base of this descent, a hundred and fifty feet perhaps below the stand of the young sportsman, flowed the dark arrowy stream – a wild and perilous water. As clear as crystal, yet as dark as the brown cairngorm, it came pouring down among the broken rocks with a rapidity and force which showed what must be its fury when swollen by a storm among the mountains, here breaking into wreaths of rippling foam where some unseen ledge chafed its current, there roaring and surging white as December's snow among the great round-headed rocks, and there again wheeling in sullen eddies, dark and deceitful, round and round some deep rock-rimmed basin.

Here and there, indeed, it spread out into wide, shallow, rippling rapids, filling the whole bottom of the ravine from side to side, but more generally it did not occupy above a fourth part of the space below, leaving sometimes on this margin, sometimes on that, broad pebbly banks, or slaty ledges, affording an easy footing and a clear path to the angler in its troubled waters.

After a rapid glance over the well-known scene, Jasper plunged into the coppice, and following a faint track worn by the feet of the wild-deer in the first instance, and widened by his own bolder tread, soon reached the bottom of the chasm, though not until he had flushed from the dense oak covert two noble black cocks with their superb forked tails, and glossy purple-lustred plumage, which soared away, crowing their bold defiance, over the heathery moorlands.

Once at the water's edge, the young man's tackle was speedily made ready, and in a few minutes his long line went whistling through the air, as he wielded the powerful two-handed rod, as easily as if it had been a stripling's reed, and the large gaudy peacock-fly alighted on the wheeling eddies, at the tail of a long arrowy shoot, as gently as if it had settled from too long a flight. Delicately, deftly, it was made to dance and skim the clear, brown surface, until it had crossed the pool and neared the hither bank; then again, obedient to the pliant wrist, it arose on glittering wing, circled half round the angler's head, and was sent fifteen yards aloof, straight as a wild bee's flight, into a little mimic whirlpool, scarce larger than the hat of the skilful fisherman, which spun round and round just to leeward of a grey ledge of limestone. Scarce had it reached its mark before the water broke all around it, and the gay deceit vanished, the heavy swirl of the surface, as the break was closing, indicating the great size of the fish which had risen. Just as the swirl was subsiding, and the forked tail of the monarch of the stream was half seen as he descended, that indescribable but well-known turn of the angler's wrist, fixed the barbed hook, and taught the scaly victim the nature of the prey he had gorged so heedlessly.

With a wild bound he threw himself three feet out of the water, showing his silver sides, with the sea-lice yet clinging to his scales, a fresh sea-run fish of fifteen, ay, eighteen pounds, and perhaps over.

On his broad back he strikes the water, but not as he meant the tightened line; for as he leaped, the practised hand had lowered the rod's tip, that it fell in a loose bight below him. Again! again! again! and yet a fourth time he bounded into the air with desperate and vigorous soubresaults, like an unbroken steed that would dismount his rider, lashing the eddies of the dark stream into bright bubbling streaks, and making the heart of his captor beat high with anticipation of the desperate struggle that should follow, before the monster would lie panting and exhausted on the yellow sand or moist greensward.

Away! with the rush of an eagle through the air, he is gone like an arrow down the rapids – how the reel rings, and the line whistles from the swift working wheel; he is too swift, too headstrong to be checked as yet; tenfold the strength of that slender tackle might not control him in his first fiery rush.

But Jasper, although young in years, was old in the art, and skilful as the craftiest of the gentle craftsmen. He gives him the butt of his rod steadily, trying the strength of his tackle with a delicate and gentle finger, giving him line at every rush, yet firmly, cautiously, feeling his mouth all the while, and moderating his speed even while he yields to his fury.

Meanwhile, with the eye of intuition and the nerve of iron, he bounds along the difficult shore, he leaps from rock to rock alighting on their slippery tops with the firm agility of the rope-dancer, he splashes knee deep through the slippery shallows, keeping his line ever taut, inclining his rod over his shoulder, bearing on his fish ever with a killing pull, steering him clear of every rock or stump against which he would fain smash the tackle, and landing him at length in a fine open roomy pool, at the foot of a long stretch of white and foamy rapids, down which he has just piloted him with the eye of faith, and the foot of instinct.

And now the great Salmon has turned sulky; like a piece of lead he has sunk to the bottom of the deep black pool, and lies on the gravel bottom in the sullenness of despair.

Jasper stooped, gathered up in his left hand a heavy pebble, and pitched it into the pool, as nearly as he could guess to the whereabout of his game – another – and another! Aha! that last has roused him. Again he throws himself clear out of water, and again foiled in his attempt to smash the tackle, dashes away down stream impetuous.

But his strength is departing – the vigour of his rush is broken. The angler gives him the butt abundantly, strains on him with a heavier pull, yet ever yields a little as he exerts his failing powers; see, his broad, silver side has thrice turned up, even to the surface, and though each time he has recovered himself, each time it has been with a heavier and more sickly motion.

Brave fellow! his last race is run, his last spring sprung – no more shall he disport himself in the bright reaches of the Tamar; no more shall the Naiads wreathe his clear silver scales with river-greens and flowery rushes.

The cruel gaff is in his side – his cold blood stains the eddies for a moment – he flaps out his death-pang on the hard limestone.

"Who-whoop! a nineteen pounder!"

Meantime the morning had worn onward, and ere the great fish was brought to the basket, the sun had soared clear above the mist-wreaths, and had risen so high into the summer heaven that his slant rays poured down into the gorge of the stream, and lighted up the clear depths with a lustre so transparent that every pebble at the bottom might have been discerned, with the large fish here and there floating mid depth, with their heads up stream, their gills working with a quick motion, and their broad tails vibrating at short intervals slowly but powerfully, as they lay motionless in opposition to the very strongest of the swift current.

The breeze had died away, there was no curl upon the water, and the heat was oppressive.

Under such circumstances, to whip the stream was little better than mere loss of time, yet as he hurried with a fleet foot down the gorge, perhaps with some ulterior object, beyond the mere love of sport, Jasper at times cast his fly across the stream, and drew it neatly, and, as he thought, irresistibly, right over the recusant fish; but though once or twice a large lazy Salmon would sail up slowly from the depths, and almost touch the fly with his nose, he either sunk down slowly in disgust, without breaking the water, or flapped his broad tail over the shining fraud as if to mark his contempt.

It had now got to be near noon, for, in the ardour of his success, the angler had forgotten all about his intended breakfast; and, his first fish captured, had contented himself with a slender meal furnished from out his fishing-basket and his leathern bottle.

Jasper had traversed by this time some ten miles in length, following the sinuosities of the stream, and had reached a favourite pool at the head of a long, straight, narrow trench, cut by the waters themselves in the course of time, through the hard schistous rock which walls the torrent on each hand, not leaving the slightest ledge or margin between the rapids and the precipice.

Through this wild gorge of some fifty yards in length, the river shoots like an arrow over a steep inclined plane of limestone rock, the surface of which is polished by the action of the water, till it is as slippery as ice, and at the extremity leaps down a sheer descent of some twelve feet into a large, wide basin, surrounded by softly swelling banks of greensward, and a fair amphitheatre of woodland.

At the upper end this pool is so deep as to be vulgarly deemed un-fathomable; below, however, it expands yet wider into a shallow rippling ford, where it is crossed by the high-road, down stream of which again there is another long, sharp rapid, and another fall, over the last steps of the hills; after which the nature of the stream becomes changed, and it murmurs gently onward through a green pastoral country, unrippled and uninterrupted.

Just in the inner angle of the high-road, on the right hand of the stream, there stood an old-fashioned, low-browed, thatch-covered, stone cottage, with a rude portico of rustic woodwork overrun with jasmine and virgin-bower, and a pretty flower-garden sloping down in successive terraces to the edge of the basin. Beside this, there was no other house in sight, unless it were part of the roof of a mill which stood in the low ground on the brink of the second fall, surrounded with a mass of willows. But the tall steeple of a country church, raising itself heavenward above the brow of the hill, seemed to show that, although concealed by the undulations of the ground, a village was hard at hand.

The morning had changed a second time, a hazy film had crept up to the zenith, and the sun was now covered with a pale golden veil, and a slight current of air down the gorge ruffled the water.

It was a capital pool, famous for being the temporary haunt of the very finest fish, which were wont to lie there awhile, as if to recruit themselves after the exertions of leaping the two falls and stemming the double rapid, before attempting to ascend the stream farther.

Few, however, even of the best and boldest fishermen, cared to wet a line in its waters, in consequence of the supposed impossibility of following a heavy fish through the gorge below, or checking him at the brink of the fall. It is true, that, throughout the length of the pass, the current was broken by bare, slippery rocks peering above the waters, at intervals, which might be cleared by an active cragsman; and it had been in fact reconnoitered by Jasper and others in cool blood, but the result of the examination was that it was deemed impassable.

Thinking, however, little of striking a large fish, and perhaps desiring to waste a little time before scaling the banks and emerging on the high-road, Jasper threw a favourite fly of peacock's herl and gold tinsel lightly across the water; and, almost before he had time to think, had hooked a monstrous fish, which, at the very first leap, he set down as weighing at least thirty pounds.

Thereupon followed a splendid display of piscatory skill. Well knowing that his fish must be lost if he once should succeed in getting his head down the rapid, Jasper exerted every nerve, and exhausted every art to humour, to meet, to restrain, to check him. Four times the fish rushed for the pass, and four times Jasper met him so stoutly with the butt, trying his tackle to the very utmost, that he succeeded in forcing him from the perilous spot. Round and round the pool he had piloted him, and had taken post at length, hoping that the worst was already over, close to the opening of the rocky chasm.

And now perhaps waxing too confident, he checked his fish too sharply. Stung into fury, the monster sprang five times in succession into the air, lashing the water with his angry tail, and then rushed like an arrow down the chasm.

He was gone – but Jasper's blood was up, and thinking of nothing but his sport, he dashed forward, and embarked, with a fearless foot, in the terrible descent.

Leap after leap he took with beautiful precision, alighting firm and erect on the centre of each slippery block, and bounding thence to the next with unerring instinct, guiding his fish the while with consummate skill through the intricacies of the pass.

There were now but three more leaps to be taken before he would reach the flat table-rock above the fall, which once attained, he would have firm foot-hold and a fair field; already he rejoiced, triumphant in the success of his bold attainment, and confident in victory, when a shrill female shriek reached his ears from the pretty flower-garden; caught by the sound, he diverted his eyes, just as he leaped, toward the place whence it came; his foot slipped, and the next instant he was flat on his back in the swift stream, where it shot the most furiously over the glassy rock. He struggled manfully, but in vain. The smooth, slippery surface afforded no purchase to his griping fingers, no hold to his labouring feet. One fearful, agonising conflict with the wild waters, and he was swept helplessly over the edge of the fall, his head, as he glanced down foot foremost, striking the rocky brink with fearful violence.

He was plunged into the deep pool, and whirled round and round by the dark eddies long before he rose, but still, though stunned and half-disabled, he strove terribly to support himself, but it was all in vain.

Again he sunk and rose once more, and as he rose that wild shriek again reached his ears, and his last glance fell upon a female form wringing her hands in despair on the bank, and a young man rushing down in wild haste from the cottage on the hill.

He felt that aid was at hand, and struck out again for life – for dear life!

But the water seemed to fail beneath him.

A slight flash sprang across his eyes, his brain reeled, and all was blackness.

He sunk to the bottom, spurned it with his feet, and rose once more, but not to the surface.

His quivering blue hands emerged alone above the relentless waters, grasped for a little moment at empty space, and then disappeared.

The circling ripples closed over him, and subsided into stillness.

He felt, knew, suffered nothing more.

His young, warm heart was cold and lifeless – his soul had lost its consciousness – the vital spark had faded into darkness – perhaps was quenched for ever.

AKSAKOV ON FISHING
Arthur Ransome

1929

SERGEI AKSAKOV was born in 1791 and died in 1859. His father was the only son of one of the first Russian serf-owners who crossed the Volga, bought large tracts of land from the Bashkir nomads, and, bringing with them their serfs, settled down in the foot-hills of the Urals. To this day that country of wide steppes and fruitful river valleys is sparsely populated. The life of the colonizing Russians was like that of the early North American settlers, except that the Bashkirs were a milder people than the Red Indians. In 1773, however, there was the great Pugatchev rebellion, led by a Cossack Robin Hood, who raised the poor against the rich, killed many landlords and made others fly for their lives, including the Aksakovs. But after Pugatchev had been captured, taken in a cage to Moscow, tortured and killed, the Aksakovs returned to their estate and by the time Aksakov's father was old enough to marry memory of that eruption had died away, the order of the society seemed fixed for all time and the landowners were able to enjoy a pastoral life which was hardly disturbed until near the end of Aksakov's own life. He died, a little distrustful of the future, just two years before the long-promised emancipation of the serfs. His father was a simple colonial squire of noble rank, delighting in the open air and country life and especially in fishing. His mother was a provincial blue-stocking from Ufa, then the capital of the province, with a contempt for all country interests, a feeling that her intellect was wasted in a log-built farm-house of the steppes, and a great interest in her own health and in that of her children. This contrast between his mother's contempt for fishing and his father's and his own delight in it is a constantly recurring thread throughout the series of hardly disguised memoirs which have made Aksakov one of the best beloved and most widely read of Russian classics.

I propose by translating fragments from his books to allow Aksakov to speak for himself and so to give to fishermen in England some of the great pleasure he has given me on journeys, usually with a fishing rod, in Russia. These fragments are almost all concerned with his childhood as a fisherman. The first is taken from his account of a long journey by road which he made with his father and mother, from the town of Ufa, to the estate of his grandfather. This journey must have been about the year 1794, when he was a very small boy.

HIS FIRST FISH

The road was sandy. We drove at a foot's pace and the servants walked. They broke boughs and twigs from the different trees and handed them into the carriage and I examined them with great satisfaction and noticed how they differed one from another. The day was very hot and when we had driven fifteen versts, we stopped to bait the horses and, particularly, so that my mother should not be too tired by the journey and the crossing of the river. This first rest (after leaving Ufa and crossing the Belebey) took place not in the open country but in some Russian village which I hardly remember. But father promised that next day we should bait on the banks of the Dema, when he would show me fishing, something of which I knew only from what he had told me. During the time of our rest, in a shed in a peasant's farmyard, my father busied himself in making up tackle for me and for himself. This again was a new delight to me. Hairs were pulled from the horses' tails and we set ourselves to twisting lines. I myself held the hairs fastened together and father twisted them into the fine thread called a line. Ephrem Evseyitch, a kind servant who was very fond of me, helped us. He did not make his line in the ordinary way, but somehow, on his knee, twisted stout lines for big fish. Weights and hooks, which had been brought with us, were fastened and tied on, and all this apparatus, now seen by me for the first time, was wound on little sticks, wrapped in paper, and put for safe-keeping in my box. With what attention and curiosity I looked at these novel objects, and how easily and surely I learnt their names.

That night they camped at the roadside, making a fire with the use of flint and tinder. The children, Aksakov and his little sister, slept with their mother in the carriage, their father in a cart, the servants, of course, on the ground. It was hardly light in the morning before they were on the move again. The children, half asleep, hardly noticed the harnessing of the horses, fell instantly asleep again and did not wake until they were already half-way across a broad, treeless plain. For forty versts they passed no human dwelling-place. His mother made the little boy read aloud, but his mind was elsewhere. At last, "Trofim, the coachman, shaking up the reins, called out joyfully to his horses, 'Eh, my dears, stir yourselves! It's not far to the Dema!' And our good horses hurried forward at a trot." Far ahead, beyond the dry, parched plain, a broad strip of green showed where the river must lie. Then they could see the grey felt tents of the Bashkir nomads and their herds pasturing about them in the green valley. There, spread out beneath them glittered the winding river, lakes here and there and the old channel of the Dema.

The descent into the valley from the plateau they had crossed was steep and dangerous. They had to put drags on the wheels, while the little Aksakov was flinging himself from window to window of the carriage, until he was told to be quiet.

At last we were by the ferry on the bank of the Dema. The carriage turned aside and stopped under the shade of a gigantic black poplar, the doors were opened and the first one out was I – and in such a hurry that I left my box with the tackles behind. Father, smiling, reminded me of

them, but when I begged to go fishing at once, told me not to be in a
hurry but to wait till he had put things in order for my mother and
arranged for the baiting of the horses.

"You go for a walk with Ephrem, have a look at the ferry and get the
worms ready." I took Ephrem's hand and we walked down to the ferry.
The majestic Dema, full, not too wide, not too fast, quiet, smooth, level
with its banks, stretched away before me. Fish, big and little, leapt continually. My heart drummed in my breast and I shook at every splash,
when a pike or other predatory fish shot up to the surface in pursuit of
the small fry.

On each side of the river a stout post had been driven into the ground.
Between these posts was firmly fastened a wet rope as thick as a man's
arm. Along this rope moved the raft, built like the wooden floor of a
room, founded on two enormous hollowed-out logs, here called *komyagi*. I
was soon shown that a single man could easily shift his raft from one side
of the river to the other. The two ferrymen were Bashkirs, with sharp-
pointed felt hats. They talked broken Russian. Ephrem, or Evseyitch, as
I used to call him, holding me firmly by the hand went on the raft with
me and said to one of the Bashkirs, "Come on, friend, over with us to the
other side!" And the Bashkir, gripping with his muscular hands, standing facing the opposite bank and without moving his feet, very willingly
began pulling on the rope with both hands, when the raft, leaving the
shore, floated out across the river. In a few minutes we were on the other
bank. Here Evseyitch, still holding on to me, looked for good places for
the fishing he passionately loved. Presently he re-crossed the river with
me in the same way. Then he began talking with the two ferrymen, who
lived in a wattled hut on the bank. Mercilessly distorting the Russian
language, thinking so to make it easier for the Bashkirs, mixing with it
Tartar words, he asked them where he could find worms for our fishing.
One of the Bashkirs soon guessed what he wanted and replied, "*Ekshi,
Ekshi, batchka*, right! Come along!" and took us under a small shelter
where a couple of horses were standing for protection from the sun.
There, in great quantities, we found what we wanted. Going up to the
carriage, I saw that everything was in order. Mother had been placed in
the shade of a bushy black poplar, our hamper had been opened and the
samovar was boiling. All the provisions for our dinner had been bought
the evening before in the Tartar village, not forgetting oats for the horses,
for whom also fresh newly cut grass had been bought from the
Bashkirs. . . .

As soon as ever we had drunk tea (at the end of the meal) I began to beg my father to show me the fishing. At last we set out and Evseyitch with us. He had already cut some elm rods. They made floats of thick green reed, fastened the lines on and began to fish from the ferry-raft, trusting the Bashkirs, who said, "Ai, Ai, fish bite very well." Evseyitch made the lightest of the rods ready for me and fastened to it a thin line with a small hook. He baited it with a scrap of kneaded up bread, cast out the tackle and put the rod into my right hand. My left was firmly held by my father. On the instant the float stood on end and then sank down into the water. "Pull! pull!" cried Evseyitch and with a great struggle I pulled out a fair-sized roach. I trembled all over as if in a fever and was beside myself with joy. I seized my prey with both hands and ran to show it to mother. Evseyitch went with me. Mother would not believe that I was capable of catching a fish myself, but, panting and gasping with excitement I assured her, calling Evseyitch to witness, that I had actually, myself pulled out this splendid fish. Evseyitch confirmed what I said. Mother had no inclination towards fishing, indeed disliked it and I was very much hurt that she met my joy so coldly. But worse was to come. Seeing me so excited, she said that it was bad for me and added that she would not let me go back until I had calmed down. She made me sit beside her and sent Evseyitch to tell my father that she would send Serezha (diminutive of Sergei) when he had rested and come to himself. This was an unexpected blow for me. Tears poured from my eyes, but mother had the firmness not to let me go until I was completely calm. After waiting a little time, father came for me himself. Mother was displeased. She said that when she had let me go she had not imagined that I was myself to fish. But father urged her to let me this time catch a few more, and mother, though not at once, agreed. How I thanked my father! I do not know what would have happened to me if I had not been allowed to go. I think I should certainly have fallen ill from misery. My sister begged to go with me and, as the fishing was only fifty yards away, she was allowed to go with her nurse and watch us catching fish. When we came back to the river, father showed me some big perch and roach which he had caught in my absence; other fish were not biting at this time because it was already late in the year and hot, so Evseyitch explained. I caught a few more small roach, each one with almost as much delight as the first. But, as mother had given me leave only for a short time, we soon went back to her. Father ordered Makei, the cook, to boil and fry a few big perch and gave all the rest to the servants to boil themselves a kettle of fish soup.

Fishing simply sent me out of my mind. I could neither think nor talk of anything else, so that mother was angry and said that she would not let me fish again because I might fall ill from such excitement. Father assured her that this happened only on a first occasion and that my excitement would pass. As for me I was sure that it would never pass, and my heart stood still while I heard my fate being decided. The tackle, the quivering and sinking float, the bending rod, the fish tugging at the line – the mere memory of these things threw me into a transport of delight. For the rest of our stay at this place I was unhappy. I dared not talk of fish either with my father or my sister. Everyone was as if displeased at something. In this mood we continued our journey.

His mother's disapproval spoilt his second day's fishing. They had stayed some time on his aunt's estate and were on the way to his grandfather's when they had to cross the Ika. His father had told him that it was a river as good as the Dema and promised that they should camp for the night on its banks and fish. However, when they were still some way from the river, his mother announced that she would prefer to stop in a Chuvash village, from which there was a fine view. "What were fine views to me?" says Aksakov bitterly. "All my dreams of fishing in the evening, when, as my father had told me, the fish bit so well, in a river as good as the Dema, dissolved like smoke and I stood as if sentenced to some kind of punishment." However, his father borrowed a spare horse and drove on to the river. The wretched woman, who deserves for all ages the reprobation of all true fishermen, gave the little boy leave to go with his father so unwillingly and with such conditions that she took away the whole of his pleasure. He went with his father, caught a perch, but was unable to forget his mother's disapproval, fished as if in disgrace and in the end wept and returned to their stopping-place.

There are many of these journeys described in Aksakov's books and always his chief interest while travelling was in the rivers they crossed. He draws the portrait of one river after another, at all seasons of the year, as the frozen road of winter, as the quiet stream of summer, with the mist covering it in the evening, or at dawn steaming until the light wind rolls up the mist and lets the hot sun through. One of these river pictures illustrates better than any abstract statement could the difference between the Russian and English climates, that violent contrast of the seasons, the prolonged immobility of the river in winter that, as the months drag out, piles up almost unbearably the fisherman's longing for the summer. Expectancy is stretched until it can stretch no more and then, as if it were a snapped bowstring, there is a sudden miraculous release. It is as if the heart had frozen with the river and was freed by the thawing of the water. In Russia, it is sometimes said, there is no spring. There is winter, when the country is under snow and the rivers are sledge-roads. Then suddenly comes the thaw. In the streets of the towns the gutters sing like becks in spate carrying down to the river the accumulated snow of the winter. Then the snow melts over the fields. The tributary streams are freed and the rapidly rising water lifts the frozen winter river until at last the whole huge belt of ice moves between the river banks. "The river stirs." Then comes the breaking up of the ice. Huge masses lift and grind and crash against each other as they are washed down, sometimes carrying bridges with them. Then, full with all the waters of the melted snow-fields, the rivers spread far over the surrounding country. By the time they are once more within the river's banks it is already green summer. Near Leningrad and Moscow I used to think I was lucky if I had my first day's fishing in the first week of May. In October winter was upon us again. Aksakov describes the stirring of the river as he saw it when a small boy in the town of Ufa in 1795. He had been promised that as soon as the summer came they should move to an estate called Sergeievka, where there was a lake full of fish. His passion for fishing had been too strong for his mother and, in spite of her, he and his father talked of nothing else.

"THE RIVER STIRS"

The river Bielaya could be seen from the steps of our house and I impatiently awaited its opening. Every time I asked father or Evseyitch, "When shall we be going to Sergeievka?" they answered, "As soon as the river stirs."

At last there came this longed-for day and hour. Evseyitch looked hurriedly into my nursery and said, with a voice full of joy and excitement, "The Bielaya has stirred!" Mother gave me permission and, in a moment, warmly dressed, I was standing on the steps and greedily following with my eyes the long strip of blue, dark and sometimes yellow ice moving between the motionless banks. Already the road across the frozen river had floated far away and an unlucky black cow was running to and fro on it, as if mad, from one bank to the other. The women and girls standing round me accompanied with exclamations of pity each unsuccessful movement of the hurrying animal. I could hear its lowing and was very sorry for it. A bend of the river took it round a high cliff behind which disappeared the road and the black cow running upon it. Suddenly two dogs were seen on the moving ice, but their anxious scurrying aroused not pity but laughter in the people standing about me, for all were sure that the dogs would not drown but would leap or swim ashore. I could easily believe this, and, forgetting the poor cow, laughed with the rest. The dogs were not long in justifying the general expectation and soon got across to the bank. The ice still moved in a powerful, solid, unbroken, endless mass. Evseyitch, fearing the hard cold wind, said to me, "Let's go indoors, little hawk, the river won't break up for some time yet and you will catch a chill. Better if I come and tell you when the ice begins to crack." Very unwillingly I obeyed, but mother was very pleased and praised both Evseyitch and me. And indeed it was not until an hour later that Evseyitch came to tell me that the ice on the river was breaking up. Once more mother let me go for a short time and dressing up still more warmly, I went out and saw yet another new picture that I had never seen before. The ice split and broke into separate blocks. Water splashed between them. They collided one with another. The bigger and stronger submerged the weaker, but, if it met with much resistance, it rose with one edge on high. Sometimes it floated for a long time in that position. Sometimes both blocks broke up into fragments with a crash and sank in the water. A dull roar, sometimes with noises in it like a creaking or a distant groaning, came distinctly to our ears. After watching for some time this tremendous and terrible spectacle I went back to mother and told her feverishly and at length all that I had seen. Father came home from his office (he was at that time a minor official) and with fresh eagerness I set myself to describe to him how the Bielaya had stirred, and told him about it at greater length and more excitedly than I had told mother, because somehow he listened more willingly. From that day the Bielaya was the object of my daily observations. The river began to spread beyond its banks and to submerge the meadows. Every day the picture changed and at last the floods, spreading over some eight versts, mingled with the horizon. To the left was to be seen an infinite expanse of water, clear and smooth as a mirror, while immediately in front of our house it was as if sown with the tops of trees, with here and there huge half drowned oaks and elms and black poplars, the height of which was thus shown. They were like small floating islands. . . .

The floods were long in going down and even when the river was once more within its banks, so that it was possible to cross it, the roads were impassable mud. At last, however, the family set out for Sergeievka, where a wooden farm-house was to be their summer residence. Aksakov's account of their arrival is a delightful illustration of all their characters as well as of the simplicity of Russian country life in those days.

The farmhouse consisted of two cottages; a new one and an old, joined by a covered passage. Not far from these was a cottage for the servants, not yet roofed. The rest of the courtyard was filled by a long straw shelter to serve instead of a barn for the carriages and instead of a stable for the horses. Instead of steps before the cottages a couple of stones had been laid one above another. In the newer cottage there were no doors or windows but only the holes that had been cut to receive them. Mother was not altogether pleased and scolded father, but I liked everything much better than our town house in Ufa. Father assured her that the windows would be brought the next day and that they could be nailed on from outside without waiting for the frames which were not yet ready and advised her to hang up rugs instead of the doors. They began to unpack and to settle in. Chairs, beds and tables had been brought in advance. We soon sat down to dinner. The food, made almost ready beforehand, on a trivet in a hole in the ground dug close to the stockade, seemed to us very tasty. They intended in this hole to make a summer cooking stove of clay. Mother calmed down, grew cheerful and let me go with father to the lake, the object of all my thoughts and hopes. Evseyitch went with us, carrying in his hands the tackles he had pre-pared. Mother laughed when she looked at us and said merrily, "No windows and no doors, but your fishing tackle is all ready." I could not feel my feet under me for joy. I could not walk but ran and skipped along, so that I had to be held by the hand. There it was, at last, my long expected, long yearned for, splendid lake, and splendid it actually was. . . .

More than the tackle had been prepared, and though the servants' cottage was without a roof and their own was without doors and windows, a boat was ready on the lake and small stages for fishing had already been set up, because near the banks in some places the water was shallow and without such stages it would have been awkward to fish. The boat was meant for use in netting.

THE LAKE

The lake was full of all kinds of fish and very big ones. In flood time the
river Bielaya overflowed into it and later when the water began to go
down the Meshtcheryaks (a local tribe) used to close with wattled
hurdles the narrow shallow channel that joined lake and river, so that all
the fish stayed in the lake until the next spring. Huge pike and *zherichs*
(*Aspius rapax*, a predatory fish unknown in England. Modern Russian
fishermen take it by spinning a small spoon) broke the water, chasing the
smaller fish, which were ceaselessly on the move. In places by the banks
and weed-beds the water was rippled by the shoals of fish crowding on
the shallows and sometimes even jumping out on the shore; these fish,
they told me, were spawning. The commonest fish in the lake were perch
and bream.

We unwound our tackles and set to fishing. Father took the biggest rod
with a stout line, put on some sort of unusually fat worm, and cast out as
far as ever he could; he was wanting to catch a big fish. Evseyitch and I
fished with medium-sized tackles and baited with small midden worms.
The fish began to bite at once. One after another our baits were taken by
medium-sized perch and little bream, which latter fish I had not seen
before. I got into such a state of excitement, into such a frenzy, as
Evseyitch said, that my hands and feet shook and I hardly knew what I
was doing. We made such a terrible noise what with continually hauling
out fish and casting out our tackles, what with my shouts and Evseyitch's
instructions and efforts to restrain my childish transports, that father,
saying, "No, there is no catching anything good with you here," got into
the boat with his big rod, rowed off a few score yards, lowered a stone to
the bottom by a rope fastened to the boat, and began to fish once more.
The quantity of our catch and the ease with which we got it, cooled
however my eagerness and that of my *dyadka* [here used for a male
nurse], who, to tell the truth, had been as excited as I was. He began to
think how we too could catch bigger fish. "Let's fish on the bottom, little
hawk," said he, "and put on bigger worms, and I'll put out a third rod
with a bait of bread." I, of course, willingly agreed. We moved our floats
up the line so that they did not stand on end but lay flat on the water; we
put on bigger worms and Evseyitch even put a dozen at once on his hook;
he baited the third tackle with a lump of kneaded bread almost as big as
a hazel nut. The fish suddenly stopped biting and, so far as we were concerned, there began a period of absolute quiet. As if on purpose to justify

my father's saying that nothing good was to be caught in our company, he had a bite from some sort of big fish. He played it for a long time, and Evseyitch and I, standing on the landing stage, watched with lively interest. Suddenly my father exclaimed, "Lost him!" and lifted his barren tackle from the water. The hook, however, was undamaged. "Evidently I did not give him time to get it well down," said he with vexation, and baited his hook and cast out afresh. Evseyitch was very sad about it. "What a misfortune," he said, "Another won't take it now. Once the first has got away there'll be no more luck." I, on the other hand, not having seen the fish, because father had not brought it to the top of the water, not having felt the weight of it, because I had not had the rod in my hands, and not understanding that one can judge of the size of a fish by the bending of the rod, did not take this loss so bitterly to heart and even said that perhaps it was a little one. For some time we sat absolutely quiet without a touch from a fish. I began to find it dull and begged Evseyitch to set my tackle as it had been before. He did as I asked; my float stood up once more, and fish began to bite at once, but Evseyitch did not alter his own tackles and his floats lay quietly on the top of the water. I caught over a score of fish, two of which I could not pull out without Evseyitch's help. Indeed, he was doing nothing else but unhooking fish, putting them in the bucket of water, and baiting my hook with fresh worms. He had no time to look after his own rods and so did not notice that one of them was no longer on the jetty until a fish of some sort had dragged it forty yards away. Evseyitch raised such a yell that he frightened me. Evseyitch begged and prayed my father to catch the floating rod. Father hurriedly did so; he pulled his stone into the boat and, rowing now to the right, now to the left, soon caught up Evseyitch's rod, hauled out a very big perch, put it in the boat without unhooking it and brought it to us on the landing stage. In this incident I took a much more lively interest; Evseyitch's yells and anxiety excited me; I jumped for joy when we carried the perch to the bank, unhooked it and put it in the bucket. Probably the noise and the coming of the boat to the landing stage had frightened the fish; they stopped biting and we sat for a long time in vain expecting a further catch. It was not until near evening, when the sun had already begun to go down, that my father landed an enormous bream, which he kept with him in the boat so as not to frighten off the fish who were clearly about. He only held the bream up in both hands to show it to us from afar. The small bream had begun to bite again at my worms, when father suddenly observed that a mist was rising from the water and told Evseyitch to take me home. I did not at all want to go; but I had already so much enjoyed the fishing that I did not dare to ask permission to stay, and, with both hands helping Evseyitch to carry the bucket full of water and fish – though there was no sort of need for my help, which was probably a hindrance to him – I went back joyfully to mother, who was expecting me.

'While I had been actually fishing, pulling out a fish, or watching the movements of my float, expecting that the very next moment there would be a bite, I had felt nothing but the excitement of fear, hope and a sort of hunter's greed; true satisfaction, complete joy, I felt only now, in remembering all the details with delight and in telling them over again to Evseyitch, who had himself taken part in my fishing and consequently knew all about it just as well as I did, but, being a genuine sportsman, also found pleasure in repeating and recalling all the incidents of the day. We walked along, both shouting aloud, interrupting each other with our stories and even stopped sometimes and put the bucket on the ground to finish some excited reminiscence of how the float moved, how it was carried off, how the fish struggled or broke away; then we picked up the bucket again and hurried homewards. Mother, sitting on the stone steps, or rather on the two stones that took the place of steps in our new still unfinished dwelling, heard us returning while we were still far away and was surprised that it was so long before we arrived. "What were you and Evseyitch so loudly discussing?" she asked when we came up to her. I began to tell her the story all over again, and Evseyitch too. Although I had more than once noticed that mother listened very unwillingly to my passionate descriptions of fishing, at that moment I forgot altogether. In confirmation of our tale, Evseyitch and I took out of the bucket first one and then another fish, until, difficult though it was, we had in the end emptied the whole of our catch on the ground. But our fish made no sort of impression on my mother. When I had calmed down from my story I noticed that a little fire had been made in front of my mother and that two or three logs were smouldering there, the smoke from which was carried towards her. I asked what that was for? Mother replied that she did not know how to get away from the mosquitoes, and only then, looking in my face she cried out, "See what the mosquitoes have done to you! Your whole face is swollen and bleeding." And indeed I had been so bitten by the mosquitoes that my face, neck and hands were swollen up. And all this I had not even noticed, such was my passionate delight in fishing. . . .

The two months that he spent in the unfinished house on the shore of the lake shone out in his memory even as an old man. Then for the first time he went out shooting with his father. Then for the first time he watched the netting of the quails lured to their end by the notes of a whistle-pipe. He watched the netting of fish in the lake, with its accompanying tumult, saw a draught of fish taken so big that there was danger of breaking the net and the men took buckets into the water and filled them with fish to lessen the weight and in the end filled a cart with their spoils. He showed himself even then a true fisherman, resenting the catching with a net of good fish that might be caught on rod and line, and even lamenting aloud that so many fish had been caught that the fishing would be spoilt. Evseyitch comforted him and indeed on the day after the netting the fish bit better than ever. The netting, said Evseyitch, had driven them in the right direction. Indeed they caught so many that his passion slackened and he wondered what they should do with them, and though Evseyitch told him they would all be dried or smoked, he lost interest and gave up fishing sooner than usual. He always looked back to those two months as to the experience that had confirmed him as a fisherman. He was a delicate child and had been in weak health when they left the town. His mother wanted him to drink *koumiss* (mare's milk) to put flesh on his bones, but he was much against it. "To tell the truth, I think I could have reconciled myself to the *koumiss* if I had not been afraid that the use of it and the morning walks which that entailed would take from me the best time for fishing. The desire to catch fish grew in me from hour to hour; it was only from fear that my mother would forbid me to sit by the lake with a rod that with forced diligence I busied myself with reading and writing and the first two rules of arithmetic which my father had taught me. I remember that I pretended rather cleverly and often entered into long discussions with my mother while my mind was occupied with no other thoughts than of how quickest to run away with my rod to the landing stage, and each minute's delay was a severe trial for me." In the very hot weather he was not allowed out in the middle of the day and had to be home from his fishing by ten in the morning. "How I prayed for dull days when mother would let me fish till dinner-time and the fish bit more greedily. What happiness it was to sit quietly with Evseyitch on the landing-stage, to bait the hooks, to cast, to watch the floats, without being afraid that it was time to go home but looking merrily at Surka (his dog) who always sat or slept, stretched out in the sun, on the bank. But, as a result, reading, writing and arithmetic progressed very stiffly and childish games with my sister began to lose their interest and pleasure." When, at the end of the two months, the family moved back into the town he found himself valuing the friendship of Surka more than that of his sister, because the little dog had shared his happiness and reminded him continually of his life by the lake.

In the winter of 1796 his grandfather died, his father succeeded to the estate of Aksakovo and in the summer of 1797, much against the will of Aksakov's mother, his father resigned his official post in Ufa and the family moved into the country. Aksakov describes their characteristic arrival at Aksakovo, his mother lamenting her town life, sulking in one corner of the carriage while his father sat in the other. "He seemed unhappy, too, but I noticed that at the same time he could not disguise his satisfaction on seeing the reedy lakes opening out before us, the green woods, the village and the house." There was much fuss over their settling in. His self-pitying mother would have nothing to do with the housekeeping, which was left to the old grandmother and an unmarried aunt, who had a character of her own, some choice in books and a delight like her brother's in fishing. She, indeed, is the first female angler to be mentioned in Russian literature.

At this time I did no reading or writing and every day mother let me go fishing with Evseyitch; by now she had learnt to trust his devotion and care. My passion for fishing grew daily, and daily I discovered new beauties in Bagrovo (the pseudonym given to Aksakovo in the book). In the deep places by the garden and along the mill-dam we caught perch and such big roach that I was often unable to get them out without Evseyitch's help. From the summer kitchen to the mill, where the river divided in two and was shallow, we caught gudgeon and other small fish. At this time of the year the bigger fish, such as orfe, chub and tench, were already not biting, or rather (this of course, I learnt much later) we did not know how to fish for them. In general, fishing was then in a most primitive infantile state. Above all I loved the island. There one could catch both large fish and small. In the old channel, still and fairly deep, bites were to be had from big fish and on the other side where the river Buguruslan ran shallow over a clean bottom of sand and pebbles, gudgeon used to take splendidly. Besides, to sit in the shade of the birches and lime-trees, even without a rod, on the sloping green bank was so jolly that even now I cannot remember it without emotion. The island was also my aunt's favourite place, and she would sometimes sit there and fish with me; she was a very keen fisherwoman.

When he was eight years old, the little Aksakov was taken to Kazan. His mother, in order to spare him, slipped away and said her final farewell by letter. Then, when she had already driven sixty miles on the way home to Aksakovo, she had the carriage turned round and drove back to Kazan to see him again. It may be imagined what manner of schooldays were his. He and his mother had become absolutely dependent on each other. He was unhappy and fell ill and in the end his mother, quarrelling with some of his masters and getting round others, removed him on medical grounds. He fished on the way home at one of the river crossings. For the last stage of the long journey he was allowed to sit by the coachman. He thus returned to Aksakovo and was allowed to spend an entire year in the country. Whatever his illness was, which is not clear, it did not prevent his fishing.

HIS FIRST BIG FISH

Every day in the morning, before it was yet hot, I went off to fish with Evseyitch. The best fishing was in our own garden because below Aksakovo, in the Mordvin village of Kivatskoe, there was a mill and a great dam, so that the banked-up water reached almost to our garden. Here the river might be described as the upper part of the Kivatskoe mill-dam and all fishermen know that such a place is very good for fishing. Here for the first time I tasted the highest pleasure of the fisherman, in the catching of a big fish; up to that time I had caught only roach, perch and gudgeon; of course roach and perch grow to a considerable size, but somehow the big ones had not come my way and if they had I should not have been able to pull them out, because I fished with a fine line and a small hook. Evseyitch twisted me two lines, each of twenty hairs, tied strong hooks to them, fastened them to powerful rods and took me to his secret place in the garden, which he called "the golden spot." He put on the hook a lump of kneaded black bread as big as a large hazel nut, cast out my tackle so that it should lie on the bottom close under a bush and put out his own by the bank near some weeds and reeds. I sat still and dared not for a second take my eyes off my float, which moved quietly to and fro because, just here, the water eddied under the bank. Suddenly Evseyitch jumped up, shouting, "There he is, batiushka!" and began a tussle with a big fish, holding his rod with both hands. He had no sort of inkling of art in fishing and lugged away with all his force, as they say "Straight from the shoulder"; the fish probably was stuck in the weeds or reeds, the rod was simply a pole, and the line broke. We did not have a chance of seeing what sort of fish it was. Evseyitch fell into such a frenzy that I almost trembled to look at him. He swore and declared that it was a bigger fish than ever he had seen in his life; probably, however, it was an ordinary orfe or chub that had got caught in the weeds and therefore seemed very heavy. Unwinding my second tackle, my *dyadka* cast it out as quickly as he could in the place where the fish had taken and saying, "Yes, I did get a bit excited, this time I will not pull so hard," sat down to await another victim, but in vain. It was my turn next. Fate was willing to please me and my float began to rise a little and then to lie down again and at last stood on end and disappeared below the surface. I struck and a huge fish began to move heavily about as if resisting in the water. Evseyitch rushed to help me and grabbed at my rod but I, remembering what he had just said, ceaselessly urged him to pull gently, and in the end, thanks to a new, strong line and a not very flexible rod, which I did not let out of my hands, we, somehow or other by our joint efforts, dragged out on the bank a most gigantic orfe, on which Evseyitch fell at full length, shouting out "That's him, little hawk! now he won't get away!" I shook with delight, as if I were in a fever, and this, by the way, has happened to me since then on landing a big fish; for a long time I could not control myself, and kept running again and again to look at the orfe, which lay in the grass on the bank, in a safe place. We cast out again, but there were no more bites. In half an hour we went home, for I had been given leave to fish only for a short time. . . . In those days we were not in the habit of weighing big fish, but I think that I never again caught an orfe of such a size and that it must have weighed seven pounds at least.

With one more quotation from his reminiscences of this year in the country I will bring this account of the fishing of Aksakov's boyhood to a close. It is not in itself particularly interesting, but I read it with satisfaction because it showed that although Aksakov's mother had spoilt much of his father's pleasure in fishing, there was one year at least in which he was able to find some excuse for returning to the sport that had been one of the chief enjoyments of his life, as it was to be for his son. During this year some changes (that proved in the end to be ill-advised) were made in the mill. Much of the water was let out of the dam, so that the fish were crowded together in the water that remained.

The fish were as thick as in a caldron of good fish soup. A fabulous fishing began. Evseyitch and I were always at the dam and fished nowhere else; even my father, who had been too busy to fish much, could now fish from morning till night because he had to spend a great part of the day at the mill superintending the work that was going on. He was able to fish without losing sight of the building in progress and could go from time to time to inspect it. Chub, orfe, tench, perch, pike and big roach (three pounds and over) bit continually at all hours of the day. The size of the fish depended on the size of the bait. Whoever used big baits caught big fish. I remember that my father, who particularly liked fishing for perch and pike, fastened two hooks on a single line and, baiting with little fish, used to catch two perch at once and, on one occasion a perch and a pike at the same time. Most of the pike, however, were caught on trimmers, baited with fair-sized roach and perch. It was not unusual to catch an eighteen-pounder. It goes without saying that in spite of our strong hooks and lines, since our skill in fishing was small and we did not use a landing net, the biggest fish often got away, smashed rod or hook or broke the line. My Evseyitch, who even as an old man often amused me by his vehemence in fishing, suffered more than any of us from these unhappy losses and, thanks to his kindness, I, too, often lost a good fish because without his help I could not pull it out and his help was almost always disastrous. The very best fishing lasted from the spring until half-way through July (Old Style; end of July by our reckoning) when the larger fish stopped biting. I mean the orfe, chub and tench; all the others bit splendidly, and probably these would have taken as well, if we had then known of the bait of a whole moulted crayfish.

He went back to school at Kazaɳ at the end of the year. His love of the country strengthened as he grew older. Dissatisfied with the only book of natural history he had, he filled an exercise book with his own descriptions of animals, birds and fishes. Presently to his fishing he added another sport, shooting, on which he wrote a book late in his life. He delighted also in hawking, mushroom gathering and butterfly collecting, the subject of one of the most charming of his essays. He left the newly founded University of Kazan (of which he was one of the first pupils) in 1807. The next year he went to St. Petersburg with his parents and entered the civil service. In 1816 he married and retired to Aksakovo. He had fourteen children, and partly on account of his increasing family and his growing interest in literature and the theatre, he applied in 1826 for a post in Government service and entered the Censorship Department. He fished, of course, continually and in 1829 published an idyll in verse called *The Fisherman's Sorrow*, in which one fisherman comforts another for having lost a large chub by catching hold of the line. In 1832 he met Gogol; and Gogol, much his junior, greatly influenced his writing. For a second time he retired from Government Service. He lived thenceforward on an estate at Abramzevo, not far from Moscow, where he had fishing close at hand and could keep in touch with the writers and theatres of Moscow. He never revisited Aksakovo. For many years he had contributed critical work to the Moscow papers. He now began to write the books which made him famous, *Notes on Fishing* (1847), *Notes of a Sportsman in the Orenburg District, Tales and Recollections of a Sportsman, A Family Chronicle, Reminiscences,* and *The Childhood of Bagrov the Grandson.* He died in 1859, while writing a Life of his sister. Three editions of his *Notes on Fishing* were published in his lifetime. The second contained many additions and changes due, as he said, to six years of fishing "with less abandonment and greater care," but in the course of the three years that followed he had found little to add, so that the third edition may fairly be taken as representative of his final views on a sport which occupied his leisure to the end of his life. It is pleasant to think that most of the passages I have already quoted, those vivid memories of his childhood, are taken from the last book he published, when he was very nearly seventy years old.

HIS "NOTES ON FISHING"

He wrote his *Notes on Fishing* "to refresh his memories for his own delight." His health was breaking and he was settling down to a dozen years of illness and authorship. To write on fishing in Russia in 1847 was a bold act for a man who was taking serious part in the tumult of a new-born literature in a country on the eve of great social changes. Aksakov pointed out in self-defence that no book on fishing existed in Russia, whereas in France and England there were many great works on the subject and in London even a club devoted to the perfection of the sport. Difference of climate and fish, he thought, made it useless to translate the foreign books. It may be said that this same difference makes it useless for Englishmen to read Aksakov. It does, I think, make it useless to translate his book in full, as I at one time intended. Many of the Russian fish are not found in England. We have, for example, nothing comparable to the *Som* (*Siluris glanis*) which weighs up to 400 pounds and is to be caught with baits of big fish, huge lumps of meat, half-plucked ducks and hens or sucking pigs. The Orfe (*Idus melanotus.* Russian *Yaz*) is known to us only as an alien import. The *Zherich* (*Aspius rapax*) the pride of the Moscow River, where it is caught on cockchafers, night-moths and by spinning, is not known to us at all. But the English fish are known in Russia and to read of Aksakov's methods of fishing for them is almost to take a glimpse at the English fishing of the seventeenth century. Walton and Aksakov could have gone fishing together and neither would have found anything to wonder at in the equipment of the other.

Like Walton, Aksakov felt it necessary to begin his book with a defence of fishing. He had not forgotten his own and his father's difficulties and armed fishermen old and young with arguments to use against their wives and mothers. "Let us begin at the beginning," he says. To call fishermen idle and lazy is altogether unjust. The true fisherman must be both healthy and active. It is by no means to the taste of a lazy man to rise early, often before the dawn, to bear the heat of noon or damp and cold weather, to be tirelessly attentive while actually fishing, to seek out the good places, for which purpose it is often necessary to try a great many, to walk a long way, or to row a long way in a boat. If there are idle fellows who, without a true vocation to fishing, simply not knowing where to go or how to fill in their time, prefer sitting on the bank with a rod to running about in the marshes with a gun, can they be called sportsmen? How is fishing to blame because such persons take it up? Baseless too is the assertion that angling is an amusement for children and dotards. No one ever became a genuine sportsman-angler in old age who was not one in youth. Of course children nearly always begin with fishing because other sports are less possible at their age; but is it in fishing alone that children imitate the amusements of their elders? As for the fact that a weak old man or an invalid, sometimes without the use of his legs, can fish and find in fishing some consolation for his wretched existence, it is precisely this that constitutes one of the important and valuable advantages of angling against the statement that it is an occupation for half-wits and fools. But, my God, where are they not? What is there that they do not do? Where are the wise and useful undertakings in which fools do not meddle? It does not follow from this that all the other people who are engaged in the same activities as the fools are themselves stupid. To show the absurdity of such a suggestion, one may name famous historical personages who cannot be suspected of stupidity and were passionate lovers of angling. It is known that Rumiantsev, our celebrated general, was passionately devoted to this sport. Everyone knows his reply made with pretended humility to one who asked him an important diplomatic question: "That is not my business. My business is only to catch fish and take fortresses."

FISHERMAN'S LUCK

There is no denying that in fishing as in all else much depends on luck and that there are lucky fishermen as there are lucky card-players. Otherwise, how explain the unearned success of some and the undeserved failure of others? But just as the lucky card-player, if he is without skill, often loses, so the lucky fisherman without skill catches little. Both must have firmness, patience and knowledge of how to profit by their luck when it comes to them. The impatient fisherman, vexed because his neighbour, fishing in a bad place, with coarse tackle and a stupid unseasonable bait, has continual bites, whereas his own tackles, prepared by a master, baited by a sportsman, lie untouched, often abandons a good place that he has baited up, moves to another, to a third, lets the time of the take slip by and returns home with empty hands; while his neighbour, moving to the place that he has left, regardless of his bad tackle and his lack of skill (through which, of course, he loses half his fish) returns home with a full bag. This, however, is a matter of character more than of skill in fishing. Generally, we should never be resentful of failure. I have known many fishermen who if something goes wrong at the beginning of the day, if they tangle their cast, or get caught up, worst of all if their first good fish breaks away, get angry, begin baiting g their hooks carelessly, strike too soon and too hard, and even give up fishing. These impatient fisherman, being in this way themselves in the wrong all round, commonly put the blame on their ill luck.

But is is not for his moral reflections, nor yet for his practical advice, that we read Aksakov, but for the pleasure he took in fishing and in fish which glows in every page he wrote about them. It shines clearest perhaps in those memories of his childhood's fishing but it is unmistakable even in such a detail as his description of the bite of a perch as "definite, sincere and *conscientious.*" He may be wrong, but there is something delightful in his eagerness to add, in a footnote to his third edition, not long before he died, the news that "Pike shed their teeth annually, in the month of May, a fact which I learnt to my surprise quite recently." There never was a man who understood so well the pleasure not of fishing only, but of being near water and of watching fish. Let me end with a passage on this subject.

THE FISHERMAN GROWING OLD

Almost all young fish, especially of the smaller kinds, are so beautiful, or, to be more precise, so pretty, active and clean, that the people of the south of Russia use the word *ruibka* (little fish) as a word of affection and tenderness in praise of maidenly beauty and charm." . . . He quotes from his favourite Gogol the pasage in which the young Cossack begs his love, "Heart of mine, my little fish, my jewel! Look at me! Put out through the lattice if only thy little white hand! . . .' He goes on: "For the peasant of Great Russia that is too delicate; but he too loves to watch every kind of fish, sparkling merrily on the surface of the water, flashing its silver or golden scales, its rainbow stripes; sometimes swimming quietly, secretly, sometimes still and motionless on the bottom of the river! Not a peasant, old or young, will pass by river or pond without looking to see "how the free fishes play" and often a peasant travelling on foot hurrying somewhere on necessary business forgets for a time his working life and, leaning over a dark blue pool looks earnestly into the shadowy depths, admiring the quick movements of the fish, especially when it is playing and splashing, when, coming to the top, suddenly with a sharp turn and a blow of its tail it goes down again, leaving a swirling circle on the surface, the margins of which, gradually spreading, do not at once efface themselves in the quiet smoothness of the water; or when, with only its back fin cutting the surface, the fish flies like an arrow in some one direction and in pursuit of it there runs a long wave which, dividing into two, offers the strange figure of a widening triangle. . . . Is there need to say after this that the fisherman watches every kind of fish with a still greater and a special love and sees a large or unusual fish with ecstasy and a joyful throbbing of the heart? These expressions, perhaps, may seem laughable to non-fishermen – I shall not be offended; I am talking to fishermen and they will understand me! Each one of them, growing old, finds pleasure in remembering the lively feeling that inspired him in youth when, rod in hand, forgetting sleep and tiredness, he gave himself up passionately to his beloved sport. Each one of them, surely, remembers with satisfaction that golden time. . . . And I too remember it as a long ago, sweet, and not quite clear dream. I remember the sultry noons, the banks overgrown with tall, scented herbs and flowers, the shadow of the alder tree quivering on the water, the deep pool of the river, and the young fisherman clinging to an overhanging bough, his hair hanging down, motionlessly gazing with charmed eyes into the dark blue but clear depths. . . . And how many fish were crowded there. . . . What orfe, what chub, what perch! . . . And how the heart of the boy stood still and his breath caught. . . . Long ago it was, very long ago. But even now young fishermen are tasting the same experience and God grant them long to preserve that lively innocent feeling of the passionate fisherman.

Aksakov kept it all his life, and few writers on fishing have known better than he how to share that feeling with others.

IZAAK WALTON
Herbert E. Palmer

1933

IZAAK WALTON, a sort of distant kinsman of Simon Peter, and the spiritual father of modern English anglers, was born in the reign of Queen Elizabeth, 1593, and died at the hale old age of ninety in the reign of Charles II, 15th December 1683 – over two and a half centuries ago. But he was many things besides angler. During his busiest years he kept a draper's shop at the corner of Chancery Lane and Fleet Street; and also – wonderful for a commercial man – won a high reputation as scholar and writer. His book of "Lives" is still valuable biography, and his quaint fresh prose a continual delight. He was much loved and honoured, and included among his many friends such formidable clerical and literary people as George Herbert, John Donne, and Sir Henry Wotton.

His most famous work, *The Compleat Angler, or the Contemplative Man's Recreation*, with excellent woodcuts (and a text from the Bible about Simon Peter on the title-page), was first published in 1653. It was only a slim volume, but it was very successful, and the delighted author was so pleased with himself that he kept on adding to it as he republished it – the edition that we read to-day being the fifth, issued in 1676. To this edition Charles Cotton, a companion poet and angler, added a second part.

But Izaak Walton's *Compleat Angler* was not quite the first angling book. Angling had been esteemed as a contemplative man's recreation as far back as the Middle Ages, particularly among the clergy, who even fished for trout with artificial flies made of coloured wools, silks, and feathers. There is an old treatise included in the re-issue of *The Boke of St. Albans*, published soon after the end of the Wars of the Roses, which gives information about fish and fishing, flies and rods. It is entitled *The Treatise of Fysshynge with an Angle*, and its authorship has been attributed to Dame Juliana Berners, a lady of noble family, and prioress of the nunnery of Sopwell of St. Albans. But Izaak Walton's *Compleat Angler* is a much vaster work, and completely takes the wind out of its sails as a piece of deliciously written entertainment, a book for Christians and nature lovers, as well as for all classes of anglers, from bait-fishers to fly-fishers.

Actually Izaak Walton was more of a bait-fisher than a fly-fisher, and ought to be the pond and canal angler's patron saint. He gives vast detailed information about baits; but he was so honest as to confess that the greater part of what he wrote on the subject of fly-fishing for trout and grayling was not out of his own experience, but was communicated to him by a Mr Thomas Barker, a gossiping old man who had been a cook in great men's families. In any case Dame Juliana's medieval list of flies had been made use of. These flies, of course, were of very large size, and though they will sometimes catch trout in this sophisticated age, they are more likely to frighten them out of their wits. The trout of to-day are fewer in numbers and are highly educated. They have quite lost their medieval and Elizabethan innocence, and more often than not have to be lured with small artificial flies which exactly imitate the real insects upon which they are feeding.

Izaak Walton's fishing-rod was a very long rod – from fourteen to twenty feet. It was made in two pieces, which he spliced together with string when he got to the waterside. If he could come back he would be very surprised to see our short, stiff, feather-weight, expensive, dry-fly rods; only seven to nine feet in length, but very far-reaching, as they will cast thirty to sixty feet of line.

But Izaak Walton was obliged to use a long tackle, and with his line fastened to the end of the top joint, he had to trust to a long length of elasticity in the rod to prevent large fish from breaking the line. But reels and running tackle were creeping into use, because he tells us that the salmon anglers had found them very convenient. His line was made of brown and white twisted horsehair; and as silk-worm gut was not then known, the hair lengths near the hook had to be white and transparent. He says in his book that the thickness of the line must not "exceed three or four hairs at the most . . . but if you can attain to angle with one hair you shall have more rises and catch more fish." But horsehair has not entirely gone out of use; and until just after the 1914–18 War many of the Wharfedale anglers preferred it to fine gut.

Izaak Walton in his book tells his angling pupil to throw his rod into the water to prevent a breakage if the fish is very large – a most laughable and primitive course of action. And yet one should not laugh too loud, for he must have been an unusually skilful fellow to have landed three-pounders on single horsehair without the help of running tackle and reel. But probably the capture of large fish was not an everyday occurrence, for one gets the impression from his quaint and charming pages that he spent nearly as much time in praising God and gossiping with milkmaids as in actual angling.

When Izaak Walton was a business man in London he fished for the most part in the Hertfordshire Lea; and also (we can infer) in the neighbouring Colne, and its little tributary the Ver, which flows past St. Albans Abbey. These streams yielded an abundance of trout, pike, roach, and dace. But when he fixed his thoughts *specially* on trout he took the coach into Hampshire, whose chalk streams always abounded with large trout. After he retired from business he travelled a great deal about the country visiting his friends, and it is rather certain that he fished a great deal in Derbyshire (especially in the River Dove), a county which his friend, Charles Cotton, specially recommends for its clear streams. Fishing was free and open nearly everywhere. Only in a very few instances was it necessary to ask permission.

Izaak Walton raised angling almost to the height of a sacrament. In one place he says very seriously, if somewhat ungrammatically: "And for you that have heard many grave serious men pity anglers, let me tell you, sir, there be many men that are by others taken to be serious and grave men, whom we contemn and pity. Men that are taken to be grave, because nature hath made them of a sour complexion; money-getting men, men that spend all their time, first, in getting, and next, in anxious care to keep it, men that are condemned to be rich, and then always busy or discontented; for these poor-rich men, we anglers pity them perfectly."

But Izaak Walton to-day if he came back to life, might use rather stronger language than "we anglers pity them perfectly." The country is not as alluring as it was. Too much of it is soiled and ugly, or the atmosphere of mystery has gone away. And three-quarters of the destruction is the fault of the "money-getting men," the men of "a sour complexion," the "poor-rich men" who have spent too much time in "getting." Throughout the Victorian age the country was often quite unnecessarily defiled with polluting factories and ugly cottage and slum buildings; while to-day the alluring brown, yellow, and grey-white roads, which used to thread the green landscape like ribbons, have been so blackened and hardened with tar that the eye aches to look at them. The tar has not only destroyed nearly all the fish in those streams near London in which Izaak used to angle, but it has shamefully scarred and sullied the green landscape. And how he would shudder at the sight of the new ugly pretentious houses and cottages, built without any attempt to beauty or pleasing architecture. How he would cry out for his old thatched cottages and charming manor houses! How gloomily he would stare at the landscape and into some of these polluted streams, remonstrating and telling us that so much of the dirt and ugliness might have been avoided without unduly inconveniencing us or in any way impoverishing the country. And almost certainly he would go down on his knees and with uplifted hands pray and beg us to control the machine before it destroys us and all that makes life worth living.

BORROW AND THE QUAKER

George Borrow

1851

I SAT UPON the bank, at the bottom of the hill which slopes down from "the Earl's home"; my float was on the waters, and my back was towards the old hall. I drew up many fish, small and great, which I took from off the hook mechanically and flung upon the bank, for I was almost unconscious of what I was about, for my mind was not with my fish. I was thinking of my earlier years – of the Scottish crags and the heaths of Ireland – and sometimes my mind would dwell on my studies – on the sonorous stanzas of Dante, rising and falling like the waves of the sea – or would strive to remember a couplet or two of poor Monsieur Boileau.

"Canst thou answer to thy conscience for pulling all these fish out of the water, and leaving them to gasp in the sun?" said a voice, clear and sonorous as a bell.

I started and looked round. Close behind me stood the tall figure of a man, dressed in raiment of quaint and singular fashion, but of goodly materials. He was in the prime and vigour of manhood; his features handsome and noble, but full of calmness and benevolence; at least, I thought so, though they were somewhat shaded by a hat of finest beaver, with broad drooping eaves.

"Surely that is a very cruel diversion in which thou indulgest, my young friend," he continued.

"I am sorry for it, if it be, sir," said I, rising; "but I do not think it cruel to fish."

"What are thy reasons for not thinking so?"

"Fishing is mentioned frequently in Scripture. Simon Peter was a fisherman."

"True; and Andrew and his brother. But thou forgettest; they did not follow fishing as a diversion, as I fear thou doest. Thou readest the Scriptures?"

"Sometimes."

"Sometimes? not daily? that is to be regretted. What profession dost thou make? I mean to what religious denomination dost thou belong, my young friend?"

"Church."

"It is a very good profession – there is much of Scripture contained in its liturgy. Dost thou read ought besides the Scriptures?"

"Sometimes."

"What dost thou read besides?"

"Greek, and Dante."

"Indeed! then thou hast the advantage over myself; I can only read the former. Well, I am rejoiced to find that thou hast other pursuits besides thy fishing. Dost thou know Hebrew?"

"No."

"Thou shouldst study it. Why dost thou not undertake the study?"

"I have no books."

"I will lend thee books, if thou wish to undertake the study. I live yonder at the hall, as perhaps thou knowest. I have a library there, in which are many curious books, both in Greek and Hebrew, which I will show to thee, whenever thou mayst find it convenient to come and see me. Farewell! I am glad to find that thou hast pursuits more satisfactory than thy cruel fishing."

And the man of peace departed, and left me on the bank of the stream. Whether from the effect of his words, or for want of inclination to the sport. I know not, but from that day I became less and less a practitioner of that "cruel fishing."

UNDER THE SYCAMORE

Izaak Walton

1653

VENATOR O my good master, this morning walk has been spent to my great pleasure and wonder: but, I pray, when shall I have your direction how to make artificial flies, like to those that the trout loves best; and, also, how to use them?

PISCATOR My honest scholar, it is now past five of the clock: we will fish till nine, and then go to breakfast. Go you to yonder sycamore-tree, and hide your bottle of drink under the hollow root of it; for about that time, and in that place, we will make a brave breakfast with a piece of powdered beef, and a radish or two, that I have in my fish-bag: we shall,

I warrant you, make a good, honest, wholesome, hungry breakfast. And I will then give you direction for the making and using of your flies: and in the meantime, there is your rod and line; and my advice is, that you fish as you see me do. And let's try which can catch the first fish.

VENATOR I thank you, master. I will observe and practise your direction as far as I am able.

PISCATOR Look you, scholar; you see I have hold of a good fish; I now see it is a trout. I pray, put that net under him; and touch not my line, for if you do, then we break all. Well done, scholar; I thank you.

Now for another. Trust me, I have another bite. Come, scholar, come lay down your rod, and help me to land this as you did the other. So now we shall be sure to have a good dish of fish for supper.

VENATOR I am glad of that; but I have no fortune: sure, master, yours is a better rod and better tackling.

PISCATOR Nay, then take mine, and I will fish with yours. Look you, scholar, I have another. Come, do as you did before. And now I have a bite at another. Oh me! he has broke all; there's half a line and a good hook lost.

VENATOR Aye, and a good trout, too.

PISCATOR Nay, the trout is not lost; for pray take notice, no man can lose what he never had.

VENATOR Master, I can neither catch with the first nor second angle: I have no fortune.

PISCATOR Look you, scholar, I have yet another. And now, having caught three brace of trouts, I will tell you a short tale as we walk towards our breakfast. A scholar (a preacher I should say) that was to preach to procure the approbation of a parish that he might be their lecturer, had got from his fellow pupil the copy of a sermon that was first preached with great commendation by him that composed it; and though the borrower of it preached it, word for word, as it was at first, yet it was utterly disliked as it was preached by the second to his congregation: which the sermon-borrower complained of to the lender of it, and was thus answered: "I lent you, indeed, my fiddle, but not my fiddlestick; for you are to know, that every one cannot make music with my words, which are fitted for my own mouth." And so, my scholar, you are to know, that as the ill pronunciation or ill accenting of words in a sermon spoils it, so the ill carriage of your line, or not fishing even to a foot in a right place, makes you lose your labour; and you are to know, that though you have my fiddle, that is, my very rod and tacklings with which you see I catch fish, yet you have not my fiddlestick, that is, you yet have not skill to know how to carry your hand and line, nor how to guide it to a right place: and this must be taught you (for you are to remember, I told you angling is an art) either by practice or a long observation, or both.

But now let's say grace, and fall to breakfast. What say you, scholar, to the providence of an old angler? Does not this meat taste well? And was not this place well chosen to eat it, for this sycamore-tree will shade us from the sun's heat?

VENATOR All excellent good, and my stomach excellent good too. And I now remember, and find that true which devout Lessius says, That poor men, and those that fast often, have much more pleasure in eating than rich men and gluttons, that always feed before their stomachs are empty of their last meat and call for more; for by that means they rob themselves of that pleasure that hunger brings to poor men. And I do seriously approve of that saying of yours, That you had rather be a civil, well-governed, well-grounded, temperate, poor angler, than a drunken lord. But I hope there is none such; however, I am certain of this, that I have been at many very costly dinners that have not afforded me half the content that this has done, for which I thank God and you.

PISCATOR And now, scholar, I think it will be time to repair to our angle-rods, which we left in the water to fish for themselves; and you shall choose which shall be yours; and it is an even lay, one of them catches.

And, let me tell you, this kind of fishing with a dead rod, and laying night-hooks, are like putting money to use; for they both work for the owners when they do nothing but sleep, or eat, or rejoice, as you know we have done this last hour, and sat as quietly and as free from cares under this sycamore, as Virgil's Tityrus and his Meliboeus did under their broad beech-tree. No life, my honest scholar, no life so happy and so pleasant as the life of a well-governed angler; for when the lawyer is swallowed up with business, and the statesman is preventing or contriving plots, then we sit on cowslip-banks, hear the birds sing, and possess ourselves in as much quietness as these silent silver streams, which we now see glide so quietly by us. Indeed, my good scholar, we may say of angling, as Dr Boteler said of strawberries, "Doubtless God could have made a better berry, but doubtless God never did"; and so if I might be judge, God never did make a more calm, quiet, innocent recreation than angling.

I'll tell you, scholar, when I sat last on this primrose-bank, and looked down these meadows, I thought of them as Charles the Emperor did of the city of Florence: That they were too pleasant to be looked on, but only on holy-days. As I then sat on this very grass, I turned my present thoughts into verse: 'twas a wish, which I'll repeat to you:

THE ANGLER'S WISH

I in these flow'ry meads would be:
These crystal streams should solace me;
To whose harmonious bubbling noise
I with my angle would rejoice:
Sit here, and see the turtle-dove
Court his chaste mate to acts of love:
Or, on that bank, feel the west wind
Breathe health and plenty: please my mind,
To see sweet dew-drops kiss these flowers,
And then washed off by April showers:
Here hear my Kenna sing a song;
There see a blackbird feed her young,
Or a leverock build her nest:
Here give my weary spirits rest,
And raise my low-pitch'd thoughts above
Earth, or what poor mortals love:
Thus, free from law-suits and the noise
Of princes' courts, I would rejoice:
Or, with my Bryan, and a book,
Loiter long days near Shawford-brook;
There sit by him, and eat my meat,
There see the sun both rise and set:
There bid good morning to next day;
There meditate my time away,
And angle on; and beg to have
A quiet passage to a welcome grave.

WALDEN
Henry David Thoreau

1854

THE SCENERY of Walden is on a humble scale, and, though beautiful, does not approach to grandeur, nor can it much concern one who has not long frequented it or lived by its shore, yet this pond is so remarkable for its depth and purity as to merit a particular description. It is a clear and deep green well, half a mile long and a mile and three quarters in circumference and contains about sixty-one and a half acres; a perennial spring in the midst of pine and oak woods, without any visible inlet or outlet, except by the clouds and evaporation. The surrounding hills rise abruptly from the water to the height of forty to eighty feet, though on the south-west and east they attain to about one hundred and one hundred and fifty feet respectively, within a quarter and a third of a mile. They are exclusively woodland. All our Concord waters have two colours at least, one when viewed at a distance, and another, more proper, close at hand. The first depends more on the light and follows the sky. In clear weather, in summer, they appear blue at a little distance, especially if agitated, and at a great distance all appear alike. In stormy weather they are sometimes a dark slate colour. The sea, however, is said to be blue one day and green another without any perceptible change in the atmosphere. I have seen our river, when the landscape being covered with snow, both water and ice were as green as grass. Some consider blue "to be the colour of pure water, whether liquid or solid" but, looking directly down into our waters from a boat, they are seen to be of very different colours. Walden is blue at one time and green at another, even from the same point of view. Lying between the earth and the heavens, it partakes of the colour of both. Viewed from a hill-top it reflects the colour of the sky but near at hand it is of a yellowish tint, next the shore where you can see the sand, then a light green, which gradually deepens to a uniform dark green in the body of the pond. In some lights, even from a hill-top, it is a vivid green next the shore. Some have referred this to the reflection of the verdure; but it is equally green there against the railroad sandbank, and in the spring, before the leaves are expanded, and it may be simply the result of the prevailing blue mixed with the yellow of the sand. Such is the colour of its iris. This is that portion also, where in spring, the ice being warmed by the heat of the sun reflected from the bottom and also transmitted through the earth, melts first and forms a narrow canal about the still frozen middle. Like the rest of our waters, when much agitated, in clear weather, so that the surface of the waves may reflect the sky at the right angle, or because there is more light mixed with it, it appears at a little distance of a darker blue than the sky itself; and at such a time, being on its surface, and looking with divided vision, so as to see the reflection, I have discerned a matchless and indescribable light blue, such as watered or changeable silks and sword blades suggest, more cerulean than the sky itself, alternating with the original dark green on the opposite sides of the waves, which last appeared but muddy in comparison. It is a vitreous greenish blue, as I remember it, like those patches of winter sky seen through cloud vistas in the west before sundown.

Yet a single glass of its water held up to the light is as colourless as an equal quantity of air. It is well known that a large plate of glass will have a green tint, owing, as the makers say, to its "body" but a small piece of the same will be colourless. How large a body of Walden water would be required to reflect a green tint I have never proved.

The water is so transparent that the bottom can easily be discerned at the depth of twenty-five and thirty feet. Paddling over it, you may see many feet beneath the surface, the schools of perch and shiners, perhaps only an inch long, yet the former easily distinguishable by their transverse bars and you think that they must be ascetic fish that find a subsistence there.

Once in the winter, many years ago, when I had been cutting holes through the ice in order to catch pickerel, as I stepped ashore I tossed my axe back on to the ice, but some evil genius had directed it, it slid four or five rods directly into one of the holes, where the water was twenty-five feet deep.

Out of curiosity I lay down on the ice and looked through the hole, until I saw the axe a little on one side, standing on its head, with its helve erect and gently swaying to and fro with the pulse of the pond, and there it might have stood erect and swaying till in the course of time the handle rotted off if I had not disturbed it. Making another hole directly over it with an ice chisel which I had, and cutting down the longest birch which I could find in the neighbourhood with my knife, I made a slip noose, which I attached to its end, and, letting it down carefully, passed it over the knob of the handle, and drew it by a line along the birch, and so pulled the axe out again.

The shore is composed of a belt of smooth rounded white stones like paving stones, excepting one or two short sand beaches, and is so steep that in many places a single leap will carry you into water over your head; and were it not for its remarkable transparency, that would be the last to be seen of its bottom till it rose on the opposite side. Some think it is bottomless. It is nowhere muddy, and a casual observer would say there were no weeds in it; and of noticeable plants, except in the little meadows recently overflowed, which do not properly belong to it, a closer scrutiny does not detect a flag or a bulrush, nor even a lily, yellow or white, but only a few small heart leaves and potamogetons, and perhaps a water target or two; all of which however a bather might not perceive, and these plants are clean and bright like the element they grow in."

[Thoreau goes on to describe the rise and fall of the pond and how these periodic fluctuations stunted the trees and bushes which fringe its shores.]

By this fluctuation in the pond asserts its title to the shore, and thus the *shore* is *shorn*, and the trees cannot hold it by right of possession. These are the lips of the lake on which no beard grows. It licks its chaps from time to time. There have been caught in Walden, pickerel, one weighing 7 lb. to say nothing of another which carried off a reel with great velocity, which the fisherman safely set down at 8 lb., because he did not see him; perch and pouts, some of each weighing over 2 lb., shiners, chivins or roach (*Leuciscus pulchellus*), a very few breams, and a couple of eels, one weighing 4 lb. – I am thus particular because the weight of a fish is commonly its only title to fame, and these are the only eels I have heard ‹f› here – also I have a faint recollection of a little fish some 5 inches long with silvery sides and a greenish back, somewhat dacelike in character. Nevertheless, this pond is not very fertile in fish. Its pickerel, though not abundant, are its chief boast. I have seen at one time, lying on the ice, pickerel of at least three different kinds, a long shallow one, steel coloured, most like those caught in the river; a bright golden kind, with greenish reflections and remarkably deep, which is the most common here, and another golden-coloured and shaped like the last, but peppered on the sides with small dark brown and black spots, intermixed with a few faint blood red ones, very much like a trout . . . these are all very firm fish and weigh more than their size promises. The shiners, pouts, and perch also, and indeed all the fishes which inhabit this pond, are much cleaner, handsomer and firmer-fleshed, than those in the river and most other ponds, as the water is purer, and they can easily be distinguished from them.

A lake is the landscape's most beautiful and expressive feature. It is the earth's eye, looking into which the beholder measures the depth of his own nature. . . .

An old man who used to frequent the pond nearly sixty winters ago, when it was dark with surrounding forest tells me that in those days he sometimes saw it all alive with ducks and other waterfowl, and that there were many eagles about it. He came here a-fishing, and used an old log canoe which he found on the shore. It was made of two white pine logs dug out and pinned together, and was cut off square at the ends. It was very clumsy but lasted a good many years before it became waterlogged, and perhaps sank to the bottom. He did not know whose it was, it belonged to the pond.

. . . Early in the morning, while all things are crisp with frost, men come with fishing reels and slender lunch, and let down their fine lines through the snowy field (the frozen lake) to take pickerel and perch; wild men, who instinctively follow other fashions and trust other authorities than their townsmen, and by their goings and comings stitch towns together in parts where else they would be ripped. They sit and eat their luncheon in stout fear-naughts on the dry oak leaves on the shore, as wise in natural lore as the citizen is artificial. They never consulted with books and know and can tell much less than they have done. The things which they practise are said not to be known. Here is one fishing for pickerel with grown perch for bait. You look into his pail with wonder as into a summer pond, as if he kept summer locked up at home, or knew where she had retreated. How, pray, did he get these in mid-winter? Oh, he got the worms out of rotten logs since the ground froze, and so he caught them. His life itself passes deeper into Nature than the studies of the naturalist penetrate, himself a subject for the naturalist.

The latter raises the moss and bark gently with his knife in search of insects; the former lays open logs to their core with his axe, and moss and bark fly far and wide. He gets his living by barking trees. Such a man has some right to fish, and I love to see Nature carried out in him. The perch swallows the grub worm, the pickerel swallows the perch, and the fisherman swallows the pickerel and so all the chinks in the scale are filled.

When I strolled around the pond in misty weather I was sometimes amused by the primitive mode which some ruder fisherman adopted. He would perhaps have placed alder branches over the narrow hole in the ice, which were four or five rods apart, and equal distances from the shore, and having fastened the end of his line to a stick to prevent its being pulled through, having passed the slack line over a twig of the alder, a foot or more above the ice, and tied a dry oak leaf to it, which being pulled down, would show when he had a bite. These alders loomed through the mist at regular intervals as you walked round the pond.

Ah! those pickerel of Walden! When I see them lying on the ice or in the well which the fishermen cuts in the ice, making a little hole to admit the water, I am always surprised at their rare beauty, as if they were fabulous fishes, they are so foreign to the streets, even to the woods, foreign as Arabia to our Concord life. They possess a quite dazzling and transcendent beauty, which separates them by a wide interval from the cadaverous cod and haddock whose fame is trumpeted in our streets. They are not green, like the pines, nor grey like the stones, nor blue like the sky, but they have, to my eyes, if possible, yet rarer colours, like flowers and precious stones, as if they were pearls, the animalised *nuclei* or crystals of the Walden water. They, of course, *are* Walden all over and all through; are themselves small Waldens in the animal kingdom of Waldenses. It is surprising that they are caught here – that in this deep and capacious spring, far beneath the rattling teams and chaises and tinkling sleighs that travel the Walden road, this great gold and emerald fish swims. I never chanced to see its kind in any market; it would be the cynosure of all eyes there. Easily with a few convulsive quirks, they give up their watery ghosts, like a mortal translated before his time to the thin air of heaven. . . .

. . . Occasionally, after my hoeing was done for the day, I joined some impatient companion who had been fishing on the pond since morning, as silent and motionless as a duck or a floating leaf, and after practising various kinds of philosophy, had concluded commonly, by the time I arrived, that he belonged to the ancient sect of Coenobites. There was one older man, an excellent fisher and skilled in all kinds of woodcraft, who was pleased to look upon my house as a building erected for the convenience of fishermen and I was equally pleased when he sat in my doorway to arrange his lines. Once in a while we sat together on the pond, he at one end of the boat and I at the other, but not many words passed between us, for he had grown deaf in his later years, but he occasionally hummed a psalm, which harmonised well enough with my philosophy. Our intercourse was thus altogether one of unbroken harmony, far more pleasing to remember than if it had been carried on by speech. When, as was commonly the case, I had none to commune with, I used to raise the echoes by striking with a paddle on the side of my boat, filling the surrounding woods with circling and dilating sound, stirring them up as a keeper of a menagerie his wild beasts, until I elicited a growl from every wooded vale and hillside.

In warm evenings I frequently sat in the boat playing the flute, and saw the perch, which I seemed to have charmed, hovering around me, and the moon travelling over the ribbed bottom, which was strewn with the wrecks of the forest. Formerly I had come to this pond adventurously, from time to time, in dark summer nights, with a companion, and making a fire close to the water's edge, which we thought attracted the fishes, we caught pouts with a bunch of worms strung on a thread and when we had done, far into the night, threw burning brands high into the air like sky rockets, which, coming down into the pond, were quenched with a loud hissing, and we were suddenly groping in total darkness. Through this, whistling a tune, we took our way to the haunts of men again. But now I had made my home by the shore.

Sometimes, after staying in a village parlour till the family had all retired, I have returned to the woods, and partly with a view to the next day's dinner, spent the hours of midnight fishing from a boat by moonlight, serenaded by owls and foxes, and hearing, from time to time, the creaking note of some unknown bird close at hand. These experiences were very valuable and memorable to me – anchored in forty feet of water, and twenty or thirty rods from the shore, surrounded sometimes by thousands of small perch and shiners, dimpling the surface with their tails in the moonlight, and communicating by a long flaxen line with mysterious nocturnal fishes which had their dwelling forty feet below, or sometimes dragging sixty feet of line about the pond as I drifted in a gentle night breeze, now and then feeling a slight vibration along it, indicative of some life prowling about its extremity, of dull uncertain blundering purpose there, and slow to make up its mind. At length you slowly raise, pulling hand over hand, some horned pout, squeaking and squirming in the upper air. It was very queer, especially in dark nights, when your thoughts had wandered to vast and cosmogonal themes in other spheres, to feel this faint jerk, which came to interrupt your dreams and link you with Nature again. It seemed as if I might next cast my line upwards into the air, as well as downwards into this element which was scarcely more dense. Thus I caught two fishes, as it were, with one hook.

PATRONAGE
Thomas Barker

1657

To The Right Honourable Edward Lord Montague, Generall of the Navy, and one of the Lords Commissioners of the Treasury.

NOBLE LORD,

I Do present this my book as I have named it *Barker's Delight*, to your Honour. I pray God send you safe home to your good Lady and sweet Babes. *Amen, Amen*. If you shall find anything delightfull in the reading of it, I shall heartily rejoyce, for I know you are one who takes delight in that pleasure and have good judgement and experience, as many noble persons and Gentlemen of true piety and honour do and have. The favour that I have found from you, and a great many more that did and do love that pleasure, shall never be bury'd in oblivion by me. I am now grown old, and am willing to enlarge my little book. I have written no more but mine own experience and practice, and have set forth the true ground of Angling, which I have been gathering these three score years, having spent many pounds in the gaining of it, as is well known in the place where I was born and educated, which is *Bracemeale* in the Liberty of *Salop*, being a Freeman and Burgesse of the same City. If any noble or gentle Angler, of what degree soever he be, have a mind to discourse of any of these wayes and experiments, I live in *Henry* the 7th's Gifts, the next doore to the Gatehouse in *Westm.*, my name is *Barker*, where I shall be ready, as long as please God, to satisfie them, and maintain my art, during life, which is not like to be long; that the younger fry may have my experiments at a smaller charge than I had them, for, it would be too heavy for every one that loveth that exercise to be at that charge as I was at first in my youth, the losse of my time, with great expences. Therefore I took it in consideration, and thought fit to let it be understood, and to take pains to set forth the true grounds and wayes that I have found by experience both for the fitting of rods and tackles both for ground-baits and flyes, both for day and night, with the dressing, wherein I take as much delight as in the taking of them, and to show how I can perform it, to furnish any Lords table, onely with trouts as it is furnished with flesh, for 16 or 20 dishes. And I have a desire to preserve their health (with help of God) to go dry in their boots and shooes in angling, for age taketh the pleasure from me. My Lord, I am,

Your Honours most Humble Servant,
THOMAS BARKER, 1657

SOME VIEWS ON THE COMPLEAT ANGLER

A DISSENTING VIEW FROM RICHARD FRANK

He stuffs his Book with Morals from Dubravius and others, not giving us one Precedent of his own practical Experiments, except otherwise where he prefers the Trencher before the Troling-rod; who lays the stress of his Arguments upon other Men's Observations, wherewith he stuffs his indigested *Octavo*; so brings himself under the Angler's Censure, and the common Calamity of a Plagiary, to be pitied (poor Man) for his loss of Time, in scribling and transcribing other Men's Notions. These be the drones that rob the hive, yet flatter the bees they bring them honey.

SIR WALTER SETS THE RECORD STRAIGHT

Probably no readers while they read the disparaging passages in which the venerable Izaac is introduced, can forbear wishing that the good old man, who had so true an eye for Nature, so simple a taste for her most innocent pleasures, and withal, so sound a judgment, both concerning men and things, had made this northern tour instead of Franck; and had detailed in the beautiful simplicity of Arcadian language, his observations on the scenery and manners of Scotland. Yet we must do our author the justice to state, that he is as much superior to the excellent patriarch Izaac Walton, in the mystery of Fly-fishing, as inferior to him in taste, feeling, and common sense. Franck's contests with salmon are painted to the life, and his directions to the angler are generally given with great judgment.

BYRON IS AGAINST IT

Whatever Izaak Walton sings or says;
The quaint, old, cruel coxcomb, in his gullet
Should have a hook, and a small trout to pull it.

It would have taught him humanity at least. This sentimental savage, whom it is a mode to quote (amongst novelists) to show their sympathy for innocent sports and old songs, teaches how to sew up frogs, and break their legs by way of experiment, in addition to the art of angling, the cruelest, the coldest, and the stupidest of pretended sports. They may talk about the beauties of Nature, but the angler merely thinks about his dish of fish; he has no leisure to take his eyes from off the streams, and a single *bite* is worth to him more than all the scenery around. Besides, some fish bite best on a rainy day. The whale, the shark, and the tunny fishery have somewhat of noble and perilous in them; even net fishing, trawling, etc., are more humane and useful. But angling! No angler can be a good man.

CHARLES LAMB IS FOR IT

I shall expect you to bring me a brimful account of the pleasure which Walton has given you, when you come to town. It must square with your mind. The delightful innocence and healthfulness of the Angler's mind will have blown upon yours like a Zephyr. Don't you already feel your spirit *filled* with the scene – the banks of rivers – the cowslip-beds – the pastoral scenes – the neat ale-houses – and hostesses and milkmaids as far exceeding Virgil and Pope as the *Holy Living* is beyond Thomas à Kempis. Are not the eating and drinking joys painted to the Life? Do they not inspire you with an immortal hunger? Are you not ambitious of being made an Angler?

From a letter from CHARLES LAMB to his friend,
ROBERT LLOYD, 7th February 1801

ANDREW LANG SAYS IT WITH FLOWERS

A bait-fisher *may* be a good man, as Izaak was, but it is easier for a camel to pass through the eye of a needle. As coarse fish are usually caught only with bait, I shall not follow Izaak on to this unholy ground, wherein, none the less, grow flowers of Walton's fancy, and the songs of the old poets are heard. *The Compleat Angler*, indeed, is a book to be marked with flowers, marsh-marigolds and fritillaries, and petals of the yellow iris, for the whole provokes us to content, and whispers that word of the apostle, "Study to be quiet."

THE COMPLEAT ANGLER – A POEM BY J.WESTWOOD

What, not a word for thee, O little tome,
Brown-jerkined, friendly faced, of all my books
The one that wears the quaintest, kindliest looks –
Seems most completely, cosily at home
Amongst its fellows. Ah! if thou couldst tell
Thy story – how, in sixteen fifty-three,
Good Master Marriott, standing at his door,
Saw anglers hurrying – fifty – yea, three score,
To buy thee, ere noon pealed from Dunstan's bell:
And how he stared and . . . shook his sides with glee.
One story, this, which fact or fiction weaves.
Meanwhile, adorn my shelf, beloved of all –
Old book! with lavender between thy leaves,
And twenty ballads round thee on the wall.

. . . and William Hazlitt

The English nation are naturally "brothers of the angle." This pursuit implies just that mixture of patience and pastime, of vacancy and thoughtfulness, of idleness and business, of pleasure and of pain, which is suited to the genius of an Englishman, and, as I suspect, of no one else in the same degree. He is eminently gifted to stand in the situation assigned by Dr Johnson to the angler, "at one end of a rod with a worm at the other." I should suppose no other language than ours can show such a book as an oft-mentioned one, Walton's *Compleat Angler* – so full of naivete, of unaffected sprightliness, of busy trifling, of dainty songs, of refreshing brooks, of shady arbours, of happy thoughts, and of the herb called *Heart's Ease*! Some persons can see neither the wit nor wisdom of this genuine volume, as if a book as well as a man might not have a personal character belonging to it, amiable, venerable from the spirit of joy and thorough goodness it manifests, independently of acute remarks or scientific discoveries; others object to the cruelty of Walton's theory and practice of trout-fishing – for my part, I should as soon charge an infant with cruelty for killing a fly, and I feel the same sort of pleasure in reading his book as I should have done in the company of this happy, childlike old man, watching his ruddy cheek, his laughing eye, the kindness of his heart, and the dexterity of his hand in seizing his finny prey!

THE FIRST FLIES
Dame Juliana Berners

1486

MARCHE – The donne flye, the body of the donne woll and the wyngis of the pertryche. Another doone flye: the body of blacke woll: the wynges of the blackyst drakc: and the jay under the wynge and under the tayle.

APRYLL – The stone flye, the bodye of blacke wull: and yelawe under the wynge, and under the tayle and the wynges of the drake. In the begynnynge of May a good flye, the body of roddyd wull and lappid abawte wyth blacke sylke: the wynges of the drake and of the redde capons hakyll.

MAY – The yelaw flye, the body of yelaw wull: the wynges of the redde cocke hakyll and of the drake lyttyd yelaw. The blacke lauper, the body of blacke wull and lappyd abawte wyth the herle of y pecok tayle: and the wynges of y redde capon with a blewe heed.

JUNE – The donne cutte: the body of blacke wull and a yelaw lyste after eyther syde: the wynges of the bosarde bounde on with barkyd hempe. The mauve flye, the body of dolke wull, the wynges of the blackest mayle of the wylde drake. The tandy flye at saynt Wyllyams daye, the body of tandy wull and the wynges contrary eyther ayenst other of the whitest mayle of y wylde drake.

JUYLL – The waspe flye, the body of blacke wull and lappid abawte with yelaw threde; the winges of the bosarde. The shell fly at saynt Thomas daye, the body of greene wull and lappyd abawte wyth the herle of the pecoks tayle: wynges of the bosarde.

AUGUST – The drake flye, the body of blacke wull and lappid abawte wyth blacke sylke: wynges of the mayle of the black drake wyth a blacke heed.

CURIOSITIES OF FISH
R. B. Gent

1637

Q. Wherefore is it, that oysters, cockles, and the like shell fish doe open against the Tyde, although they be farre from the sea?

A. Either out of custome which they had, when they were in their maratime habitacles, at the certainty of the Tydes so to doe: or else that, naturally they feele in themselves the motion of the Sea, by which they, by their opening, desire to feed and refresh themselves.

Q. Wherefore is it, that Sea-fish is usually better than that of fresh water?

A. The same may be demanded why River-fish is better than Pond-fish, and Pond-fish better than Ten-fish, and this better than Dike-fish: Because these taste more of muddy impurity, than those of the Sea: for the Sea working, admits no mudde; and this appeares in River-mussels, (*vulgo*) Horse-mussels, which savour of rankness of filth; and the Sea-mussels are admitted for humane food, the others rejected.

Q. Wherefore is it, that fresh water Fishes have wind bladders, the Sea-fish none?

A. Because it was necessary for the fresh Fish, for its better navigation, (as I may say) to have in it an ayery vessell, to have its body floating, by the reason of the tenuity of the fresh water; but the salt water Fish not, by the reason of a grosser and stronger nature of the Sea, and more apt for their swift and gliding supporation.

ST ANTHONY TO THE FISHES
Translated by Joseph Addison

c. 1200 (trans. 1705)

WHEN THE HERETICS would not regard his preaching, St Anthony betook himself to the seashore, where the river Marecchia disembogues itself into the Adriatic. He here called the fish together in the name of God, that they might hear his holy word. The fish came swimming towards him in such vast shoals, both from the sea and from the river, that the surface of the water was quite covered with their multitudes. They quickly ranged themselves, according to their several species, into a very beautiful congregation, and, like so many rational creatures, presented themselves before him to hear the word of God. St Anthony was so struck with the miraculous obedience and submission of these poor animals, that he found a secret sweetness distilling upon his soul, and at last addressed himself to them in the following words.

"Although the infinite power and providence of God (my dearly beloved Fish) discovers itself in all the works of his creation, as in the heavens, in the sun, in the moon, and in the stars, in this lower world, in man, and in other perfect creatures; nevertheless the goodness of the Divine Majesty shines out in you more eminently, and appears after a more particular manner, than in any other created beings. For notwith-standing you are comprehended under the name of reptiles, partaking of a middle nature between stones and beasts, and imprisoned in the deep abyss of waters; notwithstanding you are tost among billows, thrown up and down by tempests, deaf to hearing, dumb to speech, and terrible to behold: notwithstanding, I say, these natural disadvantages, the Divine Greatness shows itself in you after a very wonderful manner. In you are seen the mighty mysteries of an infinite goodness. The holy scripture has always made use of you, as the types and shadows of some profound sacrament.

"Do you think that, without a mystery, the first present that God Almighty made to man, was of you, O ye Fishes? Do you think that without a mystery, among all creatures and animals which were appointed for sacrifices, you only were excepted, O ye Fishes? Do you think there was nothing meant by our Saviour Christ, that next to the paschal lamb he took so much pleasure in the food of you, O ye Fishes? Do you think it was by mere chance, that when the Redeemer of the World was to pay a tribute to Caesar, he thought fit to find it in the mouth of a fish? These are all of them so many mysteries and sacraments, that oblige you in a more particular manner to the praises of your Creator.

"It is from God, my beloved Fish, that you have received being, life, motion, and sense. It is he that has given you, in compliance with your natural inclinations, the whole world of waters for your habitation. It is he that has furnished it with lodgings, chambers, caverns, grottoes, and such magnificent retirements as are not to be met with in the seats of kings, or in the palaces of princes. You have the water for your dwelling, a clear transparent element, brighter than crystal; you can see from its deepest bottom everything that passes on its surface; you have the eyes of a lynx, or of an argus; you are guided by a secret and unerring principle, delighting in everything that may be beneficial to you, and avoiding everything that may be hurtful; you are carried on by a hidden instinct to preserve yourselves, and to propagate your species; you obey, in all your actions, works and motions, the dictates and suggestions of nature, without the least repugnancy or contradiction.

"The colds of winter, and the heats of summer, are equally incapable of molesting you. A serene or a clouded sky are indifferent to you. Let the earth abound in fruits, or be cursed with scarcity, it has no influence on your welfare. You live secure in rains and thunders, lightnings and earthquakes; you have no concern in the blossoms of spring, or in the glowings of summer, in the fruits of autumn, or in the frosts of winter.

You are not solicitous about hours or days, months or years; the variableness of the weather, or the change of seasons.

"In what dreadful majesty, in what wonderful power, in what amazing providence did God Almighty distinguish you among all the species of creatures that perished in the universal deluge! You only were insensible of the mischief that had laid waste the whole world.

"All this, as I have already told you, ought to inspire you with gratitude and praise towards the Divine Majesty, that has done so great things for you, granted you such particular graces and privileges, and heaped upon you so many distinguishing favours. And since for all this you cannot employ your tongues in the praises of your Benefactor, and are not provided with words to express your gratitude; make at least some sign of reverence; bow yourselves at his name; give some show of gratitude, according to the best of your capacities; express your thanks in the most becoming manner that you are able, and be not unmindful of all the benefits he has bestowed upon you."

He had no sooner done speaking, but behold a miracle! The fish, as though they had been endued with reason, bowed down their heads with all the marks of a profound humility and devotion, moving their bodies up and down with a kind of fondness, as approving what had been spoken by the blessed Father St Anthony.

The legend adds, that after many heretics, who were present at the miracle, had been converted by it, the saint gave his benediction to the fish, and dismissed them.

THE FISHERMAN'S DREAM
Theocritus

3rd Century B.C.
Translated by Charles Stuart Calverlye

Want quickens wit: Want's pupils needs must work,
O Diophantus: for the child of toil
Is grudged his very sleep by carking cares:
Or, if he taste the blessedness of night,
Thought for the morrow soon warns slumber off.

Two ancient fishers once lay side by side
On piled-up sea-wrack in their wattled hut,
Its leafy wall their curtain. Near them lay
The weapons of their trade, basket and rod,
Hooks, weed-encumbered nets, and cords and oars,
And, propped on rollers, an infirm old boat.
Their pillow was a scanty mat, eked out
With caps and garments: such the ways and means,
Such the whole treasury of the fishermen.
They knew no luxuries: owned nor door nor dog;
Their craft, their all, their mistress Poverty:
Their only neighbour Ocean, who for aye
Round their lorn hut came floating lazily.

Ere the moon's chariot was in mid-career,
The fishers girt them for their customed toil,
And banished slumber from unwilling eyes,
And roused their dreamy intellects with speech:

Asphalion
"They say that soon flit summer-nights away,
Because all lingering is the summer day:
Friend, it is false; for dream on dream have I
Dreamed, and the dawn still reddens not the sky.
How? am I wandering? or does night pass slow?"

His Comrade
"Asphalion, scout not the sweet summer so.
'Tis not that wilful seasons have gone wrong,
But care maims slumber, and the night seems long."

Asphalion
"Didst thou e'er study dreams? For visions fair
I saw last night; and fairly thou shouldst share
The wealth I dream of, as the fish I catch.
Now, for sheer sense, I reckon few thy match;
And, for a vision, he whose motherwit
Is his sole tutor best interprets it.
And now we've time the matter to discuss:
For who could labour, lying here (like us)
Pillowed on leaves and neighboured by the deep,

132

Or sleeping amid thorns no easy sleep?
In rich men's halls the lamps are burning yet;
But fish come alway to the rich man's net."

Comrade
"To me the vision of the night relate;
Speak, and reveal the riddle to thy mate."

Asphalion
"Last evening, as I plied my watery trade,
(Not on an o'erfull stomach — we had made
Betimes a meagre meal, as you can vouch),
I fell asleep; and lo! I seemed to crouch
Among the boulders, and for fish to wait,
Still dangling, rod in hand, my vagrant bait.
A fat fellow caught it (e'en in sleep I'm bound
To dream of fishing, as of crusts the hound):
Fast clung he to the hooks; his blood outwelled;
Bent with his struggling was the rod I held:
I tugged and tugged: my efforts made me ache:
'How, with a line thus slight, this monster take?'
Then gently, just to warn him he was caught,
I twitched him once; then slacked and then made taut
My line, for now he offered not to run;
A glance soon showed me all my task was done.
'Twas a gold fish, pure metal every inch
That I had captured. I began to flinch:
'What if this beauty be the sea-king's joy,
Or azure Amphitrite's treasured toy?'
With care I disengaged him — not to rip
With hasty hook the gilding from his lip:
And with a tow-line landed him, and swore
Never to set my foot on ocean more,
But with my gold live royally ashore.
So I awoke: and, comrade, lend me now
Thy wits, for I am troubled for my vow."

Comrade
"Ne'er quake: you're pledged to nothing, for no prize
You gained or gazed on. Dreams are nought but lies.

Yet may this dream bear fruit; if, wide-awake
And not in dreams, you'll fish the neighbouring lake.
Fish that are meat you'll there mayhap behold,
Not die of famine, amid dreams of gold."

THE FIRST FLY
Claudius Aelianus

3rd Century AD

THERE IS a form of fishing in Macedonia of which I have heard and have
knowledge. Between Beroea and Thessalonica runs a river called the
Astraeus containing fish of a speckled colouring: as to their local name
you had better ask the Macedonians. They feed on flies which hover
about the river – peculiar flies, quite unlike those found elsewhere – not
resembling wasps in aspect, nor can one match them rightly in shape
with what are called anthedons or wild bees, nor with hive bees: but they
have something in common with all these. They rival in boldness an
ordinary fly: in size you might rank them with wild bees: their colour is
modelled from the wasp, and they buzz like bees. The people of the place
invariably call them horsetails.

These flies settle on the stream in search of their special food, but
cannot avoid being seen by the fish swimming below. When, therefore, a
fish detects a fly floating on the surface, he swims towards it very quietly
under water, taking care not to stir the water above, which would scare
his prey. So coming close up on the side away from the sun, the fish
opens its mouth, snaps the fly down its gullet, like a wolf seizing a lamb
from the fold, or an eagle seizing a goose from the farmyard: and then
retreats under the ripple.

Anglers are aware of the whole procedure, but never by any chance
use the natural fly as bait: for when the flies are handled, they lose their
proper colour, their wings are battered, and the fish refuse to feed upon
them. Anglers accordingly leave the flies alone, resenting their cursed
behaviour when captured: but they get the better of the fish by a clever
and wily contrivance of their art. They wrap dark red wool round a hook
and tie on to it two feathers which grow under the wattles of a cock and

resemble wax in colour. The fishing rod is six feet in length and the line the same. When the tricky fly is lowered, a fish is attracted by the colour and rises madly at the pretty thing that will give him a rare treat, but on opening his jaws is pierced by the hook and finds poor enjoyment of the feast when he is captured.

TWIXT CUP AND LIP
Richard Franck

1694

THEOPHILUS (*a tyro*) Shall we spread the water this morning with our angling artillery, and examine the fords before we feast ourselves? Resolve this morning's exercise, my benevolence; only stand by, and furnish me with directions.

ARNOLDUS (*the mentor*) Your motion inclines me to promote the adventure, and the rather because to introduce you into the anglers' society. Hold forth your hand, and grasp this rod; take also this box, and this dubbing bag of flies, and select a choice. The complexion of the water must also be considered; and depths and shallows are necessary observations. But, above all, mind carefully the clifts of those craggy rocks, from whence you must expect the head of your game, if you angle for trout. And be circumspect and cautious when and how you strike, lest peradventure passion provoke your discretion, so indanger the loss of what you labour for.

THEOPHILUS These are soveraign admonitions.

ARNOLDUS Mind, therefore, your directions, and fish like an artist; for here, if your line but reach the water, you raise a trout, or, it may be, a salmon. Where, note, if you be indigent of this generous art, and unskilful to manage so eminent an encounter, perchance you'l sacrifice your labours to loss, so in conclusion lose your reputation.

THEOPHILUS I shall be mindful of that.

ARNOLDUS Then direct your eye to those bubbling streams, at whose murmuring descents are most profound deeps. But then, again, there's cataracts and falls of water; from whose fair invitations neither doubt nor despair of incomparable entertainments. That's the Sirene's seat of trophies, where trouts tumble up and down for diversion. Don't you see them pick, and cast themselves on the surface of the streams amongst those knotty stumpy rocks, almost drown'd in water? Lay but your line in at the tail of that stream, where it's sheltred with craggy rocky stones, and manage your game with art and discretion, I'le uphold you sport enough; but be circumspect (be sure) and look well to your line, lest peradventure your tackle be torn to pieces.

THEOPHILUS Doubt not of my care and circumspection.

ARNOLDUS Then take your lot, and cast in your line; and flourish your fly, for it's dub'd with bear's hair; and the point of your hook, it's so snug and so sharp, that, as it ought, it must always hang downward. Moreover, it's proportioned of an excellent compass, wing'd also with the dapple feather of a teal; a dangerous novel to invite a desperate fish; and sutable to the day and season, in regard it's bright.

THEOPHILUS Why thus to capitulate? Let us in amongst them.

ARNOLDUS Two words to a bargain; be better advised.

THEOPHILUS It's past that now, and I'm past my senses, to feel such trepidations on a sudden invade me. What's the matter with me that I'm thus out of order?

ARNOLDUS I perceive you disordred, but not much deliciated.

THEOPHILUS If I were, it's folly to complain, when past all hope to expect redress.

ARNOLDUS How know you that?

THEOPHILUS I know you won't tell me what it is that tugs thus.

ARNOLDUS It may be a trout; or it may be a salmon.

THEOPHILUS Or it may be both, for ought I know; for it's almost impossible that one single fish should raise the water to such eruptions.

ARNOLDUS And impossible for you (I perceive) to reclaim him.

THEOPHILUS Do but resolve me what it is, and then I'le resolve myself what to do.

ARNOLDUS Make your own choice, what would you have it?

THEOPHILUS I would have it a fish.

ARNOLDUS So it is; and it may be a fish of the largest size; therefore, look well about you.

THEOPHILUS I may look which way I will, and despair at last; what makes the water swell with ebullitions?

ARNOLDUS Nothing I suppose but a change of elements, the fish has no mind to come ashore.

THEOPHILUS And I have as little inclination to go to fetch him.

ARNOLDUS Then were your hazards equal; and hitherto, as I apprehend, you have much the odds.

THEOPHILUS Odd or even, I know not how to manage him.

ARNOLDUS Would you put a force upon Neptune, to compel his subjects ashore?

THEOPHILUS Had I skill enough, I would certainly do it.

ARNOLDUS So I perceive; but you'r now almost at a stand. Pull.

THEOPHILUS On the other hand, he strives to pull all in pieces; which he will certainly do, if I do not reclaim him. But where is he now?

ARNOLDUS Gone to the bottom, it may be.

THEOPHILUS And it may be, I begin to smell the plot; he courts the deep for self-security.

ARNOLDUS Then you fancy the streams won't protect him; because there's no plot in them.

THEOPHILUS Plots for the most part, you know, lie deepest; so he sinks to the bottom for self-preservation, and creeps to death as if of old acquaintance.

ARNOLDUS Rash results reap repentance; mistake not your self by dooming his death; he's but slipt to the bottom to recruit himself, and indenture with stones to oblige their protection.

THEOPHILUS What, must we have now another vagary? Is my scaly companion surrounded and compounded of nothing but frolicks? which, for ought I know, may cost him his life, if he is not mindful to look to his hitts.

ARNOLDUS And you must be advised to look well to yours; for he'l not come ashore to beg his life. Stand fast, therefore, and call to mind your former rudiments; for trust me, I shall give you no other supply than some friendly admonishments to reconcile you together.

THEOPHILUS What, no directions; nor any farther instructions?

ARNOLDUS If two to one be odds at football, and against the rules and law of fair play, the very thought on't would make me blush, and appear shamefac'd, if but to think two anglers should at once consult together to encounter one fish.

THEOPHILUS Then I'le fight him myself, and run my own destiny. See where he comes, tumbling and tossing, and volting himself in the stiffest streams. Can no element contain his active violence? Will he twist his tail to cut my line for an experiment? But this kind of cunning may perchance defeat him; he may prick his chaps and yet miss my bait.

ARNOLDUS And you may miss him, that won't stand upon a trifle.

THEOPHILUS A trifle did you say? I'le trifle him no longer. Ha, boys! he's gone again.

ARNOLDUS I suppose he's gone where you can't come at him; and that's to the bottom for another insurrection.

THEOPHILUS So it appears, for he's invisible in a moment. This is a kind of *hocus pocus*: Surely I fancy he has outliv'd his time.

ARNOLDUS Flatter not yourself with that fly-blown opinion; for I'm apt to perswade myself he'l live beyond the art of your exercise; this I know and perceive by his working, that if you work not wisely, he'l work a reprieve.

THEOPHILUS Then I'le work with him, and trifle him ashore, to examine the point, and exchange of elements. I see he's convulst by fluttering his fins; and I'm sure he's half dead by rigling his tail; nay, more than that, he lies still without motion: And are not all these mortal signs of submission?

ARNOLDUS And if he submits, he dies without redemption; and death, you know, is a total submission.

THEOPHILUS I'le kill this fish, or forfeit my reputation.

ARNOLDUS Take your chance, for I know you are resolute.

THEOPHILUS I'le take my chance, and return victorious.

ARNOLDUS But there's no triumph, you know, till possest of the trophies.

THEOPHILUS And I am pretty near them, was it not that one or two stratagems strangely amuse me; the one of them is the casting himself on the surface, as if designing thereby to cut my line; and the other, his fastning himself in the bottom, thinking, as I apprehend, to tear all in pieces; which, if he do, I lose my reputation: besides I grow weary, and would fain horse him out.

ARNOLDUS You may do what you please, you are lord of your own exercise; the law is in your hand, manage with discretion.

THEOPHILUS I'le manage it with all the industry I have.

ARNOLDUS Do so, and you will see the event.

THEOPHILUS Then have at all.

ARNOLDUS And what have you got?

THEOPHILUS I have got nothing but the foot-steps of folly.

ARNOLDUS And nothing out of nothing is folly in the abstract; was not I prophetick?

THEOPHILUS An oracle too true to confirm my loss; for what have I left? Nothing but folly, to lament and condole this fatal conclusion: to be rob'd by a fish that I reckoned my reward: is not this felony, to steal my tackle, and ruin an angler?

THE
COMPLETE ANGLER

BIG TWO-HEARTED RIVER

Ernest Hemingway

1925

PART ONE

THE TRAIN WENT ON up the track out of sight, around one of the hills of burnt timber. Nick sat down on the bundle of canvas and bedding the baggage man had pitched out of the door of the baggage car. There was no town, nothing but the rails and the burned-over country. The thirteen saloons that had lined the one street of Seney had not left a trace. The foundations of the Mansion House hotel stuck up above the ground. The stone was chipped and split by the fire. It was all that was left of the town of Seney. Even the surface had been burned off the ground.

Nick looked at the burned-over stretch of hillside, where he had expected to find the scattered houses of the town and then walked down the railroad track to the bridge over the river. The river was there. It swirled against the log spiles of the bridge. Nick looked down into the clear, brown water, colored from the pebbly bottom, and watched the trout keeping themselves steady in the current with wavering fins. As he watched them they changed their positions by quick angles, only to hold steady in the fast water again. Nick watched them a long time.

He watched them holding themselves with their noses into the current, many trout in deep, fast moving water, slightly distorted as he watched far down through the glassy convex surface of the pool, its surface pushing and swelling smooth against the resistance of the log-driven piles of the bridge. At the bottom of the pool were the big trout. Nick did not see them at first. Then he saw them at the bottom of the pool, big trout looking to hold themselves on the gravel bottom in a varying mist of gravel and sand, raised in spurts by the current.

Nick looked down into the pool from the bridge. It was a hot day. A kingfisher flew up the stream. It was a long time since Nick had looked into a stream and seen trout. They were very satisfactory. As the shadow of the kingfisher moved up the stream, a big trout shot upstream in a long angle, only his shadow marking the angle, then lost his shadow as he came through the surface of the water, caught the sun, and then, as he went back into the stream under the surface, his shadow seemed to float down the stream with the current, unresisting, to his post under the bridge where he tightened facing up into the current.

Nick's heart tightened as the trout moved. He felt all the old feeling.

He turned and looked down the stream. It stretched away, pebbly-bottomed with shallows and big boulders and a deep pool as it curved away around the foot of a bluff.

Nick walked back up the ties to where his pack lay in the cinders beside the railway track. He was happy. He adjusted the pack harness around the bundle, pulling straps tight, slung the pack on his back, got his arms through the shoulder straps and took some of the pull off his shoulders by leaning his forehead against the wide band of the tump-line. Still, it was too heavy. It was much too heavy. He had his leather rod-case in his hand and leaning forward to keep the weight of the pack high on his shoulders he walked along the road that paralleled the railway track, leaving the burned town behind in the heat, and then turned off around a hill with a high, fire-scarred hill on either side onto a road that went back into the country. He walked along the road feeling the ache from the pull of the heavy pack. The road climbed steadily. It was hard work walking up-hill. His muscles ached and the day was hot, but Nick felt happy. He felt he had left everything behind, the need for thinking, the need to write, other needs. It was all back of him.

From the time he had gotten down off the train and the baggage man had thrown his pack out of the open car door things had been different. Seney was burned, the country was burned over and changed, but it did not matter. It could not all be burned. He knew that. He hiked along the road, sweating in the sun, climbing to cross the range of hills that separated the railway from the pine plains.

The road ran on, dipping occasionally, but always climbing. Nick went on up. Finally the road after going parallel to the burnt hillside reached the top. Nick leaned back against a stump and slipped out of the pack harness. Ahead of him, as far as he could see, was the pine plain. The burned country stopped off at the left with the range of hills. On ahead islands of dark pine trees rose out of the plain. Far off to the left was the line of the river. Nick followed it with his eye and caught glints of the water in the sun.

There was nothing but the pine plain ahead of him, until the far blue hills that marked the Lake Superior height of land. He could hardly see them, faint and far away in the heat-light over the plain. If he looked too steadily they were gone. But if he only half-looked they were there, the far-off hills of the height of land.

Nick sat down against the charred stump and smoked a cigarette. His pack balanced on the top of the stump, harness holding ready, a hollow molded in it from his back. Nick sat smoking, looking out over the country. He did not need to get his map out. He knew where he was from the position of the river.

As he smoked, his legs stretched out in front of him, he noticed a grasshopper walk along the ground and up onto his woolen sock. The grasshopper was black. As he had walked along the road, climbing, he had started many grasshoppers from the dust. They were all black. They were not the big grasshoppers with yellow and black or red and black wings whirring out from their black wing sheathing as they fly up. These were just ordinary hoppers, but all a sooty black in color. Nick had wondered about them as he walked, without really thinking about them. Now, as he watched the black hopper that was nibbling at the wool of his sock with its fourway lip, he realized that they had all turned black from living in the burned-over land. He realized that the fire must have come the year before, but the grasshoppers were all black now. He wondered how long they would stay that way.

Carefully he reached his hand down and took hold of the hopper by the wings. He turned him up, all his legs walking in the air, and looked at his jointed belly. Yes, it was black too, iridescent where the back and head were dusty.

"Go on, hopper," Nick said, speaking out loud for the first time. "Fly away somewhere."

He tossed the grasshopper up into the air and watched him sail away to a charcoal stump across the road.

Nick stood up. He leaned his back against the weight of his pack where it rested upright on the stump and got his arms through the shoulder straps. He stood with the pack on his back on the brow of the hill looking out across the country, toward the distant river and then struck down the hillside away from the road. Underfoot the ground was good walking. Two hundred yards down the hillside the fire line stopped. Then it was sweet fern, growing ankle high, to walk through, and clumps of jack pines; a long undulating country with frequent rises and descents, sandy underfoot and the country alive again.

Nick kept his direction by the sun. He knew where he wanted to strike the river and he kept on through the pine plain, mounting small rises to see other rises ahead of him and sometimes from the top of a rise a great solid island of pines off to his right or his left. He broke off some sprigs of the heathery sweet fern, and put them under his pack straps. The chafing crushed it and he smelled it as he walked.

He was tired and very hot, walking across the uneven, shadeless pine plain. At any time he knew he could strike the river by turning off to his left. It could not be more than a mile away. But he kept on toward the north to hit the river as far upstream as he could go in one day's walking.

For some time as he walked Nick had been in sight of one of the big islands of pine standing out above the rolling high ground he was crossing. He dipped down and then as he came slowly up to the crest of the ridge he turned and made toward the pine trees.

There was no underbrush in the island of pine trees. The trunks of the trees went straight up or slanted toward each other. The trunks were straight and brown without branches. The branches were high above. Some interlocked to make a solid shadow on the brown forest floor. Around the grove of trees was a bare space. It was brown and soft underfoot as Nick walked on it. This was the over-lapping of the pine needle floor, extending out beyond the width of the high branches. The trees had grown tall and the branches moved high, leaving in the sun this bare space they had once covered with shadow. Sharp at the edge of this extension of the forest floor commenced the sweet fern.

Nick slipped off his pack and lay down in the shade. He lay on his back and looked up into the pine trees. His neck and back and the small of his back rested as he stretched. The earth felt good against his back. He looked up at the sky, through the branches, and then shut his eyes. He opened them and looked up again. There was a wind high up in the branches. He shut his eyes again and went to sleep.

Nick woke stiff and cramped. The sun was nearly down. His pack was heavy and the straps painful as he lifted it on. He leaned over with the pack on and picked up the leather rod-case and started out from the pine trees across the sweet fern swale, toward the river. He knew it could not be more than a mile.

He came down a hillside covered with stumps into a meadow. At the edge of the meadow flowed the river. Nick was glad to get to the river. He walked upstream through the meadow. His trousers were soaked with the dew as he walked. After the hot day, the dew had come quickly and heavily. The river made no sound. It was too fast and smooth. At the edge of the meadow, before he mounted to a piece of high ground to make camp, Nick looked down the river at the trout rising. They were rising to insects come from the swamp on the other side of the stream when the sun went down. The trout jumped out of water to take them. While Nick walked through the little stretch of meadow alongside the stream, trout had jumped high out of water. Now as he looked down the river, the insects must be settling on the surface, for the trout were feeding steadily all down the stream. As far down the long stretch as he could see, the trout were rising, making circles all down the surface of the water, as though it were starting to rain.

The ground rose, wooded and sandy, to overlook the meadow, the stretch of river and the swamp. Nick dropped his pack and rod-case and looked for a level piece of ground. He was very hungry and he wanted to make his camp before he cooked. Between two jack pines, the ground was quite level. He took the ax out of the pack and chopped out two projecting roots. That leveled a piece of ground large enough to sleep on. He smoothed out the sandy soil with his hand and pulled all the sweet fern bushes by their roots. His hands smelled good from the sweet fern. He smoothed the uprooted earth. He did not want anything making lumps under the blankets. When he had the ground smooth, he spread his three blankets. One he folded double, next to the ground. The other two he spread on top.

With the ax he slit off a bright slab of pine from one of the stumps and split it into pegs for the tent. He wanted them long and solid to hold in the ground. With the tent unpacked and spread on the ground, the pack, leaning against a jackpine, looked much smaller. Nick tied the rope that served the tent for a ridge-pole to the trunk of one of the pine trees and pulled the tent up off the ground with the other end of the rope and tied it to the other pine. The tent hung on the rope like a canvas blanket on a clothesline. Nick poked a pole he had cut up under the back peak of the canvas and then made it a tent by pegging out the sides. He pegged the sides out taut and drove the pegs deep, hitting them down into the ground with the flat of the ax until the rope loops were buried and the canvas was drum tight.

Across the open mouth of the tent Nick fixed cheesecloth to keep out mosquitoes. He crawled inside under the mosquito bar with various things from the pack to put at the head of the bed under the slant of the canvas. Inside the tent the light came through the brown canvas. It smelled pleasantly of canvas. Already there was something mysterious and homelike. Nick was happy as he crawled inside the tent. He had not been unhappy all day. This was different though. Now things were done. There had been this to do. Now it was done. It had been a hard trip. He was very tired. That was done. He had made his camp. He was settled. Nothing could touch him. It was a good place to camp. He was there, in the good place. He was in his home where he had made it. Now he was hungry.

He came out, crawling under the cheesecloth. It was quite dark outside. It was lighter in the tent.

Nick went over to the pack and found, with his fingers, a long nail in a paper sack of nails, in the bottom of the pack. He drove it into the pine tree, holding it close and hitting it gently with the flat of the ax. He hung the pack up on the nail. All his supplies were in the pack. They were off the ground and sheltered now.

Nick was hungry. He did not believe he had ever been hungrier. He opened and emptied a can of pork and beans and a can of spaghetti into the frying pan.

"I've got a right to eat this kind of stuff, if I'm willing to carry it," Nick said. His voice sounded strange in the darkening woods. He did not speak again.

He started a fire with some chunks of pine he got with the ax from a stump. Over the fire he stuck a wire grill, pushing the four legs down into the ground with his boot. Nick put the frying pan on the grill over the flames. He was hungrier. The beans and spaghetti warmed. Nick stirred them and mixed them together. They began to bubble, making little bubbles that rose with difficulty to the surface. There was a good smell. Nick got out a bottle of tomato catchup and cut four slices of bread. The little bubbles were coming faster now. Nick sat down beside the fire and lifted the frying pan off. He poured about half the contents out into the tin plate. It spread slowly on the plate. Nick knew it was too hot. He poured on some tomato catchup. He knew the beans and spaghetti were still too hot. He looked at the fire, then at the tent, he was not going to spoil it all by burning his tongue. For years he had never enjoyed fried bananas because he had never been able to wait for them to cool. His tongue was very sensitive. He was very hungry. Across the river in the swamp, in the almost dark, he saw a mist rising. He looked at the tent once more. All right. He took a full spoonful from the plate.

"Chrise," Nick said, "Geezus Chrise," he said happily.

He ate the whole plateful before he remembered the bread. Nick finished the second plateful with the bread, mopping the plate shiny. He had not eaten since a cup of coffee and a ham sandwich in the station restaurant at St. Ignace. It had been a very fine experience. He had been that hungry before, but had not been able to satisfy it. He could have made camp hours before if he had wanted to. There were plenty of good places to camp on the river. But this was good.

Nick tucked two big chips of pine under the grill. The fire flared up. He had forgotten to get water for the coffee. Out of the pack he got a folding canvas bucket and walked down the hill, across the edge of the meadow, to the stream. The other bank was in the white mist. The grass was wet and cold as he knelt on the bank and dipped the canvas bucket into the stream. It bellied and pulled hard in the current. The water was ice cold. Nick rinsed the bucket and carried it full up to the camp. Up away from the stream it was not so cold.

Nick drove another big nail and hung up the bucket full of water. He dipped the coffee pot half full, put some more chips under the grill onto the fire and put the pot on. He could not remember which way he made coffee. He could remember an argument about it with Hopkins, but not which side he had taken. He decided to bring it to a boil. He remembered now that was Hopkins's way. He had once argued about everything with Hopkins. While he waited for the coffee to boil, he opened a small can of apricots. He liked to open cans. He emptied the can of apricots out into a tin cup. While he watched the coffee on the fire, he drank the juice syrup of the apricots, carefully at first to keep from spilling, then meditatively, sucking the apricots down. They were better than fresh apricots.

The coffee boiled as he watched. The lid came up and coffee and grounds ran down the side of the pot. Nick took it off the grill. It was a triumph for Hopkins. He put sugar in the empty apricot cup and poured some of the coffee out to cool. It was too hot to pour and he used his hat to hold the handle of the coffee pot. He would not let it steep in the pot at all. Not the first cup. It should be straight Hopkins all the way. Hop deserved that. He was a very serious coffee drinker. He was the most serious man Nick had ever known. Not heavy, serious. That was a long time ago. Hopkins spoke without moving his lips. He had played polo. He made millions of dollars in Texas. He had borrowed carfare to go to Chicago, when the wire came that his first big well had come in. He could have wired for money. That would have been too slow. They called Hop's girl the Blonde Venus. Hop did not mind because she was not his real girl. Hopkins said very confidently that none of them would make fun of his real girl. He was right. Hopkins went away when the telegram came. That was on the Black River. It took eight days for the telegram to reach him. Hopkins gave away his .22 caliber Colt automatic pistol to Nick. He gave his camera to Bill. It was to remember him always by. They were all going fishing again next summer. The Hop Head was rich. He would get a yacht and they would all cruise along the north shore of Lake Superior. He was excited but serious. They said good-bye and all felt bad. It broke up the trip. They never saw Hopkins again. That was a long time ago on the Black River.

Nick drank the coffee, the coffee according to Hopkins. The coffee was bitter. Nick laughed. It made a good ending to the story. His mind was starting to work. He knew he could choke it because he was tired enough. He spilled the coffee out of the pot and shook the grounds loose into the fire. He lit a cigarette and went inside the tent. He took off his shoes and trousers, sitting on the blankets, rolled the shoes up inside the trousers for a pillow and got in between the blankets.

Out through the front of the tent he watched the glow of the fire, when the night wind blew on it. It was a quiet night. The swamp was perfectly quiet. Nick stretched under the blanket comfortably. A mosquito hummed close to his ear. Nick sat up and lit a match. The mosquito was on the canvas, over his head. Nick moved the match quickly up to it. The mosquito made a satisfactory hiss in the flame. The match went out. Nick lay down again under the blanket. He turned on his side and shut his eyes. He was sleepy. He felt sleep coming. He curled up under the blanket and went to sleep.

PART TWO

In the morning the sun was up and the tent was starting to get hot. Nick crawled out under the mosquito netting stretched across the mouth of the tent, to look at the morning. The grass was wet on his hands as he came out. He held his trousers and his shoes in his hands. The sun was just up over the hill. There was the meadow, the river and the swamp. There were birch trees in the green of the swamp on the other side of the river.

The river was clear and smoothly fast in the early morning. Down about two hundred yards were three logs all the way across the stream. They made the water smooth and deep above them. As Nick watched, a mink crossed the river on the logs and went into the swamp. Nick was excited. He was excited by the early morning and the river. He was really too hurried to eat breakfast, but he knew he must. He built a little fire and put on the coffee pot.

While the water was heating in the pot he took an empty bottle and went down over the edge of the high ground to the meadow. The meadow was wet with dew and Nick wanted to catch grasshoppers for bait before the sun dried the grass. He found plenty of good grasshoppers. They were at the base of the grass stems. Sometimes they clung to a grass stem. They were cold and wet with the dew, and could not jump until the sun warmed them. Nick picked them up, taking only the medium-sized brown ones, and put them into the bottle. He turned over a log and just under the shelter of the edge were several hundred hoppers. It was a grasshopper lodging house. Nick put about fifty of the medium browns into the bottle. While he was picking up the hoppers the others warmed in the sun and commenced to hop away. They flew when they hopped. At first they made one flight and stayed stiff when they landed, as though they were dead.

Nick knew that by the time he was through with breakfast they would be as lively as ever. Without dew in the grass it would take him all day to catch a bottle full of good grasshoppers and he would have to crush many of them, slamming at them with his hat. He washed his hands at the stream. He was excited to be near it. Then he walked up to the tent. The hoppers were already jumping stiffly in the grass. In the bottle, warmed by the sun, they were jumping in a mass. Nick put in a pine stick as a cork. It plugged the mouth of the bottle enough, so the hoppers could not get out and left plenty of air passage.

He had rolled the log back and knew he could get grasshoppers there every morning.

Nick laid the bottle full of jumping grasshoppers against a pine trunk. Rapidly he mixed some buckwheat flour with water and stirred it smooth, one cup of flour, one cup of water. He put a handful of coffee in the pot and dipped a lump of grease out of a can and slid it sputtering across the hot skillet. On the smoking skillet he poured smoothly the buckwheat batter. It spread like lava, the grease spitting sharply. Around the edges the buckwheat cake began to firm, then brown, then crisp. The surface was bubbling slowly to porousness. Nick pushed under the browned under surface with a fresh pine chip. He shook the skillet sideways and the cake was loose on the surface. I won't try and flop it, he thought. He slid the chip of clean wood all the way under the cake, and flopped it over onto its face. It sputtered in the pan.

When it was cooked Nick regreased the skillet. He used all the batter.

It made another big flapjack and one smaller one.

Nick ate a big flapjack and a smaller one, covered with apple butter. He put apple butter on the third cake, folded it over twice, wrapped it in oiled paper and put it in his shirt pocket. He put the apple butter jar back in the pack and cut bread for two sandwiches.

In the pack he found a big onion. He sliced it in two and peeled the silky outer skin. Then he cut one half into slices and made onion sandwiches. He wrapped them in oiled paper and buttoned them in the other pocket of his khaki shirt. He turned the skillet upside down on the grill, drank the coffee, sweetened and yellow brown with the condensed milk in it, and tidied up the camp. It was a good camp.

Nick took his fly rod out of the leather rod-case, jointed it, and shoved the rod-case back into the tent. He put on the reel and threaded the line through the guides. He had to hold it from hand to hand, as he threaded it, or it would slip back through its own weight. It was a heavy, double tapered fly line. Nick had paid eight dollars for it a long time ago. It was made heavy to lift back in the air and come forward flat and heavy and straight to make it possible to cast a fly which has no weight. Nick opened the aluminum leader box. The leaders were coiled between the damp flannel pads. Nick had wet the pads at the water cooler on the train up to St. Ignace. In the damp pads the gut leaders had softened and Nick unrolled one and tied it by a loop at the end of the heavy fly line. He fastened a hook on the end of the leader. It was a small hook; very thin and springy.

Nick took it from his hook book, sitting with the rod across his lap. He tested the knot and the spring of the rod by pulling the line taut. It was a good feeling. He was careful not to let the hook bite into his finger.

He started down to the stream, holding his rod, the bottle of grasshoppers hung from his neck by a thong tied in half hitches around the neck of the bottle. His landing net hung by a hook from his belt. Over his shoulder was a long flour sack tied at each corner into an ear. The cord went over his shoulder. The sack flapped against his legs.

Nick felt awkward and professionally happy with all his equipment hanging from him. The grasshopper bottle swung against his chest. In his shirt the breast pockets bulged against him with the lunch and his fly book.

He stepped into the stream. It was a shock. His trousers clung tight to his legs. His shoes felt the gravel. The water was a rising cold shock.

Rushing, the current sucked against his legs. Where he stepped in, the water was over his knees. He waded with the current. The gravel slid under his shoes. He looked down at the swirl of water below each leg and tipped up the bottle to get a grasshopper.

The first grasshopper gave a jump in the neck of the bottle and went out into the water. He was sucked under in the whirl by Nick's right leg and came to the surface a little way down stream. He floated rapidly, kicking. In a quick circle, breaking the smooth surface of the water, he disappeared. A trout had taken him.

Another hopper poked his face out of the bottle. His antennae wavered. He was getting his front legs out of the bottle to jump. Nick took him by the head and held him while he threaded the slim hook under his chin, down through his thorax and into the last segments of his abdomen. The grasshopper took hold of the hook with his front feet, spitting tobacco juice on it. Nick dropped him into the water.

Holding the rod in his right hand he let out line against the pull of the grasshopper in the current. He stripped off line from the reel with his left hand and let it run free. He could see the hopper in the little waves of the current. It went out of sight.

There was a tug on the line. Nick pulled against the taut line. It was his first strike. Holding the now living rod across the current, he brought in the line with his left hand. The rod bent in jerks, the trout pumping against the current. Nick knew it was a small one. He lifted the rod straight up in the air. It bowed with the pull.

He saw the trout in the water jerking with his head and body against the shifting tangent of the line in the stream.

Nick took the line in his left hand and pulled the trout, thumping tiredly against the current, to the surface. His back was mottled the clear, water-over-gravel color, his side flashing in the sun. The rod under his right arm, Nick stooped, dipping his right hand into the current. He held the trout, never still, with his moist right hand, while he unhooked the barb from his mouth, then dropped him back into the stream.

He hung unsteadily in the current, then settled to the bottom beside a stone. Nick reached down his hand to touch him, his arm to the elbow under water. The trout was steady in the moving stream, resting on the gravel, beside a stone. As Nick's fingers touched him, touched his smooth, cool, underwater feeling he was gone, gone in a shadow across the bottom of the stream.

He's all right, Nick thought. He was only tired.

He had wet his hand before he touched the trout, so he would not disturb the delicate mucus that covered him. If a trout was touched with a dry hand, a white fungus attacked the unprotected spot. Years before when he had fished crowded streams, with fly fishermen ahead of him and behind him, Nick had again and again come on dead trout, furry with white fungus, drifted against a rock, or floating belly up in some pool. Nick did not like to fish with other men on the river. Unless they were of your party, they spoiled it.

He wallowed down the stream, above his knees in the current, through the fifty yards of shallow water above the pile of logs that crossed the stream. He did not rebait his hook and held it in his hand as he waded. He was certain he could catch small trout in the shallows, but he did not want them. There would be no big trout in the shallows this time of day.

Now the water deepened up his thighs sharply and coldly. Ahead was the smooth dammed-back flood of water above the logs. The water was smooth and dark; on the left, the lower edge of the meadow; on the right the swamp.

Nick leaned back against the current and took a hopper from the bottle. He threaded the hopper on the hook and spat on him for good luck. Then he pulled several yards of line from the reel and tossed the hopper out ahead onto the fast, dark water. It floated down towards the logs, then the weight of the line pulled the bait under the surface. Nick held the rod in his right hand, letting the line run out through his fingers.

There was a long tug. Nick struck and the rod came alive and dangerous, bent double, the line tightening, coming out of water, tightening, all in a heavy, dangerous, steady pull. Nick felt the moment when the leader would break if the strain increased and let the line go.

The reel ratcheted into a mechanical shriek as the line went out in a rush. Too fast. Nick could not check it, the line rushing out, the reel note rising as the line ran out.

With the core of the reel showing, his heart feeling stopped with the excitement, leaning back against the current that mounted icily his thighs, Nick thumbed the reel hard with his left hand. It was awkward getting his thumb inside the fly reel frame.

As he put on pressure the line tightened into sudden hardness and beyond the logs a huge trout went high out of water. As he jumped, Nick lowered the tip of the rod. But he felt, as he dropped the tip to ease the strain, the moment when the strain was too great; the hardness too tight. Of course, the leader had broken. There was no mistaking the feeling when all spring left the line and it became dry and hard. Then it went slack.

His mouth dry, his heart down, Nick reeled in. He had never seen so big a trout. There was a heaviness, a power not to be held, and then the bulk of him, as he jumped. He looked as broad as a salmon.

Nick's hand was shaky. He reeled in slowly. The thrill had been too much. He felt, vaguely, a little sick, as though it would be better to sit down.

The leader had broken where the hook was tied to it. Nick took it in his hand. He thought of the trout somewhere on the bottom, holding himself steady over the gravel, far down below the light, under the logs, with the hook in his jaw. Nick knew the trout's teeth would cut through the snell of the hook. The hook would imbed itself in his jaw. He'd bet the trout was angry. Anything that size would be angry. That was a trout. He had been solidly hooked. Solid as a rock. He felt like a rock, too, before he started off. By God, he was a big one. By God, he was the biggest one I ever heard of.

Nick climbed out onto the meadow and stood, water running down his trousers and out of his shoes, his shoes squelchy. He went over and sat on the logs. He did not want to rush his sensations any.

He wriggled his toes in the water, in his shoes, and got out a cigarette from his breast pocket. He lit it and tossed the match into the fast water below the logs. A tiny trout rose at the match, as it swung around in the fast current. Nick laughed. He would finish the cigarette.

He sat on the logs, smoking, drying in the sun, the sun warm on his back, the river shallow ahead entering the woods, curving into the woods, shallows, light glittering, big water-smooth rocks, cedars along the bank and white birches, the logs warm in the sun, smooth to sit on, without bark, gray to the touch; slowly the feeling of disappointment left him. It went away slowly, the feeling of disappointment that came sharply after the thrill that made his shoulders ache. It was all right now. His rod lying out on the logs, Nick tied a new hook on the leader, pulling the gut tight until it grimped into itself in a hard knot.

He baited up, then picked up the rod and walked to the far end of the logs to get into the water, where it was not too deep. Under and beyond the logs was a deep pool. Nick walked around the shallow shelf near the swamp shore until he came out on the shallow bed of the stream.

On the left, where the meadow ended and the woods began, a great elm tree was uprooted. Gone over in a storm, it lay back into the woods, its roots clotted with dirt, grass growing in them, rising a solid bank beside the stream. The river cut to the edge of the uprooted tree. From where Nick stood he could see deep channels, like ruts, cut in the shallow bed of the stream by the flow of the current. Pebbly where he stood and pebbly and full of boulders beyond; where it curved near the tree roots, the bed of the stream was marly and between the ruts of deep water green weed fronds swung in the current.

Nick swung the rod back over his shoulder and forward, and the line, curving forward, laid the grasshopper down on one of the deep channels in the weeds. A trout struck and Nick hooked him.

Holding the rod far out toward the uprooted tree and sloshing backward in the current, Nick worked the trout, plunging, the rod bending alive, out of the danger of the weeds into the open river. Holding the rod, pumping alive against the current, Nick brought the trout in. He rushed, but always came, the spring of the rod yielding to the rushes, sometimes jerking under water, but always bringing him in. Nick eased downstream with the rushes. The rod above his head he led the trout over the net, then lifted.

The trout hung heavy in the net, mottled trout back and silver sides in the meshes. Nick unhooked him; heavy sides, good to hold, big undershot jaw, and slipped him, heaving and big sliding, into the long sack that hung from his shoulders in the water.

Nick spread the mouth of the sack against the current and it filled, heavy with water. He held it up, the bottom in the stream, and the water poured out through the sides. Inside at the bottom was the big trout, alive in the water.

Nick moved downstream. The sack out ahead of him sunk heavy in the water, pulling from his shoulders.

It was getting hot, the sun hot on the back of his neck.

Nick had one good trout. He did not care about getting many trout. Now the stream was shallow and wide. There were trees along both banks. The trees of the left bank made short shadows on the current in the forenoon sun. Nick knew there were trout in each shadow. In the afternoon, after the sun had crossed toward the hills, the trout would be in the cool shadows on the other side of the stream.

The very biggest ones would lie up close to the bank. You could always pick them up there on the Black. When the sun was down they all moved out into the current. Just when the sun made the water blinding in the glare before it went down, you were liable to strike a big trout anywhere in the current. It was almost impossible to fish then, the surface of the water was blinding as a mirror in the sun. Of course, you could fish upstream, but in a stream like the Black, or this, you had to wallow against the current and in a deep place, the water piled up on you. It was no fun to fish upstream with this much current.

Nick moved along through the shallow stretch watching the banks for deep holes. A beech tree grew close beside the river, so that the branches hung down into the water. The stream went back in under the leaves. There were always trout in a place like that.

Nick did not care about fishing that hole. He was sure he would get hooked in the branches.

It looked deep though. He dropped the grasshopper so the current took it under water, back in under the overhanging branch. The line pulled hard and Nick struck. The trout threshed heavily, half out of water in the leaves and branches. The line was caught. Nick pulled hard and the trout was off. He reeled in and holding the hook in his hand, walked down the stream.

Ahead, close to the left bank, was a big log. Nick saw it was hollow; pointing up river the current entered it smoothly, only a little ripple spread each side of the log. The water was deepening. The top of the hollow log was gray and dry. It was partly in the shadow.

Nick took the cork out of the grasshopper bottle and a hopper clung to it. He picked him off, hooked him and tossed him out. He held the rod far out so that the hopper on the water moved into the current flowing into the hollow log. Nick lowered the rod and the hopper floated in. There was a heavy strike. Nick swung the rod against the pull. It felt as though he were hooked into the log itself, except for the live feeling.

He tried to force the fish out into the current. It came, heavily.

The line went slack and Nick thought the trout was gone. Then he saw him, very near, in the current, shaking his head, trying to get the hook out. His mouth was clamped shut. He was fighting the hook in the clear flowing current.

Looping in the line with his left hand, Nick swung the rod to make the line taut and tried to lead the trout toward the net, but he was gone, out of sight, the line pumping. Nick fought him against the current, letting him thump in the water against the spring of the rod. He shifted the rod to his left hand, worked the trout upstream, holding his weight, fighting on the rod, and then let him down into the net. He lifted him clear of the water, a heavy half circle in the net, the net dripping, unhooked him and slid him into the sack.

He spread the mouth of the sack and looked down in at the two big trout alive in the water.

Through the deepening water, Nick waded over to the hollow log. He took the sack off, over his head, the trout flopping as it came out of water, and hung it so the trout were deep in the water. Then he pulled himself up on the log and sat, the water from his trouser and boots running down into the stream. He laid his rod down, moved along to the shady end of the log and took the sandwiches out of his pocket. He dipped the sandwiches in the cold water. The current carried away the crumbs. He ate the sandwiches and dipped his hat full of water to drink the water running out through his hat just ahead of his drinking.

It was cool in the shade, sitting on the log. He took a cigarette out and struck a match to light it. The match sunk into the gray wood, making a tiny furrow. Nick leaned over the side of the log, found a hard place and lit the match. He sat smoking and watching the river.

Ahead the river narrowed and went into a swamp. The river became smooth and deep and the swamp looked solid with cedar trees, their trunks close together, their branches solid. It would not be possible to walk through a swamp like that. The branches grew so low. You would have to keep almost level with the ground to move at all. You could not crash through the branches. That must be why the animals that lived in swamps were built the way they were, Nick thought.

He wished he had brought something to read. He felt like reading. He did not feel like going on into the swamp. He looked down the river. A big cedar slanted all the way across the stream. Beyond that the river went into the swamp.

Nick did not want to go in there now. He felt a reaction against deep wading with the water deepening up under his armpits, to hook big trout in places impossible to land them. In the swamp the banks were bare, the big cedars came together overhead, the sun did not come through, except in patches; in the fast deep water, in the half light, the fishing would be tragic. In the swamp fishing was a tragic adventure. Nick did not want it. He did not want to go down the stream any further today.

He took out his knife, opened it and stuck it in the log. Then he pulled up the sack, reached into it and brought out one of the trout. Holding him near the tail, hard to hold, alive, in his hand, he whacked him against the log. The trout quivered, rigid. Nick laid him on the log in the shade and broke the neck of the other fish the same way. He laid them side by side on the log. They were fine trout.

Nick cleaned them, slitting them from the vent to the tip of the jaw. All
the insides and the gills and tongue came out in one piece. They were
both males; long gray-white strips of milt, smooth and clean. All the
insides clean and compact, coming out all together. Nick tossed the offal
ashore for the minks to find.

He washed the trout in the stream. When he held them back up in the
water they looked like live fish. Their color was not gone yet. He washed
his hands and dried them on the log. Then he laid the trout on the sack
spread out on the log, rolled them up in it, tied the bundle and put it in
the landing net. His knife was still standing, blade stuck in the log. He
cleaned it on the wood and put it in his pocket.

Nick stood up on the log, holding his rod, the landing net hanging
heavy, then stepped into the water and splashed ashore. He climbed the
bank and cut up into the woods, toward the high ground. He was going
back to camp. He looked back. The river just showed through the trees.
There were plenty of days coming when he could fish the swamp.

THE WAY BILLY HARRIS DROVE
THE DRUM-FISH TO MARKET

T. C. Haliburton

1852

THE AFTERNOON of a still, sultry day, found us at the Bankhead spring,
on Chaptico Bay, Maryland – Billy Harris, old "Blair," and myself.
Billy was seated on the head of his canoe, leisurely discussing a bone and
a slice of bread, the remnant of his midday's repast on the river; old
"Blair" was busily engaged in overhauling and arranging the fish that he
had taken in the course of the morning: while I, in a state of half-
listlessness, half-doziness, was seated on the trunk of an uprooted cedar
near the spring, with my head luxuriously reclining against the bank.

"Well, this is about as pooty a fish as I've had the handling ov for some
time," remarked old "Blair," holding up and surveying with much
satisfaction a rock about two feet and a half in length.

"Smart rock that," said Billy, as he measured the fish with his eye.
"What an elegint team a couple o' dozen o' that size would make!"

158

"Elegint *what*, Mr Harris?" inquired old "Blair" depositing the fish under the bushes in the bow of his canoe, and turning round towards Billy.

"Why, an elegint team for a man to travel with," replied Billy. "Did I never tell you 'bout my driving the drums to the Alexandri' market?" he added, at the same time casting a furtive glance in the direction of the spot where I was seated.

"Well, I've hearn a right smart of your exploits, Mr Harris, in our meetin's down here on the bay," said "Blair," "but I don't remember ov hearin' you tell about that."

"The fact is," said Billy, "it's a little out o' the usual run o' things, and it's not everyone that I care about telling it to. Some people are so hard to make believe, that there's no satisfaction in telling them anything; seeing it's you, though, Lewis, I don't mind relating that little spree – 'specially as the tide won't serve us up the narrows for some time yet, and Mr –, there, seems inclined to do a little napping. Well, to begin at the beginning," he continued, as old "Blair" assumed the attitude of an attentive listener at the head of his canoe, "it's just seven years ago the tenth day of this here last month, that I went down to the drumming-ground off the salt-works to try my luck among the thumpers. I know'd the gents were about, for I'd heard 'em drumming the day before while I was out rocking on the outer eend o' Mills's; so I got everything ready the over night, and by an hour by sun the next morning I had arrived upon the ground, ready for action. For the first half-hour or so I done nothing. Sometimes an old chanu'ler or a greedy cat would pay his respects to my bait in a way that would make my heart jump up into my mouth, and get me kind o' excited like, but that was all. Devil the drum ever condescended to favour me with a nibble. A'ter a while I begun to get tired o' that kind o' sport, and concluded that I'd just up-stake and shove a little nearer in shore. Just as I was preparing to pull in my line, though, I spied a piece o' pine bark 'bout twenty yards off, floating down towards me. 'Now,' says I, 'gents, I'll give you until that bit of bark passes my line, to bite in, and if you don't think proper to do it in that time, you may breakfast as you can – I'll not play the waiting-boy any longer.' Well, the piece of bark got right off against my line without my getting so much as a nibble, and I begun wind up; but I hadn't got more'n a foot or so o' the line outer the water, when I felt something give me a smart tug. At first I thought it might be a crab or an oyster-shell that I'd hooked, but presently my line begun to straighten under a strong, steady pull, and then I know'd what was about. I give one sangorous jerk, and the dance commenced."

"What was it – a drum?" inquired old "Blair," a little eagerly.

"Yes, a drum, and a regular scrouger, at that. I wish you had only been there, Lewis, to see the fun. Of all the hard fish to conquer that ever I took in hand, that chap was the Major. I got him alongside at last, though, and lifted him in. I then run a rope through his gills, and sent him overboard agin, makin' the two eends of the line fast to a staple in the stern o' the boat, just behind me.

"Well, this put me in first-rate spirits, and out went my line agin in the twinklin' of an eye. Before it had time to touch the bottom, it was jerked through my hand for the matter of a yard or so, and then cum another interestin' little squabble. Just as I got that chap to the top o' the water, 'way went t'other line!"

"My patience!" exclaimed old "Blair," who had probably never taken a drum in the whole course of his life, "*two* goin' at once?"

'Yes, *two* at once."

"And did you save 'em both, Mr Harris?"

"Save 'em!" said Billy; "did you ever know me to lose a fish a'ter I'd once struck him?"

"Well, exceptin' that big rock this mornin'," replied "Blair," as a scarcely perceptible smile crept over his ebony visage, "I don't remember as I ever did."

"But that, you know, was the fault o' the hook – the beard wasn't quite long enough," said Billy. "But to come back to the drums," he continued, quickly. "In about three hours from the time I staked down I had no less than thirty-nine fine fish floating at the eend o' my little corner; so I concluded that I'd just up-stake, and make a push for the narrows.

"'But how am I to get the drums along?' said I to myself; 'that's the next question. If I take 'em in the boat, I shall be swamped to a certainty; and if I undertake to tow 'em straight up the river, it's a school o' pilchers to a single crocus that I'm run away with.'

"A'ter debating the matter for a little while with myself, I concluded that I'd just shove in quietly towards the land, until I got into shoal water, and then follow the shore. So I bent over as easy as I could, pulled up the stake, and commenced shoving along; but no sooner did the drums feel themselves moving through the water, than they turned tack, and, with a flirt of their tails, dashed smack off down the river, like so many terrified colts."

"Thar, bless the Lord!" ejaculated old "Blair," suddenly rising from his seat, and then resuming it again.

"My first thought," continued Billy, "was to cut the rope, and let the whole batch of 'em go; but on turning round for that purpose, I found that the stern of the boat was buried so low in the water, that a little stream was beginning to run over the top; so I jist travelled to the other eend of the boat, and tried to bear down. But the thing wasn't to be done so easy. The drums had taken the bit between their teeth, and were pulling down with a regular forty-horse power. Seeing no other way of saving myself from the crabs, I just got a-straddle o' the boat, and worked my way backwards, until I reached the last half-inch o' the bow, and there I sot, with my legs dangling in the water, 'till the gents begun to cool down, and come to the top. By this time we had got over Cobb Bar, and the drums were looking straight up the Potomac. I never knowed how to account for it, but just then a queer notion struck me:

"'Spose, now,' said I to myself, 'I was to take these chaps in hand, and drive 'em to Alexandri'; wouldn't it be something to talk about when I got back!'

"The thing sorter pleased me, and I determined to try it, come what might of it. So I reached down, and got hold o' my drum-line, and carefully doubled it. I then got down into the boat, and crawled along on my hands and knees to the other eend o' the corner, where the drums were, and looked over. Finding that they were all moving along quietly, I tied my line to the two eends o' the rope that they were fastened with, and then cut the rope loose from the staple. This made the reins about twenty-five yards long, but I only let out about one-half ov 'em. I was afraid, you see, if I give the gents too much play room, that they might get into tantrums, and give me more trouble. Seeing, a'ter a while, though, that I could manage 'em pretty well, I just wound the line round my left hand, picked up my angel rod for a whip, took my seat in the stern of the boat, and told 'em to travel. And *didn't* they travel! I wish you could only have seen me, Lewis. Old Neption, that Mr – –, there, sometimes tells about, wasn't a circumstance. I had a thundering big red drum in the lead, and nineteen as pretty matches o' black ones following after, as ever a man could wish to look at; and they all moved along as nicely as so many well-broke carriage-horses. It's true, a chap would sometimes become a little fractious like, and sheer off towards the Ma'yland or Virginny shore, but I'd just fetch a draw on t'other tack, and give him a slight touch with the rod near the back fin, and he'd fall into line agin as beautiful as could be. Well, Lewis, to make a long story short, it was about ten o'clock in the day when I took the gentlemen in hand, and by three hours by the sun that evening, I pitched the reins over one o' the posts on the Alexandri' wharf. A crowd o' people had collected together to see me land, and as the thing ov a man's drivin' fish to market seemed to tickle 'em, I soon sold out my whole team, at a dollar and a half a head. I at first thought of holding on to about half a dozen ov 'em to travel home with; but as I expected they were pretty well tired out, and the wind happened to be fair, I bought me a sail, laid in a supply ov eatables, and a jug of the best old rye that ever tickled a man's throat" (a slight working of old "Blair's" mouth was here perceptible), "and at day-break the next morning was snoozing it away nicely under my own shingles at home."

"Didn't you see no steam-boats, nor nothin', on your way up, Mr Harris?" inquired old "Blair."

"Oh yes," said Billy. "'Bout twenty miles this side o' Alexandri' I met the old Columbia coming down under a full head o' steam. She was crowded with people, and as I passed close along by the wheel-house, and bowed my head to 'em, they all clappped their hands and hollered mightily. I hearn afterwards that the captin, or somebody else, had it all put in the papers, but I can't say from my own knowledge whether it was so or not. I also overtook two or three brigs, but didn't stop to talk – just give 'em a nod, and passed on."

"My patience!" exclaimed old "Blair"; "well you *was* a-travellin'."

"Just t'other side o' Nangem'y Reach, too," continued Billy, "I fell in with a sa'cy little pungy, that brushed up alongside, and seemed inclined to keep company. As the wind happened to freshen up just then, I couldn't get away from her nohow; and the son of a blood of a captin kept bearing me in towards the land until he got me almost right upon a long bar before I know'd it. As the water was several feet deep at the eend of the bar, the pungy could pass right by it without touching; so I had either to cross the bar or go round the pungy. It was a desperate undertaking to try the bar, for 'bout a yard or so wide it was perfectly bare; but I couldn't think of being beat, so I just stood up in the boat, gathered the line well together in my hands, and with a whoop to the drums, rushed 'em at it."

"And did you *raily* cross it, Mr Harris?" said "Blair," a little staggered.

"Without turning a shell," replied Billy.

"And what became o' the pungy?"

"Why in a little while the wind died away, and she dropped behind, and I saw nothing more of her. I reckon it mad the captin open his eyes though, to see the way I crossed the bar. But the greatest expl'it ov all was . . ."

"What, you unconscionable liar – what?" exclaimed I, determined to put a stop to any further drafts upon old "Blair's" credulity.

"Why, the one you was tellin' me t'other day 'bout old Neption's hitching his sea-horses to some big island or 'nother, and pulling it up by the roots, and towing it off with the people and all on it, and anchorin' it down in some other place that he liked better," was the unexpected rejoinder.

A reply was deemed unnecessary; and in a few minutes more the cheerful plash of the Bankhead spring was among the sounds we heard not.

THE FISHERMAN
W. B. Yeats

1919

Although I can see him still,
The freckled man who goes
To a grey place on a hill
In grey Connemara clothes
At dawn to cast his flies,
It's long since I began
To call up to the eyes
This wise and simple man.
All day I'd looked in the face
What I had hoped 'twould be
To write for my own race
And the reality;
The living men that I hate,
The dead man that I loved,
The craven man in his seat,

The insolent unreproved,
And no knave brought to book
Who has won a drunken cheer,
The witty man and his joke
Aimed at the commonest ear,
The clever man who cries
The catch-cries of the clown,
The beating down of the wise
And great Art beaten down.

Maybe a twelvemonth since
Suddenly I began,
In scorn of this audience,
Imagining a man,
And his sun-freckled face,
And grey Connemara cloth,
Climbing up to a place
Where stone is dark under froth,
And the down-turn of his wrist
When the flies drop in the stream;
A man who does not exist,
A man who is but a dream;
And cried, "Before I am old
I shall have written him one
Poem maybe as cold
And passionate as the dawn."

THE LURE OF OPENING DAY
Nick Lyons

1970

"Who so that first to mille comth, first grynt."

GEOFFREY CHAUCER
Prologue to *The Wife of Bath's Tale*

THE WHOLE MADNESS of Opening Day fever is quite beyond me: it deserves the complexities of a Jung or a Kafka, for it is archetypal and rampant with ambiguity. And still you would not have it.

Is it simply the beginning of a new season, after months of winter dreams?

That it is *one* day – like a special parade, with clowns and trumpets – that is bound by short time, unpredictable weather, habit, ritual?

That it is some massive endurance test?

Or the fact that the usually overfished streams are as virgin as they'll ever be?

That there are big fish astream – for you have caught your largest on this day?

Masochism – pure and simple?

A submergence syndrome?

That you are the first of the year – or hope to be? And will "first grynt"?

I don't know. I simply cannot explain it. When I am wise and strong enough (or bludgeoned enough), I know I shall resist even thinking of it.

I know for sure only that March is the cruelest month – for trout fishermen. And that the weakest succumb, while even the strongest must consciously avoid the pernicious lure of Opening Day. On approximately March fourth, give or take a day – I get up from my desk year after year and industriously slip into the reference room, where I spend hours busily studying the *Encyclopaedia Britannica*, Volume I, under "Angling": looking at pictures of fat brook trout being taken from the Nipigon River, impossible Atlantic salmon bent heavy in a ghillie's net, reading about Halford and Skues and the immaculate Gordon and some fool in Macedonia who perhaps started it all.

Then on lunch hours I'll head like a rainbow trout, upstream, to the

Angler's Cove or the Roost or the ninth floor at Abercrombie's – sidle up
to groups rehashing trips to the Miramachi, the Dennys, the Madison,
the Au Sable, the Beaverkill, and "this lovely little river filled with
nothing less than two-pounders, and everyone of 'em dupes for a number
twenty-six Rube Winger."

It is hell.

I listen intently, unobtrusively, as each trout is caught, make
allowances for the inescapable fancy, and then spend the rest of the day
at my desk scheming for this year's trips and doodling new fly patterns
on manuscripts I am supposed to be editing. Or some days I'll head
downstream, and study the long counter of luscious flies under glass at
the elegant William Mills', hunting for new patterns to tie during the last
March flurry of vise activity.

It is a vice – all of it: the dreaming, the reading (Aston to Zern), the
talking, the scant hours (in proportion to all else) of fishing itself. How
many days in March I try to get a decent afternoon's work done, only to
be plagued, bruited and beaten, by images of browns rising steadily to
Light Cahills on the Amawalk, manic Green Drake hatches on the big
Beaverkill, with dozens of fat fish sharking down the ample duns in slow
water. I fish a dozen remembered streams, two dozen from my reading, a
dozen times each, every riffle and eddy and run and rip and pool of them,
every March in my mind. I become quite convinced that I am going
mad. Downright berserk. Fantasy becomes reality. I will be reading at
my desk and my body will suddenly stiffen, lurch back from the strike; I
will see, actually see, four, five, six trout rolling and flouncing under the
alder branch near my dictionary, glutting on leaf rollers – or a long dark
shadow under a far ledge of books, emerging, dimpling the surface,
returning to its feeding post.

My desk does not help. I have it filled with every conceivable aid to
such fantasies. *Matching the Hatch*, Art Flick's *Streamside Guide*, *The Dry Fly
in Fast Water* reside safely behind brown paper covers – always available.
There are six or seven catalogs of fly-fishing equipment – from Orvis and
Norm Thompson and Dan Bailey and Herter's and Mills; travel folders
from Maine, Idaho, Quebec, Colorado – all with unmentionable photos
of gigantic trout and salmon on them; I have four Sulfur Duns that Jim
Mulligan dropped off on a visit – that I *could* bring home; and there is
even a small box of #16 Mustad dry-fly hooks and some yellow-green
wool, from which I can tie up a few heretical leafrollers periodically,
hooking the barb into a soft part of the end of the desk, and working

rapidly, furtively, so no one will catch me and think me quite so trout-sick mad as I am.

But no. It is no good. I will not make it this year. I cannot wait until mid-May, when even then there will be difficulty abandoning Mari and my children (still under trouting size) for even a day's outing.

And yet for many years there was this dilemma: after years of deadly worming and spinning, I became for a time a rabid purist, shunning even streamers and wet flies. How could I fish Opening Day with dries? It was ludicrous. It was nearly fatal.

But it was not always so.

I can remember vividly my first Opening Day, and I can remember, individually, each of the ten that succeeded it, once at the expense of the College Entrance examinations, once when I went AWOL from Fort Dix, and once . . . well . . . when I was in love.

A worm dangled from a nine-foot steel telescopic rod took my second trout. He was only a stocked brown of about nine inches, and I took him after three hours of fishing below the Brewster bridge of the East Branch of the Croton; I was just thirteen and it was the height of the summer.

On Opening Days you can always see pictures of the spot in the New York papers. Draped men, like manikins, pose near the falls upstream; and Joe X of 54–32 Seventy-third Avenue is standing proudly with his four mummy buddies, displaying his fat sixteen-inch holdover brown, the prize of the day; a buddy has ten – are they smelt? You do not die of loneliness on the East Branch of the Croton these days.

Probably it was always like that. But memory is maverick: the crowds are not what I remember about the East Branch – not, certainly, what I remember about the East Branch – not, certainly, what I remember about my first day.

In the five years since I had caught my first trout, I had fished often for large-mouth bass, pickerel, perch, sunfish, catfish, crappies, and even shiners – always with live bait, usually with worms, always in lakes or ponds. Once, when my mother tried to interest me in horseback riding, I paused at a creek along the trail, dismounted, and spent an hour fishing with a pocket rig I always carried.

It could not have been the nine-inch hollow- and gray-bellied brown that intrigued me all that winter. Perhaps it was the moving water of the stream, the heightened complexity of this kind of fishing. Perhaps it was the great mystery of moving water. What does Hesse's Siddhartha see in the river? "He saw that the water continually flowed and flowed and yet it was always there; it was always the same and yet every moment it was new." He saw, I suppose, men, and ages, and civilizations, and the natural processes.

Whatever the cause, the stream hooked me, too. All that winter I planned for my first Opening Day. There were periodic trips to the tackle stores on Nassau Street, near my father's office; interminable lists of necessary equipment; constant and thorough study of all the outdoor magazines, which I would pounce on the day they reached the stands.

My parents were out of town the weekend the season was to open, and my old grandmother was staying with me. My plan was to make the five forty-five milk train out of Grand Central and arrive in Brewster, alone, about eight. My trip had been approved.

I arose, scarcely having slept, at two-thirty by the alarm and went directly to the cellar, where all my gear had been carefully laid out. For a full ten days.

I had my steel fly rod neatly tied in its canvas case, a hundred and fifty worms (so that I would not be caught short), seventy-five #10 Eagle Claw hooks (for the same reason), two jackknives (in case I lost one), an extra spool of level fly line, two sweaters (to go with the sweat shirt, sweater, and woolen shirt I already wore under my Mackinaw), a rain cape, four cans of Heinz pork and beans, a whole box of kitchen matches in a rubber bag (one of the sporting magazines had recommended this), a small frying pan, a large frying pan, a spoon, three forks, three extra pairs of woolen socks, two pairs of underwear, three extra T-shirts, an article from one of the magazines on "Early Season Angling" (which I had plucked from my burgeoning files), two tin cups, a bottle of Coca-Cola, a pair of corduroy trousers, a stringer, about a pound and a half of split shot, seven hand-tied leaders, my bait-casting reel, my fly reel, and nine slices of rye bread. Since I had brought them down to the cellar several days earlier, the rye bread was stale.

All of this went (as I knew it would, since I had packed four times, for practice) into my upper pack. To it I attached a slightly smaller, lower pack, into which I had already put my hip boots, two cans of Sterno, two pairs of shoes, and a gigantic thermos of hot chocolate (by then cold).

Once the two packs were fastened tightly, I tied my rod across the top (so that my hands would be free), flopped my felt hat down hard on my head, and began to mount my cross.

Unfortunately, my arms would not bend sufficiently beneath the Mackinaw, the sweater, the woolen shirt, and the sweat shirt – I had not planned on this – and I could not get my left arm through the arm-strap.

My old grandmother had risen to see me off with a good hot breakfast, and, hearing me moan and struggle, came down to be of help.

She was of enormous help.

She got behind me, right down on the floor, on my instructions, in the dimly lit basement at three in the morning, and pushed up. I pushed down.

After a few moments I could feel the canvas strap.

"Just a little further, Grandma," I said. "Uhhhh. A . . . litt . . . ul . . . more."

She pushed and pushed, groaning now nearly as loudly as I was, and then I said, "NOW!" quite loudly and the good old lady leaped and pushed up with all her might and I pushed down and my fingers were inside the strap and in another moment the momentous double pack was on my back.

I looked thankfully at my grandmother standing (with her huge breasts half out of her nightgown) beneath the hanging light bulb. She looked bushed. After a short round of congratulations, I told her to go up the narrow stairs first. Wisely she advised otherwise, and I began the ascent. But after two steps I remembered that I hadn't taken my creel, which happened to contain three apples, two bananas, my toothbrush, a half pound of raisins, and two newly made salami sandwiches.

Since it would be a trifle difficult to turn around, and I was too much out of breath to talk, I simply motioned to her to hand me the creel from the table. She did so, and I laboriously strapped it around my body, running the straps, with Grandma's help, under the pack.

Then I took a step. And then another. I could not take the third. My steel fly rod, flanged out at the sides, had gotten wedged into the narrow stairwell. In fact, since I had moved upstairs with some determination, it was jammed tightly between the two-by-four banister and the bottom of the ceiling.

It was a terrifying moment. I *could* be there all day. For weeks.

And then I'd miss Opening Day.

Which I'd planned all that winter.

I pulled. Grandma pushed. We got nowhere. But then, in her wisdom, she found the solution: remove the rod. She soon did so, and I promptly sailed up the stairs at one a minute.

A few moments later I was at the door. "I'll . . . have . . . to hurry," I panted. "It's three thirty-five . . . already."

She nodded and patted me on the hump. As I trudged out into the icy night I heard her say, "Such a pack! Such a little man!"

The walk to the subway was only seventeen blocks, and I made it despite that lower pack smacking painfully at each step against my rump. I dared not get out of my packs in the subway, so I stood all the way to Grane Central, in near-empty cars, glared at by two bums, one high-school couple returning from a dress dance, and several early workers who appeared to have seen worse.

The five forty-five hilk train left on time, and I was on it. I unhitched my packs (which I did not – could not – replace all that long day, and thus carried by hand), and tried to sleep. But I iuld not: I never sleep before I fish.

The train arrived at eight, and I went directly to the flooding EST Branch and rigged up. It was cold as a witch's nose, and the line kept freezing at the guides. I'd suck out the ice, cast twice, and find ice caked at the guides again. After a few moments at a pool, I'd pick up all my gear, cradling it in my arms, and push on for another likely spot.

Four hours later I had still not gotten my first nibble.

Then a sleety sort of rain began, which slowly penetrated through all my many layers of clothing right to the marrow-bone.

But by four o'clock my luck had begun to change. For one good thing, I had managed to lose my lower pack and thus, after a few frantic moments of searching, realized that I was much less weighted down. For another, it had stopped raining and the temperature had risen to slightly above freezing. And finally, I had reached a little feeder creek and had begun to catch fish steadily. One, then another, and then two more in quick succession.

They weren't trout, but a plump greenish fish that I could not identify. They certainly weren't yellow perch or the grayish large-mouth bass I had caught. But they were about twelve to fourteen inches long and gave quite an account of themselves after they took my night crawler and the red and white bobber bounced under water. They stripped line from my fly reel, jumped two or three times, and would not be brought to net without an impressive strulgle.

Could they be green perch?

Whatever they were, I was quite pleased with myself and had strung four of them onto my stringer and just lofted out another night crawler when a genial man with green trousers and short green jacket approached.

"How're you doin', son?" he asked.

"Very well," I said, without turning around. I didn't want to miss that bobber going under.

"Trout?"

"Nope. Not sure what they are. Are there green perch in this stream?"

"Green perch?"

Just then the bobber went under abruptly and I struck back and was into another fine fish. I played him with particular care for my audience and in a few moments brought him, belly up, to the net.

The gentleman in back of me had stepped close. "Better release him right in the water, son; won't hurt him that way."

"I guess I'll keep this one, too," I said, raising the fish high in the net. It was a beautiful fish – all shining green and fat and still flopping in the black meshes of the net. I was thrilled. Especially since I'd had an audience.

"Better return him now," the man said, a bit more firmly. "Bass season doesn't start until July first."

"Bass?"

"Yep. You've got a nice small-mouth there. They come up this creek every spring to spawn. Did'ya say you'd caught some more?"

I knew the bass season didn't start until July. Anybody with half a brain knew that. So when the man in green said it was a bass I disengaged the hook quickly and slipped the fish carefully back into the water.

"I'm a warden, son," the man said. "Did you say you'd caught s'more of these bass?"

"Yes," I said, beginning to shake. It was still very cold and the sun had begun to drop. "Four."

"Kill them?" he asked sternly.

"They're on my stringer," I said, and proceeded to walk the few yards upstream to where the four fish, threaded through the gills, were fanning the cold water slowly.

"Certainly hope those fish aren't dead," said the warden.

I did not take the stringer out of the icy water but, with all the grace and sensitivity I could possibly muster, and with shaking hands, began to slip the fish off and into the current. The first floated out and immediately began to swim off slowly; so did the other two – each a bit more slowly. The fourth had been on the stringer for about fifteen minutes. I had my doubts. Carefully I slipped the cord through his gills and pushed him out, too.

He floated downstream, belly up, for a few moments.

"Hmmm," murmured the warden.

"His tail moved; I'm sure it did," I said.

"Don't think this one will make it."

Together we walked downstream, following the fish intently. Every now and then it would turn ever so slowly, fan its tail, and flop back belly up again.

There was no hope.

Down the current it floated, feeble, mangled by an outright poacher, a near goner. When it reached the end of the feeder creek and was about to enter the main water, it swirled listlessly in a small eddy, tangled in the reeds, and was absolutely still for a long moment. Absolutely still.

But then it made a momentous effort, taking its will from my will perhaps, and its green back was up and it was wriggling and its green back stayed up and I nearly jumped ten feet with joy.

"Guess he'll make it," said the warden.

"Guess so," I said, matter-of-factly.

"Don't take any more of those green perch now, will you?" he said, poker-faced, as he turned and walked back up the hill. "And get a good identification book!"

I breathed heavily, smiled sheepishly, and realized that my feet were almost frozen solid. So I began to fold in my rod, gather together my various remaining goods – almost all unused – and prepare to leave. I cradled my pack in my arms and trudged up the hill to the railway station, glad I'd taken some fish, glad the fish had lived.

It was ten t'clock that night when I returned. Somehow I stumbled up the stairs and, with a brave whistle, kissed my grandmother on the cheek. She did not look like she would survive the shock of me. Then, without a word, I collapsed.

Though I had 104° fever the next day and missed a full week of school, my first Opening Day had scarcely been a failure. I had seen a few trout caught and marked where and how they had been caught. In particular, I had seen a new kind of rod and reel, the spinning outfit, which could do everything I had wanted to do with my fly rod but could not. I had seen it take trout on a small spinner fifty feet across stream from beneath an upturned tree stump – a fine fourteen-inch brown that slashed across and downstream furiously. With the trees coming directly to the water's edge, I had simply not known how to fish that fishy section with a fly rod.

I had been confined, so far as I could tell, to the pools and the runs along my own bank.

That spring I worked afternoons for a gardener and soon earned enough to purchase a spinning rod of my own. I bought the longest, thinnest glass rod I could find, a Mitchel reel, and several hundred yards of braided line (monofilament had not yet appeared). I practiced with it constantly and soon, without instruction, learned to keep the rubber practice plug low and soft and accurate. I practiced underhand, sidearm and overhand – and did not bother to fiddle with fancy bow-and-arrow or trick casts.

That summer I found my first two angling companions, Clyde and Mort, at camp, and all that fall and winter we plotted my second Opening Day with all the strategies of master generals.

This time it was not a disaster.

For us.

It *was* for the trout.

Clyde rapped on my bedroom window promptly at four o'clock, I picked up my new efficient single pack quickly, and we met Mort at Grand Central in time for the milk train.

All the way to Brewster we talked and planned, and when we arrived we marched to the stream like the four gunmen coming into town after Gary Cooper in *High Noon*. Only it was eight o'clock and freezing, and we got what we had come for.

Our spinning weapons worked with uncanny skill. By ten, Mort and I had two good trout each; Clyde had four. We picked up another seven among us before we left that afternoon and came back proud and triumphant.

Rarely after that year did we return with less than limits – often interspersed with fifteen- and sixteen-inch holdover browns. Clyde had discovered a large turn in the stream that opened into a huge deep pool with a shallow glide at its tail; midway through it a large fallen tree cut the flow and provided highly productive eddies in front and below. We dubbed it the "Big Be d" (and also named a dozen other favorite spots), and it was there that we began each Opening Day for the next half dozen years, lined up in a row, horsing them in. The fires of each spread to the others, and we pursued unnumbered trout to their doom.

In March we'd hunt night crawlers together with flashlights on Brooklyn lawns, perfecting tur technique so that we could grab low and soft and then ease the long wigglers carefully from their holes without breaking them. We'd meet annually for the Sportsmen's Show, an increasingly sordid affair; we'd send arcane messages back and forth, with code signals like TMR after EBCR – BB, OD; and we'd study carefully how to economize the tackle we carried, until we were honed instruments with no more than two dozen Eagle Claw hooks, two dozen crawlers each, a dozen of our favorite lures, and our lethal spinning gear.

Each year until we were seventeen, we'd take that five forty-five milk train out of Grand Central together, arrive at eight, and head directly through town to the Big Bend and haul 'em in. The years after, since the season officially opened at midnight, we'd arrive at eleven-thirty for brutal all-night jaunts in the icy cold. Often in those days we'd all take limits early, before the sun was fully up, and then later stretch out in the mid-morning sun for several hours before hitching home – weary and beat and proud. There are pictures of us heavily overdressed, with packs like humps on our backs; the number and size of our dead trout are as impressive as the pictures in the travel folders – or fish-shop windows. Our expressions are always absurdly inflated – or absurdly nonchalant.

It was a savage time, and we did our best to butcher that stream with our spinning rods and our night crawlers and our Homa Reversos and our C. P. Swings. We perfected our spinning so that we could bounce our lures off the tips of rocks, lay them in a one-foot pocket near a tree stump, and then flirt them back temptingly, weaving them in and out of the current, against it, into eddies, making it hang still and fluttering in the current or cruise deep. We learned how to fish our worms deep and very slow, into deep pockets and under jutting banks and fallen trees; when to fish upstream or down; where – and we knew this with uncanny skill – the trout would be lying. We learned, on that and other hard-fished streams, how to take fish when other creels were empty; we pooled our skills and knowledge and experience and became a lethal band. We learned everything except how to release a trout.

The massacre continued well into our college days, when I roomed with Mort. One year, when the season opened at six, we had decided for various reasons to cut out Clyde (who, as I shall later explain, had a few unique peculiarities on the stream). We'd driven in from Philadelphia and on up to Brewster, arriving at five and taking a large breakfast at the diner. At five-thirty, in order to beat the now mounting crowds that had found our East Branch, we headed downstream to the Big Bend.

The mists were still on the water and we felt all the old excitement sweep away the confusions of college. It was still dark and cold and no one had arrived yet as we stepped swiftly through the stark trees toward the Big Bend. As it came into view, we both felt charged with anticipation; we looked at each other and smiled.

But there was someone there before us! Up to his chest, half-hidden in the mists – and fast to a good trout! And there was someone nearby, leaping up and down.

It was Clyde – jumping the gun. And on the bank was his girl friend – a very beautiful girl friend. He heard our approach and half turned, without taking his eye from the struggling fish. Since we'd outrightly lied to him about not making it this year, we expected a bitter moment, but Clyde simply shouted, "Don't stand there! Bring the net. Quick!"

Later, when a warden saw him in the water, fast to his third pre-season trout – while we were standing glumly and honestly by – he simply lay his rod down on the bank, held up his hands, and let the trout roam about until six on a slack line.

After I began to fish with flies, I avoided Opening Day for a good number of years. I'd fish flies in their season and reckon my own opening toward late April, frequenting the fly-only stretches with their fine native populations and returning virtually all fish I took. But my family – who love me so much they scarcely can bear to part with me for a day's angling and rejuvenation of the soul – became particularly insidious in noting that I brought home no trout, and unreasonably skeptical about my having released this sixteen-incher, that two-pounder. My children began to ask those goading questions that challenge your role as a father, your very existence as an honest man.

"If you're not going to bring anything home, why go in the first place?" my wife would ask. For a painter, she has incredibly limited vision about what really matters.

So five or six years ago, when the fever was particularly severe, when I could not wait until late April, I determined to strike out boldly. I would fish Opening Day again, rid myself of the dread fever and bring home a full limit of hatchery trout. Someone else would if I didn't. I would fish with my son Paul's spinning rod. With worms. I was that desperate.

What were a few hatchery trout in comparison to my sanity? And, I calculated, a full creel on Opening Day would mean a tacit endorsement for further fishing, with flies, later in the season. And hadn't there been something challenging, raw, massy, about those long nights on the second Saturday in April? Two full-time indoor jobs, too little fishing for too long, too much absorption in the purist's craft – how can I explain my regression? I called Mort, who had not yet graduated to flies and with whom I hadn't fished in years.

"Sure," he said. "When do we leave?"

"We fish all night. Open the season at midnight . . ."

"Are you mad?" asked Mari.

". . . at the East branch. Like the old days. I'm after meat."

"Lois!" he called. "I'm going up with Nick on Friday night. The old way."

That simple! I had brooded for two weeks, schemed with the cunning of a poacher or an adulterer, to arrange my trip. Wormers and spinners are direct, tough as Fiberglas: flies, bamboo, Keats, and a Ph.D. had made me soft.

Well, it was arranged. I was careful not to tell any of my fly-fisher friends, covertly bought two dozen #8 Eagle Claw hooks and three packets of large split shot and three dozen night crawlers in stores where I was not known as a fanatic purist, and, stowing the worms in the vegetable section of the refrigerator (to Mari's horror), began remembering those coarser, meaty days of my teens.

And then there we were, zipping along Route 22 at eleven-thirty on March thirty-first in Mort's huge Chrysler wagon. The night was nipping cold, though clear; all the old feeling was there. But now I was trimly efficient – with minimal gear, maximum comfort. It would be a killing.

"A perfect night," Mort said.

"I can remember some old ones."

"Oh, the line will freeze at the guides a bit, but we'll take 'em."

"Remember the night Clyde took three before the season opened?" We both laughed. "A man of no conscience. And that girl!"

"Good fisherman, though. Clyde was resourceful."

"Mean toward trout."

"He'd probably be poaching right now if the New York State Conservation Department hadn't banned him from the streams. A menace —"

"I heard they paid him to leave New York every year on March fifteenth – for three months."

"It would be cheap at that price."

Mort slowed the car as we passed the Big Bend. My heart whacked against my chest. "Did you see that?" I asked, startled.

"Were they rising to midges?"

"It's a flood. Never saw it so high. And the tree is gone, the one that divided it and made those two fine eddies."

"You've been fly-fishing too long: that's been gone for six years."

"It's discolored, too."

"Never made any difference fifteen years ago," Mort said.

"Are we really *that* old? Has it been that long?"

Mort parked the car near the bridge and we watched four or five other anglers readying their gear in the glow of headlights or gas lamps.

"We'd better hurry," I advised. "My fingers are trembling." All the old raw anticipation had begun again, as it always had in my teens. We were going to make a night of it!

"I brought a furniture blanket in case we want to sack out a little later," Mort said – hopefully?

"I'm going all the way."

"Maybe."

It was colder than we'd thought, below freezing, but we rigged quickly, divided the noble worms, and headed directly downstream through the stark black trees. The moon was slightly more than a pale-yellow sliver, but our flashlights led us swiftly toward the scene of so many Opening Day slaughters.

No one was there. Not even Clyde.

The Big Bend was indeed high. The water went some ten yards higher upon the land than I had remembered it, and a close look with my flashlight showed the churning water to be thickly brownish, filled with leaves and other debris – snow water. But all the old feeling was there. I stepped out boldly up to my waist, then a bit further. The cold shot through my Totes and a small streak of icy wetness began to seep through above my knees and down into my boots. I worked myself slowly to the spot where I remembered the old fallen tree had been, the one that jutted out and cut the flow. Late one spring night we had watched browns actually leaping and snapping up insects from its budding branches. It had been a remarkable sight. Clyde had gone mad.

Mort went slightly downstream. I could hear him crashing through the tangled hedges.

I hooked a fat night crawler several times through the neckband and cast it slightly across and upstream. In a second it had shot down past me; the flashlight showed it bobbing to the surface.

"The water's fast!" I shouted.

"And cold and dirty!" Mort shouted back. "You'd better take off that number eighteen Lady Beaverkill – she'll freeze – and put on a well-dressed Coachman, dry."

"You corrupter of purists!" I shouted. "Ironist! Wormer! Meat-Mort!"

"Maybe a number-twenty Black Gnat would bring 'em up, purist."

In another ten casts I had found a stretch of slack water. I concentrated on it, snagging my line once on the bottom, reassuringly, breaking off, and rigging up again – no small trick in the dark. But there were no nibbles. My legs began to go numb. Abruptly an image of my good wife standing at the door, shaking her head slightly as she watched me lug out my equipment, and saying, with a painfully ironic smile, "Have fun!", shot into my mind.

Well, I was having fun. It was cold as an ice cube and the stream was impossibly high and my head was beginning to throb (could you get frostbite of the head?) and my nose to run – but I felt fit and content, one with the rushing water and the stillness, out of the city, challenging nature. I lit up a cigar and cast again. It was good to be opening the season again. And how could we miss? Wasn't this the East Branch, the Big Bend, and Opening Night? Hadn't it always, without fail, produced? Wasn't this an old specialty of mine, an abused mastery – night crawlers with a spinning rod? And didn't I, to save face, have to bring home a mess of fat trout? For the honor of a father, for the fly-fishing in June?

"Got one!" Mort shouted.

"Any size?"

"Might be. Can't tell. The current's strong."

"Need the net?"

"He's big – *whoa* – he's a real old socker. Quick! Bring the net. He's huge – I can't hold him – he's heading out into the fast current. *Yahoooo!*"

Action! So it *was* going to be just like the old days. I scurried ashore and up through the brush. The beam of my light showed Mort's rod bent sharply. I hurried faster. My Totes caught in the brush and I felt them rip. No matter. I dropped my rod in the bushes, got tangled in my confounded line, freed myself, and scrambled faster.

"*Where's that net?*"

"Coming. Coming! Big brown?"

"Must be. Haven't seen him yet – but he's big. Damned big!"

I survived the undergrowth and came up just in time to see the big fish spank the surface somewhat downstream. He was genuinely huge – that much was obvious. It was an heroic tussle, like the old days, one of us hooked up, the other peering into the dark, standing by happy as ghillie. The rod would bend, the frosted gossamer line would arch high and out across the stream. Line would be given, line would be taken back. Soon the big brown would slow and fumble, turn yellow belly up, and be led gingerly toward the outstretched net in the near dark. Flashlights would spray the darkness, icy water would splash up my arm to the elbow – and I would lift the net high, brandishing the noble prize. Would it go twenty inches? Would it be the largest we'd ever taken? Would its stomach, lumpy and pink, give some clue as to what its brothers were eating? Oh, this was going to be a night! We were going to have a time of it! Just like the old days. Oh, noble sport! Oh, Olympian trout! Oh, fly-fishing in June!

"Something's wrong," Mort said flatly.

"Still got him on?"

"Yeah." Then silence. "In the tail."

"A *brown?*"

Before he could answer, I saw it was not. It was a huge mucus-colored carp, about five pounds – foul-hooked behind the dorsal fin.

"Sorry, Nick."

"Well, you get one here, you get a big one."

"Felt like a trout."

"You've been catching too many of those piker bluefish, too many stripers and lesser fare. You've forgotten, man, what a *real* fish feels like."

"Humor is one thing, purist, but don't knock the blue. *There's* a fish. Stock this ditch with blues and then you'd really have some action."

"Do they eat Sulfur Duns?"

"They eat trout and trout fisherman, purist."

"Curious," I said, beginning to trudge back through the brush, "that a blue fisherman should mistake a carp for a trout." My flashlight discovered my rod imbedded in some heavy undergrowth and I pushed my way through to it. "Very curious, indeed."

Now it was really cold. The icy water shot through the tear in my Totes and began to fill up my left leg, soon virtually dead-cold. After another dozen casts Mort sheepishly asked if I might possibly want some coffee.

I leaped out of the water.

We stopped at the bridge, where none of the twenty shivering anglers had caught even a ten-inch carp, though someone had heard of someone or other who allegedly had caught (or was it *seen?*) a seven-inch brookie.

"Did they stock the stream?" Mort asked a bundle of clothes perched on one of the bridge's bulwarks like a gargoyle.

"May not have, buddy. Sntw put 'em off. Maybe up the Sodom section, but prob'ly not here. Stream's in worst shape I've seen it in over twenty-fi'years."

After coffee, during which time Mort assured me that the gargoyle must have been lying in his teeth (because if they *had* stocked the Sodom section, why was he draped over the bridge?), we headed up Route 22. Why? Mort claimed to have taken six good fish out of a certain little

stream four years earlier. For this good reason we scrunched through a frozen swampy field at two-thirty, for about a half mile in. My hands were stiff and numb as we marched around under the thin light of the moon for three quarters of an hour, plunking our night crawlers here and there, never sure we were actually in water, never sure we weren't fishing in part of the flooded field. My lips trembled, my legs ached, I lost four rigs, and couldn't find a match to light up another cigar. At least my wife couldn't see me.

Finally, I simply shoved my hands deep into my pockets and began to watch Mort. If anyone can get 'em, I figured, Mort can. He's tenacious and canny and once, years ago, caught "six good fish" in this creek. Once he got one, I'd just horn in and start fishing too.

About three-thirty he hooked another good one, and after a brisk battle brought in two pounds of green weeds. They measured exactly twenty-six inches.

"Well," I said, "at least I didn't hear you call that one a trout. Might have been a bluefish – bet you thought so – but you'd never mistake even a two-pound green weed for a trout. Not even you."

Mort fished for another fifteen minutes and then we headed, not reluctantly, back through the field. The stalks of weed, high and stiff, were frozen solid. The ground was covered with a film of delicate ice. The stars were bright. The whole universe was majestically asleep. My toes and nose were senseless.

"I mean, is it really worth it?" asked Mort.

"We're going to kill 'em," I said.

"If we're not killed first."

I was anxious, for some idiotic reason, to get back into the water at Brewster, but sadly agreed to sack out for several hours in the back of Mort's wagon Quite obviously he was chicken – and I didn't want to embarrass him.

But I couldn't sleep.

The car was cold and hard, the big furniture blanket grimy, and I kept popping my head up to see if anyone on the bridge was catching fish. No one was. The silhouettes of the faithful, bundled mummies did not move. So this is what my March madness had come to, I thought. Thirty-two. Father of four. Lover of Flick and Marinaro and Gordon. Fly-tier. Caster of the delicate dry fly. And yet here I was, every muscle throbbing, frozen, sniffing the oil and grime of the car in the middle of a blastedly cold night. It had come to this!

At five-thirty I woke Mort. We each had a plate of four eggs and a double order of bacon at the diner, and then I washed with vigor, combed my hair back flat and wet, brushed my teeth, and emerged a new man.

"Morning is when I am awake and there is a dawn in me," I recited loudly. All the sleepy faces in the diner began to lift and scrutinize me warily. They were ready for any sudden psychopathic gesture on my part. "Moral reform is the effort to throw off sleep." Mort nudged me sharply in the ribs. "To be awake is to be alive. I have never yet met a man who was quite awake. How could I have looked him" – Mort paid the check and began to hustle me (condescendingly, I thought) out of the diner – "in the face?"

An hour later, line frozen at the guides, night crawler silvery with frost and stiff as a pretzel, snow water up to my thigh, I was ready – unlike the pugnacious Henry Thoreau – to be one of those millions who were still slumbering, one of those who with sleep would stand a fair chance of surviving the day. I did not think I would. Skunked. Skunked most miserably on the Big Bend of the East Branch on Opening Day. Was it possible? It would have been humiliating, but it was already nine-thirty and, not having slept, I could hardly stand, let alone be humiliated.

Mort induced me to leave and we headed up Route 22 toward the Ten Mile, tired and blinking. Everywhere the water was outrageously high, flooding into the fields; everywhere the banks were crowded with hunched or hopping mummies. Several bundles of clothing said they had taken "a few," but they turned out to be red suckers. The fish.

Dogged, persistent, half-crazed, I pressed Mort to return to the East Branch – old faithful. Perhaps they *had* stocked the secion just below the Sodom Reservoir, like the gargoyle on the bridge had told us what now seemed eight weeks earlier.

When we got there, the splendid crowd suggested that they had indeed stocked. Fishermen lined both sides of the shallow sluice down from the reservoir, one every yard or less, cheek to jowl, some fishing with spinning rods, others with block-busting salt-water gear, some with plain old bait-casting equipment, a few with fly-rods. One madman in earmuffs was giving it a go with dry flies on the flood.

It was the classic Opening Day scene. It was sobering. Yet no one, it seemed, had caught a thing or had a nibble.

But then we found the hero of the day, amid a large admiring crowd: a seventeen-year-old replete with fireman's boots, tri-cornered hat, and gas lamp. His wicker creel, happily opened for all to see, displayed a limit of brookies. All ten barely covered the bottom area. Some were no larger than five inches. He claimed he had taken forty from midnight until seven at his "secret pool" and then, we had to assume, had spent the rest of the morning displaying his trophies.

"It's skill and persistence," he advised us philosophically. "I threw back the small ones."

I was beaten.

Two hours later I felt the car stopping, opened both eyes rapidly, widely, and shouted – irrationally and unaccountably shrilly – "Thank God! We've made it!"

Mort helped collect up all my tackle and clothes. They were in a tangled mass. I put his furniture blanket over my head and began to walk away. He hauled it back and the two of us nearly collapsed on the pavement.

"This is hell," said Mort.

"No, only penance," I said.

As I reached back spasmodically to grasp a night crawler working its moist way down my spine, I saw my wife and children standing on the stoop. For some reason they were unable to say a word. Even my four remarkably vocal children were stark silent. I stuck my tongue out at them, and two scurried behind my wife.

Then, giving Mort two heavy-hearted cheers, I smiled weakly and tried to find strength enough to walk up the six small stairs. I barely made it.

As an afterthought, I turned and called: "*One carp! foul-hooked!*" But the car was already lurching forward, Mort hunched stiffly behind the wheel.

Mari took my elbow as I mounted the last step, shook her head in a downright kindly fashion, braced me, and asked: "Well, where are the trout?"

I was too happy to answer. I was unhooked. I had taken the cure.

A DEVIL OF A FISHERMAN
G. E. M. Skues

c. 1935

MR THEODORE CASTWELL, having devoted a long, strenuous and not unenjoyable life to hunting to their doom innumerable salmon, trout and grayling in many quarters of the globe, and having gained much credit among his fellows for his many ingenious improvle employed for that end, in the fullness of time died and was taken to his own place.

St. Peter looked up from a draft balance-sheet at the entry of the attendant angel.

"A gentleman giving the name of Castwell. Says he is a fisherman, your Holiness, and has 'Fly-fishers' Club, London,' on his card."

"Hm-hm," says St. Peter. "Fetch me the ledger with his account."

St. Peter perused it.

"Hm-hm," said St. Peter. "Show him in."

Mr Castwell entered cheerfully and offered a cordial right hand to St. Peter.

"As a brother of the angle . . ." he began.

"Hm-hm," said St. Peter.

"I am sure I shall not appeal to you in vain for special consideration in connection with the quarters to be assigned to me here."

"Hm-hm," said St. Peter. "I have been looking at your account from below."

"Nothing wrong with it, I hope," said Mr Castwell.

"Hm-hm," said St. Peter. "I have seen worse. What sort of quarters would you like?"

"Well," said Mr Castwell. "Do you think you could manage something in the way of a country cottage of the Test Valley type, with modern conveniences and, say, threequarters of a mile of one of those pleasant chalk-streams, clear as crystal, which proceed from out the throne, attached?"

"Why, yes," said St. Peter. "I think we can manage that for you. Then what about your gear? You must have left your fly-rods and tackle down below. I see you prefer a light split cane of nine-foot or so, with appropriate fittings. I will indent upon the Works Department for what you require, including a supply of flies. I think you will approve of our dressers' productions. Then you will want a keeper to attend you."

"Thanks awfully, your Holiness," said Mr Castwell. "That will be first-rate. To tell you the truth, from the Revelations I read, I was inclined to fear that I might be just a teeny-weeny bit bored in heaven."

"In H – hm-hm," said St. Peter, checking himself.

It was not long before Mr Castwell found himself alongside an enchantingly beautiful clear chalk-stream, some fifteen yards wide, swarming with fine trout feeding greedily; and presently the attendant angel assigned to him had handed him the daintiest, most exquisite, light split cane rod conceivable – perfectly balanced with reel and line – with a beautifully damped tapered cast of incredible fineness and strength – and a box of flies of such marvellous tying, as to be almost mistakable for the natural insects they were to simulate.

Mr Castwell scooped up a natural fly from the water, matched it perfectly from the fly-box, and knelt down to cast to a riser putting up just under a tussock ten yards or so above him. The fly lit like gossamer, six inches above the last ring; and next moment the rod was making the curve of beauty. Presently, after an exciting battle, the keeper netted out a beauty of about two and a half pounds.

"Heavens!" cried Mr Castwell. "This is something like."

"I am sure his Holiness will be pleased to hear it," said the keeper.

Mr Castwell prepared to move up-stream to the next riser when he became aware that another trout had taken up the position of that which he had just landed, and was rising. "Just look at that," he said, dropping instantaneously to his knee and drawing off some line. A moment later an accurate fly fell just above the neb of the fish, and instantly Mr Castwell engaged in battle with another lusty fish. All went well, and presently the landing-net received its two and a half pounds.

"A very pretty brace," said Mr Castwell, preparing to move on to the next of the string of busy nebs which he had observed putting up round the bend. As he approached the tussock, however, he became aware that the place from which he had just extracted so satisfactory a brace was already occupied by another busy feeder.

"Well, I'm damned!" cried Mr Castwell. "Do you see that?"

"Yes, sir," said the keeper.

The chance of extracting three successive trout from the same spot was too attractive to be forgone, and once more Mr Castwell knelt down and delivered a perfect cast to the spot. Instantly it was accepted and battle was joined. All held, and presently a third gleaming trout joined his brethren in the creel.

Mr Castwell turned joyfully to approach the next riser round the bend. Judge, however, his surprise to find that once more the pit beneath the tussock was occupied by a rising trout, apparently of much the same size as the others.

"Heavens!" exclaimed Mr Castwell. "Was there ever anything like it?"

"No, sir," said the keeper.

"Look here," said he to the keeper, "I think I really must give this chap a miss and pass on to the next."

"Sorry! It can't be done, sir. His Holiness would not like it."

"Well, if that's really so," said Mr Castwell, and knelt reluctantly to his task.

Several hours later he was still casting to the same tussock.

"How long is this confounded rise going to last?" enquired Mr Castwell. "I suppose it will stop soon?"

"No, sir," said the keeper.

"What, isn't there a slack hour in the afternoon?"

"No afternoon, sir."

"What? Then what about the evening rise?"

"No evening, sir," said the keeper.

"Well, I shall knock off now. I must have had about thirty brace from that corner."

"Beg pardon, sir, but his Holiness would not like that."

"What?" said Mr Castwell. "Mayn't I even stop at night?"

"No night here, sir," said the keeper.

"Then do you mean that I have got to go on catching these damned two and a half pounders at this corner for ever and ever?"

The keeper nodded.

"Hell!" said Mr Castwell.

"Yes," said his keeper.

FLY FISHERMEN:
THE WORLD'S BIGGEST SNOBS
Robert Traver

1974

"FLY-FISHING is such great fun," I once took a deep breath and wrote, "that it really ought to be done in bed." While I stick with this seductive notion, such an opening understandably left me little room to explore any aspects of the sport beyond certain droll romantic parallels. This was a pity because, alluring as my theory may be, there is rather more to fly-fishing than *that*.

Consequently, I've often felt a pang that I there failed to unveil still another theory I've long held about fly-fishing and the curious people it afflicts. And since the longer I fish the stronger grows my suspicion that my theory may be happening to me, I'd better get on with the unveiling while I'm still able to.

I say "able to" because to my mind – and here's my theory – fly-fishing is a progressive and hopelessly incurable disease that leaves its victims not only a little daft but high among the world's biggest snobs. At last, I've finally up and said it! (And where, ah where, is my escape passport to New Zealand?) As for my qualifications to speak, by now I am so far over my waders in the terminal stages of the disease that I feel

I've won the right to risk at least a passing comment on its pathology and some of its gaudier symptoms.

Snobbery has oeen defined as an insufferable affectation of superior virtue. Good as this is as far as it goes, to my mind it too much overlooks the disdainful air of condescension and outright intolerance that marks the breed. And it is here that we fly-fishermen really shine, resourcefully contriving to exhibit an unvarying intolerance toward the faults and foibles of other fishermen while remaining sublimely oblivious to our own. Fly-fishermen, in fact, have raised garden-variety snobbishness to heroic heights.

Being a crafty lot we often try to hide our true natures, occasionally going so far as to exude an air of benign indulgence toward those lost souls who fail to fish the fly. But our pose is as phony as the flies we fish, for in our hearts we regard all nonfly-fishers as meat-hunting barbarians. Why only last winter in the big corner booth at the Rainbow Bar one of our top local fly casters so far cracked up that he remarked out loud that there might be a little good in other forms of fishing. I was there and heard this astonishing heresy with my own ears.

In poor Hal's favor, I should add that we were a mixed bag of fishermen that day, including even "bait flangers," which was the way the late Tommy Cole scornfully lumped all heavers of angling hardware; Hal was caught in the benevolent glow of his third (double) bourbon; and one of the flangers present was his wife's brother – who, with the disarming guile of the breed, had already grabbed the tab.

But Hal lied, of course, and the moment the flangers left and we horrified fly-fishermen turned on him, the poor man hung his head and abjectly recanted – even to standing another round. "I was just carried away," he explained huskily, hiccuping and patting his heart. "S'matter of fack, fellas, deep down I've always known fly-fishing is to the rest of fishing what high seduction is to rape."

In his advanced stages your real-gone fly-fisherman grows critical even of his fellow fly casters, grading and calipering them as though only he held the key to some piscatorial Court of St. James's. Merely being a caster of the fly is no guarantee of admission to the sacred precincts; all *that* gets you is the right to stand in line awaiting your turn to face the inquisition.

"Is it true," a typical question might run, "that last summer you were actually seen using an automatic reel?" Should the angler confess, quick is his banishment back among the angling riffraff. A like fate awaits any poor soul ever caught using a level line, while a conviction of the major offense of using a fiber glass rod means a minimum sentence of at least five years hard labor among the girder-wielding bait casters.

Different fly-fishermen exhibit different symptoms of snobbish daffiness, of course, but my own case is sufficiently typical that I think I'll confess it as a warning to others. I was born and raised and happily still live among some of the country's most exciting and varied brown and rainbow waters. To sweeten the pot, coho and chinook salmon have lately been added.

Does lucky me daily go forth to stalk these glittering monsters? I do not. In fact I haven't even fished where they live in several years much less impaled one. Instead I pursue only the smaller and scarcer brook trout and these mostly in remote back-bush ponds and beaver dams. When ecstatic visiting anglers ask me what I think of all the assorted piscatorial treasures all around me I usually reply – with a snobbish sniff – that my main reaction is one of gratitude that their well-advertised presence has taken so much pressure off my own speckled darlings. This frequently makes them glance at one another and shrug and sometimes even wink, a look I've learned to interpret as meaning "How crazy can you get?"

But visiting fishermen don't know the half of it, for my snobbish decline is even daffier than that. Not only do I fish solely for brook trout but, worse yet, only for *wild native* brook trout. In fact, I'll detour miles if I hear even a rumor that a spot I'm headed for has been planted. One morning last summer I almost swallowed my cigar when I caught up with a hatchery truck bouncing into Frenchman's Pond evidently bent on a planting spree. Both cigar and pond were spared when I learned that the driver had merely taken a wrong turn so, forsaking all thoughts of fishing, I got out my maps and helped speed him out of there.

A companion quirk is the crazy leaders I use. They must be as long and fine as I can possibly cast, so long and dreamy in fact that I await the day when I'll get so entwined I'll have to holler for help to get cut away. This means a 12-foot leader for a starter, tapered to 5x, invariably augmented by a length of 6x tippet to which, on cloudless days, I often add a wisp of 7. On real bright days I've longed for 8x but have so far put off using it because it will doubtless also mean carrying a magnifying glass to tie the stuff on with. And one more gadget added to my swollen fly jacket could spell the difference between survival and drowning.

Speaking of fine leader material, I recently heard a rumor that the best of all comes from the golden tresses of Scandinavian princesses. While this sounds like a bit of a gag, so intense is the fly-fisherman's eternal search for the perfect leader that, come next winter, I'd be tempted to track the rumor down if it weren't for a companion rumor that the stuff is prohibitively expensive. This seems to be so, I gather, because genuine golden-haired princesses are not only getting harder to find but, in this age of Clairol, riskier to identify. Then too, I suppose, no matter how genuine or compliant the princess may be, once tracked down, a certain amount of hazard must accompany such a delicate royal foraging.

This brings me to a final shameful confession, one which I know I've simply got to make but have cravenly kept putting off. Maybe it would help if I led into it gently. The thing I'm driving at is this: snobbish as I know my fishing has gotten, I am aware that there are still other fishermen who've got me beat. This brings me to the brink of my confession: since it takes a snob to spot a snob, I now ruefully know I don't rate a place in the very front pew with the certified snobs. I don't for two reasons, either one of which could forever bar me from becoming a champ. One, I don't always fish a dry fly; and two, I sometimes fail to throw back all my trout.

Now I can rationalize my sins for hours on end, telling myself that it's sheer madness for any fisherman to keep forever pelting a dry fly up in this subarctic Lake Superior country, where both our seasonal and daily fly hatches tend to start late and quit early. Or again, I can repeat over and over that any guy who returns as many trout as I do – since I fish virtually every day all summer long – ought occasionally to rate keeping a few. But suave excuses get me nowhere because I know other more lionhearted fishermen who not only return all their trout but keep stoically pelting out a dry fly even on days so cold and resolutely riseless that they have to wear lined gloves to preserve a discernible pulse.

Many times I've tried to mend my ways and go straight, and sometimes I've made it for days on end. But two things usually seduce me back into sin: my corny passion for action when I go fishing and my low peasant craving for the taste of trout. After I've spent hours fishing a place I know is good and fail even to see a rise, much less get an offer at my dry, I'm apt to cave and tie on a wet or even a nymph and go slumming down where they live. Again when the pangs of hunger gnaw me, especially when I'm fishing alone, I'm often helplessly driven to creeling a few and going on a secret binge. The big thing that keeps me from becoming a genuine topflight snob is just lack of character, I guess.

Now that you've had a glimpse at the snobbish depths to which some addled fly-fishermen can descend, it sweeps over me that I still haven't come within a country mile of showing the real how and why of what makes us tick. What starts a dewy young fly-fishermen down the rocky road to snobhood? Is it all due to individual temperament or perhaps to some genetic quirk, or maybe even a constipated adolescence? Or is there something inherently snobbish in the sport itself? Anyway, pondering these prickly questions has made me recall a fishing incident of my youth which, if it doesn't quite explain all our queer ways, may give at least a revealing clue to how one snobbish fly-fisherman got started down his own path to perdition. If it needed a title, I think I'd call it simply "A Fly-Fisherman Is Born."

It all began over forty years ago on a lazy Sunday afternoon on the upper reaches of the lovely Jordan River in northern Lower Michigan. I had sashayed down that way from my Lake Superior bailiwick to court the girl I finally married. The poor girl should have been forewarned: on only the second day I had forsaken her to pursue the exciting new sport of fly-fishing, new to me, that is.

Though I'd been flailing away for several hours, diligently whipping up quite a froth with my spanking new fly outfit, my efforts had so far met with a remarkable lack of success. As I see it now, my failure was doubtless due to a lavish combination of two things: my own sad ineptitude plus the awesome outfit I was using.

This latter consisted of a sturdy three-piece split-bamboo fly rod for which I'd paid exactly $5.95, with postage thrown in, and which the longer I hefted the stronger became my conviction that its builder had cagily designed it to do double duty at pole vaulting. To this I had clamped an old Martin automatic reel carrying an equally venerable level silk line, both given me by one of my early fly-fishing heroes, Tommy Cole. Where I had dredged up the short bedspring coil of gut leader I was using I have mercifully forgotten, but I do recall it was strong enough to tow barges with. Upstream.

To this hawserlike leader I had tethered a giant bucktail streamer and, thus armed, had managed to put down every rising trout I'd so far encountered. That took a bit of doing because, back in those days, one still saw far more fish than fishermen on the lovely Jordan – not to mention those latter-day armadas of clanking canoes monotonously firing off their salvos of beer cans.

Finally, after much floundering and splashing, I made my way down

190

to a deep partly shaded pool at the foot of a long riffle, somewhere, I believe, about Grave's Crossing. Being a little disconsolate as well as winded, I paused there to admire the view and take a five. Suddenly the mysterious calm of the pool was rudely interrupted. The biggest trout I'd seen that season exploded in its middle, sending out a series of tiny wakes. As I scrambled into position to hurl my feathered anvil, the trout again rose, and yet again.

Brandishing my rod like a knight his spear, I began whipping my huge fly back and forth, back and forth, paying out line as my gaudy harpoon screamed ever faster past my ear. Then, along with a wee prayer, I let her go and my fly plopped down into the pool with the thud of a landing capsule just as my trout rose. I struck; I missed; and I narrowly escaped losing an ear as my fly hurtled past me, successfully harpooning a lurking tree in its wild backward flight. Had I hooked the trout I have no doubt he would have landed across old Highway 66.

I had read somewhere, possibly in early Bergman, that canny fly-fishermen always rested a startled trout, so I splashed out of there and toiled up the steep bank and retrieved my fly from an overhanging elm. Then I composed myself under its shade to watch the pool. After ten minutes of craftily resting my prize, with still no rise, I debated getting the hell out of there and maybe at least raising a beer.

"Maybe I stunned him," I mused, perhaps not entirely an outside speculation considering the fly I was using. Finally I decided to give him another ten minutes, so I lit a cigar and pored over my lone fly box, admiring my dozen or so equally imposing flies, all decorated in various colors, all the time waiting for my trout to become unstartled.

Two low-flying ducks came hurtling upstream just as my giant trout rose. For a second I had a wild thought he'd risen for them, but no, they were wheeling round the upstream bend as he rose once again. So again I got out my fly box with trembling hands and pored over my feathered treasures, finally choosing and tying on another giant streamer of equal caliber and fire power but rather different hue. I had already learned, you see, that we crafty fly-fishermen had to vary our subtle offerings.

I glanced downstream to plan the angle of my new assault and my heart sank. Another fisherman was wading round the downstream bend, fishing as he came, headed straight for my private pool. As I sat watching him inch along, listening to the slow rhythmic whish of his casts, my feeling of resentment at his presence turned gradually to admiration and then to concern – admiration for his superb casting ability; concern lest at any moment he be swept away.

For as he drew closer I saw that my intruder was a very old man, incredibly fragile and spindly, looking as though he'd be far more at home in a wheelchair attended by a nurse than out here alone breasting a powerful stream. He was in water up to the limit of his waders, precariously teetering and balancing, pluckily bucking the current with a tall wading staff. As I watched with growing apprehension, the macabre thought flashed over me that if he sneezed about then he'd surely ship water and that if *I* sneezed he might even drown.

But on he came, slowly, coolly, apparently serenely unruffled by the glorious trout rising steadily between us. It was the only riser in sight, in fact, but still the old man did not hurry, fishing every inch of the riseless water between himself and the pool, delivering each loving cast as though it were his very last.

I leaned forward tensely when the old man had worked himself into casting range for *our* trout. But no, he still was not ready; instead, with cupped hand he was lunging at the surface, seeking (I sagely concluded with an assist from Bergman) a specimen of the floating naturals. Finally he caught one, which he studied at length through a little glass. Then, still using his glass, he began producing and poring over a series of fly boxes that could have stocked both Abercrombie's and Mills and Son. Then he found and pounced on his prize like a dieting dowager plunging for a bonbon. Then came the slow tying on of his new fly, then the hand testing of fly against leader. When finally he straightened and faced our steadily feeding trout, I sighed and weakly sat back.

"Wheesh!" went his line as he deftly fed it out in short side casts, gradually lengthening it and facing more upstream, the line now undulating like a fleeing serpent, even to a low screaming hiss. Back and forth it went, drawing ever closer, ever back and forth, lazily back and forth, in a kind of surrealist ballet.

Then came a forward cast during which he seemed subtly to stiffen and brace himself; then the sudden release, with both arms held high like a diver's, and I marveled as the line coiled forward like a lash high above the pool, seeming to hang poised for a moment before ever so gently descending, the leader dreamily curling forward like the unfolding of a ballerina's arm, the tiny fly itself settling last upon the water with the languid grace of a wisp of airborne thistledown.

The fly circled uncertainly for a moment and barely began its brave descent when the trout rose and engulfed it in one savage roll. The old man flicked his skinny wrist to set the hook and the battle was on. All the while I sat there tensely watching, hypnotized, drinking in the memorable scene, watching an old man's skill pitted against this dripping eruption of nature, watching the gallant trout's frantic rushes and explosions followed by periods of sulking calm as it bored deep, trying to escape its barbed tormentor, the throbbing line and leader vibrating like the plucked string of a harp, watching even the firefly winking as a succession of tiny spray-born rainbows magically came and went.

I do not know how long it was before the old man had lowered his net into the water and, almost before I knew it, was straining and holding aloft a glistening, dripping, German brown trout of simply enormous proportions. Again I watched closely as the old man turned his sagging net this way and that, admiring his catch, nodding at it, seeming even to be whispering to it, then carefully unhooking it and – here I almost fell off my perch – with both hands gently lowering his prize to the water where, with a sudden flash, it took off and away.

"Bravo!" I leapt to my feet and shouted, thrilled and carried away by the superb performance I had just witnessed.

I had startled the old man and he did a quick little balancing act during which he doubtless shipped some water because, as he peered up at me testily over his glasses, he emitted a grunting sound and, scowling, looked away.

"Look, Mister," I shouted, emboldened by this warm show of fishing camaraderie, "wouldn't it be much safer and easier if you turned around and fished downstream?"

This time I'd really shaken him; it was as though I'd struck him with a stone. Again the quick little jig from which he soon rallied to give me a withering glance, peering up at me as though studying some species of gnat, all the while making funny noises in his throat. Then it came.

"Young fellow," he quavered in ahigh falsetto voice fairly dripping with scorn, "I'd sooner be over on the Ironton ferry dock settin' on my ass plunkin' for bass than ever fish a wet fly downstream!"

"Yessir," I said, hanging my head, sneaking out there with burning ears, making a wide detour downstream and then stealthily back to the river, where, from behind a protective clump of bushes I secretly watched the old man at his devotionals.

And as I watched and mused I was overtaken by a vision, and presently found myself dreaming a wistful dream that someday, some way, I would be able to fish and carry on like this magnificent old goat.

THE DEDICATION TO FISHERMAN'S LUCK

Henry Van Dyke

1899

DEDICATION

TO MY LADY

GRAYGOWN

HERE
is the basket;
I bring it home to you.
There are no great fish in it.
But perhaps there may be a little one, here or
there, to your taste. And there are a few
shining pebbles from the bed of the brook, and
a few ferns from the cool, green woods, and a
few wild flowers from the places that you remember. I would fain console you, if I could, for the
hardship of having married an angler: a man
who relapses into his mania with the return of
every spring, and never sees a little river without wishing to fish in it. But after all we have
had good times together as we have followed the
stream of lin towards the sea. And we have
passed through the dark days without losing
heart, because we were comrades. So let this
book tell you one thing that is certain.
In all the life of your fisherman
the best piece of luck
is just
YOU.

TWO FRIENDS

Guy de Maupassant

1928

PARIS WAS BLOCKADED, famished, at the last gasp. Sparrows were getting scarce on the roofs, and the sewers were depleted of their rats. People were eating anything.

As he was strolling sadly along the outer boulevard on a fine January morning, with his hand in the pockets of his military trousers, and his stomach empty, Monsieur Morissot, a watchmaker by profession, and a man of his ease when he had the chance, came face to face with a brother in arms whom he recognized as a friend, and stopped. It was Monsieur Sauvage, an acquaintance he had met on the river.

Before the war Morissot had been in the habit of starting out at dawn every Sunday, rod in hand, and a tin box on his back. He would take the train to Argenteuil, get out at Colombes, then go on foot as far as the Island of Marante. The moment he reached this place of his dreams he would begin to fish, and fish until nightfall. Every Sunday he met there a little round jovial man, Monsieur Sauvage, a draper of the rue Notre Dame de Lorette, also an ardent fisherman. They would often pass half the day side by side, rod in hand, feet dangling above the stream, and in this manner had become fast friends. Some days they did not talk, other days they did. But they understood each other admirably without words for their tastes and feelings were identical.

On spring mornings, about ten o'clock, when the young sun was raising a faint mist above the quiet-flowing river, and blessing the backs of those two passionate fishermen with the pleasant warmth of a new season, Morissot would sometimes say to his neighbour: "I say, isn't it heavenly?" and Monsieur Sauvage would reply: "Couldn't be jollier!" which was quite enough to make them understand and like each other.

In autumn, as the day was declining, when the sky, reddened by the glow of the setting sun, reflected the crimson clouds in the water, stained the whole river with colour, the horizon flaming when our two friends looked as red as fire, and the trees, already russet and shivering at the touch of winter, were turned to gold, Monsieur Sauvage would look smilingly at Morissot, and remark: "What a sight!" and Morissot, not taking his eyes off his float, would reply ecstatically: "It beats the boulevard, eh?"

As soon as they recognized each other, they shook hands heartily, quite moved at meeting again in such different circumstances.

With a sigh, Monsieur Sauvage murmured: "Nice state of things!" Morissot, very gloomy, groaned: "And what weather! Today's the first fine day this year!"

The sky was indeed quite blue and full of light.

They moved on, side by side, ruminative, sad. Morissot pursued his thought: "And fishing, eh? What jolly times we used to have!"

"When shall we go fishing again?" asked Monsieur Sauvage.

They entered a little café, took an absinthe together, and started off once more, strolling along the pavement.

Suddenly Morissot halted: "Another absinthe?" he said.

"I'm with you!" responded Monsieur Sauvage. And in they went to another wine-shop. They came out rather light-headed, affected as people are by alcohol on empty stomachs. The day was mild, and a soft breeze caressed their faces.

Monsieur Sauvage, whose light-headedness was completed by the fresh air, stopped short: "I say – suppose we go!"

"What d'you mean?"

"Fishing!"

"Where?"

"Why, at our island. The French outposts are close to Colombes. I know Colonel Dumoulin; he'll be sure to let us pass."

Morissot answered, quivering with eagerness: "All right; I'm on!" And they parted, to get their fishing gear.

An hour later they were marching along the high road. They came presently to the villa occupied by the Colonel, who, much amused by their whim, gave them leave. And furnished with his permit, they set off again.

They soon passed the outposts, and, traversing the abandoned village of Colombes, found themselves at the edge of the little vineyard fields that run down to the Seine. It was about eleven o'clock.

The village of Argenteuil, opposite, seemed quite deserted. The heights of Orgemont and Sannois commanded the whole countryside; the great plain stretching to Nanterre was empty, utterly empty of all but its naked cherry-trees and its grey earth.

Monsieur Sauvage, jerking his thumb towards the heights, muttered: "The Prussians are up there!" And disquietude stole into the hearts of the two friends, looking at that deserted country. The Prussians! They had never seen any, but they had felt them there for months, all round Paris, bringing ruin to France, bringing famine; pillaging, massacre, invisible, yet invincible. And a sort of superstitious terror was added to their hatred for that unknown and victorious race.

Morissot stammered: "I say – suppose we were to meet some?"

With that Parisian jocularity which nothing can suppress, Monsieur Sauvage replied: "We'd give 'em some fried fish."

None the less, daunted by the silence all round, they hesitated to go farther.

At last Monsieur Sauvage took the plunge. "Come on! But be careful!"

They got down into a vineyard, where they crept along, all eyes and ears, bent double, taking cover behind every bush.

There was still a strip of open ground to cross before they could get to the riverside; they took it at the double and the moment they reached the bank plumped down amongst some dry rushes.

Morissot glued his ear to the ground for any sound of footsteps. Nothing! They were alone, utterly alone.

They plucked up spirit again, and began to fish.

In front of them the Island of Marante, uninhabited, hid them from the far bank. The little island restaurant was closed, and looked as if it had been abandoned for years.

Monsieur Sauvage caught the first gudgeon, Morissot the second, and every minute they kept pulling in their lines with a little silvery creature wriggling at the end. Truly a miraculous draught of fishes!

They placed their spoil carefully in a very fine-meshed net suspended in the water at their feet, and were filled by the delicious joy that visits those who know once more a pleasure of which they have been deprived too long.

The good sun warmed their shoulders; they heard nothing, thought of nothing, were lost to the world. They fished.

But suddenly a dull boom, which seemed to come from underground, made the earth tremble. The bombardment had begun again.

Morissot turned his head. Away above the bank he could see on his left the great silhouette of Mont Valérien, showing a white plume in its cap, a puff of smoke just belched forth. Then a second spurt of smoke shot up from the fort's summit, and some seconds afterwards was heard the roar of the gun.

Then more and more. Every minute the hill breathed out death, sending forth clouds of white smoke, which rose slowly to the calm heaven, and made a crown of cloud.

Monsieur Sauvage shrugged his shoulders. "At it again!" he said.

Morissot, who was anxiously watching the bobbing of his float, was seized with the sudden fury of a man of peace against these maniacs battering against each other, and he growled out: "Idiots I call them, killing each other like that!"

"Worse than the beasts!" said Monsieur Sauvage.

And Morissot, busy with a fish, added: "It'll always be like that, in my opinion, so long as we have governments."

Monsieur Sauvage cut him short. "The Republic would never have declared war –"

Morissot broke in: "Under a monarchy you get war against your neighbours; under a republic – war amongst yourselves."

And they began tranquilly discussing and unravelling momentous political problems with the sweet reasonableness of peaceable, ignorant men, who agreed at any rate on one point, that Man would never be free.

And Mont Valérien thundered without ceasing, shattering with its shells the homes of France, pounding out life, crushing human beings, putting an end to many a dream, to many an expected joy, to many a hope of happiness; opening everywhere, too, in the hearts of wives, of girls, of mothers, wounds that would never heal.

"Such is life!" declared Monsieur Sauvage.

"You mean 'Such is death'," said Morissot, and laughed.

They both gave a sudden start; there was surely someone coming up behind them. Turning their eyes they saw, standing close to their very elbows, four men, four big, bearded men, dressed in a sort of servant's livery, with flat caps on their heads, pointing rifles at them.

The rods fell from their hands and floated off downstream.

In a few seconds they were seized, bound, thrown into a boat, and taken over to the island.

Behind the house that they had thought deserted they perceived some twenty German soldiers.

A sort of hairy giant, smoking a great porcelain pipe, and sitting astride of a chair, said in excellent French: "Well, gentlemen, what luck fishing?"

Whereupon a soldier laid at his officer's feet the net full of fish, which he had carefully brought along.

The Prussian smiled. "I see – not bad. But we've other fish to fry. Now listen to me, and keep cool. I regard you as two spies sent to watch me. I take you, and I shoot you. You were pretending to fish, the better to disguise your plans. You've fallen into my hands, so much the worse for you. That's war. But, seeing that you passed through your outposts, you must assuredly have been given the password to get back again. Give it me, and I'll let you go."

Livid, side by side, the two friends were silent, but their hands kept jerking with little nervous movements.

The officer continued: "No one will ever know; it will be all right; you can go home quite easy in your minds. If you refuse, it's death – instant death. Choose."

They remained motionless, without a word.

The Prussian, calm as ever, stretched out his hands towards the water, and said: "Think! In five minutes you'll be at the bottom of that river. In five minutes. You've got families, I suppose?"

Mont Valérien went on thundering. The two fishermen stood silent.

The German gave an order in his own language. Then he moved his chair so as not to be too near his prisoners. Twelve men came forward, took their stand twenty paces away, and grounded arms.

The officer said: "I give you one minute; not a second more."

And, getting up abruptly, he approached the two Frenchmen, took Morissot by the arm, and, drawing him aside, whispered: "Quick, that password. Your friend need never know. It will only look as though I'd relented." Morissot made no answer.

Then the Prussian took Monsieur Sauvage apart, and asked him the same question.

Monsieur Sauvage did not reply.

Once again they were side by side. The officer gave a word of command. The soldiers raised their rifles.

At that moment Morissot's glance alighted on the net full of gudgeons lying on the grass a few paces from him. The sun was shining on that glittering heap of fishes, still full of life. His spirit sank. In spite of all effort his eyes filled with tears.

"Good-bye, Monsieur Sauvage!" he stammered out.

Monsieur Sauvage answered: "Good-bye, Monsieur Morissot."

They grasped each other's hands, shaken from head to foot by a trembling they could not control.

"Fire!" cried the officer.

Twelve shots rang out as one.

Monsieur Sauvage fell forward like a log. Morissot, the taller, wavered, spun around, and came down across his comrade, his face upturned to the sky; blood spurted from his tunic, torn across the chest.

The German gave another order. His men dispersed. They came back with ropes and stones, which they fastened to the feet of the two dead friends, whom they carried to the river-bank. And Mont Valérien never ceased rumbling, crowned now with piled-up clouds of smoke.

Two of the soldiers took Morissot by the head and heels, two others laid hold of Monsieur Sauvage in the same manner. The bodies, swung violently to and fro, were hurled forward, described a curve, then plunged upright into the river, where the stones dragged them down feet first.

The water splashed up, foamed, and rippled, then fell calm again, and tiny waves rolled out towards the banks.

A few bloodstains floated away.

The officer, calm as ever, said quietly: "Now it is the fishes' turn!" and went back towards the house.

But suddenly catching sight of the net full of gudgeons on the grass, he took it up, looked it over, smiled, and called out: "Wilhelm!"

A soldier in a white apron came running up. The Prussian threw him the spoil of the two dead fishermen.

"Get these little things fried at once while they're still alive. They will be delicious."

And he went back to his pipe.

LOOKING BACK
Lord Grey of Fallodon

1899

Thus, as the angler looks back he thinks less of individual captures and days than of scenes in which he fished. The luxuriance of water-meadows, animated by insect and bird and trout life, tender with the green and gay with the blossoms of early spring; the nobleness and volume of great salmon rivers; the exhilaration of looking at any salmon pool, great or small; the rich brownness of Highland water; the wild openness of the treeless, trackless spaces which he has traversed in an explorer's spirit of adventure to search likely water for sea-trout: now on one, now on another of these scenes an angler's mind will dwell, as he thinks of fishing. Special days and successes he will no doubt recall, but always with the remembrance and the mind's vision of the scenes and the world in which he fished. For, indeed, this does seem a separate world, a world of beauty and enjoyment. The time must come to all of us, who live long, when memory is more than prospect. An angler who has reached this stage and reviews the pleasure of life will be grateful and glad that he has been an angler, for he will look back upon days radiant with happiness, peaks and peaks of enjoyment that are not less bright because they are lit in memory by the light of a setting sun.

THE POACHER

Not so pleasant

Holloa, here's some d----d rascal been stealing the fish this evening, if I catch him, I'll break every bone in his skin.

SQUARING THE KEEPER

Francis Francis

1880

How I ENJOYED that day, to be sure! Some old sportsmen dearly love a little bit of poaching; for my part, it must be a very little bit to suit me. I never feel comfortable under it. In shooting, for example, I have seen some fellows who would rather pot a brace of birds off a neighbour's land than a dozen brace from their own, the stolen sweets are so particularly relishing. I never had any such feeling. If I ever was induced to break bounds, I always felt ashamed of myself from the first. My heart never was in the work, and if I got a shot I was so disturbed by my sense that I had no right to it, that the odds were two to one against the gun, though on other occasions it would be two to one on it; and if a keeper did appear, I would always rather have sneaked off by the shortest cut to my own territory than brazen it out by a bribe of 5s. I don't think, if left to my decision, I would ever willingly – never deliberately – have poached; but, on the occasion I am about to deal with I did it without intent, and cheeked it out afterwards in such a way that I often doubt in my own mind whether it could have been I, and if so, what possessed me.

We had a line from the Three Bridges Station on the Brighton line to Horsham under consideration; and I was engaged in surveying and levelling it. The line has long since been constructed. Our party, consisting of three, put up at the old-fashioned half-way house at Crawley – a queer little village, with a very remarkable old elm tree in it, the root and bole of which are hollowed out and form a small apartment. Crawley was a wonderful place in the old coaching days. The inn was a house of great grandeur and pretension; even then there were some attenuated remnants of old plate that gave one the idea of a lady-like old spinster very much reduced in circumstances. Here, formerly, dozens of coaches stopped daily, and it was rarely that they had not out from thirty to forty pair of post-horses. Now one coach called during the summer at the end of the village, and a pair of post-horses three times a week was good work; a sad falling off! Still the worthies of the village assembled nightly in the common room (greatly shorn of its glories) to have their smoke and talk, and, being a gregarious animal, I preferred to join them rather than to smoke alone. One evening I was listening to the usual Babel of conversation going on round me about pigs, beasts, and whuts, when I heard the word "trout" close at hand. I immediately pricked up my ears; two men sitting by me were talking:

"Ah, I've had many a voine un out an it, surelye."

"Out of where?" said I, breaking in upon the talk without scruple.

"Whoy, out o' the stream down agin th' steation."

"Stream! Why, you don't mean that dead ditch water that runs under the road just above the public?"

"Ah! but I doo tho! There be some voine trout in't, onlikely as't looks."

"The deuce there are! – and – and – may anyone go and fish it?"

"Ay, surelye. Whoy not?"

"Then dash my wigs if I don't go and have a turn at it to-morrow!" And, as my tackle needed looking up, I retired shortly. My stock was not extensive, for, not expecting any fishing, I had come down without any necessaries; but it so happened that, being at Horsham one day, and seeing in a small stream that flowed – or, as a Yankee would say, "flew" – through it in those days, some uncommonly fine roach, I went to the only shop in the town (a barber's I think it was) where any approach to fishing-tackle could be purchased, and bought the only rod I could get, a small, trumpery, three-joint, walking-stick rod, a dozen or so of strands of Indian grass – gut he did not possess – a yard or so of silk line, and a few hooks; no reel, no running-line, no anything else. With this I was perforce content. The fishing at Horsham did not result in much, and the place I was going to fish on the next day was pretty much as I have described it – a dead, deep, ditchy-looking bit of water, apparently with very little stream, which ran under the road and past the end of the garden appertaining to a public-house on the other side of the road. I rigged up a line of a yard and a half or so of silk, and to it fastened a strand of Indian grass some two feet long, and on this tied a No. 6 or 7 hook. I had no shot, because, the stream being almost still, the worm would suffice to carry it to the bottom. I forgot to say that worm fishing was my intent; for, even had I had fly tackle, the stream was so grown over and inclosed in a thicket that it would not have been possible to use it.

The next morning I sallied out directly after breakfast, and, having to get some bait, I stopped on the roadside just behind a gipsy's cart, where there was a mound of old road scrapings and cuttings, and, to the astonishment of sundry olive-coloured juveniles, I commenced turning the stuff up with a pointed stick, and soon got together a good stock of worms. Having put in a bit of moss out of the hedge to scour them, I again made tracks for the water, and soon reached it. There was a stile opposite the public-house, and I stepped over it. A footpath ran alongside of a dense sort of hedgerow thicket, which was some twenty or thirty yards or more deep, and in the centre of this the stream ran. Into the thicket I at once plunged, and soon got to the banks of the stream. It was sore work scrambling along them, the tangle was so thick. It did not look as if the stream was often fished. The first twenty or thirty yards or so did not seem tempting. They were straight, even, and dead, and the water looked black and very ditch-like. Presently I came to a bend, which made a sort of pool. It had a profound appearance. There might have been a fish there, and, if there was, he would likely enough be a big one; so rapidly jointing up my little poker of a rod – for it was not above eight or nine feet long – I unwound the line, stuck a worm on the hook, and dropped it into the spot. It slowly settled down out of sight into some four or five feet of water, and barely had reached the bottom when "spang" the line went, cutting the surface, out towards the opposite bank. I raised the point sharply as it ran straight out, and struck. I only got one tug, and that nearly pulled the rod out of my hand and smashed everything, and, with a boil which came up to the surface as if the rudder of a boat had been rapidly turned below, a huge fish made his escape. I collapsed. "Four or five pounds, if he was an ounce, by the boil he made!" I groaned. "When – when shall I ever have such another chance? When shall I ever hook such another?" It was a dreadful beginning. Of course the miserable grass had broken; but I doubt if even gut would have held him without a little running-line. Had I had but three or four yards of that, so as to have allowed him to reach the opposite side without breaking, no doubt I might have got on terms with him in time; but it was no use crying over spilt milk. As an Irishman would say, there might be "as good fish in the stream as *hadn't* come out of it," and luck might be in store yet; so I set to work to repair damages, and, as single-strand grass was not strong enough, I doubled it and twisted it, and so tied another hook on. It was clumsy work enough, but the water was dark and the stream shaded, and the trout apparently very unso*fish*ticated, for I soon began picking them up, here one and there one. They all ran from about ¾ lb. to 1 lb., and I got some three or four brace of them pretty quickly.

Presently I emerged from the thicket, and found that the stream ran under an arch in the railway embankment. Dropping the worm in, I let it glide off under the arch, and got a heavy lug, and, after a turn of pully-hauly, up bolted a fine trout into the open stream above the arch. He was a powerful fish, and I had all my work to play him with my fourteen feet of rod and line without letting him go down under the arch again; but I was up to my work, and by degrees I coaxed him away from it into a little gut, and as soon as he was exhausted I shelved him out with my left hand. As I was doing so a train rattled by, and a row of heads popped out to note my battle with the trout. He was a capital fish, very handsome, and weighed exactly two pounds. I then crossed the railway and plunged once more into the thicket, which was here denser and deeper than ever. It was rare tearing and scrambling work, but the stream here was livelier and shallower, and the fish more plentiful; and, having now filled my pockets, I had to hang fish on the twigs as I went along (having no basket), with a view to retrieving them as I came back; and at every place where I made my way into the stream I left two or three good trout hanging gilled on a branch. I fished on and on, and the afternoon began to grow apace, the stream to get thin and shallow, and the trout small; so I thought I would turn back and fish only a choice spot or two on my return, collecting my fish as I went. Sport had been capital, and on my return journey, though I only caught another fish or two, I filled my pockets, my hat, and my handkerchief, until I left off fishing at last, having nowhere else to stow a single fish more; and I made my way out into the footpath, having tackled up and tied up my rod. By this time I was almost exhausted, for I had had nothing to eat or drink all day; and, crossing the stile, I made for the public-house opposite to recruit the inner man. As I did so, the host came to the door.

"What! Bin a-fishin', sir?" was his accost.

"Yes," I replied, "yes, and had some very nice sport – eighteen brace and a half, and one two-pounder."

"Why, where *have* you been then?"

"Oh, up the ditch in the thicket yonder."

"What!!!" in a tone of horror. "Ditch! Why, that's the head of the Mole! Don't you know that I'm the keeper to it? And master's so dreadful particular that he won't give leave to no one, and there hain't been a single rod in there this two year" (I could well believe it) "and, by jingo, here he comes! Here, bring them fish in out of sight" (I had been untying the handkerchief to show them) "and give me that there rod. If he sees 'em, there'll be a horful row."

In we bolted, and a stout, jolly gentleman, with a white hat, drove up in a sulky, and stopped to discourse the landlord. I peeped at him from behind the curtain of the parlour window, and, as he sat flicking at a stone in the road, I thought he had a very "see-you-hanged-before-I-give-you-leave" kind of a face. They talked for a few minutes and then he drove on, when the host returned to me. I need not say that my feelings were not the most cheerful in the interval.

"Well, you air as nice a cool sort of young gent as I've met with for some time! To go an' poarch a stream right an' left like this, and then to go and walk slap into the keeper's 'ouse an' show'n the vish! What is to be done about it, danged if I knows. Ye ought to be summoned, that you did!" "Well," I replied, "all right; but first of all let's drink something, and then we'll consider about it. If you've got to do anything professional, why we shan't either of us be the worse of it for a pipe and a glass of brandy-and-water. 'You can always take up a quarrel at any time; but a limited portion of spirits and water you cannot,'" quoth I, quoting Dickens, "and, while you're mixing it, give me a biscuit." At this he shook his head; but I could see that it was like the shake of a pointer's tail when he is not certain whether he has game before him or no. So I filled up the two big rummers with a stiff dose of mahogany myself, and chirruped invitingly through a fine churchwarden pipe, before filling it with the finest of birdseye, with which my pouch was well stocked.

"Well, I be dashed if I knows what I ought to do! 'Tis clear to me as ye did'n knaw ye was doin' wrong." The pointer's tail was wagging, and unconsciously his hand stole to the big rummer, and a third of the mahogany vanished at a swig.

"Certainly not; should I have come in here to show you the fish if I had?"

"Naw, naw, that *be* trew; 't bent likely" – and I pushed the big pouch across to him, for I saw that his eyes lightened at the sight of the birdseye, for really good tobacco was by no means so general in the country then as it is now. "That be trew," he continued, filling his churchwarden in an absent kind of way, as if the question was still one of uncertainty; and he repeated, slowly, "That be ver-ry" – puff, puff – pause – "'mazin' foine backer this" – puff – "Lor'!'" – puff, puff – "it dooes one good, sich a bit o' backer as this." From that time not another word was said about the poaching, but we branched off into general sport. Mine host was a real enthusiastic sportsman at heart. He enjoyed every kind of sport, and, beyond all, loved a crack about it like the present. We went the whole round of hunting, shooting, coursing, fishing, with a touch of ratting and badger "droring," and we both enjoyed ourselves very thoroughly.

Three times were those big jorums of mahogany refilled, and twice three times the contents of the churchwardens came and went, and mine host and myself grew more and more hail fellows, and more pleased with our company. It evidently was an unusual treat for Boniface, and he looked on me as a sort of phenomenon. At length, however, it began to get late, and I rose to go. I paid my score, and left the remains of the prime birdseye for his future pleasure – a delicacy he much appreciated. His last words to me as I left the house were: "Now look here; if anybody 'ed a seed you as tha went along that theer footpath – and there was lots went along it, 'cos I seed 'em" (this was true enough, and I had heard them, too, but they did not see me), "I'd 'a lost my place, vor sartin. Now, mind, you must promise me you woan't never goo there no more" (this I readily did, and duty was satisfied). "But, lookee here" (catching hold of my arm just as I left the door, and whispering in my ear), "the next time as you cooms, goo up droo my garden, and out at the little gate at the back; there ben't no footpath at all there, and the vishin's a sight better nor 'tis down thik way."

TOM BROWN AND VELVETEENS

Thomas Hughes

1857

NOW CAME ON the may-fly season; the soft hazy summer weather lay sleepily along the rich meadows by Avon side, and the green and grey flies flickered with their lazy up and down flight over the reeds and the water and the meadows in myriads upon myriads . . .

Every little pitiful coarse fish in the Avon was on the alert for the flies, and gorging his wretched carcase with hundreds daily, the gluttonous rogues! and every lover of the gentle craft was out to avenge the poor may-flies.

So one fine Thursday afternoon, Tom, having borrowed East's new rod, started by himself to the river. He fished for some time with small success: not a fish would rise at him; but as he prowled along the bank he was presently aware of mighty ones feeding in a pool on the opposite side, under the shade of a huge willow-tree. The stream was deep there, but some fifty yards below was a shallow for which he made off hot-foot; and forgetting landlords, keepers, solemn prohibitions of the Doctor, and everything else, pulled up his trousers, plunged across, and in three minutes was creeping along on all fours towards the clump of willows.

It isn't often that great chub, or any other coarse fish, are in earnest about anything, but just then they were thoroughly bent on feeding, and in half an hour Master Tom had deposited three thumping fellows at the foot of the giant willow. As he was baiting for a fourth pounder, and just going to throw in again, he became aware of a man coming up the bank not one hundred yards off. Another look told him that it was the under-keeper. Could he reach the shallow before him? No, not carrying his rod. Nothing for it but the tree; so Tom laid his bones to it, shinning up as fast as he could, and dragging up his rod after him. He had just time to reach and crouch along a huge branch some ten feet up, which stretched over the river, when the keeper arrived at the clump. Tom's heart beat fast as he came under the tree; two steps more and he would have passed, when as ill-luck would have it, the gleam on the scales of the dead fish caught his eye, and he made a dead point at the foot of the tree. He picked up the fish one by one; his eye and touch told him that they had been alive and feeding within the hour. Tom crouched lower along the branch, and heard the keeper beating the clump. "If I could only get the rod hidden," thought he, and began gently shifting it to get it alongside of him; "willow-trees don't throw out straight hickory shoots twelve feet long, with no leaves, worse luck." Alas! the keeper catches the rustle, and then a sight of the rod, and then of Tom's hand and arm.

"Oh, be up ther', be'ee?" says he, running under the tree. "Now you come down this minute."

"Tree'd at last," thinks Tom, making no answer, and keeping as close as possible, but working away at the rod, which he takes to pieces: "I'm for it unless I can starve him out." And then he begins to meditate getting along the bank for a plunge, and scramble to the other side; but the small branches are so thick, and the opposite bank so difficult, that the keeper will have lots of time to get round by the ford before he can get out, so he gives that up. And now he hears the keeper beginning to scramble up the trunk. That will never do; so he scrambled himself back to where his branch joins the trunk, and stands with lifted rod.

"Hullo, Velveteens, mind your finger if you come any higher." The keeper stops and looks up, and then with a grin says, "Oh! be you, be it, young measter? Well, here's luck. Now I tells 'ee to come down at once, and it'll be best for 'ee."

"Thank'ee, Velveteens, I'm very comfortable," said Tom, shortening his rod in his hand, and preparing for battle.

"Werry well, please yourself," says the keeper, descending however to the ground again, and taking his seat on the bank; "I bean't in no hurry, so you may take your time. I'll larn'ee to gee honest folk names afore I've done with 'ee."

"My luck as usual," thinks Tom, "what a fool I was to give him a black. If I'd called him 'keeper' now I might get off. The return match is all his way."

The keeper quietly proceeded to take out his pipe, fill, and light it, keeping an eye on Tom, who now sat disconsolately across the branch, looking at the keeper – a pitiful sight for men and fishes. The more he thought of it the less he liked it. "It must be getting near second calling-over," thinks he. Keeper smokes on stolidly. "If he takes me up I shall be flogged safe enough. I can't sit here all night. Wonder if he'll rise at silver."

"I say, keeper," said he meekly, "let me go for two bob?"

"Not for twenty neither," grunts his persecutor.

And so they sat on till long past second calling-over, and the sun came slanting in through the willow branches, and telling of locking-up near at hand.

"I'm coming down, keeper," said Tom at last, with a sigh, fairly tired out. "Now what are you going to do?"

"Walk'ee up to School and give 'ee over to the Doctor, them's my orders," says Velveteens, knocking the ashes out of his fourth pipe, and standing up and shaking himself.

"Very good," said Tom; "but hands off, you know. I'll go with you quietly, so no collaring or that sort of thing."

Keeper looked at him a minute – "Werry good," said he at last; and so Tom descended and wended his way drearily by the side of the keeper up to the School-house, where they arrived just at locking-up. As they passed the School gates, the Tadpole and several others who were standing there caught the state of things, and rushed out, crying, "Rescue!" but Tom shook his head, so they only followed to the Doctor's gate and went back sorely puzzled.

How changed and stern the Doctor seemed from the last time Tom was up there, as the keeper told the story, not omitting to state how Tom had called him blackguard names. "Indeed, sir," broke in the culprit, "it was only Velveteens." The Doctor only asked one question.

"You know the rule about the banks, Brown?"

"Yes, sir."

"Then wait for me tomorrow, after first lesson."

"I thought so," muttered Tom.

"And about the rod, sir?" went on the keeper. "Master told me as we might have all the rods . . ."

"Oh, please, sir," broke in Tom, "the rod isn't mine." The Doctor looked puzzled; but the keeper, who was a good-hearted fellow, and melted at Tom's evident distress, gave up his claim. Tom was flogged next morning and a few days afterwards met Velveteens, and presented him with half a crown for giving up the rod claim and they became sworn friends; and I regret to say that Tom had many more fish from under the willow that may-fly season, and was never caught again by Velveteens.

SNARING PIKE
Richard Jeffries

1870

FROM THE OUTLOOK of the oak some aspen trees could be seen far up in the withy beds; and it had been agreed that there the first essay of the stream should be made. On arriving at these trees we paused, and began to fix the wires on the hazel rods. The wire for fish must slip very easily, the thinner it is, if strong enough, the better, because it takes a firmer grip. A single wire will do; but two thin ones are preferable. This copper wire is as flexible as thread. Brass wire is not so good; it is stiffer, and too conspicuous in the water.

At the shank end a stout string is attached in the middle of its length. Then the wire is placed against the rod, lying flat upon it for about six inches. The strings are now wound round tightly in opposite directions, binding it to the stick, so that at the top the lines cross and are in position to tie in the slight notch cut for the purpose. A loop that will allow four fingers to enter is about large enough, though, of course, it must be varied according to the size of the jack in view. Heavy jacks are not often wired, and scarcely ever in brooks.

For jack the shape of the loop should be circular; for trout it should be oval, and considerably larger in proportion to the apparent bulk of the fish. Jacks are straight-grown and do not thicken much in the middle; with trout it is different. The noose should be about six inches from the top of the rod. Orion said he would go twenty yards farther up; I went direct from the centre of the withy bed to the stream.

The bank rose a little above the level of the withy bed; it was a broad mound full of ash stoles and willow – the sort that is grown for poles. At that spot the vines of wild hops had killed all the underwood, leaving open spaces between the stoles; the vines were matted so thickly that they hid the ground. This was too exposed a place, so I went back and farther up till I could just hear Orion rustling through the hemlocks. Here the dead grass and some elder bushes afforded shelter, and the water could be approached unseen.

It was about six or eight inches deep; the opposite shore was bordered for several yards out with flags and rushes. The cattle nibbled their tender tops off, as far as they could reach; farther out they were pushing

213

up straight and pointed. The rib and groove of the flag so closely resembles those of the ancient bayonet that it might be supposed the weapon was modelled from that plant . . .

The rushes grew nearer the shore of the meadow – the old ones yellow, the young green; in places this fringe of rush and sedge and flag must have been six yards wide and it extended as far as could be seen up the brook. No doubt the cattle trod in the edge of the firm ground, by degrees every year to get at the water, and thus widened the marsh.

After a long look across, I began to examine the stream near at hand; the rushes and flags had forced the clear sweet current away from the meadow, so that it ran just under the bank. I was making out the brown sticks on the bottom when there was a slight splash – caused by Orion about ten yards higher up – and almost at the same instant something shot down the brook towards me. He had, doubtless, landed a jack and its fellow had rushed away. Under a large dead bough that had fallen across its top in the stream I saw the long slender fish lying a few feet from the bank, motionless save for the gentle curving of the tail edges. So faint was that waving that it seemed caused rather by the flow of the current than the volition of the fish. The wings of the swallow work the whole of the longest summer day, but the fins of the fish in running water are never still; day and night they move continuously.

By slow degrees I advanced the hazel rod, keeping it at first near to, and parallel with the bank, because jack do not like anything that stretches across them.

I imagine other fish have the same dislike for right angles. The straight shadow ever seems to arouse suspicion, no boughs are ever straight. Perhaps if it were possible to angle without a rod, there would be more success, particularly in small streams. But after getting the stick almost out far enough, it became evident that the dead branch would not let me slip the wire into the water in front of the jack in the usual way. So I had to draw it back again as gradually as it had been put forth.

With fish everything must be done gradually without a jerk. A sudden jerking movement alarms them. If you walk gently by they remain still, but start or lift the arm quickly and they dart for deep water. The object of withdrawing the rod was to get at and enlarge the loop in order that it might be slipped over his tail, since the head is protected by the bough. It is a more delicate operation to pass the wire up from behind; it has to go farther before the spot that allows a firm grip is reached, and fish are well aware that natural objects such as twigs float down with the current.

Anything therefore approaching from behind or rubbing upwards is suspicious. As this fish had just been startled it would not do to let the wire touch him at all.

After enlarging the loop I put the rod slowly forth again, worked the wire upstream, slipped the noose over his tail and gently got it up to the balance of the fish.

Waiting a moment to get the elbow over the end of the rod so as to get a good leverage, I gave a sudden jerk upwards, and felt the weight instantly. But the top of the rod struck the overhanging bough, and there was my fish, hung indeed, but still in the water near the surface. Nor could I throw it on the bank because of the elder. So I shortened the rod, pulling it quickly towards me and dragging the jack through the water. The pliant wire had cut into the scales and skin – he might have been safely left suspended over the stream all day; but in the eagerness of the moment I was not satisfied till I had him on the mound.

We did not see much of Southlands because the withy beds were on the lowest ground; but there were six jacks strung on a twisted withy when we got back to the stunted oak and rested there tasting acid sorrel leaves.

EFFECT OF STARLIGHT
UPON POACHERS
Robert H. Davis

1937

YOU KNOW HOW IT IS; worn to the quick by cares that infest the day; dulled to exhaustion with details, what with one damned thing after another, and more to come, when the welcome shadows of night enfold one in benignant embrace and Nirvana extinguishes the blinding fires of the public eye.

Curious indeed that I should have come so far from home to observe the transformations that take place among mortals so beset by weariness, when at last goaded into retaliation, they strike off the fetters of convention and enter the primitive state.

Take the case of Art and Dan and Al, three sterling and law-abiding citizens of Charlottetown, the capital of this salubrious island washed by the waters of the Atlantic and the Gulf of St. Lawrence; an empire favored of the gods and endowed with Elysian charms transcending the endowments of paradise.

It was my good fortune to partake of the unlimited hospitalities bestowed with lavish hand by Art and Dan and Al, all anglers of the highest types; dry fly casters and disciples of light tackle. Seldom is it the lot of a comparative stranger to fall within a circle of preeminent piscatorial pundits in any respect comparable with the three above mentioned Dromios. All men of action, as follows, to wit:

About 11:30 P.M., that is to say the last run of the evening's feature film, we four trickled out of a movie theater, halting on the curb to inspect the beauty of the night.

Said Art: "The sea trout are biting."

Said Dan: "Let's go."

Said Al: "You'll join us, Bob."

Said I: "You bet. When?"

Said the bunch: "Now!"

I declared my unpreparedness. No clothes, no boots, no tackle. The trio guffawed. Night angling except for black bass and eels was low down, I insisted. "You're crazy," said Dan. "We'll be on the stream by 12 M., the witching hour," said Al. "Hop in, boys," said Art, elbowing the rest of us to his car, idling at the curb. That settled it. We piled in and hit for the country.

Once beyond the city lights every star overhead burst into a beacon. Across the landscape lay an iridescence that brought trees and scattered farm-houses into soft relief against the sky line. Through a rural section where all the inhabitants were slumbering we glided swiftly, twenty miles, halting at a pasture gate. Entering, we crossed a hay field, the timothy and clover flicking against our hubs. A quick drop into a lush valley, wrapped in deep shadows. The perfume of rivers smote my nostrils. Just ahead, set against a grove of jack pines, appeared the outline of a rambling abode half concealed by the trees. A dog barked. Art doused the headlights, bringing the car to a halt in the angle of a rail fence on the edge of a marsh redolent of sweet fern. Again the dog barked, this time quite near. Dan whistled a soft call. "Come here, Prince." From the gloom stepped an Irish setter and licked the hand extended to him. "Out, boys," said Al, making his way to the rear of the car and opening a large motor trunk from which he produced gum boots, creels, rods and nets, light canvas coats and hats for all hands. "Get into these things. Step lively. Stow your town clothes and shoes in the back seat. Prince will watch them."

The subdued tone of the conversation aroused my suspicions. Could it be that poaching was the program, and that Prince even was a vicarious participant? Hinting as much, I evoked suppressed laughter, but no defense. "Anyhow," said Art, "the pool awaits us and the trout are there. Up, Prince, do your stuff; we'll be back in a couple of hours."

Into the rear seat bounded the setter to take up his guardianship.

A short walk through maples, birch, spruce and hemlock brought us to a stretch of alders. Beyond, a river bank, open and free of brush, gave casting room for all. An angler's heaven; a hundred yards of deep, slow-moving water broken by rising sea trout leaping for but never attaining the stars. By the light of the Big Dipper, Saturn, Mars and the Milky Way we coupled up our rods, tied on six foot leaders, bearing a Montreal or a Parmachenc Bell, and we went to it, each for himself alone.

Under the hypnotic influence of the night, the expanding circles born of breaking and striking trout; the faint cries of night birds passing over-head, I experienced a sense of complete detachment from all earthly things, though brought back at intervals by exclamations, mutterings and echoes of mild blasphemy from my all but invisible companions. Forward and back, fighting, netting and landing fish I visioned the triumphs that were mounting to the right and to the left of me. All the zenith shimmering in sidereal fire seemed to hold in its embrace this poacher's paradise. Alas! no mortal's pen can write the history of a dream.

A quartering moon rising in the east fixed its accusing eye upon us. As one man, under the sudden white light of guilt, we dismembered our rods, gathered up the fruits of our encroachment and vanished.

Small wonder, after counting our catch which totaled three creels full, that Art should have then and there tendered Prince a live trout for protecting poachers while his master lay asleep in the cottage under the spreading jack pines.

"That dog," said Dan, from the back seat on the way home, "always comes through like a gentleman when we take visitors fishing after dark."

"Do you suppose he knows that you're a poacher?" I asked.

"Sure," replied the night raider, "that's why he likes me."

THE FISH

SALMON BROOK

Henry David Thoreau

c. 1850

Salmon Brook,
Penichook,
    Ye sweet waters of my brain,
When shall I look,
Or cast the hook,
    In your waves again?

Silver eels,
Wooden creels,
    These the baits that still allure,
And dragon-fly
That floated by; –
    May they still endure!

THE FISH

Anton Chekhov

1922

A SUMMER MORNING. The air is still; there is no sound but the churring of a grasshopper on the river bank, and somewhere the timid cooing of a turtle-dove. Feathery clouds stand motionless in the sky, looking like snow scattered about . . . Gerassim, the carpenter, a tall gaunt peasant, with a curly red head and a face overgrown with hair, is floundering about in the water under the green willow branches near an unfinished bathing shed . . . He puffs and pants and, blinking furiously, is trying to get hold of something under the roots of the willows. His face is covered with perspiration. A couple of yards from him, Lubim, the carpenter, a young hunchback with a triangular face and narrow Chinese-looking eyes, is standing up to his neck in water. Both Gerassim and Lubim are in shirts and linen breeches. Both are blue with cold, for they have been more than an hour already in the water.

"But why do you keep poking with your hand?" cries the hunchback Lubim, shivering as though in a fever. "You blockhead! Hold him, hold him, or else he'll get away, the anathema! Hold him, I tell you!"

"He won't get away . . . Where can he get to? He's under a root," says Gerassim in a hoarse, hollow bass, which seems to come not from his throat, but from the depths of his stomach. "He's slippery, the beggar, and there's nothing to catch hold of."

"Get him by the gills, by the gills!"

"There's no seeing his gills . . . Stay, I've got hold of something . . . I've got him by the lip . . . He's biting, the brute!"

"Don't pull him out by the lip, don't – or you'll let him go! Take him by the gills, take him by the gills. . . . You've begun poking with your hand again! You are a senseless man, the Queen of Heaven forgive me! Catch hold!"

"Catch hold!" Gerassim mimics him. "You're a fine one to give orders . . . You'd better come and catch hold of him yourself, you hunchback devil . . . What are you standing there for?"

"I would catch hold of him if it were possible. But can I stand by the bank, and me as short as I am? It's deep there."

"It doesn't matter if it is deep . . . You must swim."

The hunchback waves his arms, swims up to Gerassim, and catches hold of the twigs. At the first attempt to stand up, he goes into the water over his head and begins blowing up bubbles.

"I told you it was deep," he says, rolling his eyes angrily. "Am I to sit on your neck or what?"

"Stand on a root . . . there are a lot of roots like a ladder." The hunchback gropes for a root with his heel, and tightly gripping several twigs, stands on it . . . Having got his balance, and established himself in his new position, he bends down, and trying not to get the water into his mouth begins fumbling with his right hand among the roots. Getting entangled among the weeds and slipping on the mossy roots, he finds his hand in contact with the sharp pincers of a crayfish.

"As though we wanted to see you, you demon!" says Lubim, and he angrily flings the crayfish on the bank.

At last his hand feels Gerassim's arm, and groping its way along it comes to something cold and slimy.

"Here he is!" says Lubim with a grin. "A fine fellow! Move your fingers, I'll get him directly . . . by the gills. Stop, don't prod me with your elbow . . . I'll have him in a minute, in a minute, only let me get hold of him. . . . The beggar has got a long way under the roots, there is nothing to get hold of . . . One can't get to the head . . . one can only feel its belly . . . Kill that gnat on my neck – it's stinging! I'll get him by the gills, directly . . . Come to one side and give him a push! Poke him with your finger!"

The hunchback puffs out his cheeks,holds his breath, opens his eyes wide, and apparently has already got his fingers in the gills, but at that moment the twigs to which he is holding on with his left hand break, and losing his balance he plops into the water! Eddies race away from the bank as though frightened, and little bubbles come up from the spot where he has fallen in. The hunchback swims out and, snorting, clutches at the twigs.

"You'll be drowned next, you stupid, and I shall have to answer for you," wheezes Gerassim. "Clamber out, the devil take you! I'll get him out myself."

High words follow . . . The sun is baking hot. The shadows begin to grow shorter and to draw in on themselves, like the horns of a snail . . . The high grass warmed by the sun begins to give out a strong, heavy smell of honey. It will soon be midday, and Gerassim and Lubim are still floundering under the willow tree. The husky bass and the shrill, frozen tenor persistently disturb the stillness of the summer day.

"Pull him out by the gills, pull him out! Stay, I'll push him out! Where are you shoving your great ugly fist? Poke him with your finger – you pig's face! Get round by the side! get to the left, to the left, there's a big hole on the right! You'll be a supper for the water-devil! Pull it by the lip!"

There is the sound of the flick of a whip . . . A herd of cattle, driven by Yefim, the shepherd, saunter lazily down the sloping bank to drink. The shepherd, a decrepit old man, with one eye and a crooked mouth, walks with his head bowed, looking at his feet. The first to reach the water are the sheep, then come the horses, and last of all the cows.

"Push him from below!" he hears Lubim's voice. "Stick your finger in! Are you deaf, fellow, or what? Tfoo!"

"What are you after, lads?" shouts Yefim.

"An eel-pout! We can't get him out! He's hidden under the roots. Get round to the side! To the side!"

For a minute Yefim screws up his eye at the fishermen, then he takes off his bark shoes, throws his sack off his shoulders, and takes off his shirt. He has not the patience to take off his breeches, but, making the sign of the cross, he steps into the water, holding out his thin dark arms to balance himself . . . For fifty paces he walks along the slimy bottom, then he takes to swimming.

"Wait a minute, lads!" he shouts. "Wait! Don't be in a hurry to pull him out, you'll lose him. You must do it properly!"

Yefim joins the carpenters and all three, shoving each other with their knees and their elbows, puffing and swearing at one another, bustle about the same spot. Lubim, the hunchback, gets a mouthful of water, and the air rings with his hard spasmodic coughing.

"Where's the shepherd?" comes a shout from the bank. "Yefim! Shepherd! Where are you? The cattle are in the garden! Drive them out, drive them out of the garden! Where is he, the old brigand?"

First men's voices are heard, then a woman's. The master himself, Andrey Andreitch, wearing a dressing-gown made of a Persian shawl and carrying a newspaper in his hand, appears from behind the garden fence. He looks inquiringly towards the shouts which come from the river, and then trips rapidly towards the bathing shed.

"What's this? Who's shouting?" he asks sternly, seeing through the branches of the willow the three wet heads of the fishermen. "What are you so busy about there?"

"Catching a fish," mutters Yefim, without raising his head.

"I'll give it to you! The beasts are in the garden and he is fishing! . . . When will that bathing shed be done, you devils? You've been at work two days, and what is there to show for it?"

"It . . . will soon be done," grunts Gerassim; "summer is long, you'll have plenty of time to wash, your honour. . . . Pfrrr! . . . We can't manage this eel-pout here anyhow . . . He's got under a root and sits there as if he were in a hole and won't budge one way or another. . . ."

"An eel-pout?" says the master, and his eyes begin to glisten. "Get him out quickly then."

"You'll give us half a rouble for it presently . . . if we oblige you . . . A huge eel-pout, as fat as a merchant's wife . . . It's worth half a rouble, your honour, for the trouble . . . Don't squeeze him, Lubim, don't squeeze him, you'll spoil him! Push him up from below! Pull the root upwards, my good man . . . what's your name? Upwards, not downwards, you brute! Don't swing your legs!"

Five minutes pass, ten . . . The master loses all patience.

"Vassily!" he shouts, turning towards the garden. "Vaska! Call Vassily to me!"

The coachman Vassily runs up. He is chewing something and breathing hard.

"Go into the water," the master orders him. "Help them to pull out that eel-pout. They can't get him out."

Vassily rapidly undresses and gets into the water.

"In a minute . . . I'll get him in a minute," he mutters. "Where's the eel-pout? We'll have him out in a trice! You'd better go, Yefim. An old man like you ought to be minding his own business instead of being here. Where's that eel-pout? I'll have him in a minute . . . Here he is! Let go."

"What's the good of saying that? We know all about that! You get it out!"

"But there is no getting it out like this! One must get hold of it by the head."

"And the head is under the root! We know that, you fool!"

"Now then, don't talk or you'll catch it! You dirty cur!"

"Before the master to use such language," mutters Yefim. "You won't get him out, lads! He's fixed himself much too cleverly!"

"Wait a minute, I'll come directly," says the master, and he begins hurriedly undressing. "Four fools, and can't get an eel-pout!"

When he is undressed, Andrey Andreitch gives himself time to cool and gets into the water. But even his interference leads to nothing.

"We must chop the root off," Lubim decides at last. "Gerassim, go and get an axe! Give me an axe!"

"Don't chop your fingers off," says the master, when the blows of the axe on the root under water are heard. "Yefim, get out of this! Stay, I'll get the eel-pout . . . You'll never do it."

The root is hacked a little. They partly break it off, and Andrey Andreitch, to his immense satisfaction, feels his fingers under the gills of the fish.

"I'm pulling him out, lads! Don't crowd round . . . stand still . . . I am pulling him out!"

The head of a big eel-pout, and behind it its long black body, nearly a yard long, appears on the surface of the water. The fish flaps its tail heavily and tries to tear itself away.

"None of your nonsense, my boy! Fiddlesticks! I've got you! Aha!"

A honied smile overspreads all the faces. A minute passes in silent contemplation.

"A famous eel-pout," mutters Yefim, scratching under his shoulder-blades. "I'll be bound it weighs ten pounds."

"Mm! . . . yes," the master assents. "The liver is fairly swollen! It seems to stand out! A-ach!"

The fish makes a sudden, unexpected upward movement with its tail and the fishermen hear a loud splash . . . they all put out their hands, but it is too late; they have seen the last of the eel-pout.

PETE AND THE BIG TROUT
Henry Ward Beecher

1867

PETE AIN'T GROWED AWAY from natur' so far but what he knows what's goin' on in beast and bird. There ain't his equal at fishin' in these parts. The fish just cum, I do believe, and ask him to catch 'em.

He don't take on airs about it neither. He ain't stingy. He'd just as soon take you to the best brooks and the best places as not. But then that's nothin'. Very like you can't catch a fish. The trout knows who's after 'em. They want Pete to catch 'em, not Tom, Dick, and Harry.

You mind that time he caught that trout out of Hulcomb's mill-pond, don't you? – No? Well, it had been known that there was an awful big fellow living in there. And I know a hundred folks had tried for him. Gentlemen had come up from New Haven, and from Bridgeport, and from down to New York, a-fishin', and ever so many of 'em had wound up with tryin' their luck for that big trout, and they had all sorts of riggin'. One he tried flies, and another worms; sometimes they took the mornin', and sometimes the evenin'. They knew the hole where he lay. He's been seen breaking the water for one thing and another, but allus when nobody was fishin'. He was a curious trout. I believe he knew Sunday just as well as Deacon Marble did. At any rate the deacon thought the trout meant to aggravate him. The deacon, you know, is a little waggish. He often tells about that trout. Sez he: "One Sunday morning, just as I got along by the willows, I heard an awful splash, and not ten feet from shore I saw the trout, as long as my arm, just curving over like a bow, and going down with something for breakfast. 'Gracious!' says I, and I almost jumped out of the waggon. But my wife Polly, says she: 'What on airth are you thinkin' of, Deacon? It's Sabbath-day, and you're goin' to meetin'! It's a pretty business for a deacon!' That sort of talk cooled me off. But I do say, that for about a minute I wished I wasn't a deacon. But 'twouldn't made any difference, for I came down next day to mill on purpose, and I came down once or twice more, and nothin' was to be seen, tho' I tried him with the most temptin' things. Wall, next Sunday I came along agin', and to save my life I couldn't keep off worldly and wandering thoughts. I tried to be sayin' my Catechism. But I couldn't keep my eyes off the pond as we came up to the willows. I'd got along in the Catechism as smooth as the road, to the Fourth Commandment, and was sayin' it out loud for Polly, and jist as I was sayin': 'What is required in the Fourth Commandment?' I heard a splash, and there was the trout, and afore I could think, I said: 'Gracious, Polly; I must have that trout.' She almost riz right up: 'I knew you wan't sayin' your Catechism hearty. Is this the way you answer the question about keepin' the Lord's day? I'm ashamed, Deacon Marble,' says she. 'You'd better change your road, and go to meetin' on the road over the hill. If I was a deacon, I wouldn't let a fish's tail whisk the whole Catechism out of my head'; – and I had to go to meetin' on the hill road all the rest of the summer."

Wall, Pete he worked down to the mill for a week or two – that's as long as he stays anywhere, except at Dr Wentworth's, and he lets him come and go about as he pleases. And so, one day, says he: "I'm goin' to catch that big trout." So, after the sun was gone down, and just as the moon riz and lighted up the tops of the bushes, but didn't touch the water – Pete, he took a little mouse he'd caught, and hooked his hook through his skin, on the back, so that it didn't hurt him or hinder his being lively, and he threw him in about as far as a mouse could have jumped from the branches that hung over. Of course, the mouse he put out lively to swim for his life. Quick as a flash of lightnin', the water opened with a rush, and the mouse went under; but he came up again, and the trout with him, and he weighed between three and four pound.

226

THE CUNNING OF TROUT

Alexander Urquhart

1914

IT IS POSSIBLE for a vast aggregate of thinking to be performed around a particular problem without advancing its solution. Thus, on the first brilliant Saturday afternoon in March ever since the close of the ice age the goodly army of anglers have turned a willing mind to the great question of fish. From then till October, throughout all the intervening ages, they have speculated on fish, told stories about fish, and even lied about fish. They have fondly rolled their agile conceptions of fish into and out of every corner of their crania. They have despised and mistrusted their fellowmen who are in imperfect sympathy with fish; and even the angling peasants of Cumberland looked down with lofty contempt upon Wordsworth because, as one of them put it, "there wasn't a bit o' fish in him." Yet, notwithstanding all this the psychology of trout remains in a backward state. Indeed, it is highly probable, though not subject to proof, that neolithic man, after a day of it on the river with hooks made out of thorns, black or white, said precisely the same things about trout as are said today by every little assembly of fishers gathered at a wayside station to await the last train. He paid his tribute to the great mental powers of the trout; so do they. He remarked on its great ability to learn from experience; its mastery of the disguises of hooks; its profound wisdom in old age – so do they. He wondered what trout thought about him; and today they raise conjectures on the subject of what the old fellow "is saying to himself" about them as he lurks in his favourite hole beneath the big root of the alder-tree. Neolithic man credited trout with firmly held views as to the relative safety of blackthorn hooks used with or without the bark, and his modern descendant has merely changed the mechanism of the opinion, and credits his quarry with views on tinsel or hackel of hare lug. Then, as now, the sceptical man who ventured (within reach of water) to declare that trout have no power of thinking at all, that they are as unteachable as a dead machine, would stand in imminent danger of a watery martyrdom as fit retribution for his most accursed heresy.

And yet the heretic would be very near the truth, for it is only in fables and anglers' tales that fish are creatures of intelligence. They are born with a certain endowment of fear, suspicion, and fixed utilitarian instinct, and an endowment which experience hardly, if at all, modifies up or down. When a naturalist wishes to find examples of unteachableness he goes to the fish kingdom; for though fish stand higher in the order of life than the insects and other articulated creatures, their adaptive intelligence is universally lower. A spider, for example, may be taught in ten minutes to get the better of its inherited instincts, if some disagreeable result follows the attempt to gratify them. Present one with a fly dipped in an unpleasantly tasting substance like turpentine, and after two trials it will learn to subordinate the whole teaching of its countless ancestors that a fly within reach is a thing to be pounced upon. But a fish will go on plunging at a thing which, were it a teachable creature, experience would have warned it to leave alone. There are countless examples of salmon, and even trout, taking the fly within a few minutes of being struck, and there are many cases of a salmon being caught with the hook still in its jaw which it had broken off after a mighty struggle half an hour before. But more striking experiments than these have attested the unteachableness of fish. Mr. Bateson tells how none of the fish in his aquarium seemed to get a lasting appreciation of the nature of the glass wall of the tank. The same fish again and again knocked their heads against the glass in trying to seize objects moving on the other side, and some of the oldest inhabitants continued to the last subject to the fish's natural instinct to pounce, though it meant a damaged snout every time. Even the examples of teachableness in fish only emphasize a general belief in their unteachableness, as in the well-known case of the pike which dashed itself for three months against a glass partition in the attempt to get at some minnows in the next division of the aquarium, and became at last so firmly persuaded of the danger of attacking them that, when the partition was removed, it left them quite unmolested. In this case the pike never learned anything about the partition. It merely got fixed hard in its head a dull notion that there was something about those minnows which interfered with their usefulness as articles of diet. Of course, in support of the belief of the teachableness of fish there will be cited the case of those young hatchery trout which come up in shoals to be fed on their attendant making the customary sign. This, however, is not a case of intelligence. It is but a free response to a natural impulse, the almost mechanical performance of an action in the direct sequence of a stimulus acting on one of the senses. The stupidest moth will quickly learn to respond in the same way to a scent which it associates with food. it is not in responding to, but in the inhibition of, such impulses that intelligence, and particularly the sort attributed to fish, should be shown.

How, then, is the so-called cunning of the trout to be accounted for? The question is not very difficult if one keeps steadily in mind the fact that they have been fished for since, at any rate, the days of neolithic man; and teachableness has not necessarily any part in the problem. Through all those ages man has been steadily extracting from the water the fish with an inferior original endowment of suspicion; and, considering the length of time during which the process has been going on, the surprising thing is not that fish are suspicious, but that there are any strains left with so little suspicion that they may still be deceived with a confection of steel, feathers, tinsel, and hair. There were wary and less wary fish in the waters when man began to operate with rod and line. The wary strain, or the more wary members of it, have survived to multiply their kind, while the unwary and the less wary have found their way into the basket. Thus the fish in much-fished rivers have not acquired their reputation for cunning because greater experience has taught them more, but because all the simpletons have been taken out. Nor is the case of the cunning old trout at all destructive of this theory of elimination. It is argued that this trout must have learned a lot, or he would never have grown so old. But the dangers of the old trout were just as great – they were even greater – when he was young as they are now that he is old. As he successfully eluded them then, the probability is that he was as naturally wary then as now. The theory that fish are taught great cunning by experience is hardly capable of statement in a particular case, and is, indeed, always set forth in general terms applicable to entire rivers. Just consider the amount and kind of experience necessary to teach a trout the sort of angler-defying wisdom attributed to it. It is known already that the *amount* of experience needed to teach a fish is very great, and in this case the kind of it must be actual contact with a hook. By this proposition, therefore, the fish must have been on a hook and escaped hundreds of times, if hundreds of experiments would suffice to impress the kind of brain which fails, after months of constant teaching, to learn the obstructive nature of a glass barrier. The idea that fish can learn from seeing others drawn out is absurd, since it credits them with powers both of indirect observation and logical reasoning. It may even be questioned if the so-called wisdom of fish is at all of the nature of intelligence, whether acquired by experience or by heredity, assisted by elimination. To a large extent the elusive actions of fish are mechanical responses to stimuli acting through acute senses; and when the effectiveness of the senses is reduced, as in darkness, the caution of the fish is proportionately diminished. There is nothing more certain, however, than that trout will continue to be credited with keen, conscious wisdom, accumulating with experience in old fish. It is necessary for the angler's story that it should be so, and that truth-loving person will not tamely be deprived of the groundwork of those moving dramas in which, with marvellous success, he matches his intelligence against the more than human sagacity of ancient fish.

OLD FAITHFUL

John Taintor Foote

1924

"And you never heard of Old Faithful?" George asked suddenly. "Evidently not, from what you said a while ago. Well, a lot of people have, believe me. Men have gone to the Cuddiwink district just to see him. As I've already told you, he lay beside a ledge in the pool below Horseshoe Falls. Almost nothing else in the pool. He kept it cleaned out. Worst sort of cannibal, of course – all big trout are. That was the trouble – he wanted something that would stick to his ribs. No flies for him. Did his feeding at night.

"You could see him dimly if you crawled out on a rock that jutted above the pool and looked over. He lay in about ten feet of water, right by his ledge. If he saw you, he'd back under the ledge, slowly, like a submarine going into dock. Think of the biggest thing you've ever seen, and that's the way Old Faithful looked, just lying there as still as the ledge. He never seemed to move anything, not even his gills. When he backed in out of sight he seemed to be drawn under the ledge by some invisible force.

"Ridgway – R. Campbell Ridgway – you may have read his stuff, Brethren of the Wild, that sort of thing – claimed to have seen him move. He told me about it one night. He said he was lying with just his eyes over the edge of the rock, watching the trout. Said he'd been there an hour, when down over the falls came a young red squirrel. It had fallen in above and been carried over. The squirrel was half drowned, but struck out feebly for shore. Well, so Ridgway said – Old Faithful came up and took Mister Squirrel into camp. No hurry; just came drifting up, sort of inhaled the squirrel and sank down to the ledge again. Never made a ripple, Ridgway said; just business.

"I'm telling you all this because it's necessary that you get an idea of that trout in your mind. You'll see why in a minute. No one ever had hold of him. But it was customary, if you fished the Cuddiwink, to make a few casts over him before you left the stream. Not that you ever expected him to rise. It was just a sort of gesture. Everybody did it.

"Knowing that Isabelle had never seen trout taken before, I made a day of it – naturally. The trail to camp leaves the stream just at the falls. It was pretty late when we got to it. Isabelle had her arms full of – heaven knows what – flowers and grass and ferns and fir branches and coloured leaves. She'd lugged the stuff for hours. I remember once that day I was fighting a fourteen-inch fish in swift water and she came to the bank and wanted me to look at a ripe blackberry – I think it was – she'd found. How does that strike you? And listen! I said, 'It's a beauty, darling.' That's what I said – or something like that. . . . Here, don't you pay that check! Bring it here, waiter!"

"Go on, George!" I said. "We haven't time to argue about the check. You'd come to the trail for camp at the falls."

"I told Isabelle to wait at the trail for a few minutes, while I went below the falls and did the customary thing for the edification of Old Faithful. I only intended to make three or four casts with the Number Twelve Fly and the hair-fine leader I had on, but in getting down to the pool I hooked the fly in a bush. In trying to loosen it, I stumbled over something and fell. I snapped the leader like a thread, and since I had to put on another, I tied on a fairly heavy one as a matter of form.

"I had reached for my box for a regulation fly of some sort when I remembered a fool thing that Billy Roach had given me up on the Beaverkill the season before. It was fully two inches long; I forget what he called it. He said you fished it dry for bass or large trout. He said you worked the tip of your rod and made it wiggle like a dying minnow. I didn't want the contraption, but he'd borrowed some fly oil from me and insisted on my taking it. I'd stuck it in the breast pocket of my fishing-jacket and forgotten it until then.

"Well, I felt in the pocket and there it was. I tied it on and went down to the pool. Now let me show you the exact situation." George seized a fork. "This is the pool." The fork traced an oblong figure on the tablecloth. "Here is Old Faithful's ledge." The fork deeply marked this impressive spot. "Here are the falls, with white water running to here. You can only wade to this point here, and then you have an abrupt six-foot depth. 'But you can put a fly from here to here with a long line,' you say. No, you can't. You've forgotten to allow for your back cast. Notice this bend here? That tells the story. You're not more than twenty feet from a lot of birch and what not, when you can no longer wade. 'Well then, it's impossible to put a decent fly on the water above the sunken ledge,' you say. It looks like it, but this is how it's done: right here is a narrow point running to here, where it dwindles off to a single flat rock. If you work out on the point you can jump across to this rock – situated right here – and there you are, with about a thrity-foot cast to the sunken ledge. Deep water all around you, of course, and the rock is slippery; but – there you are. Now notice this small cove, right here. The water from the falls rushes past it in a froth, but in the cove it forms a deep eddy, with the current moving round and round, like this.'' George made a slow circular motion with the fork. ''You know what I mean?'' I nodded.

''I got out on the point and jumped to the rock; got myself balanced, worked out the right amount of line and cast the dingaree Bill had forced on me, just above the sunken ledge. I didn't take the water lightly and I cast again, but I couldn't put it down decently. It would just flop in – too much weight and too many feathers. I suppose I cast it a dozen times, trying to make it settle like a fly. I wasn't thinking of trout – there would be nothing in there except Old Faithful – I was just monkeying with this doodle-bug thing, now that I had it on.

''I gave up at last and let it lie out where I had cast it. I was standing there looking at the falls roaring down, not thinking about anything in particular, when I remembered Isabelle, waiting up on the trail. I raised my rod preparatory to reeling in and the what-you-may-call-'im made a kind of a dive and wiggle out there on the surface. I reached for my reel handle. Then I realised that the thingamajig wasn't on the water. I didn't see it disappear, exactly; I was just looking at it, and then it wasn't there. 'That's funny,' I thought, and struck instinctively. Well, I was fast – so it seemed – and no snags in there. I gave it the butt three or four times, but the rod only bowed and nothing budged. I tried to figure it out. I thought perhaps a water-logged timber had come diving over the falls and upended right there. Then I noticed the rod take more of a bend and the line began to move through the water. It moved out slowly, very slowly, into the middle of the pool. It was exactly as though I was hooked onto a freight train just getting under way.

''I knew what I had hold of then, and yet I didn't believe it. I couldn't believe it. I kept thinking it was a dream, I remember. Of course, he could have gone away with everything I had any minute if he'd wanted to, but he didn't. He just kept moving slowly, round and round the pool. I gave him what pressure the tackle would stand, but he never noticed a little thing like that; just kept moving around the pool for hours, it seemed to me. I'd forgotten Isabelle; I admit that. I'd forgotten everything on earth. There didn't seem to be anything else on earth, as a matter of fact, except the falls and the pool and Old Faithful and me. At last Isabelle showed up on the bank above me, still lugging her ferns and what not. She called down to me above the noise of the falls. She asked me how long I expected her to wait alone in the woods, with night coming on.

"I hadn't had the faintest idea how I was going to try to land the fish until then. The water was boiling past the rock I was standing on, and I couldn't jump back to the point without giving him slack and perhaps falling in. I began to look around and figure. Isabelle said, 'What on earth are you doing?' I took off my landing-net and tossed it to the bank. I yelled, 'Drop that junk quick and pick up that net?' She said, 'What for, George?' I said, 'Do as I tell you and don't ask questions!' She laid down what she had and picked up the net and I told her to go to the cove and stand ready.

"She said, 'Ready for what?' I said, 'You'll see what presently. Just stand there.' I'll admit I wasn't talking quietly. There was the noise of the falls to begin with, and – well, naturally I wasn't.

"I went to work on the fish again. I began to educate him to lead. I thought if I could lead him into the cove he would swing right past Isabelle and she could net him. It was slow work – a three-ounce rod – imagine! Isabelle called, 'Do you know what time it is?' I told her to keep still and stand where she was. She didn't say anything after that.

"At last the fish began to come. He wasn't tired – he'd never done any fighting, as a matter of fact – but he'd take a suggestion as to where to go from the rod. I kept swinging him nearer and nearer the cove each time he came around. When I saw he was about ready to come, I yelled to Isabelle. I said, 'I'm going to bring him right past you, close to the top. All you have to do is to net him.'

"When the fish came round again, I steered him into the cove. Just as he was swinging past Isabelle the stuff she'd been lugging began to roll down the bank. She dropped the landing-net on top of the fish and made a dive for those leaves and grasses and things. Fortunately the net handle lodged against the bank, and after she'd put her stuff in a nice safe place she came back and picked up the net again. I never uttered a syllable. I deserve no credit for that. The trout had made a surge and shot out into the pool, and I was too busy just then to give her any idea of what I thought.

"I had a harder job getting him to swing in again. He was a little leery of the cove, but at last he came. I steered him toward Isabelle and lifted him all I dared. He came up nicely, clear to the top. I yelled, 'Here he comes! For god's sake, don't miss him!' I put everything on the tackle it would stand and managed to check the fish for an instant right in front of Isabelle.

"And this is what she did: it doesn't seem credible – it doesn't seem humanly possible; but it's a fact that you'll have to take my word for. She lifted the landing-net above her head with both hands and brought it down on top of the fish with all her might! . . . 'I didn't miss him, George,' I heard Isabelle say."

THE TROUT OF OLD
Izaak Walton

1653

You are to know, there is night as well as day fishing for a Trout, and that in the night the best Trouts come out of their holes; and the manner of taking them is, on the top of the water with a great lob or garden worm, or rather two, which you are to fish with in a place where the waters run somewhat quietly, for in a stream the bait will not be so well discerned. I say in a quiet or dead place near to some swift, there draw your bait over the top of the water, to and fro, and if there be a good Trout in the hole, he will take it, especially if the night be dark: for then he is bold and lies near the top of the water, watching the motion of any frog or water-rat or mouse that swims betwixt him and the sky; these he hunts after, if he sees the water but wrinkle or move in one of these dead holes, where these great old Trouts usually lie near to their holds: for you are to note, that the great old Trout is both subtle and fearful, and lies close all day, and does not usually stir out of his hold, but lies in it as close in the day as the timorous Hare does in her form; for the chief feeding of either is seldom in the day, but usually in the night, and then the great Trout feeds very boldly.

And you must fish for him with a strong line, and not a little hook; and let him have time to gorge your hook, for he does not usually forsake it, as he oft will in the day fishing. And if the night be not dark, then fish so with an artificial fly of a light color, and at the snap: nay, he will sometimes rise at a dead mouse, or a piece of cloth, or anything that seems to swim cross the water, or to be in motion. This is a choice way, but I have not often used it, because it is void of the pleasures that such days as these, that we two now enjoy, afford an angler.

YOUR FIRST SALMON
W. Senior (Red Spinner)

1890

THERE ARE SOME events in life never to be forgotten. You may not remember your first drubbing at school, your first stand-up collar, your first shave, your first kiss, your first client, your first appearance in print, or the incidents, weather, and so on, of your wedding day; but you cannot forget your first salmon. What a delicious remembrance it is!

There was, to be sure, something a trifle curious about mine. I was at Galway, as interesting a town as any in Ireland, and, as everyone who has looked over the railings of the bridge must know, a regular show-place for salmon. The bottom of the river seems paved with them, and you may be amused for hours, when the humour seizes the fish, by watching their antics as they shoot and circle and leap as if in the performance of a dance on the up-the-side-and-down-the-middle principle. At the eventful time to which I am referring the salmon fishing was over, for the Galway river is not one of the late kind. The proprietor of the fishery, however, with the ready courtesy of his class, freely allowed me to try my best for a brown trout, and wished me luck. This wish was gratified to my heart's content, and the little lad with the net had for a time no opportunity of dropping asleep. In the middle of the stream there was a shallow and a placid pool, surrounded by water rippling in the usual way over the stones. The fish below had ceased moving, and observing in the middle of this space the familiar expanding rings caused by a rising fish, I despatched my cast athwart.

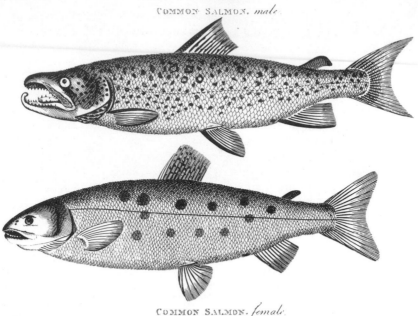

COMMON SALMON. *male*

COMMON SALMON. *female*

"Tug, tug," was instantly telegraphed down the butt of the rod: then there was a dull heavy strain.

Slowly at first, then at gathering speed, the small ebony winch made music. Straight across the pool, back again, here, there, and everywhere, the prey shot, churning the water into foam, and causing many another fish to leap into the air. Such a hullabaloo there never was. The boy shouted frantically. Workmen threw down their tools and rushed down, and in a few minutes a small crowd had collected. The fly rod was the lightest that could be made, the line finely tapered, the hooks extremely small, so that when half an hour had gone, and the evening had begun to absorb the light, and the commotion to rage as before, hope of a satisfactory finale departed. Perseverance, however, gave me the victory, although the battle would probably have been on the other side had I not prevailed upon Tim to flounder into the water and net the fish as he ran. The wonder was how a five-pound salmon could have created such a stir! Stooping to claim him, I found out the cause: he had been hooked in the back fin with a small coachman! The water was so low that in drawing the cast towards me I had fouled him in that singular manner. And this was how I caught my first salmon.

WHERE ROLLS THE ROGUE
Zane Grey

1928

THE HAPPIEST LOT of any angler would be to live somewhere along the banks of the Rogue River, most beautiful stream of Oregon. Then, if he kept close watch on conditions, he could be ready on the spot when the run of steelhead began. This peculiar and little-studied trout travels up streams and rivers flowing into the Pacific, all the way from northern California to British Columbia. During the run, which occurs at varying seasons according to locality, the steelhead are caught in abundance, on bait, salmon eggs, spinners, and spoons. But so far as I can learn they will rise to a fly in only two rivers, the Eel and the Rogue, particularly the latter. The Rogue is probably the outlet of Crater Lake, and is the coldest, swiftest, deepest stream I ever fished.

The singular difference in steelhead of different localities is probably a matter of water. The steelhead that runs up the Klamath, which is a stream of rather warm, yellow, muggy water, is less brilliantly colored than the Rogue steelhead, and certainly not to be compared with him as a game fish. Many anglers claim that rainbow trout and steelhead trout are one and the same species. My own theory is that the rainbow is a steelhead which cannot get to the sea. He is landlocked. And a steelhead is a rainbow that lives in the salt water and runs up fresh-water streams to spawn. Once the whole western part of the continent was submerged. As the land became more and more elevated through the upward thrust of the earth the salt water receded, landlocking fish in lakes and streams. The rainbow might be a species that survived.

The relation of the two fish has never been satisfactorily established. But one thing seems assured – to fly fishermen who know the Rogue River, the steelhead is the most wonderful of all fish.

I first heard of steelhead through Mr Lester, a salmon fisherman of long experience. He was visiting Long Key, Florida, and happened to tell me of his trip to Oregon and his adventure on the Rogue. He said he could not hold these steelhead – that when they were hooked they began to leap downstream through the rapids, and had to be followed. The big ones all got away. They smashed his tackle. Now this information from a noted salmon angler was exceedingly interesting. That happened six years ago. I made a trip to Oregon and found the Rogue beautiful beyond compare, but there seemed to be no fish in it. Two years ago R.C. and I ventured again, along about the end of June. Forked-tail trout and Chinook salmon had begun to appear, but no steelhead. They were expected any time. R.C. and I could not catch even the less desirable fish that had already come. We persevered, but all to no purpose.

The summer, 1922, recorded a different story. Upon our return from Vancouver and Washington we reached Grants Pass, Oregon, just when the run of steelhead was on. This was in September, and Lone Angler Wiborn had accompanied us. Fishermen friends we had made there assured us that we had struck it just right and were in for the sport of our lives. Fred Burnham, of California, surely one of the greatest of fly fishermen, was there, and he, in company with several of the native experts, kindly took upon themselves the burden of showing us how and where.

We had the finest of tackle, but only two fly-rods in the collection that would do for steelhead. Too light! And not one of our fly-reels would hold a third enough line. There were no reels of American manufacture that would do for this great fish. We had to have English reels that would hold a hundred yards of linen line besides the thirty or forty yards of casting line. These steelhead ran, we were told. All our flies were too small. Number fours and sixes were used, and Royal Coachman, Professor, Brown Hackle were advised as a start. I had a very old Kosmic fly-rod, nine and a half feet, eight ounces, that took the eye of these gentlemen anglers. Burnham had a hundred rods, but said he would cheerfully steal my Kosmic if I did not sleep with it. We rigged up seven-ounce Hardy rods for R.C. and Lone Angler. All this fuss and care and deliberation over a lot of fishing-tackle seems to many people an evidence of narrow, finicky minds. It is nothing of the kind. It is unalloyed joy of anticipation, and half of pleasure. If anyone should claim it a remarkably expensive procedure, I could not gainsay that.

Next morning we got up in the dark, and had breakfast at five o'clock in a little all-night restaurant, and were on the way up the river to Pierce Riffle before daylight. The morning was cool and gray. Forest fires were burning in the mountains and the fragrant odor of pine filled the air. Gradually the day broke, and when we turned off the road and ran down to the river the red of sunrise tipped the timbered peaks. A fringe of trees bordered the river and hid it from sight until we penetrated them.

The roar of swift, heavy waters greeted me before I saw the long green-and-white rapid that bore the name Pierce Riffle. Upstream the broad river glided round a wooded curve, and hurrying and constricting its current slid into a narrow channel with a mellow roar. A long flat bar of gravel led down to the water, and on the other shore the current rushed deep and strong, chafing at a rocky willow-skirted bank. The whole disturbance of water was perhaps a quarter of a mile long. Below the riffle opened out a magnificent broad stretch of river. The white water poured into it. There was a swift current, and dancing waves for a hundred yards, after which the water quieted and glided smoothly on toward the curve where the river disappeared. A faint violet light glimmered over the river. Most striking of all, however, were the significant widening circles and agitated spots of the placid surface upstream, and the hard splashes in the swift current before us, and below at the head of the big pool the sight of many fish breaking water, frequently several at once, trout of varying size, and steelhead that showed their beautiful colors, and occasionally a huge salmon. Certain it was that, what with trying to see all this and rig my tackle at the same time, I missed threading my line through at least two guides on my rod.

Lone Angler, true to his instincts, slipped off alone downstream; R.C. headed for the middle of the riffle, while Wharton led me up to the wide sweep of water where the river glided into the rapids. I had only hip boots and could not wade far out. Wharton wore waders and went in above his waist. Then he began to cast his fly, reaching fifty, sixty, and even seventy feet. Out there in the middle and beyond was where the steelhead lay. Even had I been able to wade out there I could not have cast far enough. At once I saw the very high degree of skill required. My spirits and hopes suffered a shock, and straightaway I felt discouraged. Nevertheless, for a while I divided my time between trying to cast my fly afar and watching Wharton at work. He claimed he was not a fine fly-caster, although he could reach the distance. But that morning the steelhead were not striking. After long patient efforts he tried one of the tiny brass spinners, without any better success. Eventually the sun grew hot and the fish stopped breaking and playing on the surface. R.C. and Lone Angler had found no luck. We gave up and started back to town. Wharton advised us to try it in the afternoon, from four o'clock until dark.

The day grew very hot and oppressive. The mountains appeared shrouded in smoke. Oregon was in the grip of a very severe hot, dry spell of weather, and was sadly in need of rain.

By two o'clock we were on our way up the river, and this time we strolled beyond Pierce Riffle to see an irrigation dam where, we had heard, salmon and steelhead congregated in great numbers and were visible. The concrete structure was indeed a fine piece of work, but we hardly more than glanced at it.

A board walk crossed the river on top of this dam. From the road, high up, we could see the fish leaping, and we ran over one another to get down on that bridge. Water was streaming through cracks in the gates. Evidently this dam had been built across a rocky formation in the river bed. Below stood up narrow ridges of rocks, and between two of these ran a channel of swift water, dropping every few rods over a ledge. This channel was alive with steelhead. First we saw them leaping up the white foamy falls; then we found them in corners and eddies of the channel, and lastly we stood right over a place where we could see hundreds of these wonderful fish. Not more than thirty feet below us! Shallow swift water ran over smooth rock, and swirled in a deep eddying pool, and then rushed on to take the first fall. Here had congregated the mass of steelhead. They had gone the wrong side of the dam to get up, for the fish ladder was at the other shore of the river. Every moment a steelhead would dart up the swift water and leap against the concrete wall, to fall back. The average weight of these fish appeared to be about six to seven pounds, but we saw many of ten and twelve pounds, and a few larger still. They were of different colors, some dark-backed, others yellow, most of them speckled gray-green. Whenever one turned on his side, then we caught the beautiful pink and silver gleam.

We crossed the river to find on the other side a wide deep pool below the apron of the dam, and up out of this led the zigzag fish ladder, an admirable waterway of many little steps, whereby the fish could get up over the dam. By watching sharply, we were able now and then to see the dark flash of fish in the white water. Hovering and wavering in the pool were large purple shadows, big salmon waiting for night to take their turn at the fish ladder. Occasionally one of these huge salmon would swoop up in the current, and lazily expose his back to the sun and to our fascinated gaze. One would have weighed more than sixty pounds. As he loomed up he gleamed purple, then darker, shading to brown, and when he came out into the light he seemed to have a greenish-black back covered with dots, and his tail looked a foot wide.

"Say, if we could only drop a line to him!" ejaculated R.C.

Speech was inadequate to express what I felt. Almost I regretted the law and the huge white sign which forbade fishing within four hundred feet of this dam. We idled there watching, and then we went back across the dam to where the steelhead were leaping and splashing. At last R.C. and Wiborn had to drag me away from there.

Five o'clock was it instead of four when we arrived at Pierce Riffle. Dusky and hot lay the somber smoky glare over the river. But the water would be like ice.

No fish appeared to be breaking. Possibly the steelhead had moved up-stream. We were told that they arrived in schools, tarried at a riffle or rapid, and passed on during the night. But any day might bring a new and fresher school.

We were on our own hook, so to speak, this afternoon, and therefore more leisurely, more independent, and less keyed up. R.C. was at the head of the riffle in less time than it takes to tell it; Lone Angler took a long while to get into new waders, and I wasted a good deal of time over my tackle. This afternoon I wore hobnailed shoes over stockings, dispensing altogether with rubber, and I was rather loath to enter that ice-cold water. Still the day had been so hot that I should have welcomed the coldest of water. My brother started out with a spinner, and he had not made a dozen casts before he raised a fish.

We did not need his yell to gather that he had apparently hooked a moving avalanche underwater. His rod jerked down and shook like a buggy-whip swinging a heavy lead. I could not hear his reel, but I did not have to hear it to know his line was flying off. Floundering out with great strides, he began to run down the gravelly shore. Right even with us then we saw a black threshing fish split the white water and disappear. R.C.'s rod sprang up like a released sapling. Gone! He waved a sorrowful hand at us and began to reel in. R.C. waded back as far as he dared into the swift heavy current, and began again to cast, quartering across the river, so that his line bagged and drifted down the current, dragging the spinner.

Lone Angler and I waded in at the head of the great pool. Industriously I plied my fly, cast after cast, sometimes executing a good one, until in half an hour I grew tired and discouraged. Steelhead began to leap in the shadow of the willow bank just opposite me. I waded in to my hips, until I had difficulty in keeping my balance in that swift current, and I cast desperately to reach the coveted distance. But always I fell short several yards.

Presently a newcomer appeared on the scene, a little man in farmer

241

garb, with an old straw hat and a pointed beard. He had a cane pole fully twenty feet long. At the butt he had a reel attached, and I saw the big shiny spinner dangling from his line. Some rods above us he labored out on a rocky point, and thrust the enormous pole out over the river. It seemed as though it might reach across. The spinner floated down the length of line he had out, about as long as his pole, and sank from sight. Then this native fisherman stood motionless like Ajax defying the lightning. I wondered skeptically and disdainfully what he imagined he was going to catch. Then in about two minutes he gave a jerk and his long pole bent. Something was pulling mighty hard on his line. But he made short shift of that fish, dragged it ashore and up on the bank, a steelhead of about five pounds. Again he thrust the huge telegraph pole out over the river. Fascinated, I watched him. Just as I feared, pretty soon he had another strike. I saw the pole jerk and curve. This fish was heavier and a fighter. I saw it smash the current and scoot through the water like an arrow. The native endeavoured to be as ruthless and violent as with his first fish. He tried literally to drag the steelhead out. I had hard work to control myself, to keep from yelling to him to play the fish. But he bent the huge pole double, dragged a big white tumbling fish in among the rocks in shallow water, and floundered after it. Disaster attended his awkward and uncouth attempt. The steelhead broke the line and got away. Then the old Oregonian exhibited some peevishness. He looked and acted as if a shabby trick had been played upon him. I was tickled and could almost hear him mutter: "Wal, by Jimmy! I'd 'a' hed thet one if he hedn't busted my line."

He disappeared in the willows and I went back to my own fishing. But presently I heard a sousing splash near me, and looked around to see another native standing in the water above me, holding out a cane pole fully as long as the other fellow's. What was more and worse, that pole was bent. This native had hooked a fish. Suddenly I felt the line rub along my legs. Amazed and angry, I waded back. Then I heard the well-known swish of a taut line cutting water. The man waded down and back, lifted his line over my head, and went ashore. He followed that fish along the shore, and presently pulled it out on the sand, a fine steelhead. Then he approached his former position. I saw him stick some kind of bait on his spinner. When he got to his place above me he cast this out and let it down, and held his rod stationary. I could see his line and it was not three feet from where I stood.

Now what would happen? I looked for Lone Angler and R.C. Both of them waved at me, and not at all sympathetically. In a few moments that native angler hooked another steelhead right by my feet. And he went ashore, and downstream with it, landing a seven-pounder in less than seven minutes. He came back, and soon he had another on. This was too much. It filled me with despair. I changed my fly for a spinner and began to cast that. It seemed to me that I might just as well have had an onion on for bait. Presently the native picked up another steelhead, right off my boots, and this one turned out to be a big one. It made a leap on the first run, a splendid diving leap, came out again fifty feet farther down, and churned the water white again. The fisherman was not able to get ashore quickly enough, so that he could run and follow this fish and it took out all his line and broke off.

"Thet there was a twelve-pounder," he told me as he came back. "Ketched two like him yestiddy down below. Ain't you hevin' any luck?"

I acquainted him with the direful state of my angling fortunes, whereupon he gave me a small crawfish and told me to put that on. Gratefully I did so. I fished alongside of him with great expectancy, but nothing happened to either of us. The steelhead had quit biting.

Sunset had passed, and the dusky violet and purple lights fell over mountains and river. R.C. reported a fish hooked and lost, and Lone Angler said he had not caught anything but scenery.

The next day found us faithfully on the job, but the morning yielded nothing. In the afternoon we went again to the dam to see the steelhead and salmon. Again we were delighted and dejected by sight of wonderful schools of fish. We idled there for two hours, and then we returned to Pierce Riffle.

The sun was westering low and showed a dull magenta through the pall of smoky haze. The river seemed a moving medium of rose and lilac, incredible to the eye. Hot and oppressive, the dry air was full of odorous penetrating fragrance. Not a single fisherman marred the beautiful landscape for us. The loneliness, the charm of the place, the mellow changing roar of the rapids, and the leaping of steelhead everywhere inspired us once more to hope and action.

R.C. got there first, and on his initial cast he raised something big. I saw his spoon hit the water, and then something strike it. A wide breaking swirl attested to the power of the fish. How incredibly fast he shot downstream! R.C. had no time to move out of his tracks before the fish was gone.

I was the last to get ready, and before I stepped into the water R.C. had another strike – missed – and Lone Angler had a steelhead on. It took him the whole length of the swift water, and farther still, not a leaping fish, but a good one of five pounds. This sudden windfall of luck changed the aspect of things. With thrilling zest we at it, and I held to my desire to catch a steelhead on a fly. The difficulties I had discovered at first hand, and the fact that few steelhead, comparatively, were taken on a fly, spurred me on to an accomplishment of that worthy feat.

R.C. soon struck another snag in the shape of a salmon. One of the heavy Chinook appropriated his spoon and started away from that place. Valiantly and wondrously my brother performed and pursued, but that salmon had a jaw of iron and an unconquerable spirit. He could not be held.

"Looks as if I were going to get mine today," said R.C. to me. "Thought I could lick anything with this tackle."

He had rigged up one of my green Leonard bait-rods, nine and one half feet, ten ounces, that I had built for bonefish, with a good-sized reel full of silk line. He waded in above me, made a wonderful cast clear across the river into the shade of the willows, and a big steelhead leaped out with the spoon in his mouth. Sharp and hard R.C. came up on him, and out he sprang again, a curved quivering opal shape, flashing the ruddy diamond drops of water. I let out a whoop and R.C. yelled, "Run, you son-of-a-gun –run!"

R.C. never moved from his tracks. He held his rod well up, and apparently lightly thumbed the reel. I could hear it screech – screech – screech. Below us stretched the hundred yards of swift water, white and choppy close at hand, and gradually quieting down into the broad deep pool. That steelhead tumbled over the white waves in the most bewildering exhibition I had ever seen. He did not seem to go under at all. He danced like a will-o'-the-wisp, like a twisting light, over and over, with a speed unbelievable. He surely ran that hundred yards in less than ten seconds. He ended this run with a big high leap. Then he sounded.

R.C. came wading down to me. His face was beaming in spite of its tensity. His eyes were alight.

"Say, did you ever see the beat of that? Sure, this steelhead game has got me," he said. "Run, you Indian! That's what all this line is for."

Before the steelhead slowed down he ran off another hundred yards of line. Then R.C. waded out and went with him downstream. Lone Angler accompanied him, and then I, unable to withstand the temptation, waded out, laid down my tackle, and joined them. R.C. gave an admirable performance with that steelhead, handling him perfectly, and eventually beaching him far around the curve of the big pool. Seven and one half pounds!

We went back to the rapid, and in a very few moments R.C. had hooked another, a different kind of fighter. He did not leap and he wanted to go upstream. What with bucking that swift current and R.C.'s strain on the line he soon tired, and gradually dropped down to the still water. There he was dragged over the shoal and landed. Six and one half pounds.

My ethical ambition expired for the time being and I put on a spinner. I made, more or less, nine hundred casts without avail. Then as I was letting my line drift, looking back at Lone Angler, totally unprepared for anything, I had a most tremendous strike. Thirty yards of fly-casting line went by the board in a flash and the green linen line followed. I burned my fingers and thumbs. All the hundred yards of linen line whizzed off the reel. Then this thunderbolt of a fish slowed up. Seizing the opportunity, I nearly drowned myself wading ashore below where I should have gone. Then I ran along the river, downstream. Soon I found that my fish had snagged the line on the bottom. How sickening was that realization! I worked for a long time to save the line, and finally did so, but the steelhead was gone. Never will I forget that strike.

The run of a bonefish, after he is hooked, is certainly great, but this strike of a steelhead is all run. You have no choice but to run yourself. That day indeed was a red-letter day along the Rogue.

Next day Burnham took us up the river, five miles beyond the dam, to a place he called the Suspension Bridge. A couple of wire cables sagged across the water between high banks, and to these were attached loops of chicken-fence wire, which in turn supported some rotten loose boards. The contrivance must have been as old as the oldest Oregon pioneer; it swayed at every step, and was certainly alarming to one unused to it. Burnham had a lot of fun leading us across this bridge, and I was sure he started it swaying by his own movements.

The stretch of Rogue River here was Burnham's favorite place. No wonder! It surpassed any stretch of fishing water I ever encountered. The bank from which we had crossed was high, a rocky rugged cliff, green with moss and vines, and covered on top with heavy timber, consisting in part of giant pines. The bank we approached was high, too, but sloping, and we descended it through thickets to the shallow rocky-floored stream. A narrow riffle roared at the head of this stretch, and sent its swift current along the far shore under the cliff, and through deep channels cut in the flat of the stream bed.

R.C. and Wiborn waded out to the riffle. I saw the former hook and lose a steelhead in the white water. Then I essayed to follow Burnham. I had a task. He stood over six feet tall and wore seven-league wading-boots, and deep or shallow was all the same to him. He worked downstream.

Nevertheless, here was a place where I could wade out as far as I liked and reach all but the farthermost spots. For a hundred yards out the water ran scarcely a foot deep over level rock, and led to where the deep ruts and channels and lanes could be reached. These deeper aisles in the rocky formation of the river bed were wonderful places to fish. The water ran dark and eddying through them. The river here was very wide, bank full, so that no bars or gravel beds or ragged rocks showed from one green shore to the other. The farther down we progressed the more beautiful grew the forest-topped cliff. Meadow larks and orioles sang melodiously in the trees, accompanied by the low murmur of the swift water. White ships of clouds sailed in the blue sky, and the sunlight shone golden on the foliage.

The steelhead were not there or would not rise. Burnham said this stretch seldom failed and we should keep on. What a wonderful sight to see him cast a fly! It fascinated me. It seemed so easy. His fly gleamed like a spark of gold in the sun. It shot out and back, forward and back, and his line seemed to wave, to undulate, to sweep up in a great curve, and at last stretch out low over the water, to drop the deceiving wisp of feathers like thistledown. He always cast quartering a little across the channel so that the bag in his line would drag the fly faster than the current. He said a steelhead rose to a fly and followed it downstream, and struck it so hard that it hooked itself. Twice he raised fish, and both times he let out a lusty yell. But he missed them, to my great disappointment.

Toward the lower end of that magnificent stretch of river the water deepened somewhat and the channels appeared harder for me to reach with a fly. I could not cast over into the shady ruts under the cliff, and it was here that Burnham was raising fish. I would make half a dozen attempts, and that meant at least six sweeps of my rod for each cast, and then I would rest my tired arm and watch Burnham.

I came to a place Burnham had left for me, a joining of two dark channels above a flat rock, behind which swirled and eddied the most haunting and beautiful little pool imaginable. It was fully sixty feet away, a prodigious cast for me. But I essayed it, more in the persistence and pride of practice than in a hope of raising a fish. Straining nerve and muscle, I swept my rod forward and back, forward and back, watching my fly, letting out more line, until I reached the limit. The fly dropped perfectly. I saw it sink and float under the surface, and then as the current caught the bag of line it dragged my fly a little more swiftly. The sight pleased me.

Then out of the dark eddying depths of that pool loomed a shape, dim at first, gathering color and life, until it became the reality of a steelhead, huge and broad as he swerved half over to follow the fly, shining pink and silver through the water. My heart leaped to my throat. Just as he reached the fly I jerked – and pulled it away from him. The action was involuntary. Then one instant I thrilled and shook, and the next my heart turned to lead and I groaned at my stupidity. Many and many a time I cast again over that pool, but all to no avail.

Suddenly my attention was attracted by Burnham's yell, and then shouts of onlookers up on the cliff opposite his position. He had hooked a steelhead. I saw it leaping. He called for me to hurry down and take the rod. I yelled back no. But he insisted. By the time I covered the goodly stretch of distance between us the fish had stopped leaping. But he had out nearly all of Burnham's line. So I took his rod, much to the amusement and interest of the audience on the cliff, and I waded after that steelhead. It took me fully a quarter of an hour to get back that line, and longer to lead the steelhead ashore. My left arm felt dead. The fish was not large, but on Burnham's light rod he was indeed heavy.

After that we fished down to the end of the stretch of good water, with no success. Then we waded to the narrow shore and headed back toward the bridge.

Next day the three of us tried Pierce Riffle again, and struck another off day. The following morning we left at daylight to motor twenty-five miles down the river to meet Burnham at the end of the road.

Our drive over the rugged bluffs above the Rogue, and the accidents we had, and the times we lost the way, would make a story. All I have space for is mention of the picturesque beauty of the Rogue River below Grants Pass. The farther we went and the higher we climbed the more beautiful grew the vistas of river, seen through the iron-walled gorges, or winding white-wreathed between dark and lofty timbered mountains, or meandering through a wide fertile valley of golden cornfields and fertile orchards.

Eventually we found the end of the road and the ranch where Burnham was staying. Late that afternoon he took us to a place called Chair Riffle, where the night before he and a Mr Carlon had taken a dozen steelhead.

Naturally we were both excited and elated. Chair Riffle owed its name to a chair-shaped stone, on which an angler could sit and fish to his heart's content. This stretch of the Rogue revealed a long wide sweep of water, running four feet deep over gravel beds, where the steelhead lay in certain currents. They loved swift water. Burnham said it was necessary to learn where they lay. This evening, however, they did not lie anywhere in that riffle. They had moved on. We were too late. But I enjoyed sitting in the stone chair, watching, and listening to the river. This was wild country. I saw cougar and bear tracks along the shore, and deer were numerous. The mountains were high, cone-shaped, heavily timbered on some slopes. From this point on through the Coast Range to the Pacific there was unsettled rugged country, full of game and fish.

Next day Burnham and Mr Carlon extended themselves in efforts to see that I hooked a steelhead on a fly. I enjoyed these kindly sportsman-like offices, but in my secret heart I did not believe the fish god himself could connect me with a steelhead. But you never can tell!

Toward sunset we motored several miles back upstream from the ranch, to Mr Carlon's favorite fishing water. It was at the foot of a rapid that foamed in many white channels around and between many little islands, all of which were covered by a long heavy green grass. Burnham took Lone Angler and R.C. up above this rapid, while Mr Carlon rowed a skiff through tortuous swift channels and in all kinds of difficult places in order to get me just where he wanted me. In half a dozen spots he held the boat and instructed me to cast here and there. What swirling eddies, and holes under shelving rocks, and little deep pools overhung by willows! Always behind us on the other side of the ledges of rock was the main roaring white channel.

At last this genial and indefatigable gentleman hauled the boat up on the edge of a rocky island, right in the middle of the lower fall of the rapid. Below us a long irregular sunken ledge of rock divided the deep-heavy water from the eddies and pools on the other side.

"Never have I failed to catch a steelhead here," he said. "You must cast farther. Watch me."

Then he swept his line out over the water without letting it touch, farther and farther, with a wonderful grace and skill. It undulated as had Burnham's, only in longer higher waves, and it seemed instinct with life. Reeling in, he took a position directly behind me, and grasping my rod hand he gave my wrist quick powerful jerks, getting my line out with the sweep that had characterized his. In a few moments he had taught me the swing of it.

"Now try it," he said, finally, turning toward the channel of swift deep water. "Cast across and down. Don't drop your fly until it is as far out as you can cast. Then let it float down along that ledge."

I complied to the best of my new-found ability, succeeding fairly well in reaching the spot designated. But I did not see my fly float under the ledge. The ruddy glow of sun on the water dazzled my eyes.

"There! You raised one!" shouted Carlon.

Then my rod sprang down, straightened by a violent tug, so energetic and electrifying that I was astounded. The scream of my reel told me what had happened. I swept up the rod to feel the strong pull of a steelhead taking line. Carlon called something that I could not distinguish above the roar of the water. But I thought he said the fish was leaping. Facing directly in the sun, I was dazzled and could not see downstream. My fish took a hundred yards of line, out into that swift channel, and there he hung. As good luck would have it, R.C. and Lone Angler with Burnham came along down the rocky shore and provided me with an inspiring audience.

If moments could be wholly all-satisfying with thrills and starts, and dreads and hopes, and vague, deep, full sense of the wild beauty of environment, and the vain boyish joy in showing my comrades my luck and my skill – if any moments of life could utterly satisfy, I experienced them then. It took what seemed a very long time to tire and lead that steelhead, but at last I accomplished it. When he bored under the ledge of rock he alarmed me considerably, and evidently worried Carlon, who wanted to take me in the boat and row around the ledge. This I feared might be needful, and was about to comply when the steelhead came out where I could lead him over the ledge. For five minutes he swam in the shallows below me, showing plainly, dark-backed, rosy-sided, gradually slowing in action until he turned on his side, his broad tail curling, his fins waving. That was the moment to have released him. I had the motive, but not the unselfish appreciation of him and his beautiful Rogue – not that time. He had been too hard to catch and there across the river stood those comrades of mine. Instead I lifted him up in the sunlight for them to see.

OL' SETTLER OF DEEP HOLE

Irving Bacheller

1900

UNCLE EB was a born lover of fun. But he had a solemn way of fishing that was no credit to a cheerful man. It was the same when he played the bass viol, but that was also a kind of fishing at which he tried his luck in a roaring torrent of sound. Both forms of dissipation gave him a serious look and manner, that came near severity. They brought on his face only the light of hope and anticipation or the shadow of disappointment.

We had finished our stent early the day of which I am writing. When we had dug our worms and were on our way to the brook with pole and line, a squint of elation had hold of Uncle Eb's face. Long wrinkles deepened as he looked into the sky for a sign of the weather, and then relaxed a bit as he turned his eyes upon the smooth sward. It was no time for idle talk. We tiptoed over the leafy carpet of the woods. As soon as I spoke he lifted his hand with a warning "Sh-h!" The murmur of the stream was in our ears. Kneeling on a mossy knoll we baited the hooks; then Uncle Eb beckoned to me.

I came to him on tiptoe.

"See that there foam 'long side o' the big log?" he whispered, pointing with his finger.

I nodded.

"Cre-e-ep up jest as ca-a-areful as ye can," he went on whispering. "Drop in a leetle above an' let 'er float down."

Then he went on, below me, lifting his feet in slow and stealthy strides.

He halted by a bit of driftwood and cautiously threw in, his arm extended, his figure alert. The squint on his face took a firmer grip. Suddenly his pole gave a leap, the water splashed, his line sang in the air, and a fish went up like a rocket. As we were looking into the tree tops it thumped the shore beside him, quivered a moment, and flopped down the bank. He scrambled after it and went to his knees in the brook, coming up empty handed. The water was slopping out of his boot legs.

"Whew!" said he, panting with excitement as I came over to him. "Reg'lar ol' he one," he added, looking down at his boots. "Got away from me – consarn him! Hed a leetle too much power in the arm."

He emptied his boots, baited up, and went back to his fishing. As I looked up at him he stood leaning over the stream jiggling his hook. In a moment I saw a tug at the line. The end of his pole went under water like a flash. It bent double as Uncle Eb gave it a lift. The fish began to dive and rush. The line cut the water in a broad semicircle and then went far and near with long, quick slashes. The pole nodded and writhed like a thing of life. Then Uncle Eb had a look on him that is one of the treasures of my memory. In a moment the fish went away with such a violent rush that, to save him, he had to throw his pole into the water.

"Heavens an' airth!" he shouted, "the ol' settler!"

The pole turned quickly and went lengthwise into the rapids. He ran down the bank and I after him. The pole was speeding through the swift water. We scrambled over logs and through bushes, but the pole went faster than we. Presently it stopped and swung around. Uncle Eb went splashing into the brook. Almost within reach of the pole he dashed his foot upon a stone, falling headlong in the current. I was close upon his heels and gave him a hand. He rose hatless, dripping from head to foot, and pressed on. He lifted his pole. The line clung to a snag and then gave way; the tackle was missing. He looked at it silently, tilting his head. We walked slowly to the shore. Neither spoke for a moment.

"Must have been a big fish," I remarked.

"Poweiful!" said he, chewing vigorously on his quid of tobacco as he shook his head and looked down at his wet clothing. "In a desp'rit fix, ain't I?"

"Too bad!" I exclaimed.

"Seldom ever hed sech a disapp'intment," he said. "Ruther counted on ketchin' thet fish – he was s' well hooked."

He looked longingly at the water a moment. "If I don't go hum," said he, "an' keep my mouth shet I'll say sumthin' I'll be sorry fer."

He was never quite the same after that. He told often of his struggle with this unseen, mysterious fish, and I imagined he was a bit more given to reflection. He had had hold of the "ol' settler of Deep Hole." – a fish of great influence and renown there in Faraway. Most of the local fishermen had felt him tug at the line one time or another. No man had ever seen him, for the water was black in Deep Hole. No fish had ever exerted a greater influence on the thought, the imagination, the manners or the moral character of his contemporaries. Tip Taylor always took off his hat and sighed when he spoke of the "ol' settler." Ransom Walker said he had once seen his top fin and thought it longer than a razor.

Ransom took to idleness and chewing tobacco immediately after his encounter with the big fish, and both vices stuck to him as long as he lived. Everyone had his theory of the "ol' settler." Most agreed he was a very heavy trout. Tip Taylor used to say that in his opinion "'twas nuthin' more'n a plain, overgrown, common sucker," but Tip came from the Sucker Brook country where suckers lived in colder water and were more entitled to respect.

Mose Tupper had never had his hook in the "ol' settler," and would believe none of the many stories of adventure at Deep Hole that had thrilled the township.

"Thet fish hes made s' many liars 'round here ye dunno who t' b'lieve," he had said at the corners one day, after Uncle Eb had told his story of the big fish. "Somebody 't knows how t' fish hed oughter go 'n ketch him fer the good o' the town – thet's what I think."

Now Mr Tupper was an excellent man, but his incredulity was always too bluntly put. It had even led to some ill-feeling.

He came in at our place one evening with a big hook and line from "down east" – the kind of tackle used in salt water.

"What ye goin' t' dew with it?" Uncle Eb inquired.

"Ketch thet fish ye talk s' much about – goin' t' put him out o' the way."

" 'Tain't fair," said Uncle Eb, "it's reedic'lous. Like leading a pup with a log chain."

"Don't care," said Mose, "I'm goin' t' go fishin' t' morrer. If there reely is any sech fish – which I don't believe there is – I'm goin' t' rassle with him an' mebbe tek him out o' the river. Thet fish is sp'ilin' the moral character o' this town. He oughter be rode on a rail – thet fish hed."

How he would punish a trout in that manner Mr Tupper failed to explain, but his metaphor was always a worse fit than his trousers – and that was bad enough.

It was just before haying, and, there being little to do, we had also planned to try our luck in the morning. When, at sunrise, we were walking down the cow path to the woods, I saw Uncle Eb had a coil of bed cord on his shoulder.

"What's that for?" I asked.

"Wall," said he, "goin' t' hev fun anyway. If we can't ketch one thing we'll try another."

We had great luck that morning, and when our basket was near full we came to Deep Hole and made ready for a swim in the water above it. Uncle Eb had looped an end of the bed cord and tied a few pebbles on it with bits of string.

"Now," said he presently, "I want t' sink this loop t' bottom an' pass the end o' the cord under the driftwood so 't we can fetch it 'crost under water."

There was a big stump, just opposite, with roots running down the bank into the stream. I shoved the line under the drift with a pole and then hauled it across, where Uncle Eb drew it up the bank under the stump roots.

"In 'bout half an hour I cal'late Mose Tupper'll be 'long," he whispered. "Wisht ye'd put on yer clo's an' lay here back o' the stump an' hold on t' the cord. When ye feel a bite give a yank er two an' haul in like Sam Hill – fifteen feet er more quicker 'n scat. Snatch his pole right away from him. Then lay still."

Uncle Eb left me shortly, going up stream. It was near an hour before I heard them coming. Uncle Eb was talking in a low tone as they came down the other bank.

"Drop right in there," he was saying, "an' let her drag down, through the deep water, deliberate like. Git clus t' the bottom."

Peering through a screen of bushes, I could see an eager look on the unlovely face of Mose. He stood leaning toward the water and jiggling his hook along the bottom. Suddenly I saw Mose jerk and felt the cord move. I gave it a double twitch and began to pull. He held hard for a jiffy and then stumbled and let go, yelling like mad. The pole hit the water with a splash and went out of sight like a diving frog. I brought it well under the foam and driftwood. Deep Hole resumed its calm, unruffled aspect. Mose went running toward Uncle Eb.

"'S a whale!" he shouted. "Ripped the pole away quicker 'n lightnin'."

"Where is it?" Uncle Eb asked.

"Tuk it away f'm me," said Mose. "Grabbed it jes' like thet," he added, with a violent jerk of his hand.

"What d' he dew with it?" Uncle Eb inquired.

Mose looked thoughtfully at the water and scratched his head, his features all a-tremble.

"Dunno," said he. "Swallered it mebbe."

"Mean t' say ye lost hook, line, sinker 'n pole?"

"Hook, line, sinker, 'n pole," he answered mournfully. "Come nigh haulin' me in tew."

" 'Tain't possible," said Uncle Eb.

Mose expectorated, his hands upon his hips, looking down at the water.

"Wouldn't eggzac'ly say 'twas possible," he drawled, "but 'twas a fact."

"Yer mistaken," said Uncle Eb.

"No, I hain't," was the answer, "I tell ye I see it."

"Then if ye see it, the nex' thing ye orter see 's a doctor. There's sumthin' wrong with you sumwheres."

"Only one thing the matter o' me," said Mose, with a little twinge of remorse. "I'm jest a natural born perfec' dum fool. Never c'u'd b'lieve there *was* any sech fish."

"Nobody ever said there was any *sech* fish," said Uncle Eb. "He's done more t' you 'n he ever done t' me. Never served me no sech trick as thet. If I was you I'd never ask nobody t'b'lieve it. 'S a leetle tew much."

Mose went slowly and picked up his hat. Then he returned to the bank and looked regretfully at the water.

"Never see the beat o' thet," he went on. "Never see sech power 'n a fish. Knocks the spots off any fish I ever hearn of."

"Ye riled him with that big tackle o' yourn," said Uncle Eb. "He wouldn't stan' it."

"Feel jest as if I'd hed holt uv a wil' cat," said Mose. "Tuk the hull thing – pole an' all – quicker 'n lightnin'. Nice a bit o' hickory as a man ever see. Gol' durned if I ever hearn o' the like o' that, *ever*."

He sat down a moment on the bank.

"Got t' rest a minute," he remarked. "Feel kind o' wopsy after thet squabble."

They soon went away. And when Mose told the story of the "swallered pole" he got the same sort of reputation he had given to others. Only it was real and large and lasting.

"Wha' d' ye think uv it?" he asked, when he had finished.

"Wall," said Ransom Walker, "wouldn't want t' say right out plain t' yer face."

" 'Twouldn't be p'lite," said Uncle Eb soberly.

"Sound a leetle ha'sh," Tip Taylor added.

"Thet fish has jerked the fear o' God out o' ye – thet's the way it looks t' me," said Carlyle Barber.

"Yer up 'n the air, Mose," said another. "Need a sinker on ye."

They bullied him – they talked him down, demurring mildly, but firmly.

"Tell ye what I'll do," said Mose sheepishly, "I'll b'lieve you fellers if you'll b'lieve me."

"What, swop even? Not much!" said one, with emphasis. "'Twouldn't be fair. Ye've ast us t' b'lieve a genuwine out 'n out *im*possibility."

Mose lifted his hat and scratched his head thoughtfully. There was a look of embarrassment in his face.

"Might a ben dreamin'," said he slowly. "I swear it's gittin' so here 'n this town a feller can't hardly b'lieve himself."

"Fur's my experience goes," said Ransom Walker, "he'd be a fool 'f he did."

"'Minds me o' the time I went fishin' with Ab Thomas," said Uncle Eb. "He ketched an ol' socker the fust thing. I went off by myself 'n got a good-sized fish, but 'twa'nt s' big 's hisn. So I tuk 'n opened his mouth 'n poured in a lot o' fine shot. When I come back Ab he looked at my fish 'n begun t' brag. When we weighed 'em mine was a leetle heavier.

"'What!' says he. ''Tain't possible thet leetle cuss uv a trout's heavier 'n mine.'

"''Tis sartin,' I said.

"'Dummed deceivin' business,' said he, as he hefted 'em both. 'Gittin' so ye can't hardly b'lieve the stillyurds.'"

255

THE
ANGLER'S WORLD

CAT FISHING IN THE OHIO RIVER

John J. Audubon

1835

IT IS WITH mingled feelings of pleasure and regret that I recall to my mind the many pleasant days I have spent on the shores of the Ohio. The visions of former years crowd on my view, as I picture to myself the fertile soil and genial atmosphere of our great western garden, Kentucky, and view the placid waters of the fair stream that flows along its western boundary. Methinks I am now on the banks of the noble river. Twenty years of my life have returned to me; my sinews are strong, and the "bow-string of my spirit is not slack;" bright visions of the future float before me as I sit on a grassy bank, gazing on the glittering waters. Around me are dense forests of lofty trees and thickly tangled undergrowth, amid which are heard the songs of feathered choristers, and from whose boughs hang clusters of glowing fruits and beautiful flowers. Reader, I am very happy. But now the dream has vanished, and here I am in the British Athens, penning an episode for my Ornithological Biography, and having before me sundry well-thumbed and weather-beaten folios, from which I expect to be able to extract some interesting particulars respecting the methods employed in those days in catching Cat-fish.

But, before entering on my subject, I will present you with a brief description of the place of my residence on the banks of the Ohio. When I first landed at Henderson in Kentucky, my family, like the village, was quite small. The latter consisted of six or eight houses; the former of my wife, myself, and a young child. Few as the houses were, we fortunately found one empty. It was a log-*cabin*, not a log-*house*; but as better could not be had, we were pleased. Well, then, we were located. The country around was thinly peopled, and all purchasable provisions rather scarce; but our neighbours were friendly, and we had brought with us flour and bacon-hams. Our pleasures were those of young people not long married, and full of life and merriment; a single smile from our infant was, I assure you, more valued by us than all the treasures of a modern Croesus would have been. The woods were amply stocked with game, the river with fish; and now and then the hoarded sweets of the industrious bees were brought from some hollow tree to our little table. Our child's cradle was our richest piece of furniture, our guns and fishing-lines our most serviceable implements, for although we began to cultivate a garden, the rankness of the soil kept the seeds we planted far beneath the tall weeds that sprung up the first year. I had then a partner, a "man of business," and there was also with me a Kentucky youth, who much preferred the sports of the forest and river to either day-book or ledger. He was naturally, as I may say, a good woodsman, hunter, and angler, and, like me, thought chiefly of procuring supplies of fish and fowl. To the task accordingly we directed all our energies.

Quantity as well as quality was an object with us, and although we well knew that three species of Cat-fish existed in the Ohio, and that all were sufficiently good, we were not sure as to the best method of securing them. We determined, however, to work on a large scale, and immediately commenced making a famous "trot-line." Now, reader, as you may probably know nothing about this engine, I shall describe it to you.

A trot-line is one of considerable length and thickness, both qualities, however, varying according to the extent of water, and the size of the fish you expect to catch. As the Ohio, at Henderson, is rather more than half a mile in breadth, and as Cat-fishes weigh from one to a hundred pounds, we manufactured a line which measured about two hundred yards in length, as thick as the little finger of some fair one yet in her teens, and as white as the damsel's finger well could be, for it was wholly of Kentucky cotton, just, let me tell you, because that substance stands the water better than either hemp or flax. The main line finished, we made a hundred smaller ones, about five feet in length, to each of which we fastened a capital hook of KIRBY and Co.'s manufacture. Now for the bait!

It was the month of May. Nature had brought abroad myriads of living beings: they covered the earth, glided through the water, and swarmed in the air. The Cat-fish is a voracious creature, not at all nice in feeding, but one who, like the vulture, contents himself with carrion when nothing better can be had. A few experiments proved to us that, of the dainties with which we tried to allure them to our hooks, they gave a decided preference, at that season, to *live toads*. These animals were very abundant about Henderson. They ramble or feed, whether by instinct or reason, during early or late twilight more than at any other time, especially after a shower, and are unable to bear the heat of the sun's rays for several hours before and after noon. We have a good number of these crawling things in America, particularly in the western and southern parts of the Union, and are very well supplied with frogs, snakes, lizards, and even crocodiles, which we call alligators; but there is enough of food for them all. and we generally suffer them to creep about, to leap or to flounder as they please, or in accordance with the habits which have been given them by the great Conductor of all.

During the month of May, and indeed until autumn, we found an abundant supply of toads. Many "fine ladies," no doubt, would have swooned, or at least screamed and gone into hysterics, had they seen one of our baskets filled with these animals, all alive and plump. Fortunately we had no tragedy queen or sentimental spinster at Henderson. Our Kentucky ladies mind their own affairs, and seldom meddle with those of others farther than to do all they can for their comfort. The toads, collected one by one, and brought home in baskets, were deposited in a barrel for use. And now that night is over, and as it is the first trial we are going to give our trot-line, just watch our movements from that high bank beside the stream. There sit down under the large cottonwood tree. You are in no danger of catching cold at this season.

My assistant follows me with a gaff hook, while I carry the paddle of our canoe; a boy bears on his back a hundred toads as good as ever hopped. Our line – oh, I forgot to inform you that we had set it last night, but without the small ones you now see on my arm. Fastening one end to yon sycamore, we paddled our canoe, with the rest nicely coiled in the stern, and soon reached its extremity, when I threw over the side the heavy stone fastened to it as a sinker. All this was done that it might be thoroughly soaked, and without kinks or snarls in the morning. Now, you observe, we launch our light bark, the toads in the basket are placed next to my feet in the bow; I have the small lines across my knees all ready looped at the end. NAT, with the paddle, and assisted by the current, keeps the stern of our boat directly down stream; and DAVID fixes, by the skin of the back and hind parts, the living bait to the hook. I hold the main line all the while, and now, having fixed one linelet to it, over goes the latter. Can you see the poor toad kicking and flouncing in the water? "No" – well, I do. You observe at length that all the lines, one after another, have been fixed, baited, and dropped. We now return swiftly to the shore.

"What a delightful thing is fishing!" have I more than once heard some knowing angler exclaim, who, with "the patience of Job," stands or slowly moves along some rivulet twenty feet wide, and three or four feet deep, with a sham fly to allure a trout, which, when at length caught, weighs half a pound. Reader, I never had such patience. Although I have waited ten years, and yet see only three-fourths of the Birds of America engraved, although some of the drawings of that work patiently made so long ago as 1805, and although I have to wait with patience two years more before I see the end of it, I never could hold a line or a rod for many minutes, unless I had – not a "nibble," but a hearty bite, and could throw the fish at once over my head on the ground. No, no – If I fish for trout, I must soon give up, or catch, as I have done in Pennsylvania's Lehigh, or the streams of Maine, fifty or more in a couple of hours. But the trot-line is in the river, and there *it* may patiently wait, until I visit it toward night. Now I take up my gun and note-book, and, accompanied by my dog, intend to ramble through the woods until breakfast. Who knows but I may shoot a turkey or a deer? It is barely four o'clock; and see what delightful mornings we have at this season in Kentucky!

Evening has returned. The heavens have already opened their twinkling eyes, although the orb of day has yet scarcely withdrawn itself from our view. How calm is the air! The nocturnal insects and quadrupeds are abroad; the bear is moving through the dark cane-brake, the land crows are flying towards their roosts, their aquatic brethren towards the interior of the forests, the squirrel is barking his adieu, and the Barred Owl glides silently and swiftly from his retreat, to seize upon the gay and noisy animal. The boat is pushed off from the shore; the main-line is in my hands; now it shakes; surely some fish have been hooked. Hand over hand I proceed to the first hook. Nothing there! But now I feel several jerks stronger and more frequent than before. Several hooks I pass; but see, what a fine Cat-fish is twisting round and round the little line to which he is fast! NAT, look to your gaff – hook him close to the tail. Keep it up, my dear fellow! – there now, we have him. More are on, and we proceed. When we have reached the end many goodly fishes are lying in the bottom of our skiff. New bait has been put on, and, as we return, I congratulate myself and my companions on the success of our efforts; for there lies fish enough for ourselves and our neighbours.

A trot-line at this period was perfectly safe at Henderson, should I have allowed it to remain for weeks at a time. The navigation was mostly performed by flat-bottomed boats, which during calm nights floated in the middle current of the river, so that the people on board could not observe the fish that had been hooked. Not a single steamer had as yet ever gone down the Ohio; now and then, it is true, a barge or a keel-boat was propelled by poles and oars; but the nature of the river is such at that place, that these boats when ascending were obliged to keep near the

Indiana shore, until above the landing of the village, (below which I always fixed my lines), when they pulled across the stream.

Several species or varieties of Cat-fish are found in the Ohio, namely the Blue, the White, and the Mud Cats, which differ considerably in their form and colour, as well as in their habits. The Mud Cat is the best, although it seldom attains so great a size as the rest. The Blue Cat is the coarsest, but when not exceeding from four to six pounds, it affords tolerable eating. The White Cat is preferable to the last, but not so common; and the Yellow Mud Cat is the best and rarest. Of the blue kind some have been caught that weighed a hundred pounds. Such fishes, however, are looked upon as monsters.

The form in all the varieties inclines to the conical, the head being diproportionately large, while the body tapers away to the root of the tail. The eyes, which are small, are placed far apart, and situated as it were on the top of the forehead, but laterally. Their mouth is wide, and armed with numerous small and very sharp teeth, while it is defended by single-sided spines, which, when the fish is in the agonies of death, stand out at right angles, and are so firmly fixed as sometimes to break before you can loosen them. The Cat-fish has also feelers of proportionate length, apparently intended to guide its motions over the bottom, whilst its eyes are watching the objects passing above.

Trot-lines cannot be used with much success unless during the middle stages of the water. When very low, it is too clear, and the fish, although extremely voracious, will rarely risk its life for a toad. When the waters are rising rapidly, your trot-lines are likely to be carried away by one of the numerous trees that float in the stream. A "happy medium" is therefore best.

When the waters are rising fast and have become muddy, a single line is used for catching Cat-fish. It is fastened to the elastic branch of some willow several feet above the water, and must be twenty or thirty feet in length. The entrails of a Wild Turkey, or a piece of fresh venison, furnish good bait; and if, when you visit your line the next morning after you have set it, the water has not risen too much, the swinging of the willow indicates that a fish has been hooked, and you have only to haul the prize ashore.

One evening I saw that the river was rising at a great rate, although it was still within its banks. I knew that the White Perch were running, that is, ascending the river from the sea, and, anxious to have a tasting of that fine fish, I baited a line with a cray-fish, and fastened it to the bough of a tree. Next morning as I pulled in the line, it felt as if fast at the bottom, yet on drawing it slowly I found that it came. Presently I felt a strong pull, the line slipped through my fingers, and next instant a large Cat-fish leaped out of the water. I played it for a while, until it became exhausted, when I drew it ashore. It had swallowed the hook, and I cut off the line close to its head. Then passing a stick through one of the gills, I and a servant tugged the fish home. On cutting it open, we, to our surprise, found in its stomach a fine White Perch, dead, but not in the least injured. The Perch had been lightly hooked, and the Cat-fish after swallowing it, had been hooked in the stomach, so that, although the instrument was small, the torture caused by it no doubt tended to disable the Cat-fish. The Perch we ate, and the Cat, which was fine, we divided into four parts, and distributed among our neighbours. My most worthy friend and relative, NICHOLAS

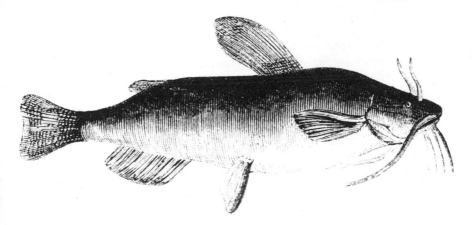

BERTHOUD, Esq., who formerly resided at Shippingport in Kentucky, but now in New York, a better fisher than whom I never knew, once placed a trot-line in "the basin" below "Tarascon's Mills," at the foot of the Rapids of the Ohio. I cannot recollect the bait which was used; but on taking up the line we obtained a remarkably fine Cat-fish, in which was found the greater part of a sucking pig!

THE FISH CHEF OF THE OLD "OLYMPIC"; THE PASSIONATE FISHERMEN OF HAUTE SAVOIE

Negley Farson

1933

IT IS A HARD CHOICE to make, but I almost believe the Frenchman is a more implacable fisherman than either the English or American. We all know de Maupassant's story of the two old comrades who went to fish outside the walls during the siege of Paris, were captured by the Germans and shot as spies, after which the jeering Germans ate their fish. And on the eve of this last war, the very last week before it, in fact, I fished in a slack water behind an island below Strasbourg with an old Frenchman in his rowboat, with the French soldiers climbing up ladders to their lookouts in the trees, staring malevolently at similar German sentries across the racing Rhine. We were using maggots to catch fish none of which could be larger than a long cigar; but this innkeeper-fisherman had invested his life's savings to buy a pub in this particular spot – so that he could follow his hobby in his off-hours (they were more off than on!) – and now, he complained bitterly, the dirty Boche would one day cross the pontoon bridge and . . . he would never fish again.

"Or perhaps they will merely use a cannon and shoot me where I am!"

He would not move, however, until that day.

I do not know whether anyone else has ever witnessed it, but I have never seen one of those French fishermen catch anything but the bottom where the Seine flows through Paris. Yet think how many businesses were being neglected, how many of those useful French wives were tending shop, while these Frenchmen, by their hundreds, sat on the banks of the Seine with the scantiest hope that they could bring something home that would justify them for a wasted day. I call that courage.

If you drive down across France in the spring, when the streams are full and the leaves are their bright vivid green, you will sometimes think that half of France must be out with rod and grub or worm. You will see (at least, you did one day) the Frenchmen sitting by their poplar-lined canals. Sometimes, with a little lead minnow with a hook in its tail. You will see them leaning over the shore-end of a bridge by some fresh river, jerking their rod up and down, up and down, up and down. . . . They are fishing for yellow perch. And many a time I have got out of my car and watched these Frenchmen. I have an affinity with them – and an equal anxiety as to what they might be about to catch. I know the black-barred perch; and the spectacle of one of these Frenchmen always recalled spring days in a canoe on the windy lake back home. Ask them a pertinent question. And the Frenchman, seeing you are a knowledgable angler, responds with a discourse on local habits.

Finally you are both rewarded; he has got one! '*Eh, bien! M'sieu – demi-kilo!*' And some stocky, jovial Frenchman of the Midi, free from all inhibitions concerning the social values of fishing, will inform you that this monster he is holding up must weigh at least a pound.

I have found, on such occasions, that if you go with this Frenchman (and his trophy) to his favourite little sidewalk café in some sunbaked village square that you will come nearer to his heart – what he really thinks about life and politics – than you possibly could by bribe or guile. He feels, as a fellow fisherman, that he can talk straight with you. You have the common bond. And if you happen to be on a journey in which time is of no importance he will introduce you in the evening to the members of his village fishing club. There is hardly a village in all France which does not have one.

These clubs are not altogether unknown in either England or America, but they are extremely rare. In France they are an institution. Many of them are for more than merely the local coarse fish; they exist in the trout regions where their democracy is just as unblemished. This is particularly true in Haute Savoie, where the swift green rivers race down through the pine forests and grey crags; and where, in most other countries, you would find every foot of such water owned by some rich proprietor. I had passed in and out of Paris for years, often with weeks to spare, wondering whether it was worth the bother to find where I could buy the right to fish for trout, and then always giving it up because it seemed too complicated. Then by an off-chance I picked a tiny village high up in the mountains of Haute Savoie to settle down in and write my book on South America. And here I found the poor trout fisherman's heaven.

As I drove past Lake Annecy I stopped at the local fishing shop to see what kind of flies they were using, and get some. I was amazed at the "elegance" of this little tackle shop, its window display, its show-cases, its long line of rods – it might have been in Pall Mall or St. James's Street.

There was such a professional competence in its air. But what gave me such a start, almost a shock, was that when the proprietor turned round to speak to me from a cast he was tying I found myself looking at the twin brother of the little bicycle-and-tackle shop man I had left only a few days before back in Somerset.

Later, when we were fishing one of the mountain rivers together, I told him about this. But this day when I waited for him to straighten up I found that he couldn't; he was a hunchback. And later, on the river, he told me why he could never stand upright again; he had been "hunchbacked" on the Somme – shot through the spine. Not only that, but when our acquaintance improved he took me to the fine little hotel he had once owned in Annecy, and had sold so that he could run just his small tackle shop. "You may think me a fool, *M'sieu*, but I am a completely happy man. In the hotel I made money – but in my shop I *live!*" On the river one luncheon time, when we ate on the bouldered bank with an eagle soaring high overhead, he told me that he was a member of the Cross of Fire, the Hooded Men, the most violent Fascist organisation in all France – and that his brother had just come out from serving three months in prison, because twenty-six rifles had been found in their house.

He was the finest fly-fisher I have ever seen.

"But these flies, *M'sieu!*" he exclaimed when I went out to my car that first day and brought back my bag, "are not the ones for here! *Pas ici!* What do you think of these?"

I told him I had never in my life seen the like of those he was showing me. He was immensely pleased. "They are," he said . . . half closing his eyes like some composer searching for a chord . . . "a few experiments that I have made myself. . . . I would suggest that you try them."

I never go into a tackle shop without coming out ruined. But on that day, because I did not know he was so genuine, I bought only three or four casts and a dozen or so of his gnat-like experiments (whose look I did not trust at all), thanking him for mere politeness' sake. When he asked me where I was going to live in the mountains, and I told him about fifty miles up, he again closed his eyes.

"Too far, *M'sieu* . . . unless you are a goat. The river is full of gorges up there. You will never get down them. Even *I* find it almost impossible."

I withheld my smile, staring at this satyr-like little creature before me, and listened patiently while he made me write down the names of some villages where, he told me, I should begin fishing lower down. Then with light sarcasm I asked him how could I fish those stretches of water – when

I was not going to live in an hotel or an inn anywhere along that lower stretch. He replied with amazement: "The Club!"

He then wrote down the name of a Frenchman in each of some five small villages and wished me good luck. "Perhaps, *M'sieu*," he said modestly, "we might have a day on the river together?"

As this is a more or less accurate account of our conversation that impatient afternoon, for I was anxious to get on, I will merely state that I noticed the name of each Frenchman he gave me was obviously the proprietor of some inn or café (for which I thought he was pimping) and that I lost his own card, which he pressed upon me, even before I reached my own little pub, The Golden Lion.

So much for snap judgments.

A few days later I slid my car down to where the gorges ceased and entered a café. Its proprietor and a hefty daughter were serving what appeared to be the village postman, its policeman, and one or two other non-uniformed gentlemen, with some demi-litres of white wine. I asked if I could speak to the president of the village fishing club. The hairy-armed man behind the bar said that this was he. Could he do anything for me? I replied that I would like to fish this stretch of river; how much would it be? I was asked for how long? I said, possibly a couple of days – maybe more. Were there any fish here?

At that I noticed that the postman, the policeman, and the other non-uniformed gents had stopped speaking since I came in. Now I saw them staring at me intently. I was being appraised. I began to feel uncomfortable. . . .

The fat, hairy-armed man behind the bar smiled. Then he shrugged his shoulders. He said – looking at the others – "There *are* fish. . . ." He left that statement hanging in the air; and if ever I have been told more plainly to my face, "There are fish – providing you know how to catch them," I don't want to be reminded of it. The others now turned from regarding me and took up their conversation again. It was a bad beginning. I paid fifteen francs a day, I think, for a week's fishing, drank a polite demi-litre of white wine, and left the hotel. It required all my courage to ask the proprietor did he mind if I left my car, for safe-keeping, before his hotel. He said no, he didn't mind. That was all.

The rivers up there are all snow-fed, many of them are glacial; so that even in mid-summer you will find long, swift stretches where it is hard to wade. Up by the Golden Lion, as the little satyr in Annecy had prophesied, there were gorges. And sides so steep that it was torture to get down to fish the few pools that lay between them. I had tried. I had slipped and slid down through the heavy pine forests (almost breaking my rod) to fish a few of these pools – but there was no way that I could find to get either down or up to fish the next pool. Nothing but a steep climb up the mountain-side, a walk along the mountain road, and then another descent to get down to fish another pool. I found it no good. Not for me. Although the proprietor of the Golden Lion (that excruciating man) did exclaim when I brought home a few fish from my first attempt: "There! You see I was not lying when I wrote to you that my hotel had kilometres of fine trout fishing!"

But down here was the beginning of orchard country, and alpine wheat. The river was broad, with long beds of grey boulders that now lay bare in the sun. There were farms on one side and slopes of steep pine forest on the other, and grey iron-streaked cliffs. An inspiring country. As I put my rod together and soaked the cast I saw long stickles and channels of water coursing between the islands made by boulders bared by the falling water. There were long broad sweeps where the river was apple-green. And, very wisely, I put on the satyr's cast.

These were light-backed trout with vivid red spots, which struck (when they did strike) with a vicious intensity. This river was not a glacial one, and in that ice-clear water I could watch a large part of their fight. In one deep stretch of river, where it was so flat and slow that it was almost like a shallow lake, I got the best fish of the afternoon by putting on an old worn Mayfly. It was a freak attempt, but continuous rises under the branches of some trees on the far side of the pool tempted me. It was about all I could do, wading out till the water seeped over into my waders (and how cold it was!), to get my fly across to them. Time and again I watched it float, unnoticed, down under the branches; then there was a quick splash. I walked backward up on to the island of boulders again. After an exciting few minutes' fight I netted a fine little fish that was over $1\frac{1}{2}$ lb.

But although I can say I have scarcely ever seen such fine trout water, I did not touch many trout. The reason explained itself about 5 o'clock, when I saw a man emerge from the bushes opposite me (I had crossed the river to the opposite side from the village) and fix a wood grub to a reel-less line that was wrapped around an ordinary bamboo rod. He pitched this grub in and let it drift down to a pool that I had been casting over, which began under a leaning tree. Dumbfounded – I recognised him as one of the non-uniformed gentlemen I had seen at mid-day sitting in the inn – dumbfounded, I say, and a little angry, I saw him pull out a nice nine- or ten-inch trout.

Such competition was too formidable. I watched Frenchman after Frenchman appear, fix on a grub (I learned they got them from Geneva) and pop it into the water. It seemed as if the whole village was down by 6 o'clock, including the postman. I gave it up. I had eight fish, none of which was up to half a pound, except the one lucky one; yet I felt I could now walk with impunity back to that village inn. And there, tired, I sat down at a table before its arboured door and ordered a litre of white wine.

The hefty daughter came out to serve me, smiling now. "*Et vous? M'sieu – bonne chance?*"

I pulled aside the grass inside my bag and showed her the big one. The next person who came out was the proprietor: "*Bien?*" he asked.

I repeated my performance – with the one big fish. He did not say anything. But, as I had not taken my rod apart – it was leaning against the car – he walked over, and picked it up. He tried it with his wrist. Then (and I watched him do that so carefully) I saw him looking at the flies. He nodded. Then he came back and sat down at the table beside me, tapping it idly with his fingers.

'Where did you get that one?" he asked, meaning my one big fish.

So that's the way it began. I was there a couple of months that summer, writing my book; and every afternoon I fished the streams or rivers around me. I have seldom found more congenial, pithy companions than these Frenchmen of the village fishing clubs. The presidency of the club, I learned, was an honour which was supposed to rotate yearly. The proprietors of the village inns or cafés always took it in turn – because it brought such customers! The return from the river always led direct to the café, where the day's luck was discussed. For this it was necessary to have a demi-litre, perhaps several demi-litres of white wine. They were not all grub fishermen. An occasional elderly man (perhaps the village doctor) would amble back with a fly rod, and make some acid remarks about the rest of the company.

But they all loved fishing. They loved talking about fishing even more, perhaps; but they loved just fishing itself so much that it was not long before I discovered that any stretch of river within an easy walk of one of these villages was simply fished to death. Talk about "too many rods on the water"; their bamboo poles looked almost like a fence at times.

And so, as his name was like a legend along the river, I called up the little hunchback down in Annecy. Should we, I asked, have a day's fishing on the river together? He asked me to wait a moment. He always called his chubby red-haired little wife "*Mon petit*" (as fat Sacha Guitry used to call his beloved Yvonne Printemps); and I could hear him cajoling her now – the discussion obviously being, would she look after the store? Then his bright voice came back to me:

"Of a certainty! Tomorrow, 9 o'clock precisely, I shall meet you at –"

He was at loss for name, for, he said, "there is no village there". But he gave me a rendezvous about fifteen miles below where I had been fishing all the time! "I shall wait for you by the road," came his eager injunction; "I have a little red Citroën coupé – stop when you see it!"

By now I had reached that place in the confidence of M. Vacheron, proprietor of the *Lion d'Or*, to know that he had been the "fish chef" on the old *Olympic*. He had cooked in the "private" restaurant, that *de luxe* dining-room, where millionaires and movie stars gorged themselves across the Atlantic. They had seventeen chefs for, on the average, only thirty-eight people. He was a distinguished man.

"Mr Pierpont Morgan", said M. Vacheron, "*always* ordered oysters *au gratin* and lobster Newberg."

This night, learning that I was to fish with the celebrated M. Croisier, he wondered if it might not be possible for me to bring some of my trout back alive – as some of the Frenchmen did in these parts with a little barrel or tin can of water on their backs. I firmly told him no; we would have to continue in our usual way. I did not intend to burden myself in these rough streams with any additional pounds of wobbling water.

"Very well," sighed M. Vacheron; "I would like to cook you the true *truite au bleu*. But for that I must have them alive. I cook them alive and then clean them afterwards. If you cannot bring them back alive, then you must mark the two or three you have caught last – the last to die – and I shall do with these. These I shall cook. The colour will not be *truite au bleu* – but they will taste almost as good."

M. Vacheron lived over his past, with the aid of many cognacs, every night; and now, dejected because of my refusal to provide him with live trout, he declared: "The golden age of cooking is over, M. Farson. It is the sauces. Truffles and cream and butter – even the big restaurants aren't so free with these any more. From our point of view (the chefs') probably the finest restaurant in the world was the old Café Royal in London when Mrs Nobel owned it . . . Ah . . . everything! . . . hundreds of truffles . . . all the

butter you wanted . . . if a dish was not precisely correct . . . you threw it in
the fire. . ."

"And some of the dishes we used to prepare. . . . The *Crêpes Veux-tu?* . . . !
They were pancakes cooked in apricot brandy . . . with lizards done on
them in meringue . . . with cherry eyes . . . and then little piles of fresh
peaches and pine-apple piled up all around. . . ! "

As we sat in his kitchen, where he held these nightly reminiscences, the
rain ran in rivers down its window panes. There had been a cloud-burst
that day. And we had seen a staggering thing – a farmhouse up on the
Alpine meadow behind us struck by lightning. It was one of those Swiss-
chalet affairs, with broad stones holding down the shingles of its roof. It
went up in one grand blaze as if a high explosive had hit it. We had
watched it from our balcony.

Its owners were away, having just taken their cattle to graze on a higher
alpine slope. "And now," said the sophisticated M. Vacheron, "they have
lost all their money – it is burning there now – for, M. Farson, you know a
French peasant never puts his money in a bank. He doesn't trust banks."

I, selfishly, was only worried about this rain; would it spoil my day
tomorrow with M. Croisier? I awoke early to a clear blue sky over the
glistening pine forest, drank my bowl of coffee, leapt into the car – and
swerved and slithered down the slippery mountain road to where I found a
little red Citroën almost lying on its side in a ditch in a deep forest twenty-
five miles below. M. Croisier was in an exultant mood: "We shall have a
fine day!"

The only habitation we passed that day was a saw-mill. For mile after
mile the river sides here were too steep for farming. That is why there were
no villages. That is why there were so many trout. But M. Croisier fished
in a peculiar way: he fished with a wet fly, up-stream, throwing the fly
directly ahead of him. He got thirty-seven trout and I got, I think,
seventeen.

But what fishing!

We cast with lines not much longer than our rods. We fished behind
every rock, boulder, ledge. And M. Croisier even took fish from dead
against the bank. Tap-Tap-Tap went M. Croisier.

"But! " I protested at first, "you don't leave your flies on the water long
enough for any fish to touch them! "

The little hunchbacked man smiled: "Do not worry, M. Farson. If the
trout are there – I shall get them."

The point was, he explained, that where the stream was so swift, and especially after this cloud-burst in the upper mountains, the trout just *couldn't* leave any lee they had found – that was why, he said, we would find so many of them right up against the bank. And again, if we let our lines rest on the water for more than an instant, we would have our casts swept back against our own waders. "No! – it must be like that!" –'and he put his flies behind a rock before us just as if they were on the end of a wand.

I have never seen anything like it.

Nor have I ever seen anything like his eagerness. There were one or two fairly large pools or riffles that we approached. But before I could get up to them the little satyr raced on ahead of me. He couldn't resist it. "*Pardon, M'sieu!*" he always said, apologising for his selfishness – then raced me to the next pool just the same. The forest, rocks, glistening racing water, were all so fresh that sun-filled morning, with the white clouds scudding across the blue sky overhead, that I felt too full of the sheer joy of living to mind what he did – but, I decided, the next time M. Croisier and I went out *I* would put on running shoes.

There was a pool by the saw-mill, with some logs in it which were waiting to be cut. Here M. Croisier put his fly rod down and took a short little rod, about the size of a section of trout rod, from his back. It was a stout little piece, with an off-cast wire loop at its tip. This, said the satyr, was a "Dandinet". He then took from his bag a wooden spreader very similar to those you see in tackle-shops around which are wound hand-lines for sale. But on this one was nothing but yards and yards of stout gut – just, let us say, some sixty or a hundred yards of a cast. And on the end of this M. Vacheron slid a little lead minnow – after which he attached a hook to the end of the gut.

"You see," he said, giving it a flick, "I can cast this anywhere."

The little lead minnow shot through the air . . . the gut unwound off the spreader as easily as a thread-line off a Silex reel, and *plunk!* the minnow fell into the pool, say, about forty yards from us. The instant it hit the water M. Croisier was already winding it in with swift revolutions of the wooden spreader. And this he did with the speed with which you would bring back your Devon with a bait-casting reel.

A fish took the minnow. When it jumped I saw the lead minnow shoot yards up the gut-line. "You see", exulted the expert M. Croisier, "when the minnow shoots up the line they have nothing to shake against. . . ."

It was purely for my amusement, he said, that he had brought the "Dandinet" along. And then to show me what he really could do with it, he shot the minnow upstream where the river entered the pool. And again he retrieved it. "But this, M. Farson . . . is not like fly fishing!"

I still had a lot of my two months to go, and this was the beginning of a friendship. M. Croisier told me that – and very plainly.

The way it came about was that at the end of the day, before we began the long walk back to our cars, for we had been fishing upriver all this time, we reached a village. Here, after a stiff climb up the river bank. M. Croisier and I rested ourselves in its small inn's yard. We had a few litres of white wine. And during this I attempted to pay for some casts and flies I had borrowed from him on the river. He held up his little hand in dismay:

"M. Farson! No! In my little shop in Annecy, I shall charge you for *everything – beaucoup!* But on the river, M. Farson . . . on the river we are comrades!"

It was a gesture from *la belle France* I shall never forget.

CANAL TRAVEL

Robert Louis Stevenson

c. 1890

IT WAS A FINE, green, fat landscape; or rather a mere green water-lane, going on from village to village. Things had a settled look, as in places long lived in. Crop-headed children spat upon us from the bridges as we went below, with a true conservative feeling. But even more conservative were the fishermen, intent upon their floats, who let us go by without one glance. They perched upon sterlings and buttresses, and along the slope of the embankment, gently occupied. They were indifferent like pieces of dead nature. They did not move any more than if they had been fishing in an old Dutch print. The leaves fluttered, the water lapped, but they continued in one stay like so many churches established by law. You might have trepanned every one of their innocent heads, and found no more than so much coiled fishing-line below their skulls. I do not care for your stalwart fellows in india-rubber stockings breasting up mountain torrents with a salmon rod; but I do dearly love the class of man who plies his unfruitful art, for ever and a day, by still and depopulated waters.

FISHING IN ABYSSINIA

Sir Samuel W. Baker

1867

IN THE AFTERNOON I arranged my tackle, and strolled down to the pool to fish. There was a difficulty in procuring bait; a worm was never heard of in the burning deserts of Nubia, neither had I a net to catch small fish; I was, therefore, obliged to bait with pieces of hippopotamus. Fishing in such a pool as that of the Atbara was sufficiently exciting, as it was impossible to speculate upon what creature might accept the invitation; but the Arabs who accompanied me were particular in guarding me against the position I had taken under a willow-bush close to the water, as they explained, that most probably a crocodile would take me instead of the bait; they declared that accidents had frequently happened when people had sat upon the bank either to drink with their hands, or even while watching their goats. I accordingly fished at a few feet distant from the margin, and presently I had a bite; I landed a species of perch about two pounds weight; this was the "boulti," one of the best Nile fish mentioned by the traveller Bruce. In a short time I had caught a respectable dish of fish, but hitherto no monster had paid me the slightest attention; accordingly I changed my bait, and upon a powerful hook, fitted upon a treble-twisted wire, I fastened an enticing strip of boulti. The bait was about four ounces, and glistened like silver; the water was tolerably clear, but not too bright, and with such an attraction I expected something heavy. My float was a large-sized pike-float for live bait, and this civilised sign had been only a few minutes in the wild waters of the Atbara, when, bob! and away it went! I had a very large reel, with nearly three hundred yards of line that had been specially made for monsters; down went the top of my rod as though a grindstone was suspended on it, and, as I recovered its position, away went the line, and the reel revolved, not with the sudden dash of a spirited fish, but with the steady determined pull of a trotting horse. What on earth have I got hold of? In a few minutes about a hundred yards of line were out, and as the creature was steadily, but slowly, travelling down the centre of the channel, I determined to cry "halt!" if possible, as my tackle was extremely strong, and my rod was a single bamboo. Accordingly, I put on a powerful strain, which was replied to by a sullen tug, a shake, and again my rod was pulled suddenly down to the water's edge. At length, after the roughest handling, I began to reel in slack line, as my unknown friend had doubled in upon me, and once more putting severe pressure upon him or her, as it might be, I perceived a great swirl in the water about twenty yards from the rod. The tackle would bear anything, and I strained so heavily upon my adversary that I soon reduced our distance; but the water was exceedingly deep, the bank precipitous, and he was still invisible. At length, after much tugging and counter-tugging, he began to show; eagerly I gazed into the water to examine my new acquaintance, when I made out something below, in shape between a coach-wheel and a sponging-bath; in a few more moments I brought to the surface an enormous turtle, well hooked. I felt like the old lady who won an elephant in a lottery: that I had him was certain, but what was I to do with my prize? It was at least a hundred pounds weight, and the bank was steep and covered with bushes; thus it was impossible to land the monster, that now tugged and dived with the determination of the grindstone that his first pull had suggested. Once I attempted the gaff, but the trusty weapon that had landed many a fish in Scotland broke on the hard shell of the turtle, and I was helpless. My Arab now came to my assistance, and at once terminated the struggle. Seizing the line with both hands, utterly regardless of all remonstrance (which, being in English, he did not understand), he quickly hauled our turtle to the surface, and held it, struggling and gnashing its jaws, close to the steep bank. In a few moments the line slackened, and the turtle disappeared. The fight was over! The sharp horny jaws had bitten through treble-twisted brass wire as clean as though cut by shears. My visions of turtle soup had faded.

VIEW OF THE SAMBRE

Robert Louis Stevenson

c. 1890

BESIDES THE CATTLE, we saw no living things except a few birds and a great many fishermen. These sat along the edges of the meadows, sometimes with one rod, sometimes with as many as half a score. They seemed stupefied with contentment; and when we induced them to exchange a few words with us about the weather, their voices sounded quiet and far-away.

There was a strange diversity of opinion among them as to the kind of fish for which they set their lures; although they were all agreed in this, that the river was abundantly supplied. Where it was plain that no two of them had ever caught the same kind of fish, we could not help suspecting that perhaps not any one of them had ever caught a fish at all. I hope, since the afternoon was so lovely, that they were one and all rewarded; and that a silver booty went home in every basket for the pot. Some of my friends would cry shame on me for this; but I prefer a man, were he only an angler, to the bravest pair of gills in all *God's* waters. I do not affect fishes unless when cooked in sauce; whereas an angler is an important piece of river scenery, and hence deserves some recognition among canoeists. He can always tell you where you are after a mild fashion; and his quiet presence serves to accentuate the solitude and stillness, and remind you of the glittering citizens below your boat.

TOM MARTIN CREEK
Richard Brautigan

1967

I WALKED DOWN one morning from Steelhead, following the Klamath River that was high and murky and had the intelligence of a dinosaur. Tom Martin Creek was a small creek with cold, clear water and poured out of a canyon and through a culvert under the highway and then into the Klamath.

I dropped a fly in a small pool just below where the creek flowed out of the culvert and took a nine-inch trout. It was a good-looking fish and fought all over the top of the pool.

Even though the creek was very small and poured out of a steep brushy canyon filled with poison oak, I decided to follow the creek up a ways because I liked the feel and motion of the creek.

I liked the name, too.

Tom Martin Creek.

It's good to name creeks after people and then later to follow them for a while seeing what they have to offer, what they know and have made of themselves.

But that creek turned out to be a real son-of-a-bitch. I had to fight it all the God-damn way: brush, poison oak and hardly any good places to fish, and sometimes the canyon was so narrow the creek poured out like water from a faucet. Sometimes it was so bad that it just left me standing there, not knowing which way to jump.

You had to be a plumber to fish that creek.

After that first trout I was alone in there. But I didn't know it until later.

LEISTERING FOR SALMON IN SCOTLAND

Sir Walter Scott

c. 1820

THIS CHASE, in which the fish is pursued and struck with barbed spears, or a sort of long-shafted trident, called a waster (or leister), is much practised at the mouth of the Esk, and in the other salmon rivers of Scotland. The sport is followed by day and night, but most commonly in the latter, when the fish are discovered by means of torches, or fire-grates, filled with blazing fragments of tar-barrels, which shed a strong though partial light upon the water. On the present occasion, the principal party were embarked in a crazy boat upon a part of the river which was enlarged and deepened by the restraint of a mill-wear, while others, like the ancient Bacchanals in their gambols, ran along the banks, brandishing their torches and spears, and pursuing the salmon, some of which endeavoured to escape up the stream, while others, shrouding themselves under roots of trees, fragments of stones, and large rocks, attempted to conceal themselves from the researches of the fishermen. These the party in the boat detected by the slightest indications; the twinkling of a fin, the rising of an air-bell, was sufficient to point out to these adroit sportsmen in what direction to use their weapon. . . .

The sportsmen returned loaded with fish, upwards of one hundred having been killed within the range of their sport. The best were selected for the use of the principal farmers, the others divided among their shepherds, cottars, dependants, and others of inferior rank who attended. These fish, dried in the turf smoke of their cabins, or shealings, formed a savoury addition to the mess of potatoes, mixed with onions, which was the principal part of their winter food. In the meanwhile, a liberal distribution of ale and whisky was made among them, besides what was called a kettle of fish, – two or three salmon, namely, plunged into a caldron, and boiled for their supper. Brown accompanied his jolly landlord and the rest of his friends into the large and smoky kitchen, where this savoury mess reeked on an oaken table, massive enough to have dined Johnny Armstrong and his merry men. All was hearty cheer and huzza, and jest and clamorous laughter, and bragging alternately, and raillery between whiles.

THE FISH AND FISHING OF
THE UNITED STATES

1885

I love the babbling brook, the placid lake,
Where spotted trout and pike their pastime take;
I love the rocky shore, the rushing stream,
Where lordly salmon leap, in sunlight gleam;
The stately river, the expansive bay,
Where striped basse and silver squeteague play;
The ocean's distant roar, the bounding wave,
Where monsters daily bask and dolphins lave;
These! these! I love, and oft away from home
Truant I stray, tempted by them to roam;
These! these! I love, and never can forsake,
For all the gold that trade or toil can make.

Anglers of the western world, you, as the lamented Power would have said, are "born to good luck." Your lot is cast in a land of many waters and many fishes. Loud should be your paeans of praise, profound your gratitude to the giver of all good, when you consider the many advantages you enjoy as anglers of the United States. Were you to traverse the circle of the globe for pleasure with the rod, you would return with an anxious step and a loving heart to the "Land of the free and the home of the brave," satisfied that no country you had visited possessed half the sporting advantages of your own; for it would occupy an ordinary lifetime, were a man, with angling implements, merely to explore the waters and make acquaintance with every variety of fish that has "a local habitation and a name" within its extended boundaries.

As the state of natural science in regard to the history and habits of our fishes is in its infancy, so also are the contrivances and arts employed in taking them, yet rude and undeveloped. But we are rapidly increasing our knowledge and refining our methods; as we *must* do when pleasure, and not profit, is the object of our pursuit, and the fish, constantly sought, become wary, and yield only to the utmost address of the angler.

Much certainly might here be said of the ordinary and extraordinary game fish inhabiting the waters of both hemispheres, which have long furnished themes to cultivated anglers and practical studies of the art. But much especially deserves to be said of the finny inhabitants of our own bright streams, which are unhappily unknown to our brotherhood in the old world. Who that ever took a striped basse or squeteague of five or ten pounds' weight can ever forget the pleasurable excitement and ecstasy of the moment; or what man, worthy the name, whose fortune has been cast among the northern lakes, can fail, even in his dreams, to remember the intense enjoyment that thrilled his sound and senses as he triumphantly drew from its pellucid waters, after a long skirmish and a doubtful struggle, a three foot trout or a large black basse? Who, too, that has made one of a party in the briny bay, and captured a mess of lively barb, or the noble sheepshead, after a vigorous contest and a beautiful play with rod and reel, wonders at the enthusiasm of the American angler, surrounded by such opportunities of enjoyment? The salmon, the trout, and the pike are almost the only game fish of Europe. It is true,

> *Their pienteous streams a various race supply:*
> *The bright eyed perch, with fins of Tyrian dye,*
> *The silver eel, in shining volumes rolled,*

The yellow carp, in scales bedropped with gold,
Swift trouts, diversified with crimson stains,
And pikes, the tyrants of the watery plains,

but we have, in addition, almost innumerable objects of sport. For the lover of the breezy ocean there is the invigorating pastime of trolling for blue fish, or of drawing from its populous depths the valued sea basse, porgie, and tautog. In larger rivers and lakes abound the mighty muskellunge, or ponderous cat-fish, and buffalo; and last, though not least, is the never-to-be-forgotten red-fish, which tenants the bays and mouths of our southern rivers. Happy and grateful then should our angler be that his lot is cast in such a land!

Surrounded by such abundance and variety of "finny attractions," is it wonderful that the angler falls into ecstasies, expatiating on his favorite subject? But we would moderate any pride of superiority we indulge in over our transatlantic brethren in respect to the quantity and quality of our game, by reasoning with ourselves and inquiring, Are our advantages to last, can they always be? You who have trod the mossy bank in pursuit of trout, and warred against the swift current when the striped basse was the object of your sport, will answer emphatically *no*. You are painfully assured that the well known haunts wherein in happy boyhood you took many a "silver side," are deserted, and the overarching banks of your favorite streams conceal your spotted friends no longer. You know that at your basse grounds you take few and still fewer fish, and that some of your former places are now never visited by the sought for game. It is the commonest complaint of the old anglers that fishing nowadays is uncertain; that it is much more difficult to take a mess of fish; there are too many after them; in short, that "times are not as they used to be," and so also says the gunner of his favorite sort of game. Now, what are the causes of this scarcity and disappearance; what the preventives and the remedy therefor?

The causes are easily seen, and almost as easily remedied, if those interested in the preservation of our game would unite their efforts to do so. The haunts of our favorite fish are *netted* by mercenary fishermen, who, in season or out of season, take large and small (for all is fish that comes to their net) to the nearest city, where they get extravagant prices for their unhallowed spoil. And this resurrectionism, for it is little better, is practised nightly in our midst. Another reason is the indiscriminate taking of fish at spawning time by boys and (what is worse) ignorant men, and also by market fishermen, who take them in great numbers from their icy retreat and spawning grounds in tide waters. Add to this the wanton waste of fish by many who call themselves anglers, who (angling not for the pleasure of fishing, but to see how many they can take) leave them to gasp and die by the stream side, and you have reasons enough for the depopulation of all the waters in creation. Trout has almost become extinct in those parts of New York, New Jersey, Pennsylvania, and many of the eastern states, that are adjacent to the principal cities and towns, and are abundant only in the less populated and accessible portions, and even there are fast decreasing, owing to the same causes.

Now what are the remedies? The rod sportsman has several advantages over the gunner. Birds fly high, are as free as air, and so are those that pursue them; "they can be seen." Every boy in the country that has arrived at the age of twelve years is a good shot, and can bag his game, in season or out, by getting out of hear-shot distance; and no obstacles can be interposed to this general and indiscriminate slaughter, except the enforcement of rigid laws, and the severe discountenance of public opinion.

But the lover of the finny race can protect his game with more certainty. Although the inhabitant of the crystal water can often be seen, there is no certainty of taking him, except it be with net or spear, and this can be prevented. A gentleman who had a fine pond, stocked with golden carp, was asked by a dealer in fish for the privilege of taking some fish from his pond. The gentleman, having been in a former instance imposed upon by the inquirer, answered, that he might come and take as many as he pleased; but immediately he set his men to work, and planted stakes throughout the pond. Much time was spent in the purchase and preparation of nets, at considerable expense; the netters went, but returned with torn nets and no fish, and a flea in their ear. A word to the wise is sufficient.

Were a few anglers in the vicinity of water netted by poachers to club together to protect it, and see that the ground was properly staked, the ponds and streams could in a measure be preserved from the depredations of such barbarians. Draw-nets and seines are the most injurious; gill-nets and fykes cannot be used with much effect without being visible, and can be watched by the vigilant angler.

In regard, then, to the protection of game, we have the same interest with the fowler; and as there are many who pursue fish and fowl, and many epicures also

> *Who love a dish*
> *Of birds or fish,*

concert of action among them could not fail to be effectual. Strong laws against taking or vending game out of season, strictly enforced by the rigorous prosecution of all offenders, would check, if not stop the growing evil.

To this end sporting clubs should be formed in the different cities, towns, and districts of the country, which might be benefited by such laws; and vigilance committees formed to correspond with and visit the sporting grounds, and see that every violation of the statutes is thoroughly dealt with. By such a course of procedure our game grounds could be preserved, our pleasures greatly increased, and a stock of nature's "best gift, our ever new delight," preserved to future generations. We can do more. Where ponds and streams have ceased to be tenated by the favorite trout, transportation and propagation can be carried on privately, at little expense, and the fish left to remain many years with safety and success. Then the streams we once loved may be made lively and joyous as in the days of our youth. There appears to be only one description of fish that we are destined to lose, and that is the king of the tribe, the salmon. The majority of our rivers being large enough to admit of all kinds of navigation, including that enemy of fish and fishing, the steamboat, we shall eventually have to bid farewell to this royal visitor. He cannot be domesticated, but roams as his instinct leads him. Other descriptions of game are ours, and in our keeping; and it behoves us, as true men and *faithful anglers*, to propagate and preserve them.

SPRING SALMON
IN THE DUBLIN DISTRICT

Arthur A. Luce

1959

IN THE IRISH ANGLER'S YEAR salmon and trout angling combine well. Our salmon are at their best, broadly speaking, when trout are at their worst, and our trout are at their best when the quality of salmon is beginning to decline. Corrib trout, taken in February on the trolled minnow, and sent to the Dublin market, are "snakes", most of them. Liffey salmon and Boyne salmon, taken on the opening days of those rivers, are lusty and strong, and glitter like bars of silver. Our springers are noble fish, excelling those of the summer and autumn in size and fighting qualities and table qualities. Many of our trout are "in the pink" by April; but they do not reach perfection till June or July.

Dublin's fair city deserves a passing word of tribute. It is a fine centre of fishing and thinking. Is there any other metropolis in which the angler can catch a salmon, and twenty minutes later be dining with the dons in cap and gown at the high table of a University. It has been done in Dublin, and it could still be done today. And if in the foregoing statement "shoot a wild duck" were substituted for "catch a salmon", the statement would still be true. Indeed in the latter part of August and September, with time allowed, all three feats might be done in a day.

The Liffey and the Boyne with its tributary, the Blackwater, are the themes of this chapter. The salmon angling in these rivers is colourful and readily accessible; it adds not a little to the panorama of Irish angling. We begin with the Liffey. The recent installation of hydro-electric works at Pollaphuca and Leixlip has altered the character of the river, and for anglers the chief point of interest is the question: has the electrification altered the salmon angling for better or for worse? I fished the Liffey regularly through the years of transition; and while I cannot offer a final answer to that question, I have some observations to make which may contribute towards an answer; for it has been most interesting to watch the gradual transformation of Anna Liffey from a quiet medium-sized river, which turned a few mills, into the motive force of a hydro-electric system which supplies Dublin and district with water, light and power.

The River Liffey rises in the Dublin mountains only thirteen miles from the sea, as the crow flies, but it makes a circuit of over eighty miles before entering the sea in Dublin bay. It is tidal up to Island Bridge, where stands the club house of the Dublin University Boat Club, overlooking the weir. The net fishing at the Island Bridge pool used to be valuable; but it was overfished (so anglers thought), and it declined in value by year, and was recently acquired by the local Salmon Anglers Association. There is a little angling in the tidal waters, and salmon are occasionally taken in the higher stretches of the river; but Island Bridge downstream and Lucan Bridge upstream are the practical limits of worth-while salmon angling. An old friend of mine had it from his father that to take a salmon in Lucan demesne or higher upstream was a rare event. There are several weirs between Chapelizod and Lucan, and by the time the running fish reaches Lucan Bridge his first *élan* is spent; he is beginning to stale and is less inclined to take the lure.

In former days the movements of the migrant fish were entirely decided by the rainfall. If sufficient rain fell to bring down a flood or a fresh, they moved up; if not they stayed put. The electrification of the river has changed all that. There is now a daily fresh, and runable water almost without intermission. The fish can now run at will. In consequence there is more fishing than formerly; whether there are more fish caught, or more fish to catch, are nice questions. I fished for several years under the new conditions, but no two years were alike; no definite trends were in evidence, and the data were insufficient to form a reliable opinion as to the net effect of electrification. I have heard that in very recent years summer grilse have begun to run in the Liffey. That is a very interesting development that may well be due directly to the daily flow of turbine water; and if the run of grilse establishes itself, it will add greatly to the angling amenities of the river. In former days salmon angling in the Liffey petered out at the end of April, or early in May, and summer grilse were few and far between.

The transition from occasional rainfall floods to daily turbine water made anglers wonder whether turbine water has the same physical and chemical properties as a flood of natural rain-water. The current looks the same, and the bait behaves in the same way in both mediums; but some anglers think that the fish are not so responsive in turbine water.

There used to be a large amount of "free fishing" in the Liffey near Dublin; but some of it has recently been acquired by the new Association. Such fishing is not "free" in a legal or technical sense. The term "free fishing" simply means water, not known to be preserved, or known not to be preserved. In such waters the angler "fished and found out"; and only rarely was he turned off. The meadows at Chapelizod were "free", and are so still, I believe. "Free", when I fished it, was "the Wren's Nest". This is a sporting pool, consisting of a weir and two or three runs, immediately opposite an old inn of that name on the Strawberry Beds road to Lucan. Fifty years ago strawberries were extensively cultivated in this warm and sheltered valley with its sandy soil. The farms that grew them were rendezvous for picnic parties from the city, and offered shilling teas with, in the season, a plate of strawberries and cream. The picturesque name for the road has outlived the industry.

Two incidents at the Wren's Nest pool stand out in memory. I once drowned a fish there. He was a fresh-run salmon, fifteen pounds in weight. He raced upstream, and there was nothing I could do about it. He turned at the torrent under the weir, and shot like a flash downstream. The current was fast and strong, and in a few seconds I was master. As soon as the pull came on his tail, he was paralysed; his head was downstream; his tail was upstream, and he could not right himself; the current was too strong for him; his gills and his fate were sealed. I reeled him up, a dead-weight, slowly; and when he reached me, there he lay in the water at my feet helpless, dead, drowned in his own element.

One morning towards the end of March I had fine sport at the same pool. It was the day of Archbishop Barton's enthronement in the Collegiate and Cathedral Church of St. Patrick. The enthronement was in the early afternoon, and it was my duty to be present; but I had the morning free. It was a balmy, gracious day; the March lamb had vanquished the lion; and the air was champagne. I reached the Wren's Nest soon after 11 am, and found conditions perfect. The sun shone; the breeze was light and southerly; the water was clearing after a flood, and a shoal of fresh-run fish was resting under the weir. I put up a two-inch gold devon, and took three fish in quick succession; and then my time was up. The pool was nowhere near fished out; water and weather were still all that angler's heart could desire; it was the chance of a lifetime; but I had to go. The struggle between pastoral duty and piscatorial inclination was sharp, and the memory still is poignant. Years afterwards I had the temerity to tell His Grace why I remembered the day of his enthronement. He was a good sportsman, and congratulated with me on my pre-prandial salmon, and condoled with me on the afternoon catch that was not caught.

The best-known stretch of the Liffey for salmon-angling, and perhaps the most productive, lies below Lucan Bridge between Hill's cloth mill and Shackleton's flour mill. A good part of this stretch lies immediately beside the Strawberry Beds roadway. You can stand actually on the side-path and cast, taking care not to hook the passers-by. The children on their way to school stop and look on, and ask, "Have you caught a fish yet, Misther?"; and their mothers, going to Lucan to shop, basket in hand, are no less interested; for angling news in Ireland is "hot news"; it has top priority after horses. The capture of a salmon at Lucan is known at Chapelizod within two hours, and *vice versa*. If you are in a fish, a gallery gathers, shouting advice and encouragement. "Hould him, Sir. Don't let him away. Mind those bushes. Watch that tree. He's bet. He's coming in. Give him the butt."

It is a handy spot to fish, if you are out for fish, and not for privacy. There are no fields to cross or awkward stiles. You just park your car, put up your rod and fish away; and if you are lucky and catch a fish, you have not far to carry him; a few steps and he is in the boot of your car, provided there is no war on, or oil crisis in the Middle East.

It is a handy spot for the local poacher, too. He soon learned the hours of the tenant of the fishing, and adjusted his own operations accordingly. One day I came down earlier than usual when I had the fishing; and there was my brave poacher on the job, with bicycle beside the road, all ready for instant flight. But there was no flight for him that day; for his bait was stuck fast in Garnett's tree on the far side of the river. This was a sunken tree under the far bank; it took its name from a tackle-shop well known to generations of Dublin anglers, whose proprietor, a sportsman and pleasant companion, was alleged to have done well out of the snag that bore his name. The poacher's bait is still, I doubt not, in Garnett's tree. The poacher, an old soldier, got the edge of my tongue; he promised amendment of life. He promised never to fish there again. He borrowed a new trace and bait from me, and went off to pastures new.

This stretch when I first knew it was "free fishing" and had been so time out of mind; but all good things come to an end. One year on the 1st of February, then the opening day, half a dozen of us anglers were spaced along the river bank, casting our devons and collies. Then the squire of Lucan, a cultured man, of ancient Irish family, took a hand. I admired the way he did it. The fishing was his; but his rights had not been enforced. It was not a pleasant job for a man in his position. He did not leave it to an agent, but came down in person and took our names and addresses. It was a dramatic little scene, and it had the desired effect. No proceedings were taken, of course; but subsequently I wrote and made an offer for the fishing which was accepted; and I rented it from him and his heirs for more than twenty years.

During this period the Pollaphuca dam was built to contain the upper waters of the Liffey and of the King's River, already mentioned. When the Power Station was in action, the turbine water began to come down daily. The effect on the fishing was considerable and, in one year, remarkable. To find the river fishable every day, no matter what the rainfall of yesterday was a novelty and a continuing joy. Previously we often never knew till we reached the river whether there would be any fishing, or not. In a dry spring weeks would pass without fish having a chance to run; but now the Power Station was giving us fresh water and a good current every day.

The first or the second year (I am not sure which) in which the turbine water came down was the *annus mirabilis* of the Lucan stretch; it yielded thirty salmon to one rod in the three months, February, March and April. A Liffey angler who took half a dozen salmon in the season would be well satisfied, as a rule. Thirty fish was beyond the dreams of the most sanguine of Liffey anglers. It was one of the war years; there was no petrol for private cars; and one made the journey to and from Lucan by bus. To carry a spring salmon to the bus was quite an undertaking. One day I had three to carry. The locals helped at the Lucan end; but one had to be one's own porter on de-bussing at O'Connell Bridge in the heart of the city. There was nothing for it but to carry the three fine fish, each neatly trussed up head and tail, across the noble thoroughfare. The guards (police) stopped the traffic, and the citizens of Dublin, who love a salmon as they love a horse, looked on approvingly.

That year stood alone; it was a flash in the pan, so far as my experience went. The turbine flow of water gave more fishing, but on the whole it did not give more fish. From the salmon angler's point of view there are drawbacks to the daily fresh and almost continuous flow; and the chief drawback is that the salmon are kept on the move all the time, and are not allowed to rest. Probably the explanation of the "wonder-year", mentioned above, was that the Power Station was not in full production; only some of the turbines were working, with the result that the supply of water down each day just suited the rather placid flow of the stretch; enough water came down to send a fish or two up each day over the weir below without sending them on a through-passage over the weir above. In subsequent years all the turbines were working; a larger head of water came down each day, and the fish tended to run through. In all rivers the run of salmon is apt to vary greatly from year to year for reasons, at present unascertained, but which have no connection with local events in a particular river. The world supply of running salmon seems to vary greatly from year to year. The broad, permanent effects of electrification on a particular river must be judged over a series of years. The effect of electrification on the Liffey salmon angling is, as I write, in doubt. Time and the records of the Salmon Anglers Association may show.

And now northwards to the historic River Boyne. The Boyne made history nearly three centuries ago; it helped to mould pre-history two to three millenniums ago. Stand on the hill of Tara, and look northwards towards New Grange and the valley of the Boyne, and you are looking out on the richest lands of Ireland, richest in soil, in memories and in archaeological remains; and those remains link the country intimately with the main stream of ancient European civilization.

The Boyne fishing is thirty miles and more from Dublin, but Dublin anglers make light of the run. They like to leave their hospitals and Inns of Court and lecture rooms and offices, and get right away for one day in the week. The Boyne is further afield than the Liffey, but is better fishing, and holds better fish. The Liffey salmon is good, but he tends to be long for his size. The Boyne salmon is one of the best in the country; he is short for his size, has deep shoulders, is shaped like a bent bow, and is as strong as a horse. His average weight is 16 to 18 lb., according to the *Angler's Guide* (1957 and earlier editions). The Boyne can provide more fishing, especially fly fishing, than does the Liffey, over a longer course; it is a bigger and wider stream with a fuller head of fast-flowing water.

The Boyne rises near Edenderry and enters the sea below Drogheda; it has a course of some seventy miles, and is fed by several large tributaries. The principal salmon angling is between Navan and Slane and Oldbridge. The tide reaches to Oldbridge, some three miles upstream from Drogheda. Near Oldbridge a fine Georgian mansion, named Townley Hall, with a superb staircase by Francis Johnston, in Olympian aloofness surveys the River Boyne and the river of time. In the narrow leafy lane that descends the hill just east of Townley Hall, on 1st July (O.S.; 12th July, N.S.) 1690 King William on his white horse held the council of war that decided the fateful issue of the Battle of the Boyne. The left-wing of his army forded the river, and how heavily-laden infantry, under fire, could do what no peaceful angler would willingly attempt today has long puzzled me. July is a wet month, a month of floods and freshes; the river is broad, and to cross it even in low water would be a hard and dangerous task; the river bed is rugged; the current is rapid, and the holes are deep.

"Trust in God, and keep your powder dry" – that famous Order of the Day would not be easy to observe in full in crossing the Boyne water.

A military historian has very kindly considered the difficulty, and he offers the following two-pronged explanation, and very reasonable it seems: (*a*) the infantry crossed at Oldbridge, but in the tidal water, and they waited for low tide, and (*b*) in those days the Boyne was wider and shallower than it is at present. The Boyne owes its present character to the Boyne Navigation Company, which operated from about the end of the eighteenth century; it made the canal, referred to below, built "ramparts", and confined the river to its present banks.

The Boyne below Navan winds through some of the richest pastures and most fertile tilth in Ireland; it skirts prehistoric barrows and the burial grounds of ancient kings; chief of them is the enormous communal sepulchre of New Grange, which dates probably from the Middle Bronze Age, and is one of the largest megalithic structures known. These structures testify to the wealth and importance of the district in those far-off days. The stones of New Grange, many of them, are profusely carved with spirals, manders and other art-forms, which two millenniums later Irish artists were to express in other mediums, above all in the superb illuminations of the Gospel-books of Durrow and Kells.

When the Boyne opens it is often too high to fish; you can hardly find it, let alone fish it. It is over its banks, spreading like a lake far and wide over the rushy water-meadows. When it first becomes fishable, there is little use for the fly rod; the spinning rod and heavy baits have it all their own way. Beginning with three-inch silver devons, the angler works down, as the water lowers and clears, to two-and-a-half inch blue and silver with its taking flash, and thence to two-inch gold; and when that stage is reached, it is time to think of changing over to the fly.

And here I must touch on a controversial matter, the law of the *medium filum*. That law was strictly observed when I first fished the Boyne, and it was part of the angler's code on honour not to trespass beyond the line. Today the law is in some stretches more honoured in the breach than the observance. The keen young angler on the far bank with his American reel and helped by a following wind drops his bait at your feet, too close to be safe or pleasant, across eighty or ninety yards of water. The change in practice is due in part to the vast improvement in the casting power of reels, which has outstripped (dare I say it?) the improvement in manners and consideration for others. On a narrow river like the Liffey the *medium filum* could not be observed without serious loss to both sides, and there, and in similar waters, by common and mutual consent in the joint interests of both banks, the letter of the law is disregarded, and both banks gain, and gain equally. That cannot be said of a broad river like the Boyne; in many reaches it is neither necessary, nor fair, to cast into the other man's water and take the other man's fish; and by doing so the one bank gains at the expense of the other bank.

Among the famous pools and reaches and fisheries of the Boyne should be mentioned Blackcastle, Dunmoe and Slane. The Blackcastle fishery extends for two miles on both banks. Its records for seventeen years (1920–36) are given and tabulated in the *Irish Free State Angler's Guide* (3rd ed., 1937), P. 178. They should be studied by all who wish to know some facts about the annual run of fish. The fluctuations are enormous, and their unpredictability shows what a deal remains to be found out about the habits and movements of *salmo salar*. The figures *per annum* range from 337 fish in 1927 to 40 fish in 1932, and from 251 fish in 1935 to 49 fish in 1936. The six years 1920–5 yielded a total of 1,163 fish, while the six years 1929–34 yielded a total of only 337 fish, the exact number taken in the one year 1927.

Dunmoe I knew well; it is a fine open piece of fishing water, about a mile long, well diversified with sharps and flats and weirs. It is some four miles from Navan, and the four miles seemed forty the evening in wartime when there was no petrol for us, and I had to "cycle" back to catch the bus in Navan, somehow managing to fit on the bicycle my rods and tackle, three fish totalling sixty pounds in weight, and (occasionally) myself. Salmon are too lordly and patrician a fish for the plebeian bicycle; they are not happy on the handle-bars; they slip off the carrier; and if you tie them to the frame, your legs cannot get fairly and squarely to the treadmill. Nominally I cycled back to Navan; actually it was a four-mile walk with the bicycle serving as wheel-barrow for my *impedimenta* for most of the way.

Along the eastern bank of Dunmoe runs a low hill, or esker, which gives welcome shelter from the sour east winds of April. Here the river is flanked by the remains of the derelict canal, mentioned above, now the home of a myriad moorhens. To get to the river you must cross the canal by a frail plank, all that time has left of the lockgate. Here is the Lock Pool, a good pool for the fly when the river is low, but unproductive in high water. A tiny church with a peaceful graveyard looks down from the hill. There, too, is a modern mansion surrounded by trees; cock pheasants crow in the plantations, and occasionally one will spread his strong wings and glorious tail, and glide, as if in conscious majesty, across the broad river.

On the western bank stand the ruins of a moated castle that in the days of the Viking invasions dominated and defended Dunmoe. Behind the castle, as far as eye can see, roll the rich pastures of County Meath, where calves, born in Kerry or the mountainy west, complete their "sad Odyssey" and fatten for the English market. In the broad, sloping pastures, bordering the river, fat cows and fierce-looking steers (Heaven send the angler there be no bull amongst them!) roam at will, or rest among the gnarled and haunted hawthorns where the fairies feast at night.

The Castle marks the upper limits of the Dunmoe fishing; here are rapids which in falling water may yield a fish. Some two hundred yards downstream is the Moerings Pool, a fast-flowing glide of water above a low weir, one of the best holding pools. A fish took me there at dusk. He was a "banker", slightly red, but tough and strong. He weighed twenty-five pounds and he played for just twenty-five minutes. He would let me reel him to my feet, and then bolt straight across the river and bump the far bank. Then slowly back he came, only to repeat the dash till his strength gave out. Why does a salmon's strength give out so soon? Their average fight of "a pound a minute" is not good considering the boundless energy they absorb in the sea, their streamlined shape, and the incredible feats of gymnastics they perform. The Erne River before the electricians harnessed it used to tumble into the Atlantic near Ballyshannon. The Assaroe Falls the spot was called; and it was a fine sight to stand there when a run was on, and watch the lordly salmon climbing almost vertically up the wall of torrent water. You would think they had a heart for any endurance test, and would never give in. His stay-at-home cousin, the brown trout, that has never had to rough it much, and that has never known the rich feeding of ocean, is, pound for pound, the better fighter of the two. Compare this stout Boyne salmon, twenty-five pounds in weight, who gave up after twenty-five minutes, with the brown trout, say fifteen pounds in weight, whose story is told below; he was undefeated after a stern struggle lasting for two hours and a half. The same holds at the lower levels. Many a five-pound grilse gives up in five minutes. I cannot see a five-pound trout in good condition giving up so soon.

At a pool without a name lower down in the Dunmoe stretch an unusual thing happened one fine and frosty morning in early March. The sun was gaining power; but the frosty nip was in the air still; the water was bitterly cold, and the reeds and rushes at the water's edge were stiff with hoar-frost. I was wading through them, breaking the thin skin of crackling ice, and spinning as I went. All of a sudden I saw among the reeds a few yards ahead of me a sight that made me rub my eyes. "What's that, Paddy?" Paddy looked, and Paddy gasped. Sure enough, it was the back fin and broad tail of a big salmon sunning himself in the shallow water right up against the bank. "Show me the gaff, Sir." "Nonsense, Paddy," said I, "he hasn't done anything to us." Paddy's face fell. He was mortal keen to get me a fish; and here was a gift of the gods. Like Juvenal's enormous turbot, *ipse capi voluit*; it wished to be caught.

Thinking the fish was sick, I crept up to him, and passing my hand under his body gently, I tickled him, as one tickles a trout. He was clearly in the pink of condition. I passed my hand under the whole length of him, and he did not stir. Was he asleep? Do fish sleep? Paddy came up quietly and did what I had done. For quite a time we stayed there, admiring and fondling him. Then Paddy went too far, and took hold of his tail. With a mighty thrash and smash our salmon drove out into the middle of the river, and Paddy nearly went with him.

We ought to do right for right's sake, and not for what we get out of it. Often virtue is its own reward, and has to be. But there is justice in things, as well as right; and no theory of disinterested virtue measures up to the facts. I suppose that fish had to go back to the Boyne; but he had left a debt behind him, and I frankly admit that I fished for the rest of that day with a glow of conscious virtue, and the North Briton's "lively expectation of favours to come". Alas, I went home empty-handed, and I could almost hear Paddy saying to himself, as I settled with him, "An, sarves ye right!" *Respice finem*, Paddy. Wait for the end of the tale. The rewards of virtue are slow, but sure. Next week when my Boyne day came round, the justice of things was strikingly vindicated. At the very self-same spot in the nameless pool just above a weir, my gold devon was sweeping round in a graceful curve, when a lovely fish, twenty pounds in weight, took it and met his fate.

St. Columba (*c.* 521–97) seems to have held somewhat similar views. St. Columba was the soldier-saint of Ireland who founded the famous monastery on the island of Iona, and from that centre helped to convert the Picts, and did the ground-work of the Irish mission to Lindisfarne and the north of England in the seventh century. The Saint was knowledgeable about salmon, and is twice credited by his biographer, Abbot Adamnan, with second sight about them; and in both cases, may I say it with all respect, the Saint seems to share the angler's healthy joy in the capture of a *large* fish. The first incident may have concerned a Boyne salmon; for it occurred "*in fluvio Sale*", which, according to some commentators, is an Irish river in the Navan district. If so, it might well have been the Blackwater, which runs through Kells where St. Columba founded a monastery; Kells, after the sack of Iona by the Vikings in A.D. 805, became the seat of authority of the Columban order. Other commentators, however, locate the river in Scotland. Wherever it was, some hardy fishermen on the River Sale had taken five fish in their net. "Cast again," said the Saint, "and you shall at once find a large fish which the Lord has provided for me." They did so, and they drew ashore a salmon of amazing size ("*mirae magnitudinis esocem*"). One can almost see the concertina action of the narrator's hands. The other incident occurred for certain in Ireland. The Saint was staying on Lough Cé in County Roscommon with some companions who were fishermen. They wished to go fishing; but the Saint restrained them for two days, saying there were no fish in the river (the Boyle). On the third day he let them go, and they took two salmon of extraordinary size ("*rarissimae magnitudinis*").

Boyne angling today has its special charm and its distinctive features: the holding pools and reaches are long and wide; the current is mostly full and strong; fishing rights are understood and respected; the fish are of fine quality, and to take one of thirty pounds weight is no uncommon event. There is great variety in the fishing. One must be reasonably active and prepared to walk a good deal to take full advantage of it; but walking is a pleasure there; the setting is that of a rich and prosperous countryside, happy, smiling and historic. The Boyne angler fishes in wide, open spaces, and feels as free as air; and to the tired city-man his day on the Boyne is a weekly tonic, fish or no fish.

To balance the picture here is an account of a famous piece of water in Navan itself, not two hundred yards from the Boyne. It, too, has tonic qualities; but the medicine is in tabloid form; for here all is narrow and compact and on a small scale. Yet it is a pool where great fish and great thrills and great experience are to be had. The pool is called the Mollies. Ask why? and I reply, Well because it *is* the Mollies. The old cricketer was asked, "Why do they call it a *yorker*?" And he replied, of course, "Because it *is* a *yorker*." All Navan anglers and most Dublin anglers know the Mollies, its name and fame. It is a pool on the Blackwater (not to be confused with the southern Blackwater), a tributary of the Boyne. It flows down from Kells, and joins the Boyne in Navan town, and the Mollies is the first considerable pool above the junction. There is no noticeable difference between a Boyne fish and a Blackwater fish; and presumably it is a matter of chance whether a running fish would turn right at the junction into the Blackwater, or continue up the Boyne to Trim. They say that salmon return to their native rivers to spawn. The dogma must be, broadly speaking, true; for rivers have their distinctive types of fish. Does the dogma, one may ask, apply to tributaries? Would a salmon parr from the Blackwater, when full grown and returning from the sea to spawn, seek to return to the tributary, or would the main river do as well? The latter alternative is probably correct. For nature acts by general tendency, and not always with mechanical precision. *De minimis non curat lex*; the law of the land does not bother about details, and the same would seem to be true of the law of instinct.

Here are some facts and figures about the Mollies, which show what a curious pool, or rather group of pools, it is, pointing the contrast with the Boyne. The total length of the Mollies is one hundred and eighty yards; its average width is nine yards, and it narrows at the waist or gut to five or six yards. It stretches from Spicer's flour mill on the south bank to Elliot's saw mill on the north bank. Every inch of it is fishable at some height of water, and every inch of it may hold a fish. Three rods on either side, six in all, can fish comfortably in high water; in low water two rods a side is enough. A total of twenty-four fish was taken from the pool on the opening day (then 12th February) some years ago. Since that time structural alterations have been made in the fish pass at the upper end, and the fish can run through more easily. As a result the Mollies, though still a good holding pool, does not hold as many salmon as it did. In the good old days whenever you looked at the water in March or April, you would see a salmon turn. The pool was often overcrowded, and there was one very sad year; a great run of fish early in the season was followed by a long, long drought. The pool was full of fish; the water got staler and staler, and furunculosis appeared; in that confined space it spread like wildfire; it was pitiable to see those noble fish a prey to the dread disease; there they were all around you, blotched, gasping, dying, and dead, by the score. On one day eighty infected fish were removed from the pool.

On the north bank the Mollies is approached through the saw mill; through the tree trunks and piles of planks and heaps of sawdust you make your way to the accompaniment of screeching saws; and the cheerful men working them shriek "tight lines" to you. The approach on the south bank is quiet, unusual, and almost romantic. The angler enters by a private garden gate through the courtesy of the owner, and crosses a trim lawn and passes through gardens of flowers and vegetables which run down almost to the water's edge. Snowdrops and scillas and a few hardy crocuses welcome us when we start work in February; rows, of sturdy cabbages and broccoli, somewhat the worse for the January snows, are bravely struggling to live and grow and thrive; the gardener is pottering about doing odd jobs, but rarely losing sight of the river; and if he sees your top joint bending, he will soon be at your side, in case you need assistance, as expert with gaff as with spade.

It is a strange situation, is it not, to be fishing here for salmon in a private garden in the heart of a country town? The fishing is varied and interesting; in one hundred and eighty yards of narrow stream you have an epitome of all the main types of angling for spring salmon from a bank. Here is fly fishing, direct casting and Spey casting, except at the very beginning of the season and in very high water. Here is bait fishing except in very low water. On the great majority of fishing days both fly rod and spinning rod are in use, if not everywhere, at least in parts of the pool. The water, too, is well varied; here you have broken water and smooth, sharps and flats, medium and slow; and each variety of water calls for some special knowledge or knack or skill in handling fly and bait.

Stand at the head of the Mollies in the shadow of Spicer's mill up at the weir, and if a run is on, you will see the big fish slipping up the ladder one by one or jumping at the falls and often tumbling back. Immediately below the weir is a seething cauldron of water in which it is futile to fish. Walk down a few yards on the narrow stony path between the river and the mill-stream, and you will find the current slower and the water fishable. Now the river widens, and leaves a stretch of slack beside the main current, and the slack water may hold a taking fish. At the bend is a sheltery pool, known as the Ladies Pool, where the current slows, and many a fish is taken in medium water. At the outflow of the Ladies Pool the banks narrow like a *v*, and the current gathers pace and pours into the gut which is the strangest feature of the Mollies. The gut at its narrowest is barely twenty feet from bank to bank. On the north side is a vertical face of rock at the base of which a narrow pathway, often flooded, winds. On the south side the mill-stream rejoins the river under a flimsy wooden bridge. The gut is a curious geological freak, but a great spot for a fish. In the lowest water there is current in it. A big conical rock sticks up in the middle of it, and salmon rest behind the rock, beside it and in front. Here a young bride, who had never fished before, hooked and killed a salmon thirty pounds in weight; her reputation as an angler was made; and, perhaps wisely, she hardly ever fished again.

Below the gut runs a fifty-yards stretch of relatively quiet water, and that is the only stretch fishable in a high flood when the river comes down brown. At the tail of this stretch a long sunken wall, well beneath the surface, running diagonally down across the stream, carries the water to the saw-mill sluice. This wall is a famous lie for fish, and a famous place for losing baits. Below the wall is "The Pool", a grand holding pool, where the river broadens, slows down, and then gathers momentum and hurtles over the weir where the Mollies ends.

The Mollies is a gold mine to dealers in angling requisites; there is hardly an inch in it where you cannot lose a bait; there is hardly an inch in it where you cannot lose a fish, no matter how well he is hooked and how strong your tackle. Rocks are everywhere, submerged, unexpected rocks, cruel catchy rocks. It is no place for a novice at angling. It is no place for a novice unless he is dead keen to learn the job. If he is keen to learn, and prepared to pay the price, the Mollies will teach him. It is a hard school, but a good school; it teaches the whole curriculum. If a man can fish the Mollies, he can fish anywhere. When he has lost a few pet baits, he will learn to read in the swirl the exact position and the depth of the sunken rock; he will feel his way to the delicate touch and the nicely-directed fling that brings the bait round, just skirting the snag where the big fish can see and take it. He may, as the gillie said, "shtick in the Republic" a time or two; and that will teach him when to reel fast, when to reel slow, when to raise the bait, and when to lower. He will learn the art of releasing a bait; he will learn the virtues of the "traveller"; and if the "traveller" fails to release him, as often as not an angler on the far bank will see his trouble, and come along like a Good Samaritan, risking his own bait, and will hook the other's line, and pull and release him and set him free.

The Mollies is the place to learn the salmon's ways; there are plenty of salmon in the pool as a rule; they often show, and close at hand. The taking rise, the sulky rise, the turn of the running fish, the uneasy sideways fling before the rain, the prospecting leap of the fish just up over the weir – these are all to be seen at close quarters, often all in the one day. In some lights on some days the way of the salmon with the fly can clearly be seen here only a few yards off; up he comes, and looks, and turns away down; up he comes, and looks, and looks once too often.

The Mollies teaches the whole art of playing your fish, and grassing him; but teaches the hard way. The angler who hooks a salmon on a broad river or a lake has usually time to look about him and to mend his hand. With a hooked fish on the Mollies there are no second chances. The angler must be "on the spot", and his tackle must be all in order, and his handling and management must be correct from the word "Go". They take so near you; there is no free line; they feel the vibration of the check instantaneously, and the vibration sets them mad, if they are that way inclined. He may be half the length of the pool away before you realize you are in a fish; and the first mad rush of a mad spring fish, just up, with the sea lice on him, is almost always to the narrow gut. A hooked fish will rush almost ashore there, and the danger of fouling the line round a rock is great.

If he takes in the lower portion of the "The Pool", the weir is the danger; he is liable to go over either in his first alarm or in his last despairing effort; and if he goes over, a loss is certain – at least so I thought till this year. My first fish this season took at the lip of the weir, and went straight over; it was impossible to stop him and impossible to follow him. I was for giving up, and cutting my losses and my line; but my friend William, a fearless young athlete, would not hear of it. So I held on; my tackle was strong, and the moil of waters beneath the weir buffeted the fish, and seemed to stun him; gradually I reeled him up into the white foam under the bushes at the foot of the fall; and there he hung half in the water, half out. William did the rest; pluckily he scrambled down the edge of the weir, and luckily he was just able to reach him with the gaff.

That salmon panicked over the weir because of the very high water; but generally in ordinary water, when hooked in "The Pool" at the edge of the weir, your salmon does not panic, and gives you time to plan. But leave nothing to chance, however quiet he seems. By draw or by pull coax him away from the weir. The "draw" is one method; the "pull" is another. You draw from above the salmon, you pull from below him. The draw can be most effective, if he has not been frightened at the strike. In the draw the reel must be very quiet, quite still if possible; if it revolves rapidly, vibrations from the check travel down the line and excite the fish. If you can manage to tighten on him without alarming him, take a step upstream, holding the line firmly with a finger on the reel, but ever ready to release it if he fights. Probably he will respond to the gentle pressure and follow you upstream. If so, repeat the movement, moving ever slowly, steadily, and without a jerk. A big, fresh fish, if handled skilfully, will be amazingly docile; and if you can draw or lead him fifteen or twenty yards upstream before he turns restive, that is half the battle won. The other method, the pull from downstream, is more primitive, but it can be most effective. Essential to its success are that (*a*) you should be well below him, and (*b*) he must be reasonably fresh and not tired. Given those conditions your fish should react to the pull like a thoroughbred.

The Mollies is a fine school for the young salmon-angler, and it can be a great comfort to the old. Not a few elderly folk fish it year by year with a feeling of gratitude. A day on the Boyne with its far and strenuous casting and its long walks from pool to pool may be too much for him; but on the Mollies he can enjoy his sport, and take his weekly tonic of fresh air, change and exercise, with little walking, no discomfort, and a fair chance of a fish or two.

A DAY'S FISHING
IN A PRUSSIAN HAFF
Herbert E. Palmer

c. 1930

ONE MORNING in early spring, awakened by the singing of the birds, I got up sooner than usual and told the Prussian squirearchy with whom I was staying that I would like to go angling. It was the spring impulse of the trout-fisher that throbbed through my veins, but there were no trout in any waters near, so there was nothing for it but coarse-fishing.

It was very late in the season, or just out of the season for coarse-fishing; but the German law gave me the right, and ere nine o'clock I had commenced the tramp of those seven monotonous miles which separated the estate from a huge sheet of water called a "Haff."

It was a jewel of a day, and the faces of all the people I passed seemed to radiate goodwill. They were driving in horse carriages and dog-carts, riding on horseback or in wagons, or walking along the road. The Germans are very polite externally, and whenever I met a schoolboy or a farm-hand hats were lifted, and I was wished "Guten Tag" as if I were the Kaiser's masterpiece. Perhaps it was the fishing-rod over my shoulder which invited their homage. At least, it was evidence that I was a person of some leisure, and could afford a day's holiday, for in busy Germany it is something out of the common to be seen seeking recreation on any day except Sunday. One man, however, of whom I asked the way, so far forgot himself as to demand a penny for his information.

The sky was a blaze of blue. No haze or mist shrouded the long expanse of plain, the brown, ploughed fields blurred with dark-green pines. Staring beyond the forest clusters I was dreamingly conscious of other landscapes – the wastes of Russia, the scintillating expanse of the Baltic. A snipe flew out of some brushwood near the roadside, a swift, darting flight, and then the long-billed creature was lost to view. I heard a gun go off near at hand. Perhaps it had been shot. An occasional deer fled forward, lissom as the wind. Here and there the white trunks of the birch-trees shone like silver. Along the level road, at regular intervals, these birch-trees were planted with strange mathematical precision. I think if I had taken a yard measure I should have found that not a single tree was a foot too far from its companions. There were no walls or hedges, no dividing lines between the great farms; but there were many windmills, all reminding me that England was a country far distant. The road, a very good one, seemed to be just a broad yellow-brown way beaten out and paved across those miles and miles of fallow land.

Past farm-houses and villages I tramped, past birch-trees and pine-trees and windmills; and then I reached the Haff. It might have been the sea; but there was no sand, no pebbled beach, and the shallows for nearly a hundred yards were choked with weeds. So it seemed impossible to fish. I passed through the picturesque fishing-village, with its hotel and pleasantly austere cottages. There was an air of order and tidiness everywhere that one seldom sees in England. The storks stood on the chimneys, stiff-legged and comfortable and puritanical, a homely sight, yet wise, deceitful, cunning looking birds, to remind the wandering Briton that leagues and leagues of level land and choppy sea divided him from his birthplace.

I went to the hotel, and drank the inevitable lager beer, and bought some black shag tobacco. Tobacco was very cheap in Germany in those days, and you could fill a large paper-bag for the equivalent of threepence or fourpence English money. A better cigar than could be bought in England for fourpence only cost a penny or twopence. But their pipe tobacco was poor stuff in quality, and my purchase was almost as bad as the vilest of French homegrown shag.

After that I strolled round the place, wondering where to begin. The edges of the Haff were hopelessly choked with weed, not orthodox rushes, but a greenish-brownish mass of furiously provoking vegetable matter. So I walked back to the village again, and then for the second time noticed a long stone wall, rather like a breakwater, jutting into the Haff for nearly a quarter of a mile. At the end near the village several fishing-boats were anchored, and their nets were spread out in the sun. The village people, though poor, looked clean and neat, and stoically content. Many of the women wore coloured blouses of chequered or striped cloth. The men were none of them dressed in corduroys, but in a dark-grey material, and some of them wore bright-coloured jackets. But they must have had hard work sometimes to make both ends meet – not of their clothes, but their lives. They were still medieval peasants, half medieval in attire, and almost entirely medieval in outlook.

Nearly every kind of freshwater fish swim in the Haffs. But there are some species, such as the zander (*Lucioperca sandra*), a voracious cannibal fish, which do not belong to English waters. This fish, which is common enough in Germany and eastern Europe, is also known as the perch-pike, or giant perch. It grows to a length of three or four feet, is something like a common perch in appearance, but proportionally less broad. It is said to be very good to eat. . . . There are also several kinds of fish which periodically leave the Baltic and enter the Haffs to spawn. These are the sturgeon, highly prized for its roe (the *caviare* of renown), the whitefish (*Coregonus*), and a species of shad (*Clupea alosa*). Among these migratory species may also be counted a few salmon.

I walked along the stone pier, wishing that my angling friends could come and see the surprising thing, this mighty estuary lake called a Haff – which is only separated from the sea by a long bar of sandy soil, often covered with pines. It might have been the sea – you could not observe the other side. But there was no horizon, no gradual blending of sky and water. You were conscious of no mystery, and could not imagine any great distance.

A high wind was blowing, flogging the water into waves. I began to fish, using a float and red worm. I tried the bait on the bttom; I tried it dangling half-way. I might have had a nibble, but really it was impossible to be sure, for the wind blew a hurricane, and made the float wobble, and sent the water hopping about in all directions, little wavelets and dimples at my feet, prophetic of bad fishing. Farther out, the lake rolled and swept before the wind as the sea might do on our coasts. Unfortunately, at the wall side the water was very shallow, only a few feet deep. I yearned for a boat, and wished that I had more money in my purse. But in spite of the bitter wind and the keen air of that early spring day, I was happy enough. It was magnificent sitting there under the blue skies, watching the silvery expanse of water tremble under the wind's turbulence.

But I wanted, above all, to catch something, and that I was not doing. So I pulled my amulet out of my pocket – namely, my pipe – for I have noticed that something nearly always comes along as soon as your brain is steeped in tobacco.

Of course it happened; I hauled out a small perch, and blessed my pipe. I was glad that I was in the country and could do as I liked, glad that I was not in Königsberg. It would have been as much as my meagre reputation was worth to have walked down the streets with a pipe in my mouth, for in Germany there was nothing quite so *infra dig.*, though you could smoke as many cigars as you liked in any part of the city.

Then the fidgets took hold of me, and I began to rove about. I dropped the worm in here; I waited ten minutes there. The way was soon strewn with matches, for the wind kept blowing them out as I tried to light my pipe for the second time. My thriftless, untidy ways were the talk of the village for a week after. The trail of match-ends evidently summed up my character pretty clearly. If you go to the place now you will possibly hear about the Englishman who wasted a whole box of matches in one morning.

Nothing more exciting occurred than trying to light a match. So, rigging up a new trace, but a non-spinning trace, with a lead minnow at the end of it, I walked to the end of the wall. I worked the minnow perseveringly up and down in the water between the stone pier and a long wooden structure that stretched still farther out. Visions of pike as long as my arm and pike-perch nearly as big as Jonah's benefactor floated before me; but although an angler likes to kill big fish, the lightness of my tackle was such that I sincerely hoped that anything too large would keep a long way off.

Suddenly, something stopped it, and I found I had caught a fish – not a very large one, but it had fins, and was quite worth keeping. It was another perch, and I laid the two down side by side and admired their bars and spines. But that was the only fish I ever caught in my life with "drop-minnow" (a non-spinning artificial bait), although many anglers say it is a good lure for perch, and the French anglers use it with occasionally excellent results.

I started worm-fishing again. Five minutes more and my float went down, for the water was not so rough here, and I could watch its movements easily. This time it was a ruff, a tiny thing; but patience warmed to hope. In a short half-hour I had caught nearly a dozen fish, but none of them was very large, and several were ruff. But ruff are a delicacy in

Germany, and sold at a high price. Some days when the boats go out the nets take in little else save ruff. The Haff fishers sell them very quickly to the squire farmers living in the neighbourhood. A ruff is to an East Prussian what a pilchard is to a Cornishman. Ruff are called *Kaulbarse*, and perch are known as *Barse*. The English word *bass*, the name for our sea-perch, is practically the same word.

I got tired of all this, flat-fishing in the waters of a flat land, and looked over the other side of the pier. I could see quite plainly a small shoal of ruff playing about in the weeds in a foot of water. So taking off the float, I hid behind a bush, and hauled out a number of them. They seemed quite fearless, and took the small red worm without hesitation. Then I pricked one, and he must have told the others, for their greed diminished and they finally went away.

The sky now began to cloud over, so I reeled up and walked home. I had caught nothing large, nor even decently middling; but an angling day often stands out for other reasons than the size of the fish which garnish it. Sometimes when every fish is diminutive and every incident trivial, the day seems an important one, so that it comes to fit into the pattern of one's life and endure in the mind.

When I got back to the estate I opened my basket and showed my catch, not exactly with pride, but with a simulation of it. My Prussian junker friends (who really seemed to have awaited my return with nothing) all exclaimed "Wundervoll" in chorus, lifting up their hands. "Good for soup," they said. So the next day most of the ruff and perch came on the table as *Kaulbars* soup, a prized preparation, a dish for German epicures.

THE ANGLER'S FATE

Ho hoy boat, help, help, get me away from this Bull.

CLOTHING FOR THE
AMERICAN SALMON FISHERMAN
Henry P. Wells

1886

THIS IS a most important part of our outfit. The American must remember that the salmon-rivers of the Atlantic seaboard lie in the direction of the North Pole. While in the direct rays of the sun it may be even shirtsleeve weather; in the shade, and especially in the morning and evening, an overcoat will not be oppressive. The angler, therefore, should clothe himself like an onion, and be prepared to peel layer after layer as the day advances, and resume them in due order as the day declines. Especially is this true when the fishing is from a boat. A boat to him who takes no part in its management, is about twenty-five degrees colder than any other known place in the same latitude. Good heavy winter underclothes, a flannel shirt, and winter trousers should form the foundation, and upon these should be reared such a superstructure of cardigan-jackets, dog-skin coats, and overcoats, as the exigencies of the occasion may require.

Be comfortable, and take whatever it is thought will conduce to this end. As long as your own back is not of necessity the means of transportation, in the matter of clothing, at all events, take all that you may need. Roughing it is all very nice for the young and inexperienced to talk of when cushioned in an easy-chair before a cheerful fire; but after a somewhat extended personal experience on my own account, and a wide observation of others, I have yet to see the person whose appetite was not more than satiated at the very first taste of the real article. A salmon-fishing expedition should be for pleasure, not penance.

A cheap felt-hat of a gray color should protect the head. It should be thick enough to laugh at the rain, wide-brimmed that it may drip elsewhere than down the back of its wearer's neck, and soft so that he may adjust it at any angle that the driving storm or the rays of the sun may require. Stiff hats are a nuisance. If such that they may be worn without embarrassment in every-day life or when travelling, they are ill adapted for fishing; while if adapted for fishing, he would indeed be a bold man who would be willing to wear one except when fishing. They are most inconvenient to pack in a trunk both from their size and shape, and though brand-new when they enter, will look when they emerge as if they had

306

been through a free fight.

A good rubber-coat is a necessity. The rubber-coat is often mis-understood, and therefore maligned. We have all seen the moisture condense from the atmosphere on the outside of an ice-pitcher. The same process takes place inside a rubber-coat. The rain cools the coat, and condenses the insensible perspiration from the body upon its interior. Thus a coat is abused as leaky which is really as tight as the ice-pitcher itself. The best rubber-coat ever made will show a wet inside under these circumstances. Coats of this description may, however, now be had in which this annoyance is met with either in a diminished degree, or not at all. This is accomplished by perforating the shoulders and upper part of the arms, and providing the coat with a short cape to exclude the water from the openings. The air is then no longer confined within the coat, the motion of the arms and body, theoretically at least, keeping up a constant circulation, and expelling the warm air before its moisture has time to condense.

Some means must also be provided to protect the legs if the fishing is from a boat. A rubber-petticoat, reaching to within four or five inches of the ground, is altogether the best device for this purpose, since it prevents the wearer from discomfort should a puddle form on his seat, as it is apt to do, and also because it is well ventilated, and easy to assume and discard. The rubber-coat should then be short. Still rubber pantaloons, or even a rubber-blanket, will answer very well, But some such protection is necessary, for no salmon-fisherman remains indoors because of rain when the fish may rise. Rubber boots, which may well be of the ventilated variety, are also advisable. When venturing into the rain, if the sleeves of the rubber-coat are not provided with straps for the purpose, – as they should be – fold each sleeve tight around the wrist, and tie them thus with a piece of twine. A rain-gauge, even though formed of the sleeve of a rubber-coat, is superfluous in salmon-fishing.

If wading is necessary, mackintosh-waders coming well up under the arms are advisable. The water will be found too cold to wade day after day with comfort or impunity, unless so protected. Those ending in stocking-feet are the best. With this caution, every trout-fisherman will understand this matter without further dilation.

Every one has heard of the black-fly. Those who have not had the pleasure of its personal acquaintance and who judge solely from the fame of its exploits, imagine something about the size of a turkey-buzzard, and armed with a proboscis like the sword of a Roman gladiator. This is a mistake. It is a most insignificant-looking little gentleman, considerably less than a quarter of an inch long. But if its appearance does not inspire respect, its action speedily will. It has a cousin, a most diminutive creature, hardly larger than the head of a pin, and so colorless as to be almost invisible. It also is a hero, and that of no mean sort. To his honor the mosquito none of us need an introduction. He stands on no ceremony, introducing himself on sight, oblivious to insult and rebuff.

Were it not for these drawbacks, salmon-fishing would be altogether too good fun for mere mortals. They are to be found in greater or less quantity on every salmon-river during the fishing season – almost absent where the banks are settled and cleared, becoming more and more abundant as the wilderness is penetrated.

The black-fly performs by daylight alone. Not until the sun is well up does he venture out on his daily avocations, and before the cool of the evening he returns home again in a most virtuous fashion.

His little cousin, on the other hand, has its business-hours in the early morning and the gloom of the twilight, though if the day be warm, damp, and gloomy – "muggy" weather in short, – he may be on hand all day long. It shuns the bright sun, for its deeds are deeds of darkness.

Both abominate the wind and vanish before it, but their weather-eye is always open, and no lull, however brief, is allowed to pass unimproved.

Should an unprepared unfortunate chance upon them when in force, though he have the hide of a rhinoceros, and the enthusiasm of Father Walton himself raised to the twenty-fourth power, neither will avail him anything. He will be subject to attacks so pertinacious and unendurable, that the necessity of self-preservation will speedily banish all thought of fishing.

The black-fly views it victim with an eye which shows a thorough knowledge of its business, and selects his tender points with the very nicest discrimination. Behind the ears, upon the eyelids and on the forehead are its favorite feeding-grounds, and for the possession of these it will do and dare anything.

The little fellow is more miscellaneous in its views, but it is by no means the more lovable on that account.

Both bear down on their prey in numbers like the hordes of Ghengis Khan – as the sands of the sea-shore in multitude. The slaughter of a few thousand more or less, if a matter of the least moment, is but an occasion for self-congratulation to the survivors in that it gives them a better chance. Let no man in the vicious pride of his youth and strength fancy that he can defy their attack, for they will rout him at last, horse, foot, and artillery, just as surely as they meet him. A thin skirmish-line he may be able to encounter though with discomfort, but a serious attack in force is beyond human endurance.

It is true different people suffer in different degrees. On some the black-fly will bring blood at every prod; on some each bite raises a swelling like a miniature volcano; others experience an intolerable itching; while others suffer all these, or any part of them, combined.

The bite of the little fellow is more uniform in result. It is followed by a burning itch, which makes one wish he could stretch his skin out on some barn-door, and go for it with a curry-comb.

Kid-gloves are advised because they are sting-proof. If the fingers are cut off no inconvenience in using the hands will be experienced. They need not become wet, since all these creatures know enough to go in when it rains. But the finger-tips and the face remain to be protected.

The soothing pipe will here add another to the long list of blessings which it bestows on mankind. But it merits and should receive its stated periods of repose. We should not crowd a really good thing too hard.

Therefore cause this lotion to be prepared, recommended to me as really sovereign by one who had annually faced the foe on the salmon-rivers of Canada for nearly forty years:

Olive-oil . . . . $\frac{1}{2}$ pint.
Creosote . . . . 1 ounce.
Pennyroyal . . . . 1 ounce.
Camphor . . . . 1 ounce.

Dissolve the camphor in alcohol, and mix.

This will be sufficient in quantity for a party of four. The bottle which contains it may find place in the grand depot of supplies. For daily use in the field, each should be provided with an oval ounce-bottleful, to be carried in the pocket at all times, ready for any and every emergency. When exposed to attack, the cork is removed from time to time, and a little of the contents of the bottle is smeared on the face with the fingers. The face need not be covered. A little here and there will suffice. Indeed, if the flies are not very numerous and aggressive, it will be enough to anoint the cloth near the face. Though not what a particular man would select as a perfume, still it is not disagreeable – certainly not when compared with fly-bites. It is a cleanly fluid, does not discolor or disorder the skin, and is readily removable by the ordinary process of washing.

The generic name for mixtures of this kind – at least throughout the wilderness which intervenes between the settlements of Maine and Canada – is "bug-juice." Human life is thought to be too short by the ranger of the wild-woods, and the articulations of his jaws are too inflexible for the terms "insect-repellant," "culexifuge," and the many other appellations in vogue in the settlements.

DIFFICULTIES
Andrew Lang

1891

I CAN'T KEEP a fly-book. I stuff the flies into my pockets at random, or stick them into the leaves of a novel, or bestow them in the lining of my hat or the case of my rods. Never, till 1890, in all my days did I possess a landing-net. If I can drag a fish up a bank, or over the gravel, well; if not, he goes on his way rejoicing. . . . A landing-net is a tedious thing to carry, so is a creel, and a creel is, to me, a superfluity. There is never anything to put in it. If I do catch a trout, I lay him under a big stone, cover him with leaves, and never find him again. I often break my top joint; so, as I never carry string, I splice it with a bit of the line, which I bite off, for I really cannot be troubled with scissors, and I always lose my knife. When a phantom minnow sticks in my clothes, I snap the gut off, and put on another, so that when I reach home I look as if a shoal of fierce minnows had attacked me and hung on like leeches. When a boy, I was – once or twice – a bait-fisher, but I never carried worms in box or bag. I found them under big stones, or in the fields, wherever I had the luck. I never tie nor otherwise fasten the joints of my rod; they often slip out of the sockets and splash into the water. Mr Hardy, however, has invented a joint-fastening which never slips. On the other hand, by letting the joint rust, you may find it difficult to take down your rod. When I see a trout rising, I always cast so as to get hung up, and I frighten him as I disengage my hook. I invariably fall in and get half-drowned when I wade, there being an insufficiency of nails in the soles of my brogues. My waders let in water, too, and when I go out to fish I usually leave my reel, or my flies, or my rod, at home. Perhaps no other man's average of lost flies in proportion to taken trout was ever so great as mine. I lose plenty, by striking furiously, after a series of short rises, and breaking the gut, with which the fish swims away.

A BORN BUNGLER
Washington Irving

c. 1820

FOR MY PART, I was always a bungler at all kinds of sport that required either patience or adroitness, and had not angled for above half an hour before I had convinced myself of the truth of Izaak Walton's opinion, that angling is something like poetry – a man must be born to it. I hooked myself instead of the fish; tangled my line in every tree; lost my bait; broke my rod; until I gave up the attempt in despair, and passed the day under the trees, reading old Izaak; satisfied that it was his fascinating vein of honest simplicity and rural feeling that had bewitched me, and not the passion for angling. My companions, however, were more persevering in their delusion. I have them at this moment before my eyes, stealing along the border of the brook, where it lay open to the day, or was merely fringed by shrubs and bushes.

I recollect also that, after toiling and watching and creeping about for the greater part of a day, with scarcely any success, in spite of all our admirable apparatus, a lubberly country urchin came down from the hills with a rod made from the branch of a tree, a few yards of twine, and, as Heaven shall help me! I believe, a crooked pin for a hook, baited with a vile earth worm – and in half an hour caught more fish than we had nibbles throughout the day!

But, above all, I recollect the "good, honest, wholesome, hungry" repast which we made under a beech-tree, just by a spring of pure sweet water that stole out of the side of a hill; and how, when it was over, one of the party read old Izaak Walton's scene with a milkmaid, while I lay on the grass and built castles in a bright pile of clouds, until I fell asleep.

ON DRY-COW FISHING
AS A FINE ART
Rudyard Kipling

1938

It must be clearly understood that I am not at all proud of this performance. In Florida men sometimes hook and land, on rod and tackle a little finer than a steam-crane and chain, a mackerel-like fish called "tarpon," which sometime run to 120 pounds. Those men stuff their captures and exhibit them in glass cases and become puffed up. On the Columbia River sturgeon of 150 pounds weight are taken with the line. When the sturgeon is hooked the line is fixed to the nearest pine tree or steamboat-wharf, and after some hours or days the sturgeon surrenders himself, if the pine or the line do not give way. The owner of the line then states on oath that he has caught a sturgeon, and he, too, becomes proud.

These things are mentioned to show how light a creel will fill the soul of a man with vanity. I am not proud. It is nothing to me that I have hooked and played seven hundred pounds weight of quarry. All my desire is to place the little affair on record before the mists of memory breed the miasma of exaggeration.

The minnow cost eighteenpence. It was a beautiful quill minnow, and the tackle-maker said that it could be thrown as a fly. He guaranteed further in respect to the triangles – it glittered with triangles – that, if necessary, the minnow would hold a horse. A man who speaks too much truth is just as offensive as a man who speaks too little. None the less, owing to the defective condition of the present law of libel, the tackle-maker's name must be withheld.

The minnow and I and a rod went down to a brook to attend to a small jack who lived between two clumps of flags in the most cramped swim that he could select. As a proof that my intentions were strictly honourable, I may mention that I was using a light split-cane rod – very dangerous if the line runs through weeds, but very satisfactory in clean water, inasmuch as it keeps a steady strain on the fish and prevents him from taking liberties. I had an old score against the jack. He owed me two live-bait already, and I had reason to suspect him of coming upstream and interfering with a little bleak-pool under a horse-bridge which lay entirely beyond his sphere of legitimate influence. Observe, therefore, that my tackle and my motives pointed clearly to jack, and jack alone; though I knew that there were monstrous big perch in the brook.

The minnow was thrown as a fly several times, and, owing to my peculiar, and hitherto unpublished, methods of fly throwing, nearly six pennyworth of the triangles came off, either in my coat-collar, or my thumb, or the back of my hand. Fly fishing is a very gory amusement.

The jack was not interested in the minnow, but towards twilight a boy opened a gate of the field and let in some twenty or thirty cows and half-a-dozen cart-horses, and they were all very much interested. The horses galloped up and down the field and shook the banks, but the cows walked solidly and breathed heavily, as people breathe who appreciate the Fine Arts.

By this time I had given up all hope of catching my jack fairly, but I wanted the live-bait and bleak-account settled before I went away, even if I tore up the bottom of the brook. Just before I had quite made up my mind to borrow a tin of chloride of lime from the farm-house – another triangle had fixed itself in my fingers – I made a cast which for pure skill, exact judgement of distance, and perfect coincidence of hand and eye and brain, would have taken every prize at a bait-casting tournament. That was the first half of the cast. The second was postponed because the quill minnow would not return to its proper place, which was under the lobe of my ear. It had done thus before and I supposed it was in collision with a grass tuft, till I turned round and saw a large red and white bald faced cow trying to rub what would be withers in a horse with her nose. She looked at me reproachfully, and her look said as plainly as words: "The season is too far advanced for gadflies. What is this strange disease?"

I replied, "Madam, I must apologise for an unwarrantable liberty on the part of my minnow, but if you will give the goodness to keep still until I can reel in, we will adjust this little difficulty."

I reeled in very swiftly and cautiously, but she would not wait. She put her tail in the air and ran away. It was a purely involuntary motion on my part: I struck. Other anglers may contradict me, but I firmly believe that if a man had foul-hooked his best friend through the nose, and that friend ran, the man would strike by instinct. I struck, therefore, and the reel began to sing just as merrily as though I had caught my jack. But had it been a jack, the minnow would have come away. I told the tackle-maker this much afterwards, and he laughed and made allusions to the guarantee about holding a horse.

Because it was a fat innocent she-cow that had done me no harm the minnow held – held like an anchor-fluke in coral moorings – and I was forced to dance up and down an interminable field very largely used by cattle. It was like salmon fishing in a nightmare. I took gigantic strides, and every stride found me up to my knees in marsh. But the cow seemed to skate along the squashy green by the brook, to skim over the miry backwaters, and to float like a mist through the patches of rush that squirted black filth over my face. Sometimes we whirled through a mob of her friends – there were no friends to help me – and they looked scandalized; and sometimes a young and frivolous cart-horse would join in the chase for a few miles, and kick solid pieces of mud into my eyes; and through all the mud, the milky smell of kine, the rush and the smother, I was aware of my own voice crying: "Pussy, pussy, pussy! Pretty pussy! Come along then, puss-cat!" You see it is so hard to speak to a cow properly, and she would not listen – no, she would not listen.

Then she stopped, and the moon got up behind the pollards to tell the cows to lie down; but they were all on their feet, and they came trooping to see. And she said, "I haven't had my supper, and I want to go to bed, and please don't worry me." And I said, "The matter has passed beyond any apology. There are three courses open to you, my dear lady. If you'll have the common sense to walk up to my creel I'll get my knife and you shall have all the minnow. Or, again, if you'll let me move across to your near side, instead of keeping me so coldly on your off side, the thing will come away in one tweak. I can't pull it out over your withers. Better still, go to a post and rub it out, dear. It won't hurt much, but if you think I'm going to lose my rod to please you, you are mistaken." And she said, "I don't understand what you are saying. I am very, very unhappy." And I said, "It's all your fault for trying to fish. Do go to the nearest gate-post, you nice fat thing, and rub it out."

For a moment I fancied she was taking my advice. She ran away and I followed. But all the other cows came with us in a bunch, and I thought of Phaeton trying to drive the Chariot of the Sun, and Texan cowboys killed by stampeding cattle, and "Green Grow the Rushes, O!" and Solomon and Job, and "loosing the bands of Orion," and hooking Behemoth, and Wordsworth who talks about whirling round with stones and rocks and trees, and "Here we go round the Mulberry Bush," and "Pippin Hill," and "Hey Diddle Diddle," and most especially the top joint of my rod. Again she stopped – but nowhere in the neighbourhood of my knife – and her sisters stood moonfaced round her. It seemed that she might, now, run towards me, and I looked for a tree, because cows are very different from salmon, who only jump against the line, and never molest the fisherman. What followed was worse than any direct attack. She began to buck-jump, to stand on her head and her tail alternately, to leap into the sky, all four feet together, and to dance on her hind legs. It was so violent and improper, so desperately unladylike, that I was inclined to blush, as one would blush at the sight of a prominent statesman sliding down a fire escape, or a duchess chasing her cook with a skillet. That flop-some abandon might go on all night in the lonely meadow among the mists, and if it went on all night – this was pure inspiration – I might be able to worry through the fishing line with my teeth.

Those who desire an entirely new sensation should chew with all their teeth, and against time, through a best waterproofed silk line, one end of which belongs to a mad cow dancing fairy rings in the moonlight; at the same time keeping one eye on the cow and the other on the top joint of a split-cane rod. She buck-jumped and I bit on the slack just in front of the reel; and I am in a position to state that that line was cored with steel wire throughout the particular section which I attacked. This has been formally denied by the tacklemaker, who is not to be believed.

The *wheep* of the broken line running through the rings told me that henceforth the cow and I might be strangers. I had already bidden good-bye to some tooth or teeth; but no price is too great for freedom of the soul.

"Madam," I said, "the minnow and twenty feet of very superior line are your alimony without reservation. For the wrong I have unwittingly done to you I express my sincere regret. At the same time, may I hope that Nature, the kindest of nurses, will in due season —"

She or one of her companions must have stepped on her spare end of the line in the dark, for she bellowed wildly and ran away, followed by all the cows. I hoped the minnow was disengaged at last; and before I went away looked at my watch, fearing to find it nearly midnight. My last cast for the jack was made at 6.23 pm. There lacked still three and a-half minutes of the half-hour; and I would have sworn that the moon was paling before the dawn!

"Simminly someone were chasing they cows down to bottom o' Ten Acre," said the farmer that evening. "Twasn't you, sir?"

"Now under what earthly circumstances do you suppose I should chase your cows? I wasn't fishing for them, was I?"

Then all the farmer's family gave themselves up to jam-smeared laughter for the rest of the evening, because that was a rare and precious jest, and it was repeated for months, and the fame of it spread from that farm to another, and yet another at least three miles away, and it will be used again for the benefit of visitors when the freshets come down in spring.

But to the greater establishment of my honour and glory I submit in print this bald statement of fact, that I may not, through forgetfulness, be tempted later to tell how I hooked a bull on a Marlow Buzz, how he ran up a tree and took to water, and how I played him along the London-road for thirty miles, and gaffed him at Smithfield. Errors of this kind may creep in with the lapse of years, and it is my ambition ever to be a worthy member of that fraternity who pride themselves on never deviating by one hair's breadth from the absolute and literal truth.

ON TALKING TO THE FISH

Arthur Ransome

1929

I WONDER WHETHER all fishermen, without knowing it, talk to their fish. When with a companion they seem in talking to him to find relief from an excitement that must otherwise come out in monologue. A gillie I know, says that all the men he has carried a gaff for, swear all the time they have a fish on, with the exception of two parsons. One of these grunts and the other "talks mush in such a way that if you did not know him you would think he was using bad language". I have heard a small boy adjuring his float to "Bob, you brute!" and a small girl who did not like taking fish off the hooks, apologizing to a perch for snatching away the bait which he was visibly on the point of taking. Pike, certainly, are seldom caught in silence. The language used to them is not polite. They look for hostility and are met with it. Many an angler more than half believes that he has heard them answer back. When a pike comes up out of the water, opens his great white mouth and shakes his head, it is hard to believe that he does not actually bark.

A month or two ago I was fortunate in overhearing nearly the whole of the catching of a salmon. I was eating my sandwiches behind a rock when a salmon fisher who did not know I was there came to the head of the pool. There was no one else in sight, and I was startled by hearing him say, not at all below his breath, "Just by the rock's the place". He began casting at once and at the second or third cast I heard "Ha! Looked at it did you? Wondered what museum I'd stolen it from and why I wanted to show it to you? Well, take another look at it. It'll be coming to you in a moment. Now where are you? Hurry up or the gates 'll be closed. Last chance of seeing the celebrated Johannes Scotus . . . There you are . . . But why not take the beastly thing? Not good enough for you? Rubbish. Now all the wise men say that I ought to offer you a smaller one of the same. But you and I know better. You want to see this one again. And you shall. Now then. Out of the smooth and into the stream. Are you waiting for it or have you gone off to lament your lack of appetite. Ha . . . One to be ready. Two to be steady. Three to decide that even if he takes it striking is a mug's game and four to . . . tighten . . . ra . . . ther . . . FIRMLY."

At this point the fisherman came down through the shallows at the head of the pool with his rod point well up, his reel screaming and his line taut to something moving rapidly far down the pool. The fisherman hurried over the boulders. "Would you? Would you?" I heard him ejaculate defiantly, evidently attributing to the fish responsibility for an awkward stumble. He got below his fish and I could see from his lips that he was talking continuously, though I could hear nothing but the stream. I picked up my gaff and, keeping well away from the river went down and took up a position not far from the fisherman, but well out of his way so that I could act as gillie for him if he wanted one. I suppose he must have heard the noise of my arrival, for he looked for half a second in my direction, but he was far too much engrossed in his contest with the fish not to forget my presence almost instantly. He and the fish were alone together. There was no one else in their world.

"Yes, my dear," I heard him say, "you are perfectly right. That big stone is the place to make for. Get the line round that and we part company. But I lost a relation of yours round that stone and just for that very reason . . . steady now . . . I am not going to lose you. No, no, my lad. You're on the wrong side. You should have gone on the other side and got the gut on the sharp edge. What? You think you'll settle down there, do you? Tire me out, eh? We'll see about that . . . Now then. This way with your head, my friend. Just feel the current on your cheek. So. Out you come. Upstream? De . . . lighted. As far as you want to go. Nothing keeping you. There's sixty yards of backing on this reel. Oh. So you don't want to go any further after all. Well, my dear, you'll have to work hard to keep where you are. There's good strong water coming down there. What? dropping already. You might have had the decency to drop this side the stream. You can't think that I'm going to lug you across. Now this little backwater here would be just the place to land you. If you won't see it, I can't make you. But . . . look here, if you go much further, you'll have to take a nasty toss into the pool below and I shall have to get down before you. Disobliging brute. Another two yards and there'll be no stopping yourself. Now then, easy, easy . . ."

The fisherman slid down over the rocks just in time to keep the line clear as the fish rolled through the fall into the low pool. Few things are more astonishing than the gymnastics of which even an elderly man finds himself capable when he has a good fish at the end of his line. The fisherman went down over those rocks like a boy and, with the fish still on, was moving steadily down the low pool before I had had time to make up my mind to follow him. I had no fish to give wings to my feet and took a minute or two to climb down.

I found the conversation still proceeding, though its tone was much less friendly. "Tired are you, now? No more tricks of that kind. You've spoilt two pools for me. Couldn't you stick to the ring and fight it out handsomely in one. Turning the best pool of the river into a circus. It'll be a couple of hours before it is worth fishing. No, enough of that. You wouldn't come into that backwater. Try this one. So. Another yard. Another foot. What? Not tired yet? Saw the gaff, did you? Didn't like the look of my face. I shouldn't have thought you had that much run left in you. Coming down again now. Turning over. Keep your head up-stream. Round again. Thank you. Inshore with you. Over it. Now, my beauty . . ." The fisherman lifted out his fish and carried it up the shingle.

He turned to me. He was very hot and rather breathless. "He's not a bad fish," he said, "Twelve or fourteen pounds. Not more." He spoke in quiet appraisement. I am sure that if I had told him that he had been talking aloud to that same fish for the last ten minutes, he would not have believed me. I wonder, is it so with us all?

ON A LONG ISLAND STREAM AND ON FISHING WITH WOMEN

Arnold Gingrich

1965

ONE BAD THING about the wonderful fishing in Europe, where I lived for the last half of the forties, was that it spoiled you for the kind of hard fishing you'd be likely to encounter most places you'd go in the over-fished and over-populated places around our big eastern cities. It was as hard to readjust as it was to readjust to American cigarettes.

When I stepped off the plane, after a mere four years of smoking *Colonials* (Maryland caporals) in Switzerland, *Gauloises* in France, *Nazionale* in Italy, *Munkacz* in Hungary and *Woodbines* in England, I naturally asked for the cigarettes I'd been smoking for more than twenty years before I went away. My first drag set in train a series of self-cocking automatic coughs that kept up as long as I puffed. I had to get weaned from the harsh workmen's cigarettes to which my taste had become accustomed, a course of treatment that led me through Picayunes to Home Runs to Sweet Caporals to Piedmonts before I could finally settle on to something as universally available as Camels, a brand that I had never smoked before but which, at that stage, was the only popular American one that I could smoke without coughing.

Much the same thing had to take place with my fishing. I found that I had acquired habits, in the course of dealing with the too permissive Austrian trout, that might possibly have been persisted in with impunity in some of our western fishing, but that could not possibly escape penalty in the East.

An added difficulty was the fact that everywhere I went with a fly rod I found myself lost in an army of hardware-heavers armed with spinning rods. In the early fifties a lot of people who really should have known better, along with a lot more who had never known how to use anything else, had suddenly discovered spinning, and few and far between were the trout waters that hadn't been literally scoured with spinning lures. I was to find it almost impossible to raise a trout to a surface fly or a nymph, right after somebody had just finished bombarding him with brass lures and silver spoons. The trout were huddled on the bottom where nothing I could do would lure them to leave.

In desperation, after a few futile tries, I began to look around for some New York equivalent of my old Fin 'n' Feather ready-made fishing of Chicago days.

In the company of a new wife who just loved fishing, but had all the patience of a wounded she-grizzly, I thought I'd better find a place where we could both go fishing and get some fish.

I was to find nothing comparable to the Fin 'n' Feather's old fishing by the pound, but I did learn of a place, just seventy miles from Manhattan, and only in its second season, which had been converted from a century-old fishing club on the Carmans River on Long Island, where Daniel Webster had according to legend once landed a forty-pound trout, which now offered fly fishing on a daily rod-fee basis.

It had, as indeed it still has, three miles of the Carmans River, a slow-moving stream, much like one of the Hampshire or Normandy chalk streams, weed-filled but with a good sand-and-gravel bottom and crystalline water. The two and a quarter miles could be easily waded, even in hip boots, while the lower three-quarters of a mile deepened into a fifty-acre lake.

The club had actually ceased to function as a club as long before as 1923, when one of its members, Anson W. Hard, had taken over its original six hundred acres as his own estate, and then added to enlarge it to its present thirteen-hundred-acre size.

Upon his death, his son Kenneth, who had been studying forestry intending to go into conservation work, decided to convert the estate for his mother's benefit into a hunting and fishing preserve.

The residence, a rambling shingle-sided dwelling with attached stables, of an impressively manor-like sprawl, was adapted to house guests in a style more baronial than nineteen out of twenty of them could possibly have known at home. And the one-time Suffolk Club became The Suffolk Lodge Game Preserve.

Going there for a weekend, back in '52, my new wife and I had the feeling of going to visit some Lord and Lady Algy, somewhere in Hampshire. We were met at the Brookhaven stop on the Long Island in a station wagon driven by Bud, one of the gamekeepers, and driven to the park-like grounds.

On the way, my wife wondered whether Bud had any other name.

"Yes ma'am," he answered, "Stuyvesant Van Veen."

If he'd said "Henry Van Dyke" I couldn't have been more surprised, or even "Washington Irving," because everything about Bud seemed Buddy-buddy, but in that sense he was typical of the establishment as a whole, because everything about the place was as shaggily friendly as a sheep-dog pup, but it all seemed old, old, old New York, and very Long Island.

Ken Hard and his wife Lee, looking like prototypes for the illustrations of an Abercrombie & Fitch catalogue, met us at the portico'd front door, which gave onto a large courtyard where you expected to see carriages drive up. He, darkly clean-cut in a way somehow reminiscent of the late Richard Barthelmess and she blonde and outdoorsy, tall and scrubbed to a bright burnish, they were both wearing shooting clothes of most casual elegance, and both looked absurdly young, as if they were playing house while the elders were out, and not really running a layout as impressive as this.

But run it they did, and do (though not Lee any more, as she and Bud subsequently wound up together as the Van Veens and Ken and a new wife from Germany carry on as the Hards), and in those early days they pampered their guests ineffably. We were driven through the preserve's then-narrow sand trails to and from the various beats on the stream in a shooting brake and brought Lucullan lunches onstream in wicker hampers, with the sparkle of the glassware only exceeded by the gleam of the silver, with hot dishes covered in stiffly immaculate napery.

The wading is easy, no more than mid-thigh deep, even for a woman of junior size, and the current gentle. In most places the stream meanders through green thickets, companionably narrow, permitting two people just enough room to fish it downstream with wet flies, side by side. Here and there are V dams where the stream is hollowed and widened enough to create good holding water for the trout, making it a near certainty to get at least one strike in the vicinity of each V dam. Other hot spots for fish action were created by long smooth glides where the stream whispers along beneath overhanging trees. Throughout the more than two miles of stream, divided into three beats, or sections, there is nothing in sight, beyond the several stream-side duck blinds and one power line to remind you that you are within a thousand miles of anything but wilderness, save for an occasional weathered sign tacked to a tree and an abandoned couple of cabins, dating from the long ago days of the Suffolk Club.

Places where you can clamber out of the stream, to answer a call of nature are mercifully frequent, though never less than a long city block or so apart, as in most sections once you're in, you're in, the margins of weed and shrubs and assorted under- and overgrowth making both sides virtually bankless.

The fishing was fine, Ken having stocked the stream weekly with fat and coony browns and bright and sassy rainbows, from eleven to twenty inches long, and there was even the admixture of some perky little native brookies, averaging eight inches, diminished but unabashed descendants of the undoubtedly sea-going whopper with which legend credits Daniel Webster. It was because of these latter denizens of the stream that Ken always bent over backward to make sure that everybody who fished his water, private and stocked and restricted though it might be, still had a New York State fishing license, in addition to his own permission, implicit in the daily rod fee. Ken set the daily creel limit at five fish, just half of that permitted by the state on its public streams, and at first tried to enforce the rule that any fish landed must be kept. Since the fishing was limited to the use of flies only, except on the lake where all forms of artificial lures were allowed, the rule seemed actually to be going counter to his own interests, and when convinced that the individual fisherman had sense enough to handle his catch carefully, so that the fish was returned to the water no worse for the experience, and possibly somewhat wiser, after being caught, Ken was willing to relax the regulation. Actually in most cases this consideration was academic, as the fishing at Suffolk Lodge was not a snap, as it had been at the Fin 'n' Feather, so that for most anglers, especially those fishing the stream for the first time, the five fish limit became a goal rather than a restriction. Certain anglers, like three priests from St. Patrick's in New York who had season rods and fished every Friday and Saturday, Sunday being their busy day and they working, as one of them put it for a very stern Boss, came to be so expert in placing a Grey Ghost in known sure-fire places in the South Section that they undoubtedly could and did reach multiples of the limit, but they were exceptional.

Why then, since the fishing was ideal, in that though the fish were abundant they were not too easy to catch, was I not altogether happy with that first season at Suffolk Lodge? The company was congenial, the meals were superb, the bedrooms and baths were par for every comfort and convenience, Ken and Lee were the best of hosts, anticipating your every least wish and yet leaving your privacy intact, and the nights were as much your own, to do what you liked, as were the days.

The answer was not in the fishing, nor yet with Suffolk Lodge with which there wasn't, nor isn't today, anything wrong. I went back there, again and again over a decade, and always found it delightful. The answer was that the fault, as was told to Brutus, was in each other.

We weren't happy with each other's fishing, and if you're not happy with each other's fishing, it will not be long before you're not happy with each other. We weren't and it wasn't.

We used to leave our gear at Suffolk Lodge through the week, to obviate the nuisance of carting it back and forth to the city, but before the next season came around I had to make a solitary trip out there, to separate the his from the hers, and see to it that hers got back to her.

An elapsed time of eight months for a marriage, *aller et retour*, is short even by today's standards. And it would be oversimplification to say that, but for fishing, that marriage might have lasted longer. Still, it might not be too wide of the mark to apply to this tender point a dictum with which General Sarnoff has been credited, "competition brings out the best in products and the worst in people."

I keep hearing about happy fishing couples, like the Lou Hartmans who catch all those muskies, and the Chauncey K. Livelys who not only fish together but keep talking about meeting other people who do too. I can only conclude either that one member of such happy couples must be a liar or, if not, that they must have in equal parts the dispositions of angels and the patience of saints.

Charlie Ritz is on record, rather wistfully I feel, to the effect that fishing is a sport and a pastime and not a competition, and that it ought to remain a sport and a pleasure, because otherwise it's worse than work. Charles Ritz is one of the happiest fishermen I know and the one who without entirely turning professional, has with evident impunity permitted his fishing to take up a measurable portion of his waking time. But it's a long time since he's been married.

We would get out on the stream at Suffolk Lodge and I'd take a fish. Mistake. I should have had sense enough to wait until she'd taken the first fish.

So the next time out, I'd try to be more thoughtful. But fish are like cats, in that the only time that you can be sure they'll come to you is when you don't want them. And a fish is even harder to shoo away, once you've hooked it, than a cat. Almost any fish will get off the hook if you're scared enough that he will, but no fish will ever get off a hook if you're afraid that he won't.

But it wasn't only the first fish that mattered. It was the same thing with every fish thereafter. I couldn't be one ahead at any time. Or if we were even then it was very impolitic to have mine be so much as a fraction of an inch larger than hers. Or if her fish, whether it was first or last or current, happened to be a rainbow, then mine had better be a rainbow, too. It didn't dare turn out to be a brown, because even if it were considerably smaller it would still outrank the rainbow, since browns had a scarcity value in the average fishing at Suffolk Lodge, as against rainbows, that might go anywhere from three to six rainbows for one brown. On the other hand, it had better not be a brookie, either, no matter how small, because the browns were stocked and the brookies were wild, so status was involved there, too.

The only thing to do, under the circumstances, was to try to fish ineptly, but that has its drawbacks, too, when you're fishing side by side. You don't dare make a fish-scaring slap with a deliberately bad cast, because in a narrow stream it will scare all the fish, and not just those on your side, bringing forth instant vituperation. So you try making as unlikely motions as possible with your line hand on the retrieve. This has its dangers, too, because sometimes all it takes to make a reluctant fish decide to take is some unorthodox jerkings of the fly to vary the monotony of the too-steady retrieve. The next expedient is to try leaving a bit of moss or grass trailing from the hook-point, but that will be noticed, no less by her than the fish, so after a time or two it gets you classified as stupid. So another gambit is to try a larger size than that of the fly on which they have last taken. This is good, but still dangerous, on the "big bait big fish" premise. Safer, is to try some utterly unlikely fly. If they've been taking a Dark Cahill wet, size 14, then try a big gaudy Parmachene Belle, size 10 or even 8 if you've got one. But that's catnip to brookies, and the smaller they are the bigger size fly they'll take. So the only safe device is to continue to spend as much time as possible getting hung up in the trees or shrubs. But not on the forward cast, for God's sake, because then you're likely to louse up the patch of stream ahead of you where she's fishing. Of course, you can always be a gentleman and offer to wait, before going ahead to try to get your fly down off the branches, until she's finished working her current spot and is ready to move on downstream. But then you're rushing her, and you know how she hates to be rushed. Safer to get hung up on your backcast, where you can dawdle around upstream getting it freed, although if you spend too much time at it you earn icy contempt for the lack of coordination which is obviously adding an insuperable handicap to your innate stupidity. Still it's the best choice, because the one time you can't catch a fish is when your fly is nowhere near the water.

The one time the lack of coordination charge may have been well founded, we were fishing in a section which, while still wadable in chest waders, was too deep for our hip boots, and Ken had given us a small aluminum pram to use. This diminutive square-ended skiff, about the size and shape of a cement mixer, could be poled or paddled about the stream, which is considerably wider in this section, and because of its platform-like bottom was considered safe to stand up in. It was close quarters, even when staying as far apart as possible, for two of us to fish from at the same time.

As we drifted into sight of an abandoned cabin, set back in the woods some fifty yards from the stream's left bank, she became curious about it, wanted to see it, and even wondered if it might be possible to fix it up enough so that some kind of deal could be worked out with Ken to let us stay in it.

I poled us over toward the left bank, started to get out on the vestigial remains of a one-time pier or dock that had been on that edge, and only realized as I jumped onto an old rafter that the rest of it was resting under the pram, which was catapulted over neatly, unfortunately with her still in it, by the leverage exerted by the rest of the board as soon as my weight hit its other end.

The pram didn't sink, though she did. I had tried to correct my mistake by attempting to jump back away from the rafter as soon as I sensed its motion, but of course missed the pram in the process, and landed in the water hardly a matter of more than a few seconds after she did.

Each of us looked funny enough to the other, when we had both scrambled to our feet and stood, respectively, waist and chest deep in the river, that involuntary laughter was the first triggered reaction.

But though we visited the abandoned cabin, as planned, it was to wring out our wet clothes, and not another word was said, then or ever, about fixing it up as a place to stay.

I had long before decided, of course, that I didn't like any form of fishing from any sort of boat, but the pram may have helped to reinforce that decision.

What I had also long thought, but now knew for certain, was that competition takes all the fun out of fishing, and makes it, as Charlie Ritz says, worse than work.

As for women and fishing, while I know that superstition and tradition are against them, as was pointed out by William Radcliffe in *Fishing from the Earliest Times*, among other places, still I have no feeling against it. Some of my best friends are women. I'm married to an ex-fisher.

Still, one of Radcliffe's citations has a certain interest: "women seem usually fatal to good catches; as one instance out of many we read in Hollinshed's *Scottish Chronicle* that if a woman wade through the one fresh river in the Lewis, there shall no salmon be seen there for a twelvemonth after."

On the other hand, some great fishermen have fished with women, even above and beyond those I've already mentioned. Al and Patti McClane fish together. But I throw that out. Al McClane can fish with anybody. And Patti McClane can fish with me, and often has and I hope will again.

The sainted Theodore Gordon himself fished with at least one woman, and I've been in love with her picture for a decade. You will find it in John McDonald's volume of the notes and letters of Gordon, *The Complete Fly Fisherman*, published by Scribner's in 1947.

There they stand together, in the Neversink in a spot that I believe I recognize as his favorite pool in Mr Hewitt's old stretch, with Gordon looking pale and wan and delicate, and she looking tall and stately as Tennyson's Maud, her long skirts in, but somehow nonetheless disdainful of, the flowing waters, and a lovelier sight I never saw.

But women fishing is one thing, and watching women fishing is another, but women watching fishing – well, in my experience, women who watch fishermen, at least stream fishermen, almost invariably remind me of a dog watching television. They have no capacity of sustained attention, no concentration whatsoever, and an eye only for the extraneous and inconsequential.

Still, there is a fairly general feeling that for some reason fishing should be a shared experience. There's industry propaganda to the effect of Take a Boy Fishing. I've taken boys fishing, and on two of them out of three it didn't take. As for just taking any boy fishing, well, why? Bless Dave Bascom of San Francisco, he who edits that hilarious fishing paper, *The Wretched Mess*, and is to my mind the funniest man on feet since W.C. Fields went horizontal. "Yes," says Dave Bascom, "Take a Boy Fishing – and throw the little bastard in."

I've known men who said they didn't go fishing any more, since their old Buddy died, or moved away or whatever. And they didn't mean their wives. I wonder if such men really ever did go fishing. Maybe they just went on what used to be called "outings," presumably because their chief attraction was that they let you out of the house. I'm all for friendship, and partnership has been a good idea since Damon and Pythias, I suppose, but if what you're setting out to do is to come, by the most permissive of definitions, within the pale of angling, then you don't need a partner. Your partner, your one true old Buddy, if you could only get it through his minimal brain, is the fish.

In its deepest self, fishing is the most solitary sport, for at its best it's all between you and the fish.

THE FISHING HOLE

Guy de Maupassant

1887

Inflicting blows and wounds causing death. Such was the charge on which M. Léopold Renard, upholsterer, appeared before the assizes.

In court were the chief witnesses, Mme Flamèche, widow of the victim; Louis Ladureau, cabinetmaker; and Jean Durdent, plumber: while close to the accused was his wife, in black – small, ugly, like a monkey dressed up as a woman.

And here is Renard (Léopold)'s account of the drama.

"As God is my witness, this is a catastrophe where, far from being the cause, I was all along the chief victim. The facts speak for themselves, My Lord. I am a decent man, a hard-working man, upholsterer these sixteen years in the same street, known, liked, respected, well thought of by all, as you've heard the neighbours say, even the house-porter, who speaks a sane word now and then. I'm fond of work, I'm fond of thrift, I'm fond of honest folk and of harmless pleasures. That's been my undoing, worse luck. Still, as I did nothing of intent, I feel no shame.

"Well, every Sunday for five years my wife here and I have spent the day at Poissy. That takes us into the open air – to say nothing of our love of fishing. Why, we're as keen on that as on spring onions! Mélie's the one that gave me the craze, the wretch, and that she's madder on it than I am, the sinner, you can see from all this trouble having come about through her, as assuredly it did, as you'll learn.

"As for me, I'm no soft one, yet I'm easy-going, without a pennyworth of wickedness. But as for her, well, well! You'd think her quite harmless, she's so small and skinny. Let me tell you, though, she's more spiteful than a cat. I'm not denying that she has her points; indeed she has, and important ones for one like me in business. But her disposition! Just you ask the neighbours, and even the house-porter, who put in a word for me a moment ago – she can tell you things.

"Day in day out she kept harping on about my softness. 'I wouldn't put up with this. I wouldn't put up with that.' Had I listened to her, My Lord, I'd have been in three scraps a month at least."

Mme Renard cut in: "Keep on. He laughs best who laughs last."

He turned towards her, not mincing his words: "Oh well, I can say what I like about you, seeing it's not you that's on trial, you."

Then turning to the judge again, he said:

"I proceed. We always went, then, to Poissy on Saturday evenings to be able to start our fishing next morning at daybreak. That custom became a kind of second nature, as the saying goes. Three years past this summer I discovered a swim – and such a swim! Shaded, eight feet of water at the least, perhaps ten. What a spot it was with its hollows under the bank – a regular lair of fishes! Talk about an angler's heaven! This hole, My Lord, I could look on as my own, seeing I was its Christopher Columbus. Everyone in the district knew it for mine, everyone – not a soul to dispute it. 'That, oh, that's Renard's spot,' they'd say, and nobody dreamt of going there, not even M. Plumeau, who is notorious, and no offence meant in saying it, for pinching the places of others.

"Well, certain always of my place, I went back and back to it just like an owner. The moment I arrived on Saturdays I boarded *Dalila* with my wife. *Dalila*, I should explain, is a Norwegian boat I had made for me by Fournaise – light yet strong. I was saying, then, that we boarded *Dalila*, and we would set about baiting the swim. As for baiting, there's no one to touch me, and well my pals all know it. You want to hear what I bait with? Well, I can't tell you. It has nothing to do with the case, I just can't tell you. It's my secret. Hundreds have asked me for it. I've been offered drinks and dainties no end to make me part with it. But just go and see if the chub come! Oh yes, they've tried to pet my patent out through my tummy. But not another soul knows it apart from my wife, and she won't tell it any more than I shall. Isn't that so, Mélie?"

The judge interrupted: "Just get to the point as soon as you can."

Whereupon the accused went on: "I'm getting to it, I'm getting to it. Well, on Saturday, the 8th of July, we left by the 5.25 train, and, as we always did on Saturdays, went before dinner to bait the swim. The weather promised to be fine. I said to Mélie: 'Great work tomorrow, great work.' And she answered: 'Looks like it.' We never talk more than that to each other.

"Then we came back to dinner. I was feeling good, and I was dry. That's where the whole trouble began, My Lord. I said to Mélie: 'Look here, Mélie, I think it would be an idea if I had a bottle of "nightcap."'" That's a light white wine we've christened so, because, if you drink too much of it, it keeps you awake and is just the opposite of a nightcap. You get the idea?

"She replied: 'Have your way, but you'll be upset again and won't be able to get up to-morrow.' There for you was truth, wisdom, prudence, discernment – I own it. Still I couldn't resist, and back I knock the bottle. Whence the whole trouble.

"Well, I couldn't sleep. Good Lord! that grape-juice nightcap kept me awake till two in the morning. Then in a twinkling, over I go, and so soundly that I'd have been deaf to the last trump itself.

"To be brief, my wife woke me at six. Out of bed I spring. On in a jiffy with my trousers and jersey, a dash of water on my mug, and into *Dalila* we jump. Too late. When I get to the swim it is already taken. Never had that happened before, My Lord, never in three years. Why, I was being robbed before my very eyes! 'Well I'm damned, I'm damned, I'm damned,' I cried. And then my wife began to rail at me: 'That's your night-cap for you. Get out, you soaker. Are you satisfied now, you stupid fool?'

"I answered nothing. Everything she said was true.

"I went ashore, however, near the spot, by way of making the best of a bad job. Perhaps the fellow wouldn't catch anything after all, and would clear out.

"He was a little skinny chap, in white drill and with a large straw hat. His wife was with him, a fat woman, who was sitting behind, sewing.

"When she saw us taking up our position near the spot, what do you think she muttered?

"'Is this, then, the only place on the river?'

"And my wife, fuming, replied:

"'People of ordinary decency usually make a point of finding out local ways. It keeps them off others' preserves.'

"As I didn't want a row, I said to her:

"'Hold your tongue, Mélie. Don't answer back, don't answer back. We'll see about this all right.'

"Well, we had tied up *Dalila* under the willows and had got out and were fishing side by side, Mélie and I, right beside the other two.

"Here, My Lord, I must go into detail.

"We hadn't been there five minutes, when down went my neighbour's line twice, thrice, and lo and behold, he hauled out a chub, big as my thigh, a bit less perhaps, but not much! My heart gave a jump, my brow broke into a sweat, and Mélie cried: 'Hi, you toper, did you see that?'

"Just then, M. Bru, the grocer of Poissy, a dab with the gudgeon, passed by in his boat and shouted:

"'So somebody's taken your place, M. Renard?' 'Yes, M. Bru,' I replied, 'there are some toughs in this world who don't know how to behave.'

"The little fellow in drill at my side pretended not to hear. His fat lump of a wife likewise, the cow."

The judge interrupted a second time: "Careful of your language. You insult the widow, Mme Flamèche, here."

Renard made excuse: "Pardon me, pardon me, my feelings ran away with me."

"Well, a quarter of an hour had hardly gone, when what should the little devil in drill do but yank out another fish, a chub, and then another on top of it, and still another five minutes later.

"I tell you I was on the verge of tears, and I could sense Mme Renard bursting with rage. She kept on rating me without pausing for breath: 'You miserable fool, don't you see you're being robbed of your fish? Don't you see it? You'll catch nothing, you, nothing, nothing, not even a frog. Don't my hands itch merely to think of it?'

"All I said, and to myself, was: 'Just wait till noon. He'll go to lunch then, this poaching fellow, and you'll get back your place.' You see, My Lord, we lunch every Sunday on the spot. We bring food with us in *Dalila*.

"Bah! Twelve struck. The wretch had a chicken wrapped up in a newspaper, and, would you believe it, while he ate he actually caught another chub!

"Mélie and I had a crumb, hardly anything. As things were, we didn't feel like it.

"Then to aid digestion I took up my newspaper. Every Sunday I read *Gil Blas* like that in the shade by the waterside. Sunday is Columbine's day, Columbine, you know, who writes articles in *Gil Blas*. I've a way of infuriating Mme Renard by pretending to know this Columbine. It's all a yarn. I don't know her at all, have never even seen her. Still she writes well, hits out and to the point, for a woman. She suits me down to the ground. After all, there're not so many of her kind.

"Well, then, I began ragging my wife, but at once she got angry, furiously angry, and then angrier still. So I said no more.

"Just at this moment our two witnesses here, M. Ladureau and M. Durdent, appeared on the other bank. We know each other by sight.

"The little fellow had begun fishing again and to such tune that I shook from sheer vexation. Then his wife said: 'This is a thundering good spot, we'll keep on coming here, Désiré.'

"A cold shiver ran down my spine, and Mme Renard kept on saying: 'Call yourself a man, call yourself a man! You chicken heart!'

"'Look here,' I said quickly, 'I'd rather clear out. I shall only do something I'll regret.'

"She hissed as if she'd scald me: 'Call yourself a man! Now you're running away, giving up your place! Run away then, you Bazaine!'

"That went home. Still I did not wince.

"Then what does the other fellow do but drag out a bream! Never had I seen such a thumper before. Never.

"And now my wife began to talk out loud – pretending to be merely thinking. You see what a she-devil she is. 'This is what one might call stolen fish,' she said, 'seeing it was we who baited the swim. They ought at least to pay us for the bait.'

"Whereupon the little drill-clad bloke's fat wife chipped in: 'Is it us you're getting at madam?'

"'I'm getting at fish thieves, those who profit by what's been spent by others.'

"'Are you calling us fish thieves then?'

"Then they began explaining – then slanging. Good Lord! they knew the words all right – real stingers. They bawled so, that our two witnesses, who were on the other bank, called out by way of a joke: 'Hi, you, over there, less row, you'll spoil your husbands' sport!'

"The fact is that the little fellow in drill and myself remained stock still. We stuck where we were, our noses glued to the water, as if we'd never heard.

"But Lord help me, we heard all right!

"'You're nothing but a liar.' – 'And you a strumpet.' – 'And you a trollop.' – 'And you a trull.' And so on and so on. A sailor couldn't have beat them.

"Suddenly I heard a noise behind me and turned round. There was the other woman, the great fat thing, belabouring my wife with her parasol. Whack! whack! Mélie took a couple. But now she was fairly roused, and when Mélie's roused she lams about, I tell you. She seized the fat dame by the hair and then smack! smack! smack! the blows fell like a shower of ripe plums.

"I'd have left them to it – the women to themselves, the men to themselves. Why mix the thing? But up like a devil comes the little drill-suit chap making to spring at my wife. 'No, no, hardly that, my hearty,' says I, and I received the old cock-sparrow flush on the end of my fist. Biff! biff! One on the nose, the other in the guts. Up go his arms, up go his legs, and he falls on his back clean in the river, right in the middle of the swim.

"Most certainly I would have fished him out, My Lord, if I'd had the time just then. But now, to crown all, the fat woman gained the upper hand and was making mincemeat of Mélie. I know well I shouldn't have rescued her while the other was drinking his fill. Still I didn't think he would be drowned. I said to myself: 'Ugh! that'll cool him down.'

"I ran, then, to separate the women. I was pommelled, scratched, bitten. Good Lord, what vixen!

"The long and the short of it was that it took me a good five minutes, nearer ten, perhaps, to part this pair of clingers.

"I turned round. There was nothing to be seen. The water was as smooth as a lake. And the fellows on the other bank kept shouting: 'Fish him out, fish him out.'

"That was all very well, but I can't swim, much less dive, believe me.

"At last, after more than a quarter of an hour it would be, the lock-keeper came along and two men with boat-hooks. They found him at the bottom of the pool, under eight feet of water, as I have said, but there he was, the little fellow in his drill suit.

"These are the facts as I swear to them. On my word of honour I am innocent."

The witnesses having testified in the same sense, the accused was acquitted.

NIGHT FISHING
Sparse Grey Hackle

1971

HEAT AND FEAR oppressed the land, for it was one of those stifling, humid August nights when the whole countryside is awake and every living thing is abroad on the business of life and death. The darkness was so thick and close that one tried instinctively to push it aside, and the air was heavy with the menace of predators and the terror of their prey. The river was soundless save for a faint spattering at my feet, a mere whisper which I could not identify until I turned on my little flashlight and discovered in the very margin of the stream, where it feathered off to nothing on a sandy beach, a dark line of what appeared to be stranded twigs and chaff. It was a horde of the tiniest of minnows, which had taken refuge in the ultimate edge of the water and still leaped frantically over each other in their efforts to be farthest from the prowling fish they knew would soon be seeking them.

I waded across the broad river to where a little cold feeder entered it and began to cast a big black wet fly on a heavy leader, for this is the season when the hellgrammites rise from the river bottom and swim ashore to pupate under stones before hatching into huge nocturnal dobson flies. It was too early yet for big fish to be feeding, but there might be a stray around, and anyway, I wanted to be fishing. So for a couple of hours I inched along silently on felt-shod feet working my fly in the cooler water along the bank, where a fish might be harboring. At midnight it was still hot and breathless. Perspiration dripped off my face, and inside my high waders I was soaked with it. I was weary of swinging the big ten-foot fly rod, too, so I went ashore and sat down for a while before I made my way up to the head of the long pool.

The sky had somehow brightened now, and the darkness, so thick and close before, appeared thin and luminous. It seemed as if I could see farther than I really could, but at least I could make out the stranded log on the far bank shining as white as bone. I replaced my wet fly with a deer-hair bug to imitate some blundering moth and began to work out line along my side of the river. It is difficult to get out in darkness just the length needed to reach one's target but not impossible if one is familiar with the water and his rod, so when I picked up the cast and pushed it straight across at the log, I was confident that my bug would drop right in front of it.

I brought my hand down hard and the bug smacked the water. A white flower of foam blossomed in front of the log, and blossomed again when I swept the tip back in a hard strike. I was into a fish! It headed down the current, and I held the rod high overhead and reeled desperately to take up the slack. I seemed to be choking, and it took me a moment to discover that it was because I was holding my breath.

Alas, the fish was strong but not strong enough; fighting but not fighting hard. Suspicion at once changed to conviction, and conviction became certainty when I brought the fish into the circle of strange pale light cast by the little flashlight which by now I held between my teeth. It was a chub — an alderman, the grandfather of all the chub in the river, a chub as round as a rolling pin, one with pretensions to rise above his class and act like a trout, but still . . . a chub.

I unhooked and returned him — gently, because I was grateful to him for providing a little action; stowed away my flashlight and felt for my pipe. Only then did I realize that my heart was pounding slowly and heavily, like a burned-out main bearing.

That is night fishing, the essence of angling, the emperor of sports. It is a gorgeous gambling game in which one stakes the certainty of long hours of faceless fumbling, nerve-racking starts, frights, falls, and fishless baskets against the off-chance of hooking into — not landing necessarily or even probably, but hooking into — a fish as long and heavy as a railroad tie and as unmanageable as a runaway submarine. It combines the wary stalking and immobile patience of an Indian hunter with sudden, violent action, the mystery and thrill of the unknown, a stimulating sense of isolation and self-reliance, and an unparalleled opportunity to be close to nature since most creatures are really nocturnal in habit.

Above all, it provides the stimulation of sudden fright at the startling things which continually occur in the dark, and in fact I incline to believe that that is the greatest lure of the sport. In all of the night-fishing experiences that I recall, the outstanding thing was always that I was scared half to death. Of these experiences, two are notable.

I used to prowl around in the deep still water where a small brook entered an ice pond, fishing for big rainbows that worked up into the stream after dark. The banks were swampy and in the stream the mud was knee-deep, but there was firm bottom under it and I could work along an inch at a time, wading almost to the top of my armpit-high waders onto the boot feet of which were strapped hobnailed leather sandals.

Saplings grew shallow-rooted on the marshy banks and were continually falling into the stream, so when, this night, I encountered the tip of one that had sunk into the mud, I thought nothing of it and backed away. The trouble was that the point of the sapling had run under the strap of my sandal and, having a knob on it, was stuck and could not be withdrawn. I soon found that I could not break the thing off because it was too flexible, nor drag the whole tree loose because it was too firmly anchored by its roots. So the situation was that I was tethered by the foot twenty feet from shore in mud so thick that I could scarcely move my feet and water so deep I had to move cautiously to avoid filling my waders. And it was darker than the inside of a coal mine.

It was a simple and rather ridiculous plight, but I could see very little about it that was humorous, particularly when I reflected that I was beyond shouting distance of a house or a road. In fact, after I had thoroughly tested the possibilities of getting loose I emitted a little cold perspiration in spite of the warmness of the night.

The only thing I could think of to do – which was to discard my rod, dive down and use my hands to free myself – was neither promising nor inviting. It would leave me flat in the stream with my waders full of water and my feet stuck deep in the mud, probably confused as to the direction in which the bank lay – and I can't swim. If I were unable to regain my feet and my balance in the darkness, and that seemed very likely indeed, I would be in a very perplexing situation. I had also to consider the possibility that I might not be able to free my foot; in that case I would have even less freedom of movement of my legs to assist me in regaining and keeping a vertical position.

I haven't the remotest idea how long I stayed there – it seemed hours – but all the while I was cogitating I was also twisting my foot and flexing the twig. Eventually it either broke off or pulled out, and although I was even keener for night fishing then than I am now and still had plenty of time left, I headed upstream to the hauling-out place at my best speed. And as soon as I got ashore I unstrapped the sandals and hurled them into the bushes. I have never since worn anything when wading at night, under or in which a stick might catch.

My other memorable experience was the result of several varieties of folly. It was early May on the Beaverkill and I had not found fish, so, misled by the warm sun and balmy air, I thought there might be night fishing in my favorite pool, the Wagon Tracks. Normally Cairns' Ford, at the head of the pool, is almost out of water except for a little channel close to the road side of the stream, but now I found it knee-deep all the way across, pants-pocket deep in the channel and of course running like a milltail. It was a tough crossing in daylight; I did not stop to think what it would be like at night.

I found that what was normally the shallow side of the pool had been scoured by floods, and in the high water I had to wade close to the bank. It was not a good sort of night water in that condition, but I was still bemused, so I put on a big stonefly nymph and started working down, casting straight across and letting the fly swing round, then fishing it back close to the bank, an inch at a time. I worked along on numbing legs for hours, staring blankly into darkness relieved only when a car passed along the road on the other side. The water was quiet, dead in fact; and then I thought I felt a light touch on the nymph, right below me, just as it would be finishing its swing. Action at last! Surely something had lipped the nymph; that was just the right point in its swing to expect it. Could I make the fish come again?

Reeling up the slack I had already worked in so that my next cast would come to exactly the same length, I chucked the nymph across the current again, and as it began to swing I unconsciously leaned forward with my arms extended in an attitude of hair-trigger alertness. The line straightened and I knew the big nymph swinging behind it was approaching the spot. Now . . .

Something, a mink perhaps, leaped off the bank and struck the water right under my outstretched arms; as it hit, a good-sized fish leaped out and made its escape.

I stood fixed; I couldn't have moved to save my life. The sweet, sickening taste which is the real flavor of fear filled my mouth and my heart hammered in my throat. I began to strangle and knew I was holding my breath, but I could not command my lungs to function.

When I had recovered the power of movement I decided that I was through, took down my rod and got my little flashlight out to go back across the ford. Now the ford ran at a diagonal and my target was a clump of bushes on the other bank. I couldn't see the bushes with my little light, but I could see the stream bottom – the shallow ford and the deeper water on either side of it. So I went along all right for perhaps a quarter of the way, and then my flashlight played out.

I had only a couple of hundred feet to go, more or less, but that is a long distance when the water is too high, the night too dark and the way too uncertain. I worked ahead feeling for the shallower water but soon got into the position familiar to every night fisherman in which one seems to be surrounded by deeper water. All right; I would stand still until a car came along to shine its headlights on my brushy marker. But this was wartime, with gasoline rationing in force, and people were not driving much at night. I think only the fact that it was Saturday night, traditional "night out" for countrymen as well as city folk, saved me.

I stood there a while beside that short, ugly rapid roaring down into deep water, remembering that I couldn't swim even without high waders and heavy hobnailed shoes to handicap me. Then a car flashed by and I found my marker and stepped out boldly until once more I seemed to be hemmed in by deep water. As I recall, I had to wait for four cars in order to reach the edge of the deeper channel, ten feet from the bank.

I stepped down into it cautiously with one foot, found a rolling stone, dislodged it, and got solid footing; I brought the other foot forward, worked it in and out of some sharp-angled pockets, and planted it beside the first. The water was halfway above my knees now, tearing at my legs, growling and foaming. The steep pounding rapid was white in the darkness and what I could see looked as bad as it sounded. I shuffled a foot forward, then brought the other one up beside it; the water was an inch deeper. I felt and withdrew with first one foot and then the other, then inched half a step downstream to get around something high and slippery. I completed another shuffling step. At last I was just two steps from safety, one into deeper water and the next up onto the bank. I put the rod joints in my mouth to have both hands free and resolved to throw myself forward and grab for bushes if I felt myself going. I took a deep breath and stepped out, and as so often happens, anticipation was worse than reality. My foot held, and in the next instant I was hauling myself out.

I sat down on the running board of my car, filled my pipe, and looked at my watch. It was 1:00 A.M. daylight saving time. My feet were numb, my legs ached, and my mouth was dry, and when I took off my waders I discovered that my knees were trembling slightly but steadily and uncontrollably. Fatigue? Not on your life. I was scared stiff.

MISERIES OF FISHING
Richard Penn

1863

I

Feeling rather unsteady whilst you are walking on a windy day over an old foot-bridge, and having occasion to regret the decayed state of the hand-rail, which once protected the passing fisherman.

II

Suddenly putting up your hand to save your hat in a high wind, and grasping a number of artificial flies, which you had pinned round it, without any intention of taking hold of more than one at a time.

III

Leading a large fish down-stream and arriving at a ditch, the width of which is evident, although the depth of it may be a matter of some doubt. Having thus to decide very quickly whether you will lose the fish and half your tackle, or run the risk of going up to your neck in mud. Perhaps both.

IV

Making a great improvement in a receipt which a friend had given you for staining gut – and finding that you have produced exactly the colour which you wanted, but that the dye has made all your bottoms quite rotten.

V

Fishing for the first time with flies of your own making – and finding that they are quite as good as any which you can buy, except that the hooks are not so firmly tied to the gut.

VI

Taking out with you as your aid-de-camp an unsophisticated lad from the neighbouring village, who laughs at you when you miss hooking a fish rising at a fly, and says with a grin, "You can't fasten 'em as my father does."

VII

Making the very throw which you feel sure will at last enable you to reach a fish that is rising at some distance – and seeing the upper half of your rod go into the middle of the river. When you have towed it ashore, finding that it has broken off close to the ferrule, which is immoveably fixed in the lower half of your rod.

VIII

Feeling the first cold drop giving notice to your great toe that in less than two minutes your boot will be full of water.

IX

Going out on a morning so fine that no man would think of taking his water-proof cloak with him – and then, before two o'clock, being thoroughly wet through by an unexpected shower.

X

When you cannot catch any fish – being told by your attendant of the excellent sport which your predecessor had on the same spot, only a few days before.

XI

Having brought with you from town a large assortment of expensive artificial flies – and being told on showng them to an experienced native, that "none of them are of any use here."

XII

After trying in vain to reach a trout which is rising on the opposite side of the river – at last walking on; and before you have gone 100 yards, looking back, and seeing a more skilful friend catch him at the first throw. – Weight 3 lbs. 2 oz.

XIII

Having stupidly trodden on the top of your rod – and then, finding that the spare top which you have brought out with you in the butt, belongs to the rod which you have left at home, and will not fit that which you are using.

XIV

Having steered safely through some very dangerous weeds a fish which you consider to weigh at least 3 lbs., and having brought him safely to the very edge of the bank, then seeing him, when he is all but in the landing net, make a plunge, which in a moment renders all your previous skill of no avail, and puts it out of your power to verify the accuracy of your calculations as to his weight.

XV

Fishing with the blowing-line when the wind is so light that your fly is seldom more than two yards from you, or when the wind is so strong that it always carries your fly up into the air, before it comes to the spot which you wish it to swim over.

XVI

Wishing to show off before a young friend whom you have been learnedly instructing in the mysteries of the art, and finding that you cannot catch any fish yourself, whilst he (an inexperienced hand) hooks and lands (by mere accident of course) a very large one.

XVII

Attempting to walk across the river in a new place without knowing exactly whereabouts certain holes, which you have heard of, are. Probing the bottom in front of you with the handle of your landing-net, and finding it very soft.

XVIII

Going some distance for three days' fishing, on the two first of which there is bright sunshine and no wind, and then finding that the third, which opens with "a southerly wind and a cloudy sky," is the day which a neighbouring farmer has fixed upon for washing two hundred sheep on the shallow where you expected to have the best sport.

XIX

Being allowed to have one day's fishing in a stream, the windings of which are so many, that it would require half a dozen different winds to enable you to fish the greater part of it, from the only side to which your leave extends.

A Good bite or Swallowing the Bait

XX

Finding, on taking your book out of your pocket, that the fly at the end of your line is not the only one by many dozen which you have had in the water, whilst you have been wading rather too deep.

XXI

Wading half an inch deeper than the tops of your boots, and finding afterwards that you must carry about with you four or five quarts in each, or must sit down on the wet grass whilst your attendant pulls them off, in order that you may empty them, and try to pull them on again.

XXII

Jumping out of bed very early every morning, during the season of the May-fly, to look at a weathercock opposite to your window, and always finding the wind either in the north or east.

XXIII

Having just hooked a heavy fish, when you are using the blowing-line, and seeing the silk break about two feet above your hand; then watching the broken end as it travels quickly through each successive ring, till it finally leaves the top of your rod, and follows the fish to the bottom of the river.

XXIV

Receiving a very elegant new rod from London, and being told by the most skilful of your brother anglers, either that it is so stiff, or that it is so pliant, that it is not possible for any man to throw a fly properly with it.

XXV

Being obliged to listen to a long story about the difficulties which one of your friends had to encounter in landing a very fine trout which has just been placed on the table for dinner, when you have no story of the same sort to tell in return.

XXVI

Hooking a large trout, and then turning the handle of your reel the wrong way; thus producing an effect diametrically opposite to that of shortening your line, and making the fish more unmanageable than before.

XXVII

Arriving just before sun-set at a shallow where the fish are rising beautifully, and finding that they are all about to be immediately driven away by five-and-twenty cows, which are preparing to walk very leisurely across the river in open files.

XXVIII

Coming to an ugly ditch in your way across a water-meadow late in the day, when you are too tired to jump, and being obliged to walk half a mile in search of a place where you think you can step over it.

XXIX

Flattering yourself that you had brought home the largest fish of the day, and then finding that two of your party have each of them caught a trout more than half a pound heavier than yours.

PERILS

H. T. Sheringham

1925

BY COMMON CONSENT fishing is the most peaceful of all forms of sport – exception might perhaps be made of snail-hunting in a well-ordered garden – but the commencing angler must not assume from this that it is wholly free from stresses and storms. There are, indeed, many occasions when it is advisable for him to walk, perhaps even to run, circumspectly. We do not think that in general there is a much better remedy for some grievous situations than circumspect (and fast) running. It is, however, an unfortunate fact that running is not possible to all men, for reasons of figure and age, and one thing and another. The following suggestions, therefore, are for occasions when running is for any cause out of the question.

A BULL

This is one of the worst of dangers. We have known even experienced hunters of lions, rhinoceroses, grizzly bears, and other formidable fauna to go with timid steps past the haunt of an English bull. The best remedy for a bull is undoubtedly a hedge of the largest size and thorniest texture. Screened by this, the angler may have a fairly easy mind.

A deep and wide dyke on the hither side of the animal is also in some sort a protection. But it must never be forgotten that bulls can and do swim and wade across streams, sometimes on very flimsy pretexts. Any dyke, therefore, chosen as a protection should be bridged by a single plank. The exact middle of this is a point of comparative safety. Should the bull be able to get too close to it, the plank may be employed as a means of swift passage from bank to bank. As the bull takes the slower route by water, the angler has a distinct advantage. If the bull shows a preference for the plank, presumably the angler then takes the other route. Or else he waits in the middle of the plank and adroitly pushes the animal off. But the contingency is one of which we have no experience.

Should there be no plank, a heap of stones of assorted sizes on the angler's bank is to be desired, and also a tree which can be easily climbed. If the stones fail to calm the animal, you must take refuge in the tree. You will probably be able to come down after nightfall and slip unostentatiously away.

It sometimes happens that you come upon a bull suddenly and without a moment for thought or plan. Then you must depend on the moral dignity of man, on a haughty brow, and a flashing eye. Do not, however, presume on your manifest superiority. Behave as one gentleman to another. If the bull is right-minded he will move slowly away. If not, if he shows a disposition to contest your passage, you must advance upon him, shouting in a great and terrible voice. If this has no effect, you are obviously in a tight place, and there is but one thing to do. Lie down at once and pretend to be dead. We are informed that bulls do not attack dead persons. Should our information be incorrect, we can only express our regret.

Other methods of managing a bull are: (1) beating him with an iron bar till he repents his sins; (2) taking him by the horns and wrestling with him till you have him at your mercy; (3) twisting his tail till he is calm. It is open to you to select either of these plans if you prefer them to the pretence of death, which, after all, lacks some of the more heroic qualities.

Cows, bullocks, heifers, and calves may be considered as milder varieties of bull. Deference is, as a rule, all that they demand. But it occasionally happens that you have to deal with a charging herd. You may (1) charge back, whooping; (2) take to the river; (3) pretend to be dead; (4) throw stones or climb a tree (given the necessary facilities). In the case of calves, we act in the manly way suggested first.

A DOG

Stones are here the specific. Nine dogs out of ten have a wholesome fear of the hurt that flies from a distance. The tenth dog is the trouble. When you meet him you may (1) give him your luncheon, murmuring "Was he, then? A good old fellow! Nice old boy, then!" (2) take your bite, and trust to getting substantial damages out of the dog's owner; (3) catch the dog's head in your landing-net, and waltz round with him till the matter is settled one way or the other. We do not know which way settlement usually goes.

A WASP

Take off your hat and beat with it till the wasp is dead or you are stung. If there are two or three wasps, walk swiftly away to another place. These creatures are, happily, infirm of purpose and do not follow very far. If you come upon a nest, walk away twice as swiftly, whirling your hat as you go.

THUNDER AND LIGHTNING

It is not necessary to take any precautions against thunder, which is quite harmless, being all bark and no bite. Lightning, however, is another matter, for a fishing rod is nothing more or less than an invitation to it. We are not in a position to give statistics as to the number of anglers who have been abolished by lightning; but no doubt there are such statistics. Nor, unfortunately, are we able to give instructions as to warding off attack. It would be well to consult an electrician.

In the event of the electrician being far away and the lightning close at hand, we should advise the angler: (1) to spike his rod 100 yards from the river, and leave it; (2) to find a portion of the river not more than 3 ft. deep and lie down in it, immersing all but his nose and eyes; (3) to duck his head when a flash comes. He should thus be able to escape notice.

SNAKES

All snakes are not adders, but against this consoling fact has to be set the consideration that all adders are snakes. This should induce the angler to order his goings with great care, and to examine bits of stick, coiling ivy roots, and the like before he places his hand on them. Beyond this we do not think any elaborate precautions are required. Snakes are of a retiring disposition. Let them retire.

ANTS

The industrious ant busies itself in making fair-seeming seats for anglers, but these seats, like those of the new art, are for show, not for use. Mr Chesterton's example, "when I find a country seat, I sit in it," admirable in all other respects, should not be held to apply to those seats mentioned. A few minutes of rest and meditation are dearly purchased at the expense of a frantic undressing in the teeth of an unsympathetic east wind. And the ants do not mind the east wind. The seats that they provide should be left to sluggards.

VAGROM MEN

Anglers do not commonly have their throats cut by bandits and other undisciplined folk, but of course it may occur to them that their traditional mildness and amiability expose them to dangers which do not beset their brethren of the gun, especially in Wales and other outlandish parts where strangers of very hirsute countenance are apt to appear suddenly in lonely places. A crag-like face fringed with red hair, framed in the gap of a hedge or projected over a bush, is, quite reasonably, a matter for apprehension.

But let the angler take heart and also counsel from the old Greek philosopher with his "Know thyself." If he studies himself in a glass just before setting out, he will soon see that he has no cause for alarm. Even the face and form of a troglodyte could not hope to vie in terrifying qualities with the be-brogued, be-wadered, be-mackintoshed, be-hatted apparition that the glass reveals. Such a figure seems ripe for the fiercest deeds, and it is almost incredible that the boldest vagabond should wish to provoke its latent ferocity.

Of course, here and there a footpad of quicker and truer perception than his fellows may exist. Should it become apparent that such a man has seen through the rugged exterior to the gentle amiability that underlies it, then the angler may briskly step into the river and wade across. The "common cursetor" has, as a rule, no great liking for water. If the river be too deep for wading, probably a shilling will meet the case.

THE THRILLING MOMENT
Henry Van Dyke

1899

EVERY MOMENT of life, I suppose, is more or less of a turning-point. Opportunities are swarming around us all the time thicker than gnats at sundown. We walk through a cloud of chances, and if we were always conscious of them they would worry us almost to death.

But happily our sense of uncertainty is soothed and cushioned by habit, so that we can live comfortably with it. Only now and then, by way of special excitement, it starts up wide awake. We perceive how delicately our fortune is poised and balanced on the pivot of a single incident. We get a peep at the oscillating needle, and, because we have happened to see it tremble, we call our experience a crisis.

The meditative angler is not exempt from these sensational periods. There are times when all the uncertainty of his chosen pursuit seems to condense itself into one big chance, and stand out before him like a salmon on the top wave of a rapid. He sees that his luck hangs by a single strand of gut, and he cannot tell whether it will hold or break. This is his thrilling moment and he never forgets it.

Mine came to me in the autumn of 1894, on the banks of the Unpronounceable River, in the Province of Quebec. It was the last day, of the open season for ouananiche, and we had set our hearts on catching some good fish to take home with us. We walked up from the mouth of the river, four preposterously long and rough miles, to the famous fishing-pool, "*la place de pêche à Boivin.*" It was a noble day for walking; the air was clear and crisp, and all the hills around us were glowing with the crimson foliage of those little bushes which God created to make burned lands look beautiful. The trail ended in a precipitous gully, down which we scrambled with high hopes, and fishing-rods unbroken, only to find that the river was in a condition which made angling absurd if not impossible.

There must have been a cloud-burst among the mountains, for the water was coming down in flood. The stream was bank-full, gurgling and eddying out among the bushes, and rushing over the shoal where the fish used to lie, in a brown torrent ten feet deep. Our last day with the land-locked salmon seemed destined to be a failure, and we must wait eight months before we could have another. There were three of us in the disappointment, and we shared it according to our temperaments.

Paul virtuously resolved not to give up while there was a chance left, and wandered downstream to look for an eddy where he might pick up a small fish. Ferdinand, our guide, resigned himself without a sigh to the consolation of eating blueberries, which he always did with great cheerfulness. But I, being more cast down than either of my comrades, sought out a convenient seat among the rocks, and, adapting my anatomy as well as possible to the irregularities of nature's upholstery, pulled from my pocket *An Amateur Angler's Days in Dove Dale*, and settled down to read myself into a Christian frame of mind.

Before beginning, my eyes roved sadly over the pool once more. It was but a casual glance. It lasted only for an instant. But in that fortunate fragment of time I distinctly saw the broad tail of a big ouananiche rise and disappear in the swift water at the very head of the pool.

Immediately the whole aspect of affairs was changed. Despondency vanished, and the river glittered with the beams of rising hope.

Such is the absurd disposition of some anglers. They never see a fish without believing that they can catch him; but if they see no fish, they are inclined to think that the river is empty and the world hollow.

I said nothing to my companions. It would have been unkind to disturb them with expectations which might never be realized. My immediate duty was to get within casting distance of that salmon as soon as possible.

The way along the shore of the pool was difficult. The bank was very steep, and the rocks by the river's edge were broken and glibbery. Presently I came to a sheer wall of stone, perhaps thirty feet high, rising directly from the deep water.

There was a tiny ledge or crevice running part of the way across the face of this wall, and by this four-inch path I edged along, holding my rod in one hand, and clinging affectionately with the other to such clumps of grass and little bushes as I could find. There was one small huckleberry plant to which I had a particular attachment. It was fortunately a firm little bush, and as I held fast to it I remembered Tennyson's poem which begins "Flower in the crannied wall," and reflected that if I should succeed in plucking out this flower, "root and all," it would probably result in an even greater increase of knowledge than the poet contemplated.

The ledge in the rock now came to an end. But below me in the pool there was a sunken reef; and on this reef a long log had caught, with one end sticking out of the water, within jumping distance. It was the only chance. To go back would have been dangerous. An angler with a large family dependent upon him for support has no right to incur unnecessary perils.

Besides, the fish was waiting for me at the upper end of the pool!

So I jumped; landed on the end of the log; felt it settle slowly down; ran along it like a small boy on a seesaw, and leaped off into shallow water just as the log rolled from the ledge and lunged out into the stream.

It went wallowing through the pool and cavorting along the rapid like a playful hippopotamus. I watched it with interest and congratulated myself that I was no longer embarked upon it. On that craft a voyage down the Unpronounceable River would have been short but far from merry. The "all ashore" bell was not rung early enough. I just got off, with not half a second to spare.

But now all was well, for I was within reach of the fish. A little scrambling over the rocks brought me to a point where I could easily cast over him. He was lying in a swift, smooth, narrow channel between two large stones. It was a snug resting-place, and no doubt he would remain there for some time. So I took out my fly-book and prepared to angle for him according to the approved rules of the art.

Nothing is more foolish in sport than the habit of precipitation. And yet it is a fault to which I am singularly subject. As a boy, in Brooklyn, I never came in sight of the Capitoline Skating Pond, after a long ride in the horse-cars, without breaking into a run along the board walk, buckling on my skates in a furious hurry, and flinging myself impetuously upon the ice, as if I feared that it would melt away before I could reach it. Now this, I confess, is a grievous defect, which advancing years have not entirely cured; and I found it necessary to take myself firmly, as it were, by the mental coat-collar, and resolve not to spoil the chance of catching the only ouananiche in the Unpronounceable River by undue haste in fishing for him.

I carefully tested a brand-new leader, and attached it to the line with great deliberation and the proper knot. Then I gave my whole mind to the important question of a wise selection of flies.

It is astonishing how much time and mental anxiety a man can spend on an apparently simple question like this. When you are buying flies in a shop it seems as if you never had half enough. You keep on picking out a half-dozen of each new variety as fast as the enticing salesman shows them to you. You stroll through the streets of Montreal or Quebec and drop in at every fishing-tackle dealer's to see whether you can find a few more good flies. Then, when you come to look over your collection at the critical moment on the bank of a stream, it seems as if you had ten times too many. And, spite of all, the precise fly that you need is not there.

You select a couple that you think fairly good, lay them down beside you in the grass, and go on looking through the book for something better. Failing to satisfy yourself, you turn to pick up those that you have laid out, and find that they have mysteriously vanished from the face of the earth.

Then you struggle with naughty words and relapse into a condition of mental palsy.

Precipitation is a fault. But deliberation, for a person of precipitate disposition, is a vice.

The best thing to do in such a case is to adopt some abstract theory of action without delay, and put it into practice without hesitation. Then if you fail, you can throw the responsibility on the theory.

Now, in regard to flies there are two theories. The old, conservative theory is, that on a bright day you should use a dark, dull fly, because it is less conspicuous. So I followed that theory first and put on a Great Dun and a Dark Montreal. I cast them delicately over the fish, but he would not look at them.

Then I perverted myself to the new, radical theory which says that on a bright day you must use a light, gay fly, because it is more in harmony with the sky, and therefore less noticeable. Accordingly I put on a Professor and a Parmacheene Belle; but this combination of learning and beauty had no attraction for the ouananiche.

Then I fell back on a theory of my own, to the effect that the ouananiche have an aversion to red, and prefer yellow and brown. So I tried various combinations of flies in which these colours predominated.

Then I abandoned all theories and went straight through my book, trying something from every page, and winding up with that lure which the guides consider infallible, – " a Jock o' Scott that cost fifty cents at Quebec." But it was all in vain. I was ready to despair.

At this psychological moment I heard behind me a voice of hope, – the song of a grasshopper: not one of those fat-legged, green-winged imbeciles that feebly tumble in the summer fields, but a game grasshopper, – one of those thin-shanked, brown-winged fellows that leap like kangaroos, and fly like birds, and sing *Kri-karee-karee-kri* in their flight.

It is not really a song, I know, but it sounds like one; and, if you had heard that Kri-karee carolling as I chased him over the rocks, you would have been sure that he was mocking me.

I believed that he was the predestined lure for that ouananiche; but it was hard to persuade him to fulfil his destiny. I slapped at him with my hat, but he was not there. I grasped at him on the bushes, and brought away "nothing but leaves." At last he made his way to the very edge of the water and poised himself on a stone, with his legs well tucked in for a long leap and a bold flight to the other side of the river. It was my final opportunity. I made a desperate grab at it and caught the grasshopper.

My premonition proved to be correct. When that Kri-karee, invisibly attached to my leader, went floating down the stream, the ouananiche was surprised. It was the fourteenth of September, and he had supposed the grasshopper season was over. The unexpected temptation was too strong for him. He rose with a rush, and in an instant I was fast to the best land-locked salmon of the year.

But the situation was not without its embarrassments. My rod weighed only four and a quarter ounces; the fish weighed between six and seven pounds. The water was furious and headstrong. I had only thirty yards of line and no landing-net.

"Holà! Ferdinand!" I cried. "Apporte la nette, vite! A beauty! Hurry up!"

I thought it must be an hour while he was making his way over the hill, through the underbrush, around the cliff. Again and again the fish ran out my line almost to the last turn. A dozen times he leaped from the water, shaking his silvery sides. Twice he tried to cut the leader across a sunken ledge. But at last he was played out, and came in quietly towards the point of the rock. At the same moment Ferdinand appeared with the net.

Now, the use of the net is really the most difficult part of angling. And Ferdinand is the best netsman in the Lake St. John country. He never makes the mistake of trying to scoop a fish in motion. He does not grope around with aimless, futile strokes as if he were feeling for something in the dark. He does not entangle the dropper-fly in the net and tear the tail-fly out of the fish's mouth. He does not get excited.

He quietly sinks the net in the water, and waits until he can see the fish distinctly, lying perfectly still and within reach. Then he makes a swift movement, like that of a mower swinging the scythe, takes the fish into the net head-first, and lands him without a slip.

I felt sure that Ferdinand was going to do the trick in precisely this way with my ouananiche. Just at the right instant he made one quick, steady swing of the arms, and – the head of the net broke clean off the handle and went floating away with the fish in it!

All seemed to be lost. But Ferdinand was equal to the occasion. He seized a long, crooked stick that lay in a pile of driftwood on the shore, sprang into the water up to his waist, caught the net as it drifted past, and dragged it to land, with the ultimate ouananiche, the prize of the season, still glittering through its meshes.

This is the story of my most thrilling moment as an angler.

But which was the moment of the deepest thrill?

Was it when the huckleberry bush saved me from a watery grave, or when the log rolled under my feet and started down the river? Was it when the fish rose, or when the net broke, or when the long stick captured it?

No, it was none of these. It was when the Kri-karee sat with his legs tucked under him on the brink of the stream. That was the turning-point. The fortunes of the day depended on the comparative quickness of the reflex action of his neural ganglia and mine. That was the thrilling moment.

I see it now. A crisis is really the commonest thing in the world. The reason why life sometimes seems dull to us is because we do not perceive the importance and the excitement of getting bait.

PICTURE CREDITS